Acts of Aid

Acts of Aid explores the interaction between politics and natural disasters after a massive earthquake hit northern India and Nepal in 1934. While famines and to some extent flood management have been written into South Asian history, government and civil society responses to 'natural' disasters remain an elusive topic. This first comprehensive historical overview of the earthquake aftermath argues that its disastrous outcome was a human and historical event shaped by existing social and economic practices.

Distribution of relief—and attempts at redistribution—as well as long-term reconstruction efforts, reflected the colonial government's political economy of aid during famines and floods. At this particular moment in history, the aftermath proved an opportunity for civil society organisations, and among them the Indian National Congress, to challenge the colonial state beyond the politics of the disaster. In the distribution of aid and attempts at changing as well as preserving established social orders, the relief process turned into a display of state-making, fuelled by nationalism and public contributions to philanthropic associations.

Focusing on the 1934 earthquake and its consequences, this book conceptualises the politics of disaster in terms of governance, civil society participation and state-making in South Asian modern history. Ultimately, it argues that efforts to implement disaster relief in various forms shaped the course of governance, state-building and the fate of communities across the region.

Eleonor Marcussen is Researcher in History at the Department of Cultural Sciences and LNU Centre for Concurrences in Colonial and Postcolonial Studies, Linnaeus University, Sweden. Her research interests include humanitarianism, historical disasters, governance and infrastructure.

Acts of Aid

Politics of Relief and Reconstruction in the 1934 Bihar–Nepal Earthquake

Eleonor Marcussen

CAMBRIDGE
UNIVERSITY PRESS

CAMBRIDGE
UNIVERSITY PRESS

University Printing House, Cambridge CB2 8BS, United Kingdom

One Liberty Plaza, 20th Floor, New York, NY 10006, USA

477 Williamstown Road, Port Melbourne, vic 3207, Australia

314 to 321, 3rd Floor, Plot No.3, Splendor Forum, Jasola District Centre, New Delhi 110025, India

103 Penang Road, #05–06/07, Visioncrest Commercial, Singapore 238467

Cambridge University Press is part of the University of Cambridge.

It furthers the University's mission by disseminating knowledge in the pursuit of education, learning and research at the highest international levels of excellence.

www.cambridge.org Information on this title: www.cambridge.org/9781108838092

First published 2022

Printed in India by Avantika Printers Pvt. Ltd.

A catalogue record for this publication is available from the British Library

Library of Congress Cataloging-in-Publication Data

Names: Marcussen, Eleonor, author.
Title: Acts of aid : politics of relief and reconstruction in the 1934 Bihar-Nepal earthquake / Eleonor Marcussen.
Description: Cambridge, United Kingdom ; New York, NY : Cambridge University Press, 2022. | Includes bibliographical references and index.
Identifiers: LCCN 2022020670 (print) | LCCN 2022020671 (ebook) | ISBN 9781108838092 (hardback) | ISBN 9781108937160 (ebook)
Subjects: LCSH: Disaster relief--Political aspects--India--Bihar--History--20th century. | Disaster relief--Political aspects--India--Bihar--History--20th century. | Earthquakes--India--Bihar. | Earthquakes--Nepal. | Bihar (India)--History--20th century. | Nepal--History--20th century. | BISAC: HISTORY / Asia / South / General | HISTORY / Asia / South / General
Classification: LCC HV600 1934.B5 M37 2022 (print) | LCC HV600 1934.B5 (ebook) | DDC 363.34/80954123--dc23/eng/20220613
LC record available at https://lccn.loc.gov/2022020670
LC ebook record available at https://lccn.loc.gov/2022020671

ISBN 978-1-108-83809-2 Hardback

Contents

Illustrations

Maps

Images

Tables

Acknowledgements

This book began its life as a doctoral thesis written at the Heidelberg University, Germany. It was submitted to Heidelberg University as a doctoral dissertation with the title 'Acts of Aid: The Politics of Relief and Reconstruction after the 1934 Bihar–Nepal Earthquake'. I am grateful for the numerous helpful and knowledgeable people who have shown their support and helped me at various stages. At the very outset, I want to thank my supervisors for their unstinting support throughout the process of research and writing. Gita Dharampal offered a warm welcome at the Department of History at the South Asia Institute. Gerrit Jasper Schenk must take special credit for inspiring my interest in historical natural disasters by inviting me into the research group 'Cultures of Disaster' at the Cluster of Excellence 'Asia and Europe in a Global Context'. I am indebted to both for unwavering intellectual support.

I am grateful for the support of colleagues at the Department of History at the South Asia Institute and at the Cluster of Excellence, 'Asia and Europe in Global Context', who gave their valuable advice and discussed ideas in workshops and colloquia. Milinda Banerjee, Somnath Batabyal, Bindu Bhadana, Amelia Bonea, Felix Eickelbeck, Ivana Gubic, Rafael Klöber, Prabhat Kumar, Manju Ludwig, Sarah Luedecke, Soumen Mukherjee, Sridevi Padmanabhan, Swarali Paranjape, Dominik Schieder, Sayed Wiqar Ali Shah and Katharina Weiler shared their research and contributed towards the completion of my project with encouragement and kind advice. I am thankful to Kristine Chalyan-Daffner, Noura Dirani and Benedict Mette for their valuable company and collaboration in researching historical disasters and images of disasters. At other institutions, I have had the pleasure to receive advice and help from many people including Shaila Bhatti, Aryendra Chakravartty, Maria Framke, Mette Gabler, Yogesh Raj and Nitin Sinha. I am thankful for advice from audiences and participants in colloquia, conferences and workshops, most notably at the Department of History, Technische Universität Darmstadt, the Department of

History, York (U.K.), South Asian Studies for Young Scholars Meet by SASNET (Falsterbo, Sweden), by the Association of South Asian Environmental Historians, the Department of History, Assam University (Silchar), and in the Fifth European PhD Workshop in South Asian Studies (Paris). I am thankful for comments by audience and participants in the conference 'Epicentre to Aftermath: Political, Social and Cultural Impacts of Earthquakes in South Asia' at SOAS University of London, where I had the opportunity to develop some thoughts around metaphors and gender, at the invitation of Michael Hutt, Stefanie Lotter, Michele Serafini and Edward Simpson. Discussions with John Whelpton and participants at the conference enriched my perspective about earthquake aftermaths in Nepal. At Leiden University I had the pleasure to discuss the politics of historical disasters at the conference 'Relocating Governance in Asia: State and Society in South- and Southeast Asia, c. 1800–2000', thanks to Girija Joshi, Maarten Manse and Sander Tetteroo. I am also grateful to Cécile Stephanie Stehrenberger for generously sharing a range of literature on body politics and disaster research. The conferences 'The Transculturality of Historical Disasters: Governance and the Materialisation of Glocalisation' and 'Imaging Disaster' organised by the research groups Cultures of Disasters and Images of Disasters, respectively, at the Excellence Initiative Asia and Europe at Heidelberg University were helpful for developing initial ideas.

I wish to sincerely thank the staff at Heidelberg University, the Heidelberg University Library, the Library of the South Asia Institute and the Max Planck Institute for Comparative Public Law and International Law in Heidelberg, Leibniz-Zentrum Moderner Orient (ZMO), Berlin, the British Library and the Library at the School of Oriental and African Studies (SOAS) University College of London for their kind service and helpful advice. In Switzerland, thanks to the kind guidance and extra effort by staff and archivists at *Bibliothèque Cantonale et Universitaire Lausanne* (Lausanne Cantonal and University Library) and *Bibliothèque de la Ville* (The Town Library) in La Chaux-de-Fonds, and Heinz Gabathuler, SCI International Archives Coordinator, I had the great opportunity to view the private papers of Pierre Cérésole and Service Civil International. In India, I am thankful to the staff at the National Archives of India, the Nehru Memorial Museum and Library (NMML), the Library of the Indian Red Cross Society (New Delhi), the West Bengal State Archives and the Indian National Library, especially the archival and newspaper sections. In Bihar, I want to thank the staff at the Bihar State Archives, the A. N. Sinha Library and the K. P. Jayaswal Research Institute (Patna) for their support and kind guidance during long research stints. I want to thank, in particular, the director and staff of the Bihar State Archives for their readiness to provide me with service and helpful advice. I am thankful to the director and staff of Khuda Bakhsh Oriental Public Library for assistance and providing accommodation during my stays in Patna. I want to thank the Asian Development Research Institute (ADRI, Patna) and Kathinka Sinha Kerkhoff for taking interest in my research. I had the pleasure to meet Surendra Gopal, who generously shared his knowledge and guided me to sources in Patna. I am grateful to the late Hetukar Jha and to Tejkar Jha for inviting me to the Darbhanga Raj Archives. The staff of the Maharajadhiraja Kameshwar Singh Kalyani Foundation provided all the support I could wish for at Darbhanga.

My research was generously supported by the German Research Council (*Deutsche Forschungsgemeinschaft*) at the Cluster of Excellence. The Cluster of Excellence also granted a scholarship for an internship at the League of Nations Archives at the United Nations Office at Geneva, where mentors and staff at UNOG, in particular Blandine Blukacz-Louisfert, Colin Wells and Jacques Oberson, generously shared their expertise about the archives. In the period leading up to the completion of this book, I benefitted from the infrastructural and financial support of NIAS SUPRA writing fellowship at Nordic Institute of Asian Studies (NIAS, Copenhagen) and from being Junior Fellow at Nalanda University (New Delhi/Rajgir) where I had the pleasure to interact with Michiel Baas, M. B. Rajani, Gopa Sabharwal, Jyoti Sapru Dar, Amartya Sen, Anjana Sharma and Aviram Sharma. An MWK-COFUND research fellowship (Marie Skłodowska-Curie grant agreement no. 665958) at the Max Weber Center for Advanced Cultural and Social Studies at the University of Erfurt was deeply enriching. As a researcher, I am glad to currently be part of the supportive environment in the Department of Cultural Sciences at the Linnaeus University and the Linnaeus University Centre for Concurrences in Colonial Postcolonial Studies in Sweden. The publication is generously funded by Sven och Dagmar Saléns Stiftelse, Linnaeus University Open Access Funding, Linnaeus University Centre for Concurrences in Colonial and Postcolonial Studies, the Department of Cultural Sciences at Linnaeus University, and Heidelberg Centre for Transcultural Studies at Heidelberg University. I am grateful to the editorial team at Cambridge University Press, in particular Qudsiya Ahmed and Sohini Ghosh, for their patience and professionalism.

Finally, I want to thank the late Staffan Lindberg (Lund University), Martin Gansten (Lund University), Mirja Juntunen (Uppsala University) and Elisabeth Pachon (University of Copenhagen) for their guidance and inspired teaching that I was fortunate to receive as a student before embarking on the PhD project.

Many friends have made the task more enjoyable. My parents and my brother have given endless love and support, without which I could not have managed. My greatest love and gratitude is owed to Niladri for unwavering exhortation and inspiration when most needed. Special acknowledgement must go to Johanna and Ethan, who both arrived in the process of researching and writing this book, for their patience and constant cheers.

Abbreviations

ABP	*Amrita Bazar Patrika*
B&O	Bihar and Orissa
BCRC	Bihar Central Relief Committee
BCUL	Bibliothèque cantonale et universitaire Lausanne (Lausanne Cantonal and University Library)
BL	British Library
BLCD	*Bihar Legislative Council Debates*
BLCP	*Bihar Legislative Council Proceedings*
BOLCP	*Bihar and Orissa Legislative Council Proceedings*
BVCF	Bibliothèque de la Ville (The Town Library) La Chaux-de-Fonds
BSA	Bihar State Archives
CID	Criminal Investigation Department
CWMG	*Collected Works of Mahatma Gandhi*
Dept	Department
DIG	Director Inspector-General
D.O.	Demi-official [letter/correspondence]
DPI	Director of Public Information
F&P	Foreign and Political Department
Foreign	Foreign Branch
Foreign-Pol.	Foreign Department, Political Branch
GOI	Government of India
HP	Home Department, Public Branch
H. Pol.	Home Department, Political Branch
IMA	Indian Medical Association
IOR	India Office Records and Private Papers
IRU	International Relief Union

INC	Indian National Congress
JFC	Joint Flood Committee
KW	Keep With
LSG	Local Self Government
MKSKF	Maharajadhiraja Kameshwar Singh Kalyani Foundation
Mss Eur	Manuscript European
NAI	National Archives of India
NMML	Nehru Memorial Museum and Library
P&J	Public and Judicial
PC	Pierre Cérésole
PS	Political Department, Special Branch
PSV	Private Secretary to the Viceroy
PSVO	Private Secretary to the Viceroy Office
PWD	Public Works Department
R-L	Revenue Department, Lands Branch
R-LR	Revenue Department, Lands/Revenue Branch
RD	Reconstruction Department
RE	Reconstruction Department, Earthquake Branch
SCI	Service Civil International
UP	United Provinces
VERF	Viceroy's Earthquake Relief Fund

Note on Transliteration

The spelling 'Behar' (Bihar) has been kept if occurring in a citation from a primary source or in a title. Transliteration of Hindi words follows the style adopted by R. S. McGregor (ed.) in *The Oxford Hindi–English Dictionary* (New Delhi: Oxford University Press, 1993). Diacritical marks have been used only in translations and not in case of proper nouns and place names. The contemporary place names have been used, for example, Monghyr instead of the more familiar modern Munger. All translations are by the author unless otherwise noted.

Introduction

Experiencing the Extraordinary and the Ordinary

Continuities and Breaks

On 15 January 1934, at around 2.13 p.m. an earthquake struck north India and Nepal.[1] In the chronicles of states, popular writers and scientists, the earthquake would be known as 'the Indian earthquake',[2] 'the great Indian earthquake',[3] 'the Bihar–Nepal earthquake',[4] 'the Bihar earthquake'[5] and in Nepal as 'the Great Earthquake'.[6] As some of these titles reveal, Bihar, which the present study focuses on, was the worst-affected region in India: the districts Muzaffarpur, Darbhanga and Champaran in north Bihar, and Monghyr, south of the Ganges, suffered the most extensive human losses and damages. In India somewhere between 7,253[7] and 20,000[8] people succumbed and approximately 8,500 died in Nepal[9] in the upheaval measuring Mw 8.1[10] to 8.4[11] according to re-evaluated historical data. The epicentre located about 10 kilometres south of Mt Everest[12] caused severe damage to infrastructure, agricultural land and a large number of houses in an area extending from the foothills of the Himalayas in Nepal to the southern bank of the Ganges (Map 1.1).[13]

The 1934 earthquake was in many ways a revolutionary event in terms of magnitude and effect: it was a large-scale disaster with an unexpected and sudden onset. Almost exactly one hundred years had elapsed since the last major earthquake occurred in the region in 1833, an event of far less impact in terms of death and destruction, with no deaths reported in India despite damages to houses.[14] After the 1934 earthquake, the 1988 Udaypur (Udaipur) earthquake[15] served as a mild precursor to the recent 25 April 2015 Gorkha earthquake that not only caused extreme destruction and about 8,700 deaths in Nepal, but also severely jolted northern India from Delhi to Kolkata.[16] In combination with findings of historical seismology, these contemporary reminders of Bihar being

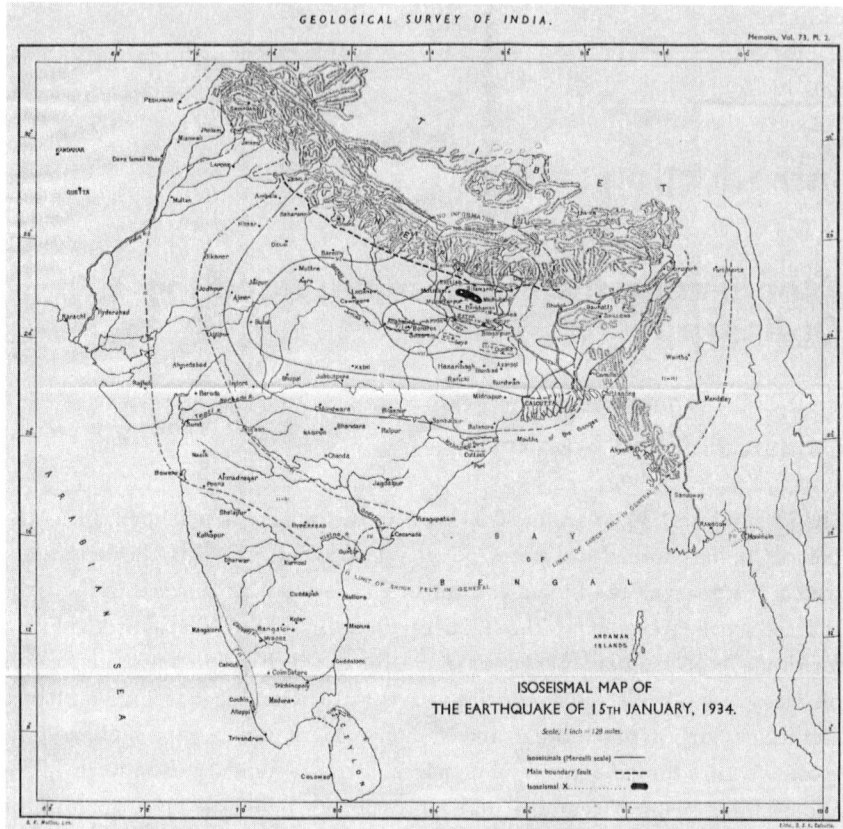

Map 1.1 Isoseismal map of the impact of the 1934 earthquake in South Asia. This detailed map was published by the GSI in 1939, while an earlier preliminary map was published by the Geological Survey of India officers J. B. Auden and A. M. N. Ghosh in 1934.

Source: Dunn et al., 'The Bihar–Nepal Earthquake of 1934', pl. 2. The earlier version was published in J. B. Auden and A. M. N. Ghosh, 'Preliminary Account of the Earthquake of the 15th January, 1934, in Bihar and Nepal', 177–239, in *Records of the Geological Survey of India* 68, pt. 2 (1934), pl. 19.

at risk in the event of regional Himalayan earthquakes have spurred research into engineering and modes of coping. Contemporary earthquake risk reduction in the Kathmandu valley aims at improving building structures and creating awareness.[17] Vital in recommending building techniques and planning dam projects and power plants is research into historical seismology, which serves to estimate location and magnitude of historical earthquakes.[18] A seismic record of the region extends back to the thirteenth century, as documented by geologists and historical seismologists of great historical and twentieth-century South Asian earthquakes.[19]

In modern South Asian history, the 1934 earthquake is foremost remembered for M. K. Gandhi's interpretation of the event as divine intervention, followed by an exchange of opinions with Rabindranath Tagore. Gandhi made the famous and disputed claim that the earthquake was a 'divine chastisement' of Bihar for the 'sin of untouchability', and Tagore contributed with a refutation of the statement as unscientific.[20] The brief discussion on whether the earthquake was caused by the treatment of Harijans, the name Gandhi used for the then untouchable castes, or whether it was a natural phenomenon detached from human actions has come to be interpreted as the manifestation of a schism between traditional beliefs and science. Scholarly works have in passing mentioned Gandhi's and Tagore's public exchange of opinions on the cause of the earthquake in order to illustrate their disparate outlooks on science and technology, most pronouncedly to prove the former's overall rejection of modern science versus the latter in its defence as a man of reason.[21] Gandhi's view of the earthquake as a divine punishment for the practice of untouchability has been taken as a case in point for proving his 'readiness to resort to harness faith'.[22] In one article his explanation of the earthquake as a punishment for sin has been described as moralistic.[23] Yet another analysis of the debate discerns an inherent theodicy in the statement by Gandhi as contrary to Tagore's rejection of divine intervention in physical phenomena.[24] Makarand R. Paranjape's article focuses entirely on their conflicting views after the earthquake, arguing that they represented 'two kinds of rationality, two ideas of science, and two approaches to modernity'.[25] Notably, the attention Gandhi's statement and Tagore's rejoinder attracted in the press then as well as later can partly be ascribed to the amount of publicity the exchange received, and partly to the historical importance of the two persons.

From a disaster studies' point of view, Gandhi's metaphysical interpretation offers an opportunity to understand how people's explanations and perceptions of human agency in disasters can affect responses.[26] Not unlike how the earthquake became incorporated into contemporary political discourse, histories of catastrophism outside the realms of 'scientific modernity' enabled people to explain, account for and rationalise loss, according to Sumathi Ramaswamy's book on the imaginary submerged Indian Ocean continent Lemuria.[27] Similarly, local knowledge in disaster myths, Urte Frömming points out in her comparative study of volcanoes in Iceland and Indonesia, is in 'modern' Western discourse regarded as magic rather than keys for understanding real-life strategies in dealing with disasters as well as perceptions of society and nature.[28] The practical usefulness of disaster interpretations is thereby lost as even anticipated and imagined disasters carry an important social potential for probation and development, cultural historians argue.[29]

If Gandhi's interpretation of the earthquake gained considerable attention in contemporary media as well as in the scholarship of today, the social psychologist Jamuna Prasad's study on the proliferation of rumours in the aftermath would come to leave a long-lasting mark on his discipline's scholarship, albeit in a different manner than intended.[30] In what appears to have been the first academic research project on the earthquake, he conducted interviews and listed observations and accounts in newspapers with the intention to understand the psychological factors underlying rumours after a disaster.[31] Prasad's contribution to the research field was in support of a 'social' approach towards rumours and challenging an analysis of the individual as independent of the 'crowd', like his contemporary Bernard Hart argued in the influential article 'The Psychology of Rumour' in 1916.[32] In 1950, Prasad published one more article based on comparisons of earthquake reports and rumours, introducing more material collected from the 1934 earthquake and later earthquakes.[33] The second article came partly in reaction to the influential study of rumour by Gordon Allport and Joseph Postman in *Psychology of Rumour* (1947), which viewed rumours as individual experiences and did not take cognizance of Prasad's article and his contrary claims on the role of the group.[34] Even though Prasad's research received limited acknowledgement by international colleagues in social psychology,[35] his study earned far wider recognition after the psychologist Leon Festinger (1919–89) used it as a key example for developing his theory of cognitive dissonance.[36] From this moment, Prasad's study would take a remarkably different academic trajectory. To prove his theory, Festinger argued that the rumours studied by Prasad had occurred outside the worst disaster area 'among people living in the area which received the shock of the earthquake but which did not suffer any damage'.[37] The 'fear-justifying rumours' served to overcome cognitive dissonance among people who felt fear but did not experience damage or death consonant with the frightening event, according to Festinger.[38] Patna, where Prasad started collecting rumours,[39] was indeed less damaged in comparison with north Bihar and Monghyr, but the district as a whole nevertheless suffered almost 150 officially recorded deaths, and Patna city saw a great number of private houses and large old buildings in ruins.[40] Both Prasad and eye-witness accounts contradicted Festinger's understanding of the earthquake rumours as detached from the worst-affected area. In this way,

Prasad's study gained fame, although not for his contribution to the role of collectives in social psychology, as the research had intended.

Perhaps less famous to a wider audience than Festinger's theory, but a classic contribution in the field of history, Ranajit Guha's *Elementary Aspects of Peasant Insurgency in Colonial India*, agrees with Prasad's social approach towards rumours in the sense that rumours are seen as a source for discerning popular mentalities and flows of information,[41] capable of triggering far-travelling panic within a very short period.[42] The seminal study on subaltern modes of communication and informal networks ascribes rumour a fundamental role.[43] By analysing rumours as an efficient communicative mode, particularly in subaltern communication,[44] Guha builds upon Prasad's argument that rumours functioned as a social medium.

Despite these significant socially embedded interpretations of a disaster and far-reaching records of earthquakes in the region, historians of South Asia have taken a sporadic interest in how society responded to earthquakes, or to natural disasters in general for that matter. Historical studies on disasters in Bihar have addressed floods,[45] and recurring floods and cyclones in Orissa,[46] the south-eastern part of the province[47] and not to forget, famines. Floods are still considered a normal and a recurrent disaster in north Bihar, one of the most flood-prone areas of the region where the Ganges and the large rivers Kosi and Gandak with tributaries criss-cross the landscape and cause regular inundations as well as major floods of varying intensity on a yearly basis.[48] Famines, the most salient and fatal of disasters from the beginning of the British East India Company Rule around 1770, are generally considered a man-made or hybrid disaster with elements of causation based on environmental conditions, weather and governance.[49] Why earthquakes have so far caught marginal attention in South Asian history may partly be explained by an inclination in historical narratives to focus on phenomena that are recurrent and lend themselves for generalisation and the gradual development traced in environmental disasters rather than singular disasters. Another reason may be a perception of catastrophes of nature as outside the scope of political history, and particularly the history of states, which would explain why historical research tends to study the role of governance in hybrid or man-made disasters rather than governance in natural hazards.[50] The lack of interest in natural disasters can, according to the pioneering work of Arno Borst, be traced to notions of modernity where a focus on societal progress led to a repression of singular events considered as abnormal interruptions in historical research.[51] Global environmental history, too, tends to focus on governance in disasters unfolding over a longer time-span, for example, famines, droughts, floods and climate change, but less so on natural disasters with a sudden onset such as earthquakes, tsunamis, typhoons, hailstorms and hurricanes.[52] The contemporary wider acceptance of human beings' agency in relation to their environs can be traced to the experience of living in the ecological epoch of the Anthropocene, defined by human geological agency and a scientific consensus on climate change being human-induced.[53] This late shift in perceptions of human agency in relation to climate change has occurred in parallel with the increasingly human toll of environmental disasters such as the dumping of toxic waste, deforestation and industrial pollution. Yet environmental disasters are largely rendered invisible, evolving during a long period and unequally distributed across the globe, termed by Rob Nixon as a form of 'slow violence' against the poor and the developing world.[54]

After a turn in geographical, anthropological and sociological research towards an understanding of natural disasters as social processes rather than natural events, cultural and historical studies have intervened to further our understanding of how people have experienced historical natural disasters and at the same time how disasters structure social life.[55] The most extreme among the constructionist approaches on disasters argues that nature and hence 'natural' disasters exist as sociocultural constructs where the natural is not purely physical or biological occurrences but depends on social and cultural understanding of nature. At the other end of the spectrum, the realist approach maintains that risk is a hazard that exists and can be measured independently of social and cultural processes, consequently not taking people's vulnerability into account. A weak constructionist approach regards risk as a hazard that usually is mediated through social and cultural processes. A strong constructionist approach, on the other hand, treats nothing as a risk in itself but as a product dependent on historical, social and political perceptions.[56] With this shift, natural disasters are the outcome of cultural and historical contexts, where social parameters, a person's socio-economic position, knowledge of resources and local environment, age, gender and social networks determine vulnerability and exposure to disaster. Thereby, a person's vulnerability is defined by the 'capacity to anticipate, cope with, resist and recover from the impact of natural hazard'.[57] Vulnerability is thereby directly related to resilience, the ability of a system, community or society to resist, absorb, accommodate to and recover from the effects of a hazard.[58] In the form of a geological event, an earthquake is a natural *hazard*; as a social experience, sociocultural constructs and human agency make it a natural or a man-made *disaster*.[59]

In line with Wisner and colleagues, who emphasise the contribution of so-called normal historical processes in producing disasters,[60] this book examines the extent to which contemporary perceptions of disasters, political agendas and governance shaped responses in the relief and reconstruction phase in Bihar in the aftermath of the 1934 earthquake. Building upon cultural and historical research into the social aspects of natural disasters, the larger aim of this book is to examine how the aftermath of a disaster demonstrates previous experiences with disasters, or a lack thereof, and the ways responses shape resilience. By studying relief and rehabilitation in the aftermath of the earthquake, the book aims to contribute to a historical understanding of 'natural' disasters as social processes, which it argues is necessary to arrive at a contextualised understanding of resilience and what it means in relation to vulnerability in future disasters. The aftermath of an earthquake is similar and yet different from other natural disasters in terms of human experience, suddenness and physical impact on built environments. Susanna M. Hoffman underlines the use of researching responses to catastrophes in order to understand the fundamental constructs that underpin the social world.[61] The ability of earthquakes to reorder society, as noted by historians, may further help us to understand how societies have adopted practices and in some instances learnt to cope with disasters. The specific scenario of an earthquake has been referred to as a form of creative destruction, a groundbreaker and an 'opportunity' for 'improvements' in the rebuilding process,[62] or cyclical renewal by reconstruction.[63] Case studies of disaster responses show how large-scale disasters have functioned as so-called focusing events on societies in terms of their ability to respond or change approaches.[64] Disaster as an opportunity to reorder society, both in the moment of crisis and in a longer aftermath, creates spaces where political legitimacy is contested or reinforced.

In order to analyse the transformative aspects of disaster, socially and historically contextualised studies are vital. These studies help us understand the trajectories of political instrumentalisation of aid,[65] individual and collective memorialisation,[66] the importance of cultural modes of coping[67] and the force of outside interventions.[68] The 2001 Bhuj earthquake and the 2004 Indian Ocean tsunami were large events. Small disasters recurring with a certain regularity, such as annual inundations or seasonal storms, may elicit responses and adaptive processes that shape institutional and organisational learning. Sociological research shows that responses to small disasters tend to result in learning which produces mitigative and preventive measures at local levels, while the policies developed for responses to large-scale disasters focus on clearing up in the aftermath.[69] Governance institutions and social science research consciously and/or purposefully make use of past experiences with disasters to improve or change responses. The development of systemic learning in responses to disasters has been differentiated into two categories that can be useful to have in mind: learning from established patterns based on previous experiences, so-called accumulative learning, or by introducing a fundamental and often innovative change.[70]

At the same time, the idea that societies and researchers can learn from history and historical disasters remains contested. Christian Pfister argues that historical disaster research can make it possible for a human to conceive risks, to make the seemingly unthinkable thinkable ['*Undenkbares denkbar*'].[71] When the implementation of knowledge repeatedly fails, as in the recent mega-disasters Hurricane Katarina and the Indian Ocean tsunami, Stewart Williams argues that large-scale disasters expose the limits of what we can know. Instead of a social constructionist approach to natural disasters, where human agency and technocratic solutions dominate, he suggests a post-social understanding of disaster as helpful in order to grasp the complexities of material realities of what he sees as non-human nature.[72] Learning from disasters is also questioned by James K. Mitchell who argues that the element of surprise in disasters such as the 2004 Indian Ocean tsunami and the 9/11 terrorist attack shows a need to plan for contingencies rather than relying on past experiences.[73] Misplaced faith in the capabilities of institutionalised scientific knowledge and technical expertise may exacerbate vulnerability, Williams writes, inspired by Ulrich Beck's influential risk thesis that modernisation by way of technological change and reflexivity has changed the notions of risk and thereby also how societies deal with hazards.[74] In his book on the long aftermath of the 2001 Bhuj earthquake, Edward Simpson suggests that instead of remembering and thereby learning from the disaster, amnesia occurs as the earthquakes are too big and too terrible to take in. Since the earthquakes are beyond the capacity of what our minds can comprehend, the enormity of the events are scaled down and in the process 'the true earthquake (...) is lost from view'.[75] As these examples show, scholars to various degrees emphasise that learning, remembering or/and forgetting at an institutional or collective level play a role in how societies respond to disaster. Historical disaster research, however, generally finds learning from the experience of disaster to be a fundamental part in explaining how societies deal with disasters differently. Jared Diamond delineates some of the most extreme ways in which societies have collapsed or survived human and environmentally induced disasters—partially choosing to learn or not to learn from past experiences.[76] Accordingly, studies of experiences with disasters can help in understanding social and environmental patterns and circumstances leading up to societal responses.[77] Gregory Clancey illustrates how in Japan, the normative machinery of governance and the unexpected natural disaster intertwined, 'creating not only states of emergency but disaster-oriented states'.[78] Cultural politics surrounding seismicity changed building techniques as well as methodology in scientific discourse.[79] As previous research on specifically cultural and religious disaster interpretations points out, disasters are not simply explained according to established narratives, but more often they make an impact on explanatory models, whether scientific, religious or governance-oriented.[80] Disasters add layers to narratives, embedded or normalised into the course of life, or featured as extraordinary events. The multiple narratives of a disaster such as the 1931 Yangtze River floods form a lens to understand how a 'disaster regime' developed in the history of modern China. The disaster regime explains how different strands of causality, both environmental and anthropogenic, intertwined to create hazards, famines and epidemics, which all translated into disaster for human beings.[81] Within this wide context of human–environmental relations, disaster learning becomes embedded within multiple practices used for interpreting and responding to emergencies. Such an analysis of disaster as a part of a larger systemic context allows for several narratives about the event and aftermath to coexist. Taking the learning experience one step further, Bas van Bavel and colleagues argue for using history, and specifically 'disaster history', as a laboratory to test and review variables and factors leading up to or preventing disasters.[82] In anthropology, disasters have long been framed as the closest thing to a natural laboratory that a student of society gets access to.[83] By analysing historical disasters, researchers argue that society can 'learn' about governance tools for responding to or preventing disasters. In contrast, historical research shows that though societies implementing changes in response to disasters frame it as a learning outcome, from the perspective of the historian, it becomes a covert instrumentalisation of the conditions a disaster creates. The literally ground-levelling effects an earthquake can have on soft and hard infrastructure feed into modernisation narratives, according to case studies from Japan and the United States. Improvements in urban reconstruction and town planning may safeguard residents in the event of a future earthquake or fire, but is primarily driven by financial interests.[84] Similarly, disasters can be used as a pretext to secure long-held political goals by installing moral values in children, Janet Borland argues in the case of the 1923 Kanto earthquake.[85]

The ability of societies to learn by adapting to disasters plays a central role in *Cultures of Disaster: Society and Natural Hazard in the Philippines* by Greg Bankoff. He suggests that societies can come to terms with hazards to the extent that disasters are not regarded as abnormal situations but rather a constant feature of life.[86] According to him, a 'culture of disaster develops and the threat is no longer a threat but becomes normalised into an extreme ecological process' if hazards recur frequently and shape responses so that mitigation and adaptation measures accommodate disaster.[87] Even in an earthquake, where the shaking ground is by most people regarded as the cause of the disaster, human agency in terms of infrastructural planning and building techniques reveal that previous experiences with disasters influence whether a natural hazard turns into a natural disaster or not.[88] And once the disaster is a fact, governance and organisation of relief work and reconstruction can prove vital to save lives and to build resilience and coping strategies, thus determining the magnitude of the disaster and the course of events in the long aftermath. The quote 'earthquakes don't kill people, buildings kill people'[89] is a pertinent example of reflection on the social dimension of an earthquake where risk can be mitigated. The present study rests upon ontological underpinnings that regard disaster as the outcome of human agency and negotiation of risks.

Accordingly, this book is about the aftermath of the earthquake. The earthquake in Bihar was a breaking point, an event, and its aftermath became a process embedded in a social context, which helps us in understanding how historical trajectories from previous disaster scenarios and contemporary social and political issues shaped responses. The disruption of *everyday routines* occurred suddenly with the earthquake in the form of casualties and physical devastation. As a process this involved coming to terms with and coping with the lasting disruptions of physical damages and sometimes mental instability, displayed as doubt in systems of belief or reliable state provisions.[90] Though the event and the aftermath of a disaster are seen as distinct entities, they are intimately linked in the disaster narrative where the event of physical destruction sets the scene for the processes of coping, relief and reconstruction in the aftermath. This book follows a sociological definition of disaster as 'the disruption of everyday routines to the extent that stability is threatened without remedial action'. The potential for disruption is contained within all social routines; each is vulnerable to breakdown.[91]

'Natural' Disasters in South Asian History

To date, there have been few studies in the field of South Asian history on the subject of natural disasters, in the sense of disasters originating from a natural hazard such as an earthquake or a cyclone. This book builds upon literature that can be classified into two categories. First, a broad group of studies that addresses the sociocultural construction of nature in the colonial period and its bearings on perceptions of natural disasters, and second, a group of dispersed studies that addresses disasters or disaster relief in a larger political context. Unlike the first group, which is constituted foremost of scholars affiliated to environmental history, and argues for a sociocultural constructionist approach to nature, the second category of literature takes an interest in disasters from the point of social, economic or political history.

Historians, and in particular environmental historians, and to some extent ethnographers pursuing research on political ecology, to varying degrees share the view that natural disasters such as landslides and floods, as well as famines, are primarily man-made disasters. By contextualising disasters as part of political economy, these studies explain causes and responses to disasters as dependent on governance and cultural constructions of nature rather than environmental, 'natural' conditions. Famines, which the colonial government analysed as the outcome of historical and environmental conditions specific to India, have been convincingly dismantled by a rich body of literature as primarily contingent on governance. From the late nineteenth century, famines became a trope within the larger nationalist critique of colonialism as a draining force. Rather than conditioned on historical and environmental circumstances, the drain theory saw famine as an evidence of the destructive force of British rule, by conquest and plunder, by the destruction of India's manufacturers and trades, by excessive land revenue demands and the heavily administrative costs that India was forced to bear.[92] Amartya Sen's ground-breaking study of the last colonial famine in India—the Great Bengal Famine—further strengthens the perception of famine as an unfolding process constituent of multiple factors and not only a decline in food caused by natural circumstances.[93] Within colonial discourse, however, natural hazards such as floods, droughts and cyclones were natural causes of famines, and accordingly famines were natural disasters.

Although natural hazards have been left out of environmental history, research on governance and nature provides a framework for how natural disasters were perceived and, arguably, conceived in the colonial period. The early works of Madhav Gadgil and Ramachandra Guha,[94] and in particular Guha's *The Unquiet Woods: Ecological Change and Peasant Resistance in the Himalaya*, which is generally acknowledged for having established South Asian environmental history in the global theatre,[95] argue that British colonialism marked an ecological watershed by altering existing food production systems and their ecological basis. Their research falls within a Marxist approach to socio-economic history in arguing that the subordination and transformation of nature were integral to colonial and economic interests.[96] Later constructionist analyses of the impact of colonial governance expand research on the complex workings of power, acknowledging not only the force of colonialism, but also its impact on the environment and the consequences of its 'expropriator approach' toward natural resources.[97] One example of such social constructionist analysis is David Arnold's influential research on how the colonial state's approach to disasters was influenced by perceptions of India as a zone of tropicality.[98] According to him, the cultural construct of the environment and climate as tropical in the gaze of the colonisers (foremost the British) during the nineteenth century manifested India as dominated by nature and void of a historical past. The appropriation of landscape as a site of improvement was repeatedly used to legitimise colonial rule and 'through nature a corresponding nature authority over human subjects'.[99] Arnold's research demonstrates how the relationship with nature became a way of trying to define, compare and. contextualise India, to render it more accessible to the European imagination and ultimately to its colonising process by interventions in the forms of science and agricultural improvements. Scholars writing on Orientalism have argued that the projection of 'the East' as different served to create a self-image of Europe that helped in maintaining imperial power in the colonies.[100] The cultural construction of nature was used to undertake 'improvement' and later projected on areas as 'impoverished sites in urgent need of "development"'.[101] The Other, in the form of disaster-prone landscapes, was— like in many studies on Others and forms of Orientalism[102]—also the target for Western intervention in the name of help and improvement.[103] Outside the realms of South Asian history, Arnold's research on geographic Otherness and tropicality as a cultural construct has contributed to Bankoff's writings on the concept of vulnerability as a product of colonial perceptions of environments.[104] According to Bankoff, contemporary discourses on vulnerability stress the natural forces at work, while denying the wider historical and social context that shape how people interact with natural hazards. In his view, the technocratic remedies prescribed to ameliorate disasters have resulted in disaster prevention as only a matter of improving scientific prediction, engineering preparedness and the administrative management of hazard.[105]

Building upon Arnold's and Bankoff's research, Upamanyu Pablo Mukherjee argues that disaster relief in the form of 'palliative imperialism' was the outcome of a fashioning of India as a disaster zone.[106] He discusses first of all Victorian disaster debates in fictional accounts and administrative documents from the nineteenth century and restricts his examples to famines and epidemics, although he refers to them in the more general term 'natural' disasters.[107] In the relationship between the 'tropical other' and the colonial state, he argues that imperialism entered a specific mode and became 'imperialism as an act of care, in fact, a relief effort—undertaken in order to fulfil Europe's historic mission of rescuing the native inhabitants from their own habitat'.[108] According to Mukherjee, the archetypical 'disaster events' of British South Asia, shaped 'understanding and practices of empire, progress, development and civilisation'. Explanations of the origins of famines and epidemics as natural or historical events demonstrate how perceptions of disasters held the Indians responsible for the suffering, while colonisers and administrators intervened and 'remedied the underdeveloped'.[109] Mukherjee's line of argument should be seen not only against the master narratives that served to justify colonialism; it also counters a Eurocentric historical scholarship built upon these narratives, epitomised perhaps foremost in *The European Miracle: Environments, Economies, and Geopolitics in the History of Europe and Asia*.[110] In the book, Eric Lionel Jones argues that disasters, disaster management and technological advances in the period 1400–1800 played a central role in the arguably successful and prosperous development of European states as compared to the corresponding failure of a number of Asian states.[111] Building upon James Morris Blaut's analysis of Jones's book as an example of Eurocentric scholarship par excellence,[112] Mukherjee, first of all, reacts to the environmental determinism and cultural superiority claimed by Jones as central to European success. Jones views the European governments as suppliers of public goods (which he refers to as 'disaster management' when addressing epidemics or 'natural' hazards) and north European agriculture as uniquely productive, and an 'intrinsically benevolent European state system' as the result of benign environments.'[113]

Turning to the second category of literature constituted of economic, social and political history, we are confronted with research that analyses society's approach to natural disasters from multiple angles. Three publications by the economic historian Tirthankar Roy provide overviews of how the market, the state and, to some extent, the 'indigenous' population responded to natural disasters during the colonial period. *Natural Disasters and Indian History* in the Oxford India Short Introduction series is a useful overview on the topic, while two articles provide case studies. Yet Roy himself states the obvious limitation of the article from 2008, as it is an 'exploration' and based upon published sources.[114] The 1934 Bihar–Nepal earthquake and the 1935 Quetta earthquake are two out of five case studies that are analysed by Roy to explore relations between the state, society and market after natural disasters, and through these studies Roy illustrates how state involvement in disaster responses gradually increased in the period 1864–1935. He proposes a transition in terms of the actors responding to natural disasters: while the market dominated responses in the nineteenth century, gradually the idea of government responsibility took root in the period leading up to the 1934 earthquake. His argument is twofold: the effectiveness of state intervention depended on compatibility between private and social goals, therefore legitimacy could affect disaster responses. In the increasingly interventionist state and simultaneous development of a critical civil society in disaster responses, Roy sees a mirroring of the political–economic context of the period. The second part of his argument is inferred from the first and proposes a general chain of events or processes. First, the initial destruction of state capacity; second, the activation of 'anarchic unregulated markets' and private actors in reaction to the temporary retreat of the state; and finally, a rebound of the state. According to Roy, the last phase was intensely contested as 'the return of the state was beset with collective actions problems, and with political conflicts of a kind engendered by late colonialism'.[115] Roy finds it 'simplistic' to explain the development of an increasingly interventionist state in the period as 'another example of "governmentality"'. Rather, he sees state control as a reaction partly to the sharp loss in control, and partly to the need for reviewing property rights in the rebuilding phase after a disaster.[116]

With regard to cyclones and flood damage, Roy refers to Braja Bandhu Bhatta's *The Natural Calamities in Orissa in the 19th Century* on the prevalence of 'natural calamities' such as floods, cyclones and famines, and responses by the colonial state in Orissa.[117] Bhatta explains revenue remission in the aftermath of floods and cyclones as a response to prevent famines. According to Bhatta, the frequency of natural calamities left people impoverished, but at the same time poverty resulted from 'high rent collection and increasing land revenue', which contributed to making people 'resourceless'.[118] In effect, the government's relaxation of taxes or rents meant a temporary relief from distress caused not only by extreme environmental conditions but also by over-taxation. Even the increase in mitigation measures such as building embankments, canals, transport systems, etc. can be interpreted either as the government's gradual realisation of its responsibility in terms of governance in turning hazards into disasters, or as a way to improve the conditions for maximising revenue profit. Bhatta's conclusion subscribes to the latter as he finds the government's mitigation measures to floods and cyclones 'partial and oriented [according] to their interests',[119] that is, the construction of canals, expanding roads and railways were meant to contribute towards agricultural improvements and thereby increase the government's revenue collection. Despite this analysis, Bhatta rather contradictorily classifies famine as a 'natural calamity' at par with floods and cyclones,[120] leaning towards a view similar to the colonial government's explanation of famines as caused by environmental conditions.[121]

In his second article, Roy suggests that the idea of government institutions as partly responsible for action in terms of prediction and understanding of disastrous events emerged in the period 1800–50, based on a comparison of responses to floods and cyclones in the Bengal delta.[122] The colonial government's introduction of a meteorological office to track cyclones and a public works department to construct embankments in protection of floods marked the beginning of the state as the 'principal agency for disaster response' in eastern Bengal.[123] Roy's economic history perspective on the emergence of a disaster response by the colonial government can be contrasted with 'the environmentalist discourse', described by him as written by historians who mainly focus on the social and environmental costs of these projects.[124] Among them, Rohan D'Souza in his acclaimed book *Drowned and Dammed: Colonial Capitalism and Flood Control in Eastern India* argues that the colonial administration of the East India Company in deltaic Orissa 'began to recast the phenomenon of inundations as chiefly a calamitous event rather than a hydraulic process'.[125] Although other research also shows the importance of water for governance structures,[126] such as the role of the state versus local management of floods and river systems,[127] D'Souza's persuasively makes the argument that flood control was integral to the strategies of empire—a strategy that led to the transformation of nature from a 'flood-dependent' agrarian regime into a 'flood-vulnerable' landscape.[128] Per se, colonial governance had brought on environmental catastrophe. Benjamin Kingsbury makes a similar argument in his study of the Bengal cyclone of 1876, in terms of the role that colonial governance played in creating disaster rather than establishing disaster management in his study of the Bengal cyclone of 1876.[129] The government chose to ignore existing knowledge about preventing, predicting and recovering from cyclones and their effects, such as epidemics and hunger, and instead took decisions based on economic policies that calculated risks and profit.[130] The failure to protect interests beyond those of the colonial state and select groups in hazards raises questions that go beyond disaster management. Can these extraordinary events offer an opportunity to examine distinctive environmental and social patterns in governance during the period?

This discussion on the socio-environmental context and responses of the colonial government to disasters leads us to a group of studies that has examined state-making or nation-building in the twentieth century. State-making is 'fundamentally about defining the forms and legitimations of government and governmentality', and thereby 'simultaneously about the making of civil society'.[131] This dialectical relationship in power between the state and civil society was perhaps nowhere as apparent as in famine relief in the nineteenth and twentieth centuries when people organised according to capacities of moral and political nature, consisting of a wide range of organisational bodies, for instance, political parties, relief associations and private enterprises.[132] Before proceeding to a set of case studies on state-making and nation-building processes in natural disasters, a body of research linking the crisis of famine with state formation and the expansion of civil society in the subcontinent are worth taking note of. While famines in terms of causation undoubtedly differ from sudden disasters, such research seems to demonstrate continuity in the critique of the failure of the colonial state in providing relief in famines as well as in natural disasters. Sanjay Sharma convincingly shows how the colonial state expanded its infrastructure through relief works for building roads and employing manual labour as a part of its processes of centralisation and expansion in north India in the early nineteenth century. Governance of famines facilitated state-building processes by strengthening the state's capacity at certain moments in history.[133] Ravi Ahuja argues that famine policy served as a way of gaining political legitimacy in the processes of state formation in south India in the early colonial era.[134] Famine became part of criticism against the state, in particular in Ireland and India, where it served as a conclusive demonstration of British indifference to people's suffering. While famine relief in terms of revenue remission, relief works and control over charitable relief was the result of colonial ideological and organisational power, it was also a 'key argument in the critique of colonialism' towards the end of the nineteenth century[135] as contemporaries saw it as a sign of the failing of the colonial state.[136] The more famine was seen as something not solely a consequence of natural causes but as man-made or at least as a phenomenon in which it was possible to intervene, the more famine was part of a 'developing critique of state power', as Arnold writes. Much of the political struggle involved countering the state's position as autocratic ruler, justified by the necessity to answer in the name of a population regarded as not yet capable.[137] As David Hall-Matthews demonstrates, the state was 'exclusively internal' in terms of accountability when inquiries remained within its boundaries, for instance, when the Government of Bombay failed to respond to the famine in 1876–78.[138] The government's increasingly interventionist stance in famines, as Lance Brennan has discussed in his analysis of the Indian Famine Codes as part of British policy, took shape in reaction to the failure of the state that the famines represented during the three first quarters of the nineteenth century.[139] If famines represented the failure of colonial governance, they also opened a space for new actors, discussions and policy changes that aimed at preventing the repetition of failures. The development of famine relief by the state and civil society in the second half of the nineteenth century forms the backdrop of an article by Georgina Brewis, who argues that famine relief at the very end of the century was used in order to channel patriotism into practical social service and contributed towards a politically active civil society. Inadequate disaster management and accountability limited to the sphere of the government and administrators in the last years of the nineteenth century and in the famine of 1900–01 marked a transition period for the formation of social service associations in the organisation of voluntary work.[140] Building upon Carey Anthony Watt's study about the role of social service activities in nation-building,[141] she emphasises, in particular, the prominent function of voluntary forces. Relief and governance of famines have thereby served to facilitate state formation as well as exposed 'bad governance', triggering state critique which strengthened nation-building activities among civil society groups.

In the context of twentieth-century earthquakes, Kokila Dang makes a similar claim on the political importance of relief in relation to nationalism, in the context of the Indian National Congress (INC) and relief work in the aftermath of the earthquake in 1934 and the 1935 Quetta earthquake.[142] Dang argues that disaster relief after the 1934 earthquake became an arena where authority was contested by the colonial state and by 'an emerging nationalism'.[143] Similarly, William Kuracina's book about the political development of the INC and the emerging state of independent India takes relief work in the 1935 Quetta earthquake as an instance of 'parallelism' in governance by the INC.[144] Compared to Kuracina, Dang's analysis bypasses the state-making and/or nation-building processes of disaster even though her dissertations directly address the political aspects of disaster relief. Yet her detailed research on the INC and civil society in the organisation of relief is an informative contribution about the larger context of the colonial state's relation to relief of various sorts. In a focused case study of the 1950 Assam earthquake, Bérénice Guyot-Réchard argues that the large-scale encounter in the relief process between communities and the Indian administration led to an 'unprecedented movement of state expansion in this strategic borderland'.[145] For the Indian state, the timing and location of the large-scale event that caused environmental and infrastructural damages resulting in landslides and flood-submerged villages posed as a major site for interventions in the form of aid. Guyot-Réchard's rich sociopolitical history refers to it as a 'significant juncture' in the geopolitical development of Assam. State-making and nation-building process following the earthquake manifested in relief and rehabilitation work, where the encounter between the central government and local communities brought them into close contact for the first time and showed the state as a potential provider of tangible goods and benefits rather than a force of control as under colonial rule.[146]

The common field of enquiry by Dang, Kuracina and Guyot-Réchard is the earthquake aftermath as a political space where the role of the state and political power can be harnessed and negotiated into efficient tools of state-making or nation-building. Besides these in-depth studies, a few publications have briefly addressed the 1934 earthquake in the context of social history. S. N. Mukherjee briefly describes the aftermath as a socio-political process and an example of how disasters are 'not just natural events, but social experiences' but unfortunately does not venture beyond comments on nationalist politicians' participation in relief work.[147] Wendy Singer's research addresses political aspects of the aftermath of the earthquake in relation to the Darbhanga Raj, local elites and peasant unrest by arguing that dissatisfaction with earthquake relief provided an opportunity for mobilisation against the authorities in 1934–37.[148] Similar to Singer, Stephen Henningham has also touched upon political loyalties and conflicts in relief and reconstruction following the earthquake in his series of publications on the Darbhanga Raj.[149] Both Singer and Henningham show how relief and reconstruction became politicised and served as a means to assert political power or contest it. These important aspects of the aftermath of the earthquake will be discussed in the context of state-making and nation-building in the course of this book. The opportunity for change that a disruptive event offers, according to these socio-political histories, rests with the agency of political actors after the physical destruction of landscape, infrastructure and human lives. The present study builds upon their suggestions that disasters can be formative in developing or shaping the state and civil society, yet, at the same time, it underlines the importance of considering responses to disasters not only in a socio-political context, but also as a part of experiences with previous hazards and disasters. Research on the sociopolitical importance of 'natural' disasters constitutes a refreshing perspective in South Asian history which this study suggests can broaden the scope of historical inquiry in order to understand better how environmental and human factors affect people in hazards.

Situating the Disaster in a Historical Perspective

This book aims to add to the existing literature on how nature and culture intersect to produce disasters as social processes. The choice of taking the

1934 Bihar–Nepal earthquake as a case study is motivated by an interest in how natural disasters were perceived and reacted upon by the state and society during the colonial period. The book focuses on the earthquake's aftermath in the geographical region that today is referred to as the state of Bihar, then a part of the province of Bihar and Orissa.[150] The earthquake of 1934 was by no means a local or even a regional disaster; the event was widely related and interpreted in media and publications across the subcontinent and also abroad. The impact of the earthquake is evident not only in records and academic publications but also from the fact that until today the earthquake serves as a time marker for births or important events,[151] and contemporary media reports a continuing memorialisation of the event.[152]

The book's first aim is thereby to join concepts from historical disaster studies with South Asian history by building upon previous research about theoretical models of disasters on the one hand, and by using a context-specific historical experience of disaster in the subcontinent on the other. By studying 'responses' after the earthquake, the book seeks to understand how the large and sudden disaster functioned as a sociopolitical event at a specific historical moment. This book argues that a sudden, unexpected and purely 'natural' disaster such as the 1934 earthquake opened a political space where political power could be contested and concentrated in relief work and rehabilitation. The book aims to understand how the earthquake and the disaster response shaped society in the aftermath. In doing so, it examines continuity and breaks with practices in previous disasters. The relationship between lessons learned and 'unlearned', between knowledge and its implementation, and between institutional adaptability and institutional change, are key issues addressed in this book. How does the response to the earthquake fit in with the larger picture of disasters in the colonial experience? To what extent can we discern a continuity with previous responses to disasters, and, or where did breaks with established practices occur? By examining responses to the 1934 earthquake, this book aims to contribute to a growing body of knowledge on how vulnerability and adaptation are shaped by historical 'natural' disasters. In doing so, the study builds upon historical research on South Asia which has dealt with disasters on a broader span and with literature addressing the role of governance, civil society and disasters.

These larger aims of the book can be further broken down into a series of questions according to the chapters. In Chapter 2, I address the government's role in the immediate aftermath by placing the official narrative of the earthquake in the larger context of colonial governance and the use of communication. What was the role of the colonial government in disaster relief? How did its perception of the earthquake as a 'natural' disaster impact the response? In Chapters 3 and 4, I examine how the collection of relief funds and distribution of aid were carried out by civil society and the colonial state on local, national and international levels. In Chapter 5, I seek to understand the allocation and distribution of relief among the victims of the earthquake. Who were the winners and losers in terms of making gains or increasingly becoming marginalised as a consequence of earthquake relief and reconstruction? In Chapter 6, I address why changes in building techniques and infrastructural construction in the aftermath did not address earthquake-safety, but instead may have increased vulnerability in future earthquakes. Can we discern any learning outcomes from the earthquake in terms of how it shaped perceptions about the built environment or how far did established ideas in urban governance prevail in reconstruction? What interests did the government and residents have in the renewal of towns and town planning? In Chapter 7, I conclude with a discussion on the patterns and ruptures discerned in responses to the earthquake and how we can understand them in relation to resilience and vulnerability. These are some of the central questions that have been dealt with throughout the course of this project.

On Methods and Approach

This book does not just construct a narrative of events but looks at some of the moments of crises that were dealt with in the aftermath. It needs to be acknowledged that the sources to a large extent are based on government archives from where correspondence, memoranda and reports have been consulted. They have served to understand why and how certain decisions of the government were taken and what implications reasoning and ideas had on the relief-response and reconstruction process. Mined from libraries and archives are also official government reports and reports by relief organisations. Although the archives have proved to be valuable sources for understanding the government's actions and its attitudes, they are often found to be dominated by an administrative or institutional 'voice' that leaves the account void of personal details and nuances. Therefore, eye-witness accounts found in poetry, private papers and manuscript collections, newspaper editorials, and accounts in regional, local and international newspapers are valuable to bridge these silences.

A real problem is a limited range of sources representing, with greater or less accuracy, the voice of people on the margins of decision-making processes in the aftermath. Any conclusions based on a limited amount of material obviously cannot make any claims to be comprehensive. This limitation entails, at times, a disproportionate focus on 'official' experiences by either the government or by relief organisations and their leaders. To counter such a misbalance, I have endeavoured to supplement and make the best use, wherever possible, of the collections of private individuals involved in the relief process, accounts in personal letters, memoirs and newspapers to provide glimpses into a variety of perceptions related to the aftermath. Nevertheless, even these sources were not always unbiased. Many times, letters, telegrams and newspapers had to be passed through government censorships before getting published, thereby making the task further complicated. Within the given constraints, using unexplored sources, it seems possible to offer a narrative of the earthquake that could help to understand responses from a variety of perspectives.

A central archival source in this research process has been correspondence, memoranda and reports emanating from the Reconstruction Department (R.D. in the notes) and the Earthquake Branch at the local government's administrative headquarters in Patna. The new department and branch centralised tasks concerning relief and reconstruction to one administrative unit since the government feared that the earthquake was likely to slow down the local government's administration by affecting 'all branches'.[153] By early February 1934, most enquiries and correspondence regarding exceptional costs, relief and damages were coordinated by the Reconstruction Department and relevant files from the other departments were renamed and transferred to the new department.[154] It processed enquiries related to damages, relief and reconstruction, except for agricultural relief which remained under the Revenue Department, and if necessary forwarded requests to the concerned departments.

A majority of the consulted files from the new department and branch contain correspondence, memoranda and reports by district officers, relief engineers and the central administration in Patna. The correspondence and participation appear to have been chaotic, not only in retrospect but also for the persons involved. District officers, experts employed for technical surveys and rural committees often had conflicting views regarding the need for reconstruction and actions to be implemented. Contrary to final accounts in the government reports, archival sources in the form of correspondence and briefings at the level of the local government administration reveal a complex and nuanced appreciation of the relief process. At the headquarters in Patna, W. B. Brett, an experienced administrator and Finance Secretary to the Government of Bihar and Orissa at the time of the earthquake, had been appointed Relief Commissioner in charge of the new Reconstruction Department in the first half of February 1934, despite the fact that he at the time of the earthquake was on leave in England.[155] Once back, he facilitated and coordinated relief measures from the local government's headquarters in Patna, with frequent visits to district towns. Though Brett did not exercise any executive powers in the district, he was often part of decisions or at least consulted on numerous issues pertaining to relief provisions and reconstruction. He was also responsible for the publication of the first government reports on the earthquake. *Report on the Progress of Earthquake Reconstruction in Bihar*, issued by Brett in June 1934,[156] was brief and intended for dissemination to specifically the Indian public through the press. It represented a culmination of publicity work that sought to promote press articles with positive accounts of the government's relief response after the publicity officer from the Department of Public Information had returned to Delhi after about two months of deputation to the government of Bihar and Orissa.[157] *A Report on the Bihar Earthquake and on the Measures Taken in Consequence Thereof up to the 31st December 1934* (henceforth referred to as *A Report on the Bihar Earthquake*), published in January 1935,[158] provided a comprehensive and summary account of the first year of relief and reconstruction and will be discussed further in the introduction of Chapter 2. The extensive use of government reports and archival sources throws light on the problem of data in terms of numbers and evidence of damages since most of these investigations of agricultural land and buildings were undertaken for the purpose of estimating the need for rehabilitation, and thereby financial compensation. The practical use of scientific reports and data collection is, for instance, demonstrated by the local government's reliance upon the Geological Survey of India (GSI), a Government of India institution.[159] The local government and not the GSI published the first 'preliminary report' of the earthquake by the GSI officers in order to provide guidelines to the public on reconstruction.[160] Despite biases, the GSI volume from 1939 dedicated to the earthquake contains a wealth of information ranging from geological investigations in the immediate aftermath to discussions on the cause of the earthquake, eye-witness accounts, images and maps. From a scientific point of view, contemporary research points to the limited data collected by the GSI officers whose work was constrained by the border between India and Nepal, and the lack of geodetic measurements in the region.[161] The same methodological issues were stated by the GSI officers themselves: investigations in Nepal were circumscribed by the special permissions granted by its government, and in India they lacked seismograms able to register the severest earthquakes (the 1934 earthquake was but one example), in addition to their perception of seismology as a neglected field in general, being looked upon as 'merely requiring the occasional attention' of the Meteorological Department and the Geological Survey of India.[162]

In addition to files of the Reconstruction Department, I have mainly consulted files of the Political Department Special Branch (sometimes referred to as 'Special Section' in the sources) and the Revenue Department Lands Branch in the Bihar State Archives (BSA).[163] The former branch addresses 'political' topics such as politically active persons, relief societies, public disturbances and disputes, and the latter mainly rural relief concerning land damages. At the National Archives of India (NAI), New Delhi, I have used various files of the Public and Political branches of the Home Department, and Foreign Department Political Branch, which address 'political' topics similar to the Political Department Special Branch at the BSA, and files from Industries and Labour, Public Works Department (PWD), about questions pertaining to the reconstruction of buildings and infrastructure. The colonial government's debates on relief and reconstruction are traced in the Historic Hansard records available online[164] and in the published *Bihar and Orissa Legislative Council Proceedings* (BOLCP) and, after Bihar and Orissa became separate provinces in 1936, in the *Bihar Legislative Council Proceedings* (BLCP) and *Bihar Legislative Council Debates* (BLCD). The council proceedings are useful for understanding conflicting interests in the reconstruction phase as well as a source of government expenditure on relief.

The India Office Records (IOR) at the British Library has also proved a valuable source for consulting government files and reports. Several narratives and accounts by prominent persons involved in the relief work and British officials' day-to-day descriptions have added alternative perspectives and viewpoints with their often personal accounts found in the European Manuscripts section. The newspaper section and the large South Asian book section provided narratives, poetry and accounts in Indian vernaculars.

In addition to government archives, officially published judicial documentation, and reports and books are available at the British Library, while the Maharajadhiraja Kameshwar Singh Kalyani Foundation (MKSKF) in Darbhanga (Bihar) hold administrative sources and private photographs of the Darbhanga Raj's reconstruction work in the aftermath. The Maharajadhiraja of Darbhanga[165] initiated the Darbhanga Improvement Trust, a scheme for town planning in Darbhanga town (see Chapter 6).[166]

Two rewarding and truly multifaceted sources for researching the aftermath have been unearthed from the Swiss archives in the form of private papers of Pierre Cérésole and the international organisational archives of Service Civil International (SCI) in Lausanne and La Chaux-de-Fonds respectively. As the founder of SCI, Cérésole ventured to Bihar three times in the aftermath (1934–37). With local cooperation partners and a small number of Europeans sent as relief workers, he set up relief centres as well as a major relocation and reconstruction project of villages endangered by the changed flood landscape.[167] Correspondence, memoranda, drawings and photo albums document the institutional network, cooperation with local organisations and the government as well as the planning and methods involved in one of the first international disaster-aid projects in South Asia.

The press disseminated news and information in the aftermath, but strict government censorship limited its scope for critical reports of relief efforts. The period 1910–45 saw a rapid growth of the vernacular press, in particular the Hindi press, which also coincided with increased pressure of the government on the vocal nationalist movement which had the support of several printing presses.[168] During the non-cooperation movements between 1919 and 1935, the government kept an eye on 'nationalist organs' such as the *Bombay Sentinel*, *Amrita Bazar Patrika* (*ABP* in notes), *Forward*, *The Searchlight*, the *Bombay Chronicle* and *Harijan*, which have been used for this research.[169] Apart from being critical of the government in general, they often voiced opinions about its response to the earthquake and highlighted actions of civil society groups. As primary sources, the newspapers provide data omitted by official records and a range of opinions by individuals and organisations regarding the management of relief. Newspapers also served as vehicles for government communiqués about relief measures undertaken and provided official data collected by government officials. They played a significant role in communicating propaganda for the sake of fund collections and drawing international attention to the earthquake. The government had support from major cosmopolitan newspapers in English, such as *The Leader*, the *Times of India* and *The Statesman*, the latter widely read, highly influential and regarded as 'unhelpful' to the nationalist cause and in the 1930s.[170]

Among the 'nationalist' newspapers, support of 'groups' or political parties formed the basis of differing opinions and rivalry in issuing statements and reporting earthquake news. The editor of the *Indian Nation*, for example, claimed that the local office of the Associated Press of India (API) deliberately withheld 'Patna news' from the newspaper in question. Even though the *Indian Nation* was a subscriber to the API, as well as being 'genuinely nationalistic', the news bureau favoured newspapers such as *The Searchlight* belonging to the same political thought, according to the editor of the *Indian Nation*.[171] Its publisher C. S. R. Somayajulu had given notice that the paper would resume publication five days after the earthquake (20 January 1934) and in laudatory acclaim of its ambition, the newspaper described itself as 'a Phoenix arising from its ashes' with the hope of working 'for the nation as a whole and not for only a particular section of it'.[172] The *Indian Nation*, first established in 1932 and published in English, was owned by the Darbhanga Raj's publishing house 'Newspapers & Publications Pvt. Ltd' and according to the government, the Maharajadhiraja of Darbhanga's mouthpiece.[173] It usually positioned itself in opposition to the INC but in May and June 1934, it published pro-Congress articles and helped to strengthen the position of the political party even though the publisher claimed to be opposed to essential parts of the Congress's political programme.[174] With its sometimes ambiguous political stance, it was considered the only moderate newspaper with any considerable circulation.[175]

The widely read Calcutta newspaper *Amrita Bazar Patrika*, branded 'extremist' by the Government of Bengal, often produced critical remarks about the government's relief response.[176] A moderate political view was expressed by the *Behar Herald*, which was published in Patna and represented the 'domiciled Bengali community'.[177] The Bihar Central Relief Committee (BCRC), a relief committee mainly run by local INC members under the leadership of Rajendra Prasad, made effective use of the 'Searchlight Press', the publishing house of the widely read newspaper *The Searchlight*[178] that was regarded by the government as the only English-medium vehicle for 'extreme nationalist opinion'.[179] It was often openly critical of the government and, as a result, faced damage suits and contempt cases.[180] The government considered it 'political', Congress-friendly and of 'influence'.[181] The Searchlight Press hosted the foundational meeting of BCRC. It issued the committee's publications, among them *Devastated Bihar: An Account of Havoc Caused by the Earthquake of the 15th January, 1934 and Relief Operation Conducted by the Committee*, which was published by late February or in the first half of March 1934.[182] The foreword described the first month of relief work, from 15 January to 15 February 1934, as 'a connected account of the devastation of the Province, of the problems facing it and the work being done to relieve the suffering of the stricken people'.[183] By providing maps, photographs and statistics, BCRC intended to provide a 'comprehensive picture' of the earthquake's aftermath for the public, who, the committee 'feared', had 'not yet been able to get an adequate conception of the havoc'.[184] The account outlined damages and relief work carried by the government as well as the committee and gave an overview of future tasks to manage. Compiled and published for the public,[185] the publication summed up and expanded on the committee's two earlier, relatively marginal publications, the short-lived weekly bulletin *Earthquake Relief* with updates from Rajendra Prasad for donors and relief workers, which ceased publication in March 1934,[186] and the summary of the weekly bulletin in a leaflet by Rajendra Prasad, *Devastated Behar: The Problem of Reconstruction*, containing suggestions on how to proceed with reconstruction already one month after the earthquake.[187] The BCRC later published a report containing data and achievements in relief work, finances and members, as well as further data on the death toll, after its second general meeting in August 1934.[188]

As noted earlier, the reports of the BCRC, as well as the Marwari Relief Society, Calcutta, served to publicise relief work undertaken and the spending of relief funds; in the case of BCRC, the committee published the reports while still appealing for funds throughout 1934. On the contrary, written records of the Ramakrishna Mission Association do not share the same wealth of information. Although librarians and administrators of the Ramakrishna Mission in Patna and Kolkata generously shared available reports and printed sources, the association's financial contributions and visibility in newspapers indicate that its presence may have been stronger than what its institutional records document.[189] Nevertheless, documentation of its work, as well as that of the Marwari Relief Society (Calcutta)[190] and BCRC, provide data and narratives on the organisation of relief work and cooperation between the government and civil society that only surfaces occasionally in the government archives. While these associations among others participated in relief work, the special status given by the local government to the Indian Red Cross and its local branch in organising emergency relief and medical aid is amply documented in the government archives and the Indian Red Cross Society's official reports.

Notes

1. The earthquake started between 2:13 p.m. and 2:14 p.m. Indian Standard Time, 15 January 1934, and continued to be felt for a period of five minutes in the central tract comprising north Bihar and Nepal, and across the Ganges, Monghyr, Patna, Barh, Jamalpur and Bhagalpur districts. John Alexander Dunn, John Bicknell Auden, A. M. N. Ghosh and D. N. Wadia (Officers of the Geological Survey of India), 'The Bihar–Nepal Earthquake of 1934', *Memoirs of the Geological Survey of India* 73 (Calcutta: Geological Survey of India, 1939; ix, 391 pp. xviii, 36 plates), 1–2. In the same volume, seismological data by S. C. Roy (Burma Meteorological Dept), 'Seismometric Study', 49–74.
2. Charles Freer Andrews, *The Indian Earthquake* (London: George Allen and Unwin Ltd, 1935).

3. William Arthur Moore (ed.), *Record of the Great Indian Earthquake: To Help the Earthquake Relief Work*, Special Issue of *The Statesman* (Calcutta: Printed and Published for *The Statesman*, 1934). Nobuji Nasu, 'No. 30, The Great Indian Earthquake of January 15, 1934', *Department Bulletin Paper* 13, no. 2, Earthquake Research Institute, Tokyo Imperial University (30 June 1935): 417–32, plate XVII–XXIII.

4. Dunn et al., 'The Bihar–Nepal Earthquake of 1934'.

5. William Bailie Brett, *A Report on the Bihar Earthquake and on the Measures Taken in Consequence thereof up to the 31st December 1934* (Patna: Superintendent, Government Printing, 1935).

6. Major General Brahma Shumsher Jung Bahadur Rana, *Nepālko Mahābhūkamp (1990 [1934])* (Nepali, 'The Great Earthquake of Nepal') (Kathmandu: Babaramahal, 1936 [first printed 1935], 249 pp., 3rd ed. by Sahayogi Press in 2041 Bikram Samvat [1984]). Nepal follows the Bikram Sambat calendar, approximately 56 years ahead of the Gregorian calendar. English translation: Major General Brahma Shumsher Jung Bahadur Rana, *The Great Earthquake in Nepal (1934 A. D.)*, trans. from Nepali by Kesar Lall (Kathmandu: Ratna Pustak Bandar, 2013, 136 pp.; rpt by Nepalaya [Kathmandu], 4th edn, 2015).

7. Brett, *A Report on the Bihar Earthquake*, 7. The same figure in Dunn et al., 'The Bihar–Nepal Earthquake of 1934', 2.

8. Twenty thousand dead according to Bihar Central Relief Committee (BCRC), *Devastated Bihar: An Account of Havoc Caused by the Earthquake of the 15th January, 1934 and Relief Operation Conducted by the Committee* (Patna: Bihar Central Relief Committee, 1934), 2.

9. Soma Nath Sapkota, Laurent Bollinger and Frédéric Perrier, 'Fatality Rates of the Mw ~8.2, 1934, Bihar–Nepal Earthquake and Comparison with the April 2015 Gorkha Earthquake', *Earth, Planets and Space* 68, no. 40 (2016): 1–9, 1. The estimates of the death toll will be discussed in Chapter 2.

10. The moment magnitude scale (Mw) is based on the seismic moment of an earthquake. It can be determined directly from instrumental observations or inferred from macroseismic intensity observations, that is, the ground-shaking strength based on reports of felt and damage effects. Emanuela Guidoboni and John E. Ebel, *Earthquakes and Tsunamis in the Past: A Guide to Techniques in Historical Seismology* (Cambridge: Cambridge University Press 2009), 526–27. Mw 8.1 or 8.2 are mentioned in Roger Bilham and Susan E. Hough, 'Site Response of the Ganges Basin Inferred from Re-evaluated Macroseismic Observations from the 1897 Shillong, 1905 Kangra, and 1934 Nepal Earthquakes', *Journal of Earth System Science* 117, no. S2 (November 2008): 773–82, 775–77.

11. Samantha Jones, Katie J. Oven and Ben Wisner, 'A Comparison of the Governance Landscape of Earthquake Risk Reduction in Nepal and the Indian State of Bihar', *International Journal of Disaster Risk Reduction* 15 (2016): 29–42, 29.

12. The geological survey of the earthquake divided the area into zones according to the Mercalli modification of the Rossi-Forel scale used for classifying earthquake intensity by measuring the physical impact of a quake on human beings and the environment. The GSI also referred to the scale as 'the Mercalli scale ... with certain additions and modifications'. Isoseismal X for the worst-affected area was located in the districts of Darbhanga, Champaran and Muzaffarpur in north Bihar, and south of the Ganges in Monghyr. Dunn et al., 'The Bihar–Nepal Earthquake of 1934', 7, and 'Chapter 2: Discussion on Scales and Isoseismals'. The authors offer yet another explanation of the scale:

    > [T]he scale normally adopted by the Geological Survey of India is the Rossi-Forel scale, which is pitched in such a way that R.-F. [Rossi-Forel scale] [isoseismal] X is roughly equivalent to Mercalli [scale] IX and X [isoseismals]. For a truer comparison to be made with some of the other Indian earthquakes, it would be better to consider the whole of the area within Mercalli isoseismal IX as that in which the earthquake was severely felt. This area is approximately 14,000 square miles or 36,200 square km in extent. (Ibid., 16)

    Pandey and Molnar refer to the scale adopted by the GSI for the Bihar–Nepal earthquake as the 'Rossi-Forel scale', referring to Dunn et al., 'The Bihar–Nepal Earthquake of 1934'. M. R. Pandey and Peter Molnar, 'The Distribution of Intensity of the Bihar–Nepal Earthquake of 15 January 1934 and Bounds on the Extent of the Rupture Zone', *Journal of Nepal Geological Society* 5, no. 1 (1988): 22–44, 24.

13. Located at 27.55°N, 87.09°N according to Wang-Ping Chen and Peter Molnar, 'Seismic Moments of Major Earthquakes and the Average Rate of Slip in Central Asia', *Journal of Geophysical Research Atmospheres* 82, no. 20 (1977): 2945–47, in Bilham and Hough, 'Site Response of the Ganges Basin', 776.

14. Roger Bilham, 'Location and Magnitude of the 1833 Nepal Earthquake and Its Relation to the Rupture Zones of Contiguous Great Himalayan Earthquakes', *Current Science* 69, no. 2 (1995): 101–28. Dunn et al., 'The Bihar–Nepal Earthquake of 1934', 116–17.

15. The 20 August 1988 earthquake measured Mw 6.6 and caused an estimated number of 1,004 deaths. S. K. Jain and N. C. Nigam, 'Historical Developments and Current Status of Earthquake Engineering in India', *Proceedings of the Twelfth World Conference on Earthquake Engineering*, Auckland, New Zealand,

30 January–4 February 2000, Paper no. 1792: 2; D. R. Nandy, A. K. Choudhury, C. Chakraborty and P. L. Narula, 'Geological Survey of India, Bihar–Nepal Earthquake, August 20, 1988', *Special Publication Geological Survey of India* 31 (1993). Udaypur (Udaipur) was also severely affected by the 1934 earthquake, according to both Nepalese and Indian primary sources (Rana, *Nepālko Mahābhūkamp (1990 [1934])*, and Dunn et al., 'The Bihar–Nepal Earthquake of 1934') in Pandey and Molnar, 'The Distribution of Intensity of the Bihar–Nepal Earthquake', 32.

16. S. Mitra, Ajay Kumar, Shashwat K. Singh, Siddharth Dey and Debacharan Powali, 'The 25 April 2015 Nepal Earthquake and Its Aftershocks', *Current Science* 108, no. 10 (25 May 2015): 1938–43. The earthquake affected mainly central Nepal and had its epicentre located 80 kilometres northwest of Kathmandu. It was followed by an Mw 7.3 earthquake northeast of the capital in Dolakha district less than three weeks later. In Bihar, only 60 people were killed. Jones et al., 'A Comparison of the Governance Landscape', 29. On the death toll of the April 2015 Gorkha earthquake, see Sapkota et al., 'Fatality Rates of the Mw ~8.2', 7.

17. Amod M. Dixit, L. R. Dwelley-Samat, M. Nakarmi, S. B. Pradhanang and B. Tucker, 'The Kathmandu Valley Earthquake Risk Management Project: An Evaluation', 12WCEE: 12th World Conference on Earthquake Engineering, Auckland, New Zealand, 30 January–4 February 2000, New Zealand Society for Earthquake Engineering, Upper Hutt, New Zealand, 2000, 8 pp. See also Anand S. Arya, *Damage Scenario under Hypothetical Recurrence of 1934 Earthquake Intensities in Various Districts in Bihar* (Patna: Bihar State Disaster Management Authority, Government of Bihar, August 2013).

18. See Pandey and Molnar, 'The Distribution of Intensity of the Bihar–Nepal Earthquake'; B. L. Jatana, 'Fail-safe Large Dams in Earthquake Prone Himalayan Region', *ISET Journal of Earthquake Technology* 36, no. 1 (1999): 1–13. For an exhaustive guide to historical seismology, see Guidoboni and Ebel, *Earthquakes and Tsunamis in the Past*. With specific reference to India, Anu Kapur provides a bibliography of reports and secondary sources on earthquakes and seismology since the mid-nineteenth century. Anu Kapur, *On Disasters in India* (New Delhi: Cambridge University Press India Pvt. Ltd., 2009), 167–75; see also Anu Kapur, *Vulnerable India: A Geographical Study of Disasters* (Shimla: Indian Institute of Advanced Study, Sage Publications, 2010).

19. Arun Bapat, R. C. Kulkarni and S. K. Guha, *Catalogue of Earthquakes in India and Neighbourhood from Historical Period up to 1979* (Roorkee: Indian Society of Earthquake Technology, 1983). R. C. Quittmeyer and K. H. Jacob, 'Historical and Modern Seismicity of Pakistan, Afghanistan, Northwestern India, and

South-Eastern Iran', *Bulletin of the Seismological Society of America* 69, no 3 (1979): 773–823. N. Ambraseys and D. Jackson, 'A Note on Early Earthquakes in Northern India and Southern Tibet', *Current Science* 84, no. 4 (2003): 570–82. N. Ambraseys, 'Three Little Known Early Earthquakes in India', *Current Science* 86, no. 4 (25 February 2004): 506–08. Sudhir K. Jain, 'Indian Earthquakes: An Overview', *Indian Concrete Journal* (November 1998): 555–61. The geologist Roger Bilham has written about historical earthquakes in north and northwestern India, among them the 1934 earthquake. Roger Bilham, 'Earthquakes in India and the Himalaya: Tectonics, Geodesy and History', *Annals of Geophysics* 47, nos. 2/3 (April/June 2004): 839–58; Roger Bilham, 'Slip Parameters for the Rann of Kachchh, India, 16 June 1819, Earthquake, Quantified from Contemporary Accounts', in *Coastal Tectonics*, ed. I.S. Stewart and C. Vita-Finzi, 295–318 (London: Geological Society, 1999); Roger Bilham, 'Slow Tilt Reversal of the Lesser Himalaya Between 1862 and 1992 at 78°E, and Bounds to the Southeast Rupture of the 1905 Kangra Earthquake', *Geophysical Journal International* 144, no. 3 (2001): 713–28; Roger Bilham, Vinod K. Gaur and Peter Molnar, 'Himalayan Seismic Hazard', *Science* 293, no. 5534 (2001): 1442–44; Bilham and Hough, 'Site Response of the Ganges Basin'; Nicholas Ambraseys and Roger Bilham, 'A Note on the Kangra $Ms = 7.8$ Earthquake of 4 April 1905', *Current Science* 79, no. 1 (10 July 2000): 45–50.

20. *Harijan*, 16 February 1934, reproduced in Krishna Dutta and Andrew Robinson (eds.), *Selected Letters of Rabindranath Tagore*, vol. 53, University of Cambridge Oriental Publications (Cambridge: Cambridge University Press, 1997), 537.

21. Shambhu Prasad confuses the year of the event, that is, 'the Bihar earthquake of 1932', when the correct year is 1934, see Shambhu Prasad, 'Towards an Understanding of Gandhi's Views on Science', *Economic and Political Weekly* 36, no. 39 (2001): 3721–32; Sunil Khilnani, 'Nehru's Faith', *Economic and Political Weekly* 37, no. 48 (2002): 4739–99, 4795–96; Sukumar Muralidharan, 'Religion, Nationalism and the State: Gandhi and India's Engagement with Political Modernity', *Social Scientist* 34, nos. 3/4 (March–April 2006): 3–36, 12–13.

22. Vinay Lal, 'The Gandhi Everyone Loves to Hate', *Economic and Political Weekly* 43, no. 40 (2008): 55–64, 58.

23. Judith M. Brown, *Gandhi: Prisoner of Hope* (New Haven: Yale University Press, 1989), 274.

24. Sabyasachi Bhattacharya (ed.), *The Mahatma and the Poet: Letters and Debates between Gandhi and Tagore 1915–1941* (New Delhi: National Book Trust, 1997), 31.

25. Makarand R. Paranjape, "'Natural Supernaturalism?" The Tagore–Gandhi Debate on the Bihar Earthquake', *The Journal of Hindu Studies* 4, no. 2 (2011): 176–204, 177, 197.

26. Eleonor Marcussen, 'Explaining the 1934 Bihar–Nepal Earthquake: The Role of Science, Astrology, and "Rumours"', in *Historical Disaster Experiences: Towards a Comparative and Transcultural History of Disasters across Asia and Europe*, ed. Gerrit Jasper Schenk, 241–66, Transcultural Research—Heidelberg Studies on Asia and Europe in a Global Context (Heidelberg: Springer, 2017).

27. Sumathi Ramaswamy, *The Lost Land of Lemuria: Fabulous Geographies, Catastrophic Histories* (Berkeley: University of California Press, 2004), 13.

28. Urte Undine Frömming, *Naturkatastrophen. Kulturelle Deutung und Verarbeitung* (Natural Disasters: Cultural Interpretation and Processing) (Frankfurt/New York: Campus Verlag, 2006), 214–15.

29. Andrea Janku, Gerrit J. Schenk and Franz Mauelshagen, 'Introduction', in *Historical Disasters in Context: Science, Religion, and Politics*, ed. Andrea Janku, Gerrit Jasper Schenk and Franz Mauelshagen, 1–14 (New York; London: Routledge, 2012), 9.

30. Jamuna Prasad trained with Fredric C. Bartlett (1886–1969) at Cambridge in the 1930s and returned to India where he engaged in social psychological research. Wade E. Pickren and Alexandra Rutherford, *A History of Modern Psychology in Context* (Hoboken, New Jersey: Wiley & Sons, 2010), 245.

31. Jamuna Prasad, 'The Psychology of Rumour: A Study Relating to the Great Indian Earthquake of 1934', *British Journal of Psychology* 26, no. 1 (1935): 1–15, 1, 9.

32. Hart's article (with the same main title as Prasad's: 'The Psychology of Rumour') was re-published as a chapter in his book *Psychopathology* from 1927, which Prasad refers to in the article from 1935. J. Prasad, 'The Psychology of Rumour', 5. See 'Preface', in Bernard Hart, *Psychopathology: Its Development and Its Place in Medicine* (Cambridge: Cambridge University Press, 1927). Prashant Bordia and Nicholas DiFonzo, 'When Social Psychology Became Less Social: Prasad and the History of Rumour Research', *Asian Journal of Social Psychology* 5, no. 1 (2002): 49–61, 51.

33. Jamuna Prasad, 'A Comparative Study of Rumours and Reports in Earthquakes', *British Journal of Psychology* 41, nos. 3/4 (1950): 129–44.

34. Bordia and DiFonzo, 'When Social Psychology Became Less Social', 51. J. Prasad, 'A Comparative Study of Rumours and Reports in Earthquakes', 133.

35. However, his research clearly inspired Durgananda Sinha (1922–98) who carried out a study of rumours in 'catastrophic situations' of landslides following unusually heavy rains in Darjeeling in June 1950. Durgananda Sinha, 'Behaviour in a Catastrophic Situation: A Psychological Study of Reports and Rumours', *British*

Journal of Psychology (General Section) 43, no. 3 (August, 1952): 200–09. Sinha was, like Prasad, a student of Bartlett at Cambridge, and returned to India as faculty in Patna where he pursued his interests in memory, cognitive processes and, not the least, anxiety which would become one of his important fields of research. Cf. Girishwar Misra, 'Obituary: Professor Durgananda Sinha (1922–1998)', *Cross-Cultural Psychology Bulletin* 32, no. 3 (September, 1998): 6–10. Interestingly, the memory of the 1934 earthquake resurfaced in rumours about disasters. Sinha, 'Behaviour in a Catastrophic Situation', 202–03.

36. According to Festinger's theory, dissonance between two conflicting beliefs and actions can be reduced or overcome by either seeking consistency, reducing the importance of both or adding more consonant beliefs to outweigh the dissonance between the two. Leon Festinger, *A Theory of Cognitive Dissonance* (Stanford, CA: Stanford University Press, 1962 [1957]), 236–37. Biographical details in Pickren and Rutherford, *A History of Modern Psychology in Context*, 245. Bordia and DiFonzo, 'When Social Psychology Became Less Social', 59n1.

37. He also compares Prasad's article from 1935 with data on rumours in Sinha's article, 'Behaviour in Catastrophic Situation.' Festinger, *A Theory of Cognitive Dissonance*, 237, 239–41.

38. Festinger, *A Theory of Cognitive Dissonance*, 238–39.

39. Prasad does not mention Patna as the site for the rumours but he personally verified the truth or fabrication of the rumours by observation in Patna while the other rumours in Darbhanga appear to have been collected from newspapers or other persons. Prasad continued collecting rumours until the end of February when road communication had been restored and the scope of damage was known, and did a follow-up study after aftershocks on 2 June and 19 August 1934. J. Prasad, 'The Psychology of Rumour', 1, 6, 9.

40. These are the official numbers that could have been accessible to Festinger, in Brett, *A Report on the Bihar Earthquake*, 8, 61, 63.

41. For reference to Prasad, see p. 257 in Ranajit Guha, *Elementary Aspects of Peasant Insurgency in Colonial India* (London, Durham: Duke University Press, 1999 [1983]).

42. Guha, *Elementary Aspects*, 253. Also, Arun Kumar, *Rewriting the Language of Politics: Kisans in Colonial Bihar* (Delhi: Manohar Publishers, 2001), 79.

43. Guha draws upon Lefebvre's work on rumours among the French peasantry during the French revolution. Georges Lefebvre, *The Great Fear of 1789: Rural Panic in Revolutionary France* (New York: Vintage Books, 1973 [French original publication 1932]). The role of rumours in communication is also discussed in Homi K. Bhabha, *The Location of Culture* (London; New York: Routledge, 1994); Kim A.

Wagner, *The Great Fear of 1857: Rumours, Conspiracies and the Making of the Indian Uprising* (Oxford: Peter Lang, 2010). For a detailed account and analysis of Guha's understanding of rumours as well as an overview of the rumours in history writing, see 'Chapter 3, Rumour: Beyond Muffled Murmurs of Dissent', in A. Kumar, *Rewriting the Language of Politics*. The communicative function of rumour 'in a predominantly illiterate society' is also mentioned in Sumit Sarkar, *Modern India, 1885–1947* (Cambridge Commonwealth series. Basingstoke: Macmillan, 1989 [1983]), 181–83.

44. Guha, *Elementary Aspects*, 254–55.

45. Praveen Singh, 'The Colonial State, Zamindars and the Politics of Flood Control in North Bihar (1850–1945)', *Indian Economic Social History Review* 45, no. 2 (2008): 239–59. Praveen Singh, '"Colonising the Rivers": Colonial Technology, Irrigation and Flood Control in North Bihar, 1850–1950', unpublished PhD dissertation, Centre for Historical Studies, School of Social Sciences, Jawaharlal Nehru University, 2003. Christopher V. Hill, *River of Sorrow: Environment and Social Control in Riparian North India, 1770–1994*, Monograph and Occasional Paper Series, No. 5. (Ann Arbor, Michigan: Association for Asian Studies, 1997). Nitin Sinha, 'Fluvial Landscapes and the State: Property and the Gangetic Diaras in Colonial India, 1790s–1890s', *Environment and History* 2, no. 20 (May 2014): 209–37.

46. Rohan D'Souza, *Drowned and Dammed: Colonial Capitalism and Flood Control in Eastern India* (New Delhi: Oxford University Press, 2006). Braja Bandhu Bhatta, *The Natural Calamities in Orissa in the 19th Century* (New Delhi: Commonwealth Publishers, 1997).

47. Bihar and Orissa formed a province from 1912 to 1936 when it was split into two separate provinces. Starting with the tax year 1936–37, Bihar and Orissa were governed as separate provinces. S. M. Wasi, *Bihar and Orissa in 1936–37* (Patna: Superintendent, Government Printing, 1938), 23–24.

48. Dinesh Kumar Mishra, 'Bihar Floods: The Inevitable Has Happened', *Economic and Political Weekly* 43, no. 26 (September 2008): 8–12.

49. Bal Mokand Bhatia, *Famines in India: A Study in Some Aspects of the Economic History of India with Special Reference to Food Problem, 1860–1990* (Delhi: Konark Publishers, 1991 [3rd ed. 1967]). Ira Klein, 'When the Rains Failed. Famine, Relief, and Mortality in British India', *The Indian Economic and Social History Review* 21, no. 2 (1984): 185–214. Aditee Nag Chowdhury-Zilly, *The Vagrant Peasant: Agrarian Distress and Desertion in Bengal; 1770–1830*. Beiträge zur Südasienforschung, Band 71 (Wiesbaden, Franz Steiner Verlag, 1982), 27–28. Most influential is the seminal study by Amartya Sen, *Poverty*

and Famines: An Essay on Entitlement and Deprivation (Oxford: Clarendon Press, 1981).

50. Lee Clarke, 'Possibilistic Thinking: A New Conceptual Tool for Thinking about Extreme Events', *Social Research* 75, no. 3, Fall (2008): 669–90.

51. Arno Borst, 'Das Erdbeben von 1348. Ein historischer Beitrag zur Katastrophenforschung', *Historische Zeitschrift* 233, no. 1 (1981): 529–68; Monica Juneja and Franz Mauelshagen, 'Disasters and Pre-Industrial Societies: Historiographic Trends and Comparative Perspectives', *The Medieval History Journal* 10, nos. 1–2 (2007): 1–31; Andreas Ranft and Stephan Selzer, 'Städte aus Trümmern: Einleitende Überlegungen' (Cities in Ruins: Introductory Considerations), in *Städte aus Trümmern: Katastrophenbewältigung zwischen Antike und Moderne*, ed. Andreas Ranft and Stephan Selzer, 9–25 (Göttingen: Vandenhoeck & Ruprecht, 2004); Gerrit Jasper Schenk, 'Historical Disaster Research: State of Research, Concepts, Methods and Case Studies', *Historical Social Research* 32, no. 3 (2007): 9–31.

52. John R. McNeill, José Augusto Pádua, Mahesh Rangarajan, *Environmental History: As If Nature Existed* (New Delhi: Oxford University Press, 2010); Richard H. Grove, *Green Imperialism: Colonial Expansion, Tropical Island Edens and the Origins of Environmentalism, 1600–1860* (Cambridge: Cambridge University Press, 1995).

53. Nigel Clark, 'Geo-Politics and the Disaster of the Anthropocene', in *Disasters and Politics: Materials, Experiments, Preparedness*, ed. Manuel Torini, Israel Rodriguez-Giralt and Michael Guggenheim, 19–37 (Oxford; West Sussex: Wiley Blackwell/ The Sociological Review, 2014), 21 (originally published in *The Sociological Review* 62, S1 [(2014]: 19–37). Dipesh Chakrabarty, 'The Climate of History: Four Theses', *Critical Inquiry* 35 (Winter 2009): 197–222. Rune T. Slettebak, 'Don't Blame the Weather: Climate-related Natural Disasters and Civil Conflict', *Journal of Peace Research* 49, no. 1: 163–76.

54. Rob Nixon, *Slow Violence and the Environmentalism of the Poor* (Cambridge, MA; London: Harvard University Press, 2011), 2–3.

55. Schenk, 'Historical Disaster Research', 19. Gerrit J. Schenk and Jens Ivo Engels (eds.), 'Historische Katastrophenforschung: Begriffe, Konzepte und Fallbeispiele' (Historical Disaster Research: Concepts, Methods and Case Studies), Theme Issue, *Historische Sozialforschung* (*Historical Social Research*) 32, no. 3 (2007). Christof Mauch (ed.), *Natural Disasters, Cultural Responses: Case Studies toward a Global Environmental History* (Lanham, MD: Lexington Books, 2009). Susanna M. Hoffman and Anthony Oliver-Smith (eds.), *Catastrophe and Culture: The Anthropology of Disaster* (Santa Fe, NM: School of American Research Press, 2002).

For comparative historical disaster studies, see Juneja and Mauelshagen, 'Disasters and Pre-Industrial Societies', 27–28. Alessa Johns (ed.), *Dreadful Visitations: Confronting Natural Catastrophe in the Age of Enlightenment* (New York and London: Routledge, 1999). For an overview of the development of disaster studies in the social sciences, mainly from a sociological perspective, see David Brunsma and J. Steven Picou, 'Disasters in the Twenty-First Century: Modern Destruction and Future Instruction', *Social Forces* 87, no. 2 (2008): 983–91. For the study of 'disaster cultures' or 'cultures of disaster' (*Katastrophenkulturen*), see Carsten Felgentreff and Wolf R. Dombrowsky, 'Hazards-, Risiko- und Katastrophenforschung', in *Naturrisiken und Sozialkatastrophen*, ed. Carsten Felgentreff and Thomas Glade, 13–29 (Berlin; Heidelberg: Spektrum Akademischer Verlag, 2008). For a literature overview over the use of disasters as an analytical category in the field of history, see Jonathan Bergman, 'Disaster: A Useful Category of Historical Analysis', *History Compass* 6, no. 3 (2008): 934–46.

56. Ben Wisner, Piers Blaikie, Terry Cannon and Ian Davis, *At Risk: Natural Hazards, People's Vulnerability, and Disasters*, 2nd ed. (London: Routledge, 2004 [1994]), 18–19. On the constructionist disaster paradigm dominating academic discourse and applied social science research, see Phil O'Keefe, Ken Westgate and Ben Wisner, 'Taking the Naturalness out of Natural Disasters', *Nature* 260, no. 5552 (1976): 566–67; and later in David Alexander, 'The Study of Natural Disasters, 1977–1997: Some Reflections on a Changing Field of Knowledge', *Disasters* 21, no. 4 (1997): 284–304. The idea that human beings play a major role in shaping the impact of 'natural' disasters is also accepted by major development agencies, see The World Bank and The United Nations, *Natural Hazards, Unnatural Disasters: The Economics of Effective Prevention* (Washington, DC: The International Bank for Reconstruction and Development/The World Bank, 2010); Janet Abramovitz, 'Unnatural Disasters', in Linda Starke (ed.), *Worldwatch Paper 158* (Washington, DC: Worldwatch Institute, October 2001).

57. Wisner et al., *At Risk*, 11. See also Ben Wisner and Henry R. Luce, 'Disaster Vulnerability: Scale, Power and Daily Life', *GeoJournal* 30, no. 2 (1993): 127–40. 'Vulnerability' is a major theme in anthropological studies of disasters. For a comprehensive overview, see, for instance, Anthony Oliver-Smith and Susanna M. Hoffman (eds.), *The Angry Earth: Disaster in an Anthropological Perspective* (London: Routledge, 1999).

58. United Nations, *2009 UNISDR Terminology on Disaster Risk Reduction* (Geneva: United Nations International Strategy for Disaster Risk Reduction), 2009), 24. Research into the concept of resilience, 'to resile from' or 'spring back from' a shock, has received criticism for emphasising a return to 'normal' rather than seeing to the

changes a disaster can bring about. Siambabala Bernard Manyena, Geoff O'Brien, Phil O'Keefe and Joanne Rose, 'Disaster Resilience: A Bounce Back or Bounce Forward Ability?' *Local Environment* 16, no. 5 (May 2011): 417–24.

59. For a discussion on 'nature' and the 'natural' in disasters, see Carsten Felgentreff and Thomas Glade, 'Naturrisiken–Sozialkatastrophen: zum Geleit', in *Naturrisiken und Sozialkatastrophen*, ed. Carsten Felgentreff and Thomas Glade, 1–10 (Berlin; Heidelberg: Spektrum Akademischer Verlag, 2008). For natural disasters as 'unnatural' from different perspectives, see Mike Davis, *Ecology of Fear: Los Angeles and the Imagination of Disaster* (New York, NY: Vintage Books, 1999); The Steinberg, *Acts of God: The Unnatural History of Natural Disaster in America* (New York, NY: Oxford University Press, 2000); Gary Stern, *Can God Intervene? How Religion Explains Natural Disasters* (West Port, Connecticut; London: Praeger, 2007).

60. Wisner et al., *At Risk*, 18.

61. Susanna M. Hoffman, 'After Atlas Shrugs: Cultural Change or Persistence after a Disaster', in *The Angry Earth: Disaster in an Anthropological Perspective*, ed. Anthony Oliver-Smith and Susanna M. Hoffman, 302–25 (London: Routledge, 1999).

62. Kevin Rozario, 'What Comes Down Must Go Up: Why Disasters Have Been Good for American Capitalism', in *American Disasters*, ed. Steven Biel, 72–102 (New York: New York University Press, 2001), 75–77. Christopher L. Dyer, 'The Phoenix Effect in Post-Disaster Recovery: An Analysis of the Economic Development Administration's Culture of Response after Hurricane Andrew', in *The Angry Earth: Disaster in Anthropological Perspective*, ed. A. Oliver-Smith and S. M. Hoffman, 278–300 (London: Routledge, 1999), 279.

63. Kai Weise, 'Summary and Commentary', in *Revisiting Kathmandu: Safeguarding Living Urban Heritage*, ed. K. Weise, 1–47, International Symposium Kathmandu Valley, 25–29 November 2013 (Paris: UNSECO, 2015), 7–8.

64. Thomas Birkland, 'Natural Disasters as Focusing Events: Policy Communities and Political Response', *International Journal of Mass Emergencies and Disasters* 14, no. 2 (1996): 221–43. Thomas Birkland, *Lessons of Disaster: Policy Change after Catastrophic Events* (Washington, D.C.: Georgetown University Press, 2006). Also see David Butler, 'Focusing Events in the Early Twentieth Century: A Hurricane, Two Earthquakes, and a Pandemic', in *Emergency Management: The American Experience, 1900–2005*, ed. Claire B. Ruben, ch. 2, 11–48 (Fairfax, VA: Public Entity Risk Institute, 2007).

65. Anu Sabhlok, 'Sewa in Relief: Gendered Geographies of Disaster in Relief in Gujarat, India', PhD dissertation, Geography and Women's Studies, Pennsylvania

State University, UMI number: 3266196, 2007. Edward Simpson, *The Political Biography of An Earthquake: Aftermath and Amnesia in Gujarat, India* (New Delhi: Oxford University Press, 2014). David Sanderson and Anshu Sharma, 'Winners and Losers from the 2001 Gujarat Earthquake', *Environment and Urbanization* 20, no. 1 (2008): 177–86; Martha Patricia Kirpes, 'Bringing Environmental Justice to Natural Hazards: An Earthquake Vulnerability and Reconstruction Case Comparison from India', PhD dissertation, Natural Resources and Environment, University of Michigan, UMI number 9825270, 1998.

66. Edward Simpson and Stuart Corbridge, 'The Geography of Things That May Become Memories: The 2001 Earthquake in Kachchh–Gujarat and the Politics of Rehabilitation in the Prememorial Era', *Annals of the Association of American Geographers* 96, no. 3 (2006): 566–85; Edward Simpson, 'The "Gujarat" Earthquake and the Political Economy of Nostalgia', *Contributions to Indian Sociology* 39, no. 2 (2005): 219–49; Edward Simpson and Malathi de Alwis, 'Remembering Natural Disaster: Politics and Culture of Memorials in Gujarat and Sri Lanka', *Anthropology Today* 24, no. 4 (2008): 6–12. Manasi Kumar, 'A Journey into the Bleeding City: Following the Footprints of the Rubble of Riot and Violence of Earthquake in Gujarat, India', *Psychology and Developing Societies* 19, no. 1 (2007): 1–36. Jayasinhji Jhala, 'In Time of Fear and Terror: Seeing, Assessing, Assisting—Understanding and Living the Reality and Consequence of Disaster', *Visual Anthropology Review* 20, no. 1 (2004): 59–69. Lyla Mehta, 'Reflections on the Kutch Earthquake', *Economic and Political Weekly* 36, no. 31 (August 2001): 2931–36.

67. Frida Hastrup, *Weathering the World: Recovering in the Wake of the Tsunami in a Tamil Fishing Village* (Oxford; New York: Berghan Books, 2011). Aaron Patrick Mulvany, 'Flood of Memories: Narratives of Flood and Loss in Tamil South India', PhD dissertation, South Asia Regional Studies, University of Pennsylvania, UMI number: 348516, 2011.

68. Emmanuel Raju, 'Exploring Disaster Recovery Coordination: Stakeholder Interfaces, Goals and Interdependencies', PhD Dissertation, Faculty of Engineering, Lund University, 2013.

69. In sociological disaster research, the term 'scaling' is used for determining the 'size' of a disaster on a range from 'everyday emergencies' to 'complete annihilation of a society'. Martin Voss and Klaus Wagner, 'Learning from (Small) Disasters', *Natural Hazards* 55, no. 3 (2010): 657–69, 662, 667.

70. Christian Pfister, 'Learning from Nature-Induced Disasters: Theoretical Considerations and Case Studies from Western Europe', in *Natural Disasters, Cultural Responses: Case Studies toward a Global Environmental History*, ed. Christof Mauch and Christian Pfister, 17–40 (Lanham, MD: Lexington Books, 2009), 20.

71. Christian Pfister, 'Die "Katastrophenluecke" des 20. Jahrhunderts und der Verlust traditionalen Risikobewusstseins', *GAIA* 18, no. 3 (2009): 239–46, 240.

72. Stewart Williams, 'Rethinking the Nature of Disaster: From Failed Instruments of Learning to a Post-Social Understanding', *Social Forces* 87, no. 2 (2008): 1115–38, 1116, 1128–31.

73. James K. Mitchell, 'Including the Capacity for Coping with Surprises in Post-Disaster Recovery Policies. Reflections on the Experience of Tangshan, China', *Behemoth. A Journal on Civilization* 1, no. 3 (2008): 21–38.

74. Williams, 'Rethinking the Nature of Disaster', 1117. Ulrich Beck, *Risk Society: Towards a New Modernity* (London: Sage Publications, 1992 [*Risikogesellschaft. Auf dem Weg in eine andere Moderne*. Frankfurt am Maine: Suhrkamp, 1986]); Ulrich Beck, 'Living in the World Risk Society', *Economy and Society* 35, no. 3 (2006): 329–45.

75. Simpson, *The Political Biography of an Earthquake*, 250.

76. Jared M. Diamond, *Collapse: How Societies Chose to Fail or Succeed* (New York: Viking, 2005). Critical review by Scott E. Page, 'Are We Collapsing? A Review of Diamond's *Collapse: How Societies Chose to Fail or Succeed*', *Journal of Economic Literature* 43, no. 4 (December 2005): 1049–62.

77. Bas van Bavel, Daniel R. Curtis and Jessica Dijkman, Matthew Hannaford, Maïka de Keyzer, Eline van Onacker and Tim Soens, *Disasters and History: The Vulnerability and Resilience of Past Societies* (Cambridge: Cambridge University Press, 2020), 1.

78. Gregory Clancey, *Earthquake Nation: The Cultural Politics of Japanese Seismicity, 1868–1930* (Berkeley: University of California Press, 2006), 4.

79. Ch. 7: 'Japanese Architecture after Nōbi', in Clancey, *Earthquake Nation*, 180–211.

80. Dieter Groh, Michael Kempe and Franz Mauelshagen, in 'Einleitung. Naturkatastrophen—wahrgenommen, gedeutet, dargestellt', in *Naturkatastrophen: Beiträge zu ihrer Deutung, Wahrnehmung und Darstellung in Text und Bild von der Antike bis ins 20. Jahrhundert*, ed. D. Groh, M. Kempe and F. Mauelshagen, 11–33 (Tübingen: Gunter Narr Verlag, 2003), 25.

81. Chris Courtney, *The Nature of Disaster in China: The 1931 Yanqzi River Flood* (Cambridge, UK: Cambridge University Press, 2018), 10–11.

82. van Bavel et al., *Disasters and History*, 43.

83. Hoffman, 'After Atlas Shrugs', 310.

84. Rozario, 'What Comes Down Must Go Up'.

85. Janet Borland, 'Capitalising on Catastrophe: Reinvigorating the Japanese State with Moral Values through Education Following the 1923 Great Kanto Earthquake', *Modern Asian Studies* 40, no. 4 (2006): 875–907.

86. Greg Bankoff, *Cultures of Disaster: Society and Natural Hazard in the Philippines* (London: Routledge Curzon, 2003), 153.

87. Ibid., 159–60.

88. Heritage conservation can be an asset in disaster risk reduction, as outlined in Rohit Jigyasu, 'From "Natural" to "Cultural" Disaster: Consequences of Post-Earthquake Rehabilitation Process on Cultural Heritage in Marathwada Region, India', UNESCO–ICOMOS Conference. Earthquake-safe: Lessons to be Learned from Traditional Construction, Istanbul, 2001. Earthquakes are geological hazards which only when they affect human societies are considered natural disasters. Wisner et al., *At Risk*, 10, 17.

89. Susan E. Hough, *Earthshaking Science: What We Know (and Don't Know) about Earthquakes* (Princeton and Oxford: Princeton University Press, 2002), 193.

90. The definition of disaster as 'event' and 'process' is from Gary A. Kreps, 'Disaster: Systemic Event and Social Catalyst', in *What Is a Disaster? Perspectives on the Question*, ed. E. L. Quarantelli, 25–50 (London, New York: Routledge, 1998), 41.

91. Robert A. Stallings, 'Disasters and the Theory of Social Order', in *What Is a Disaster? Perspectives on the Question*, ed. E. L. Quarantelli, 127–46 (London, New York: Routledge, 1998), 131.

92. See Dadabhai Naoroji, *Poverty and Un-British Rule in India* (London: Swan Sonnenschein & Co., 1901). Also in David Arnold, *Famine: Social Crisis and Historical Change* (Oxford: Basil Blackwell, 1988), 116–17; David Hall-Matthews, *Peasants, Famine and the State in Colonial Western India* (New York: Palgrave and MacMillan, 2005), 2.

93. According to Sen, so-called food availability decline does not explain why some segments of society starve during famines while others remain immune. Sen, *Poverty and Famines*.

94. Madhav Gadgil and Ramachandra Guha, *This Fissured Land: An Ecological History of India* (New Delhi: Oxford University Press, 1992), 116–18.

95. Ramachandra Guha, *The Unquiet Woods: Ecological Change and Peasant Resistance in the Himalaya* (Berkeley: University of California Press, 2000 [1989]); Mahesh Rangarajan and K. Sivaramakrishnan, 'Introduction', in *Shifting Ground: People, Animals, and Mobility in India's Environmental History*, ed. M. Rangarajan and K. Sivaramakrishnan, 1–29 (Oxford University Press: Oxford Scholarship Online, 2014, accessed 5 July 2015).

96. Gadgil and Guha, *This Fissured Land*, 116–18; Ramachandra Guha, *The Unquiet Woods*; Arnold, *The Problem of Nature*, 175–80.

97. K. Sivaramakrishnan and Gunnel Cederlöf, 'Introduction. Ecological Nationalisms—Claiming Nature for Making History', in *Ecological Nationalisms:*

Nature, Livelihoods, and Identities in South Asia, ed. Gunnel Cederlöf and K. Sivaramakrishnan, paperback ed., 1–40 (Seattle, WA: University of Washington Press, 2014 [2006]), 11.

98. David Arnold, *The Tropics and the Traveling Gaze: India, Landscape, and Science, 1800–1856* (Delhi: Permanent Black, 2005), 111. See chapter 8, 'Inventing Tropicality', and chapter 9, 'Colonizing Nature', in Arnold, *The Problem of Nature*, 141–87.

99. Arnold, *The Tropics and the Traveling Gaze*, 6.

100. Daud Ali, 'Recognizing Europe in India: Colonial Master Narratives and the Writing of Indian History, in *Contesting the Master Narrative: Essays in Social History*, ed. Jeffrey Cox and Shelton Stromquist, 95–130 (Iowa City: University of Iowa Press, 1998).

101. Arnold, *The Tropics and the Traveling Gaze*, 133.

102. Edward W. Said, *Orientalism*, Repr. with a new Afterword and new Preface (London: Penguin Books, 2003 [1978]), 1–4.

103. Arnold, *The Tropics and the Traveling Gaze*, 6.

104. For reference to David Arnold, see Bankoff, *Cultures of Disaster*, 7. Greg Bankoff, 'Rendering the World Unsafe: "Vulnerability" as a Western Discourse', *Disasters* 25, no. 1 (2001): 19–35.

105. Bankoff, *Cultures of Disaster*, 11.

106. References to Bankoff, see Upamanyu Pablo Mukherjee, *Natural Disasters and Victorian Empire: Famines, Fevers and the Literary Cultures of South Asia* (Basingstoke, UK: Palgrave Macmillan, 2013), 17, 25–26.

107. Mukherjee excludes the cyclones of 1839, 1864 and 1876 in Bengal and Orissa and instead chooses to focus on 'less visible, but arguably, more destructive disasters of recurring famines and epidemics'. Ibid., 12–13, 22.

108. 'Tropical other' Mukherjee takes from Bankoff, *Cultures of Disaster*, 7, who in turn builds upon Arnold's work on tropicality; see Mukherjee, *Natural Disasters and Victorian Empire*, 17.

109. Ibid., 18, 31, 37.

110. Eric L. Jones, *The European Miracle: Environments, Economies, and Geopolitics in the History of Europe and Asia*, 3rd ed. (New York: Cambridge University Press, 2003 [1981]).

111. Ibid., 225–27.

112. Jones's book is a case study in Eurocentric history in James Morris Blaut, *Eight Eurocentric Historians* (New York; London: The Guilford Press, 2000), ch. 5, 73–112.

113. Mukherjee, *Natural Disasters and Victorian Empire*, 14–15.

114. Tirthankar Roy, *Natural Disasters and Indian History*, Oxford India Short Introductions (New Delhi: Oxford University Press, 2012). Roy, '"The Law of

Storms": European and Indigenous Responses to Natural Disasters in Colonial India, *c.* 1800–1850', *Australian Economic History Review* 50, no. 1 (2010): 6–22. Roy, 'State, Society and Market in the Aftermath of Natural Disasters in Colonial India: A Preliminary Exploration', *Indian Economic Social History Review* 45, no. 2 (2008): 261–94.

115. Roy, 'State, Society and Market', 264.

116. Ibid., 289.

117. Ibid., 268n15.

118. Bhatta, *The Natural Calamities*, 210, 214–15.

119. Ibid., 89.

120. Ibid., xxi, 76.

121. Arnold, *Famine: Social Crisis and Historical Change*, 22.

122. Roy, '"The Law of Storms": European and Indigenous Responses'.

123. Ibid., 6–7.

124. Ibid., 12.

125. D'Souza, *Drowned and Dammed*, 84.

126. David Mosse, *The Rule of Water: Statecraft, Ecology, and Collective Action in South Asia* (Delhi: Oxford University Press, 2003).

127. A number of intersting publications on water management pertain to floods and rivers in north and northeastern India, for instance, Meena Bhargava, 'Changing River Courses in North India: Calamities, Bounties, Strategies—Sixteenth to Early Nineteenth Centuries', *The Medieval History Journal* 10, nos. 1–2 (2007): 183–208. Debojyoti Das, '"Majuli in Peril": Challenging the Received Wisdom on Flood Control in the Brahmaputra River Basin, Assam (1940–2000)', *Water History Journal* 6, no. 2 (2014): 167–185. M. A. Allison, 'Historical Changes in the Ganges-Brahmaputra Delta Front', *Journal of Coastal Research* 14, no. 4 (1998): 1269–1275. Iftekhar Iqbal, *The Bengal Delta: Ecology, State and Social Change, 1840–1943* (London: Palgrave Macmillan, 2010). Debjani Bhattacharyya, *Empire and Ecology in the Bengal Delta: The Making of Calcutta* (Cambridge: Cambridge University Press, 2018).

128. D'Souza, *Drowned and Dammed*, 51–52.

129. Benjamin Kingsbury, *An Imperial Disaster: The Bengal Cyclone of 1876* (Oxford University Press 2018).

130. Ibid., 164.

131. K. Sivaramakrishnan, *Modern Forests: Statemaking and Environmental Change in Colonial Eastern India* (Stanford: Stanford University Press, 1999), 5.

132. Sunil Khilnani, 'The Development of Civil Society', in *Civil Society: History and Possibilities*, ed. Sudipta Kaviraj and Sunil Khilnani, 11–32 (New Delhi: Cambridge University Press, 2001), 25.

133. Sanjay Sharma, *Famine, Philanthropy and the Colonial State: North India in the Early Nineteenth Century* (New Delhi: Oxford University Press, 2001), 7–9, 191.

134. Ravi Ahuja, 'State Formation and "Famine" Policy in Early Colonial South India', *Indian Economic and Social History Review* 39, no. 4 (2002): 351–80, 378–80.

135. Sharma, *Famine, Philanthropy and the Colonial State*, 2.

136. For example, early nationalists and the Poona Sarvajanik Sabha (founded in 1872) played an important role in criticising revenue and famine policies of the Government of Bombay. Christopher A. Bayly, *Origins of Nationality in South Asia: Patriotism and Ethical Government in the Making of Modern India* (Delhi: Oxford University Press, 1998), 106–07.

137. Arnold, *Famine: Social Crisis and Historical Change*, 115.

138. Hall-Matthews, *Peasants, Famine and the State in Colonial Western India*, 219–20.

139. Lance Brennan, 'The Development of the Indian Famine Codes: Personalities, Politics, and Policies', in *Famine as a Geographical Phenomenon*, ed. Bruce Currey and Graeme Hugo, 91–111 (Dordrecht: D. Reidel, 1984).

140. Georgina Brewis, '"Fill Full the Mouth of Famine": Voluntary Action in Famine Relief in India 1896–1901', *Modern Asian Studies* 44, no. 4 (2010): 887–918.

141. Carey Anthony Watt, *Serving the Nation: Cultures of Service, Association, and Citizenship* (New Delhi: Oxford University Press, 2005).

142. The 1934 and 1935 earthquakes are discussed in chapters 3 and 4 in Kokila Dang, 'The Congress and the Politics of Relief: 1920–1940', unpublished M.Phil dissertation, Centre for Historical Studies, School of Social Sciences, Jawaharlal Nehru University, 1992. Kokila Dang, 'Colonial Ideology, Nationalist Politics and the Social Organization of Relief in the Late Nineteenth and Twentieth Centuries', unpublished PhD dissertation, Centre for Historical Studies, School of Social Sciences, Jawaharlal Nehru University, 1998, ch. 11.

143. Dang, 'The Congress and the Politics of Relief', 108.

144. William F. Kuracina, *The State and Governance in India: The Congress Ideal* (New York: Routledge, 2010), 4.

145. Bérénice Guyot-Réchard, 'Reordering a Border Space: Relief, Rehabilitation, and Nation-Building in Northeastern India after the 1950 Assam Earthquake', *Modern Asian Studies* 49, no. 4 (July, 2015): 931–62, 936.

146. Guyot-Réchard, 'Reordering a Border Space', 936, 956, 950.

147. S. N. Mukherjee, 'Afterword', in *Disasters: Image and Context*, ed. Peter Hinton, 187–96 (Sydney: Sydney Studies, 1992).

148. Wendy Singer, *Creating Histories: Oral Narratives and the Politics of History-Making* (Delhi: Oxford University Press, 1997), 44–45, 134, 153n49.

149. Stephen Henningham, *Peasant Movements in Colonial India: North Bihar, 1917–1942* (Canberra: Australian National University, 1982), 140. Stephen Henningham, 'Bureaucracy and Control in India's Great Landed Estates: The Raj Darbhanga of Bihar, 1879 to 1950', *Modern Asian Studies* 17, no. 1 (1983): 35–57, 43, 47. Stephen Henningham, *A Great Estate and Its Landlords in Colonial India: Darbhanga 1860–1942* (Delhi: Oxford University Press, 1990), 128–52.

150. For research on the management of relief and reconstruction in Nepal after the earthquake, see Yogesh Raj, 'Management of the Relief and Reconstruction after the Great Earthquake of 1934' (Notes from the Archive), *Studies in Nepali History and Society* 20, no. 2 (December 2015): 375–422.

151. Referred to as the year of 'the dreadful earthquake' (*bhayanak bhukamp*), in A. Kumar, *Rewriting the Language of Politics*, 75n42. In March 2010 in Patna, people more than once told the author anecdotes of elders who were born in the year of the earthquake.

152. 'Tributes to Earthquake Victims: Residents Pay Homage to More than 1000 People Who Lost Lives in 1934', http://www.telegraphindia.com/1150116/jsp/bihar/story_8626.jsp#.VmVQOnYrLIU (accessed 12 February 2015).

153. J. S. Wilcock, *Bihar and Orissa in 1933–34* (Patna: Superintendent, Government Printing, 1935), 14. The local government financed the department. 'Presentation of the Budget for 1935–36', in *Bihar and Orissa Legislative Council Proceedings* (*BOLCP*), 13 February 1935, 32, no. 4: 261–62.

154. For instance, 'Finance Department, File No. 7/36 of 1934 P1–8, subject: 'Free Transport by Railway of Men and Stores on Earthquake Relief Work' became 'Reconstruction Department, E-33 of 1934 Part 1, subject: Railway Concessions on Occasion of Earthquake'. The files are in the present record management of BSA entered as 'General Department, Reconstruction Branch' but each individual file is marked 'Reconstruction Department, Earthquake Branch'. Local Self Government (LSG) Dept – Medical Branch, LSG Dept – Sanitation Branch, LSG Dept – LSG Branch, 1934–936 also contain files on the earthquake. Archival visits to BSA, March 2010.

155. William Bailie (W. B.) Brett was appointed Relief Commissioner 2 February 1934 (*Bihar and Orissa Gazette*, 1934, Part 1, p. 26 [BL IOR V/11/1153]), and was expected to return and take charge of the new department on 17 February 1934. D.O. 1036, James Whitty, Revenue Dept., Govt of B&O, Patna 17 February 1934, to J.W. Nicholson, BSA RE 56/1934. Brett had 'large administrative and secretarial experience and reputation for thoroughness and efficiency'. He joined the Indian Civil Service as an Assistant Magistrate and Collector in Bihar after having passed the exams in 1912, and was of a senior range with experience in

various leading positions (Private Sec. to the Governor of B&O, Sec. to the Indian Taxation Enquiry Committee, Finance Sec.) before his appointment as Relief Commissioner. 'Builders of the New Bihar', in Moore (ed.), *Record of the Great Indian Earthquake*, p. 37. 'William Bailie Brett, B.A.', in *History of Services of Gazetted and Other Officers Serving under the Government of Bihar and Orissa* (Corrected until 1st July 1930) Part I (Patna: Superintendent, Government Printing, 1930), 14–15.

156. The publication is without author and date, but W. B. Brett is mentioned as the author and the publication appeared in D.O. 'The Bihar Earthquake' (Personal and Confidential), Home Dept, GOI, to Cornelia Sorabji, Simla 21 July 1934, BL Mss Eur F165/170. He also submitted the proof copy to the Home Department by 8 June 1934. D.O. 1960 R.D., W. B. Brett to M. G. Hallett, 8 June 1934, File: 'B&O Earthquake 1934. Publicity, Relief and Reconstruction Measures in Connection therewith. Accounts of Bihar Central Relief Committee's Fund', National Archives of India (NAI) HP 34/1/1934. Published as a public report on 13 June 1934, see W. B. Brett *Report on the Progress of Earthquake Reconstruction*, S.I, 1934 (18 pp.), 18. Henceforth referred to as *RPER* in notes. Brett sent communiqués to M. G. Hallett, who except for the short spell as secretary, Home Department, GOI, 1932–36, had spent many years of his career in Bihar and Orissa and would return as Governor of Bihar 1937–39. William Gould, 'Hallett, Sir Maurice Garnier (1883–1969)', *Oxford Dictionary of National Biography* (Oxford University Press, 2004), online edition, May 2007, http://www.oxforddnb.com/view/article/67176 (accessed 16 June 2011). Sir Maurice Garnier Hallett (1883–1969): doi:10.1093/ref:odnb/67176.

157. Though the publication is without author, archival sources reveal that it was written by Brett on his own initiative. Brett started to work on the report after 'Clarke's memorandum' was sent from the same department (which is not available in the records reviewed and has not been seen by the present author). Presumably Clarke's memorandum was meant for the British public since *RPER* was for publication in India and 'much more suitable for Indian readers' according to Brett who wanted it published widely in Hindi and English. D.O. 1898 R.D., Brett to Hallett, Patna, 7 June 1934. NAI HP 34/1/1934.

158. Two thousand copies were printed 22 January 1935. Brett, *A Report on the Bihar Earthquake*.

159. Deepak Kumar, 'Economic Compulsions and the Geological Survey of India', *Indian Journal of History of Science* 17, no. 2 (1982): 289–300. For an in-depth study of Thomas Oldham, the founding father of GSI, and the role of his Irish geologists in the formation of 'British' science, see Barry Crosbie, 'Ireland, Colonial Science, and the Geographical Construction of British Rule in India, c. 1820–1870', *Historical*

Journal 52, no. 4 (2009): 963–87. Crosbie, *Irish Imperial Networks: Migration, Social Communication and Exchange in Nineteenth-Century India* (Cambridge: Cambridge University Press, 2012). Another example of the importance of GSI for the expansion of colonial power is given in Robert A. Stafford, 'Geological Surveys, Mineral Discoveries and British Expansion, 1835–71', *Journal of Imperial and Commonwealth History* 12, no. 3 (1984): 5–32.

160. See cover pager and p. 1 in J. A. Dunn, J. B. Auden and A. M. N. Ghosh, *Preliminary Report* on the North Bihar Earthquake of the 15th January 1934* (Patna: Superintendent, Government Printing, 1934) (*Certain portions of the report have been omitted).

161. Bilham and Hough, 'Site Response of the Ganges Basin', 776.

162. Dunn et al., 'The Bihar–Nepal Earthquake of 1934', 175.

163. There were no indexes available for the departments and period reviewed at the time of visiting BSA, Patna in 2010.

164. See http://hansard.millbanksystems.com/ (accessed 20 July 2015).

165. Kameshwar Singh (1907–62), Maharajadhiraj ('Great King of Kings') of Darbhanga 1929–62. His title was non-hereditary and conferred upon him by the Government of India when he inherited the Darbhanga Raj. Henningham, *A Great Estate and Its Landlords*, 128–29, 157.

166. According to indexes of the Revenue Department 1934–36, reduction of rent for earthquake-damaged lands, earthquake relief loans and the Darbhanga Improvement Trust were some of the topics relevant to the present study. The visit to the archives was made between 20 and 21 February 2010. Unfortunately, a number of relevant files in the Darbhanga State Archives were unavailable for consultation.

167. Eleonor Marcussen, 'Cooperation and Pacifism in a Colonial Context: Service Civil International and Work Camps in Bihar, 1934–1937', in *HerStory. Historical Scholarship between South Asia and Europe: Festschrift in Honour of Gita Dharampal-Frick*, ed. R. Klöber and M. Ludwig, 83–101 (Heidelberg; Berlin: CrossAsia-eBooks, 2018).

168. Ramratan Bhatnagar, *The Rise and Growth of Hindi Journalism (1826–1945)*, ed. Dhirendranath Singh (Varanasi: Vishwavidyalaya Prakashan, 2003 [1947]), 387.

169. Ibid., 387–88.

170. Established in 1875, the newspaper was British-owned and was regarded by nationalists to be a mouthpiece of British imperialism and the British community in India during the 1920s and 1930s. Even so, its editorials and contents were widely read and discussed by people holding diverse political views. Rangaswamy Parthasarathy, *Journalism in India*, rev. and enlarged ed. (New Delhi: Sterling Publishers, 1997 [4th ed., 1989]), 229–30.

171. The *Indian Nation* resumed print 24 March 1934, C. S. R. Somayajulu, *Indian Nation*, 10 April 1934.

172. 'Province Day by Day; News from the Mofussil; Earthquake Relief; Muzaffarpur; The Newest', *Indian Nation*, 25 March 1934.

173. The Political Department's perception of the press was provided in 'Notes' on the annual reports on newspapers and periodicals published in English, Oriya, Hindi and Urdu in Bihar and Orissa in 1934. P. 4 in, 'Notes', PS, File No. 1 of 1935 [s.d., printed 17 July 1935], BSA PS 1/1935.

174. D.O. D3360/34, M. G. Hallett to P. C. Tallents, Simla, 27 May 1934; Correspondence: Hallett to Tallents 30 May 1934; Somayajulu to P. C. Tallents, Patna, 7 June 1934, File: 'Re-publication of the Indian Nation. Question of Prosecution of the Editor in Connection with the Publication of the Report of the Non-official Enquiry Committee on Saran Firing', BSA PS 37/1934. According to Henningham, the newspaper was from its inception intended to provide a conservative rival viewpoint to the nationalist newspaper *The Searchlight*. It expressed 'implicit criticism of the Civil Disobedience movement', and had the support of the British official and administration. However, the Maharajadhiraja was also a 'great friend' of Rajendra Prasad and his close connections with INC leaders and donations to the party made the British administration question his political loyalties. Henningham, *A Great Estate and Its Landlords in Colonial India*, 129–31.

175. It had an annual subscription of 2,400 and 3,000 copies in circulation. 'Notes' by PS, p. 15, BSA PS 1/1935 (Appendix D, 7).

176. It had a circulation of 28,000 in 1934 and was thereby the third-largest Indian-owned newspaper in Bengal after *Ananda Bazar Patrika* (circulation 40,012) and *Dainik Basumati* (circulation 35,000). Govt of Bengal, Political Department, *Annual Report on Indian Papers Printed or Published in the Bengal Presidency: For the Year 1934*, 'Confidential' and 'For Official Use Only.' (Superintendent, Government Printing, Bengal Govt Press, Alipore, Bengal, 1935), 1, 16. BSA PS 271/1935.

177. *Behar Herald* or *Bihar Herald*, published in Patna, represented the beginning of the English Press in Bihar with its first publication in 1872. 'Appendix D', in 'Notes' by PS, pp. 3, 15, BSA PS 1/1935.

178. The committee members were: Rajendra Prasad, President, Baldeva Sahay and Syed Mohammed Hafeez, Secretaries, R. C. Pandit, Treasurer. BCRC, *Devastated Bihar*, 27. Unfortunately the spring issues of 1934 are missing from the holdings in NMML (New Delhi), Zentrum Moderner Orient (Berlin) and Cambridge University Library. Archival visits and email correspondence (Cambridge) in 2010.

179. It was one out of twelve newspapers in circulation in Patna district in 1934 and was, in terms of its opinions of the government, only matched by the Hindi newspapers *Navashakti* and *Yogi*. In Patna district, twelve newspapers were in circulation in 1934, out of which *The Searchlight, Earthquake Relief [Bulletin], Indian Nation, Behar Herald, Patna Times* and *Patna Law Times* were published in English; *Navashakti, Yogi* and *Bhandaphore* were published in Hindi; *Jamhoor* and *Ittehad* in Urdu; and *Beyapar Market Report* in English, Hindi and Bengali. 'Notes' by PS, p. 4, BSA PS 1/1935.

180. N. Kumar, *Journalism in Bihar*, Bihar District Gazetteers. Patna (Govt of Bihar, Gazetteers Branch, Revenue Department: Secretariat Press, 1971), 57–59.

181. It was published tri-weekly in English with an annual subscription of 1,500 and circulation of 4,000 copies, printed at the Searchlight Press, Patna. The proprietor was Bihar Journals Limited, Editor, Publisher and Printer Murli Manohar Prasad, Patna. 'Appendix B: Newspapers and Periodicals Started in 1934', and 'Appendix D', in 'Notes', by PS, BSA PS 1/1935.

182. BCRC, *Devastated Bihar*.

183. 'Foreword' by Baldev Sahay and Syed Mahommed Hafeez (Secretaries), in BCRC, *Devastated Bihar*.

184. Until 15 February 1934 according to 'Foreword' by Baldev Sahay and Syed Mahommed Hafeez (Secretaries), in BCRC, *Devastated Bihar*.

185. The month of publication was probably end of February or earliest mid-March. The foreword was dated 2 March 1934, see ibid. An advertisement for the publication was published in *ABP*, 22 March 1934.

186. The *Earthquake Relief Bulletin* (alternatively referred to as the *Earthquake Bulletin*), published weekly in English from the Searchlight Press in Patna. Annual subscription 300, and 1,000 in circulation, ceased publication in the first quarter of 1934. The keeper of the press was the publisher Murli Manohar Prasad, Proprietor Bihar Central Relief Committee; the editor was Professor Manorajan Prasad. ('Appendix B: Newspapers and Periodicals Started in 1934', in 'Notes' by PS, p. 18, BSA PS 1/1935). The bulletin, like BCRC's other publications, was printed at the Searchlight Press and published by BCRC's Publicity Department (ibid., 'Appendix D', 5, 14.) Also mentioned by Rajendra Prasad in *Autobiography* (New Delhi: Penguin Books India, 2010 [1946]), 355.

187. Rajendra Prasad, *Devastated Behar: The Problem of Reconstruction* (Patna: published by Publicity Officer, Bihar Central Relief Committee,d printed by Murli Manohar Prasad at the Searchlight Press, n.d. [end February to 10 March 1934]), 23 pp. In BCUL PC 1076. Pierre Cérésole had read the booklet in Switzerland in February or March 1934, after which he contacted friends in England about the idea of sending

volunteers to Bihar. Lilian Sinclair Stevenson to Pierre Cérésole, 'Information Given by C. F. Andrews to Lilian Stevenson on March 16th, in Cooldars, Gerrard's Cross' (1934), BCUL PC 990: 39.

188. BCRC, *Report for the Period Ending 30th June 1934*, 4.

189. Visits to the Ramakrishna Mission Ashram, Patna, in February 2010, and to the Ramakrishna Mission Institute of Culture, Golpark, and the Belur Math, Kolkata, March 2010.

190. The Marwari Relief Society was established and registered under the Indian Companies Act 1913. Head Office, 7–1 Jugmohan Mullick Lane, Calcutta. Honorary Sec. Kanoria, Marwari Relief Society, to Sec., Behar Govt, Calcutta 29 January 1934, File: 'Loan of Officers from Other Provinces and Appointment of a Number of B.E.s to Tender Technical Advice to Private Persons Reg. the Safety of Their Houses', BSA RE 65/1934. The Honorary Secretary was Jwalaprasad Kanoria (alt. Jwala Prasad Kanodia). According to the final report of the Marwari Relief Society, it was compiled after a document referred to as 'Preliminary Report of the Earthquake' with an audited account of its funds had been circulated to donors. Calcutta, Marwari Relief Society, *Report of the Behar Earthquake Relief Work*, published by Jwalaprasad Kanoria, General Sec. (Calcutta, March 1935), 5, 7.

2

Responses and Responsibilities in Emergency Relief

Introduction: Disrupted Communication

The damages of sudden disasters often have a paralysing effect on local government structures and systems, and at the same time, a rapid response is essential to save lives and minimise damage.[1] In this chapter, I discuss the local colonial government's response in the immediate aftermath of the 1934 earthquake and the subsequent criticism of its inadequacy in responding to the needs of the disaster-stricken population. The government's capacity and responsibilities in the aftermath revealed weak spots regarding preparedness for a major disruptive event: its security-oriented response reflected not only a fear of chaos as a possible springboard for adverse human behaviour but, perhaps more importantly, it revealed the importance of communication in maintaining control of the area. Even though the disrupted communication complicated relief and rescue work in practical terms, as discussed throughout this chapter, the central role of (disrupted) communication and (lack of) information in the government's narrative of the aftermath reflected above all the importance of communication infrastructure to the local government.

The government's response in the 1934 earthquake, S. N. Mukherjee describes, as slow and less occupied with clearing debris, saving lives and giving relief than in protecting and restoring government properties and factories. As he notes, such a security-oriented response may have been related to the Government of Bengal's concurrent efforts to strike down what were perceived as increasingly violent nationalist groups,[2] or a general apprehension towards nationalist political rivalry in the region.[3] Taking notice of the administration's priorities, Tirthankar Roy comments on the government's response in the immediate aftermath: 'Before saving lives, the civil administration had to guard the jails, the banks and the

Treasury.' As Roy notes, the government's priority was one of the reasons for criticism of its relief effort in saving the lives of those injured by or buried under debris.[4]

Mukherjee's and Roy's explanations of the local government's security-oriented response and subsequent criticism by contemporary nationalists have support in the two conflicting master narratives of the earthquake aftermath. The government's master narrative, *A Report on the Bihar Earthquake*, published by Relief Commissioner W. B. Brett, addresses every aspect of the earthquake's aftermath in a dense summary account of damages and government action in 1934. Brett based his report on an unofficial report to the Home Department in Delhi, written by P. C. Tallents, Chief Secretary to the Government of Bihar and Orissa, in August 1934.[5] Brett added excerpts from later communiqués issued by the Reconstruction Department,[6] but the summaries of the district officers' accounts of the aftermath, data from official communiqués and an outline of the response by the local government in Tallents' report formed the central narrative in Brett's report. In effect, both Tallents' and Brett's reports were collated versions of internal reports from the local government's headquarters and the district administration of affected areas, later to be further watered down in the widely available yearly report of the province, *Bihar and Orissa in 1933–34*.[7] Like Tallents' report, Brett's report described the movement of both military and armed police in the first three days after the earthquake as partially motivated by the government's fear of crimes in the aftermath: 'One of the first anxieties of [the] Government was lest there might be outbreaks of disorder and looting in the shattered towns.'[8] Unlike Tallents' report, Brett's report did not mention that the local government in Patna declared 16 and 17 January holidays, motivated 'principally' by the collapse of many banks and partially to prevent 'a run on the banks', a measure that in effect kept official institutions closed for a week.[9] The district administration in Monghyr, Muzaffarpur, Darbhanga and Motihari, and the sub-divisions Sitamarhi (Muzaffarpur district) and Madhubani (Darbhanga district) in general also prioritised exceptional security measures before organising relief. In Muzaffarpur, for instance, the administration set in motion a chain of precautionary security measures such as guarding the damaged jail and prevention of looting, for which the police were deployed, before the organisation of clearing debris. The first action by the District Officer in Monghyr was to mobilise the armed police and to arrange for an extra guard on the treasury: he then 'saw the main bazar in ruins'. Once the precautionary security measures had been taken, 'the available police and officers *then* went to help in rescue work in the town' (emphasis added).[10]

The security-oriented response reflects a belief in one of the most enduring disaster myths in public and official imagination according to sociological research on disaster aftermaths.[11] Panic, ensuing unrest, looting and the breakdown of social orders are proven to be 'exceedingly rare' following a disaster.[12] However, another perspective from disaster research argues that specifically earthquakes, with their rapid onsets, can heighten feelings of frustration more than disasters with slow onsets, such as droughts, and therefore may be more likely to stimulate conflict.[13] That does not appear to have been the case in the 1934 earthquake. Contrary to the government's expectations, Brett's report described how 'the emergency exhibited the people in a very favourable light', except for the odd case of profiteering among traders promptly put down with the support of the 'public opinion' and a few reports of looting. The absence of crimes, according to Brett, was due to 'the state of dazed stupefaction' prevailing after the earthquake and the prompt arrival of police and price control.[14] In general, apart from a request for police reinforcement by an eyewitness as 'bad characters' had attempted to create 'trouble',[15] instances of crimes were not reported in newspapers. The BCRC's *Devastated Bihar*, the official master narrative from the nationalist point of view, also reported that public order had prevailed. It did, however, state that it was maintained by 'people themselves' while the police had guarded jails, banks and government treasuries,[16] thereby implicitly criticising the unnecessary presence of the police at those sites when rescue and relief operations ought to have been a priority. According to this report, the government's response created the disaster by choosing wrong priorities, which is not an uncommon form of politicised critique of a disaster.[17] Such a critique was from the outset espoused in the nationalist counter-narrative in response to information carried in government communiqués in the newspapers. Editorials and eyewitness accounts in the *Amrita Bazar Patrika*, *The Statesman* and the *Behar Herald* called on more relief provisions, listed numbers of casualties conflicting with official data and published personal narratives criticising the government's response. The tensions and contradictions in these narratives—on the one hand were the nationalist accounts and eyewitness reports, and on the other the official version in newspaper articles and government communiqués—converged at several points in terms of damages and their impact, but disagreed regarding essential data pertaining to deaths, priorities in giving relief and the government's ability to respond in the interest of the people affected. The conflicting perspectives on the material experience of the earthquake represented a politics of narration that went beyond the aftermath.[18] Narratives of the aftermath offered a lens for criticising or advocating the current forms of governance or suggesting alternatives.

Rather than focusing on the security-oriented response of the government as a plausible *cause* of its lackadaisical approach towards relief and aid, this chapter argues that the destruction of communication infrastructure in the earthquake was the primary cause of a security-oriented response. By addressing the local colonial government's response, this chapter discusses how the government perceived communications as a fundamental part of governance. Communication served, in Bihar as elsewhere, as an important argument and tool of governance throughout the colonial period.[19] As Christopher Bayly has persuasively argued, the colonial government's initial success in the Indian subcontinent owed much less to military superiority, and was more a result of the deployment of a vast network of intelligence gathering to secure military, political and social information by using modern technological resources. 'Information panic' was characterised by 'the feeling of the fledging colonial administration that it knew nothing of the local society and that the locals were combining to deny it information'.[20] As a result, during moments of crises such as the 1934 earthquake, once the formal system of information gathering broke down, the government launched a security-oriented response. In this way, the disaster response addressed the crisis of the local government rather than that of the victims of the earthquake. In addition to the disrupted communication and flow of information, 'rumours' circulated in the immediate aftermath and although foremost concentrated on explanations of the cause of the earthquake, they were a sign of concern to the local government.[21] Rumours are a well-known phenomenon in the aftermath of a disaster, some would even argue that rumours are a universal response; most commonly, they identify scapegoats or blame the authorities for hiding information about the event that has occurred or of future disasters. These 'rumours', scientific speculations or bold new theories on metaphysics can stem both from the out-of-the-ordinary experiences that compromises a disaster and the chaos of distorted communication and governance.[22]

Communication was also a part of colonial governance that had found its way into what Upamanyu Pablo Mukherjee calls 'the classic paradigm of British administrative writing, where disasters are explained as governance glitches that can be removed as the modes of communication, knowledge gathering and self-reflection are improved'.[23] The impact of the breakdown of communication on the government's response highlights its importance in governance as well as in the colonial government's perception and interpretation of disasters. Both these aspects underline how the earthquake's aftermath was historically produced as an outcome of governance and previous experiences with disasters. The local government's emergency response highlights its dependence on communication in upholding efficient governance as well as in disaster management. As Beck has argued in his thesis on risk society, modernisation contributed to institutionalised scientific knowledge and technical expertise that exacerbate vulnerability;[24] the colonial perception of modernisation in the form of communication infrastructure shaped its notion of risk and how it responded to the earthquake.

In the following two sections, I will first examine how narratives of the aftermath addressed the disruption of communication networks and damages by the earthquake with the purpose to discuss the effect on the flow of information on the relief response. Both in Patna and in district towns, the breakdown of communication and information was central to the security and relief response. In the next two sections, I will discuss how the earthquake showed both the limits and the capacities of the government in its coordination of resources around security, relief and rescue work. The disaster response discussed in this chapter includes foremost the organisation of search and rescue teams and meeting the survivors' basic needs of medical care and shelter.[25]

The Slow Emergence of Disaster

Clear the line.
Home [Department], New Delhi.
Serious earthquake shortly after 2 p.m. today. Extensive damage caused to buildings especially High Court and General Hospital. 10 deaths known in Patna 9 in Gaya, but information still incomplete.[26]

In its brief composition, the quoted telegram informed the Secretary of State in New Delhi about a 'serious' earthquake that had struck Bihar. In the first telegrams on the day of the earthquake, the incomplete information available to the local government pertained to Patna, the provincial capital, and Gaya, an important town and railway hub. This initial communication mentioned the destruction of government buildings in Patna, the dispatcher yet to learn about the destruction in the worst-affected towns of Monghyr, south of the Ganges, and Darbhanga and Muzaffarpur in the Tirhut division in north Bihar. The first uncertain figures of the number of dead would gradually increase as the scope of the disaster gradually dawned on the local government and the public.

In the government's narrative of its relief response, the collapse of the communication system on all fronts—the telegraph system, roads and railway lines—effectively cut off the headquarters in Patna from the towns in north Bihar and from Monghyr, south of the Ganges. At the same time, the government in part explained its inability to address the earthquake aftermath adequately as the result of Bihar lacking infrastructure and the volatile 'natural' condition of its landscape. From an administrative point of view, the earthquake area was divided into three zones out of which the northern and north-eastern zones proved the most difficult to access, while the zone located south of the Ganges was, even under normal circumstances, easier to access from Patna or Calcutta.[27] In the rural and fertile agricultural land of the Tirhut division in the north, 97 per cent of its almost 11 million population resided in 14,000 villages. The division's two largest towns, Darbhanga with a population of 60,000 and Muzaffarpur with 43,000 inhabitants, had been severely hit by the earthquake. Compared to Muzaffarpur and Darbhanga, the smaller town of Motihari with about 17,000 inhabitants in the remote district of Champaran had fared better. The second earthquake zone located in the north-eastern part was less fertile and more sparsely populated than Tirhut, with the district towns Purnea and Katihar being the only towns of importance to the government. The third seriously affected zone was located in south Bihar, between the Ganges and the hills of the Chota Nagpur plateau, where Patna, the towns Monghyr, Bhagalpur and Arrah lay on or were in close proximity to the southern bank of the Ganges. Monghyr, with its 53,000 inhabitants, located 100 miles east of Patna on a peninsula in the Ganges, suffered severely in terms of loss of lives and material assets. Another 35 miles further to the east near the Ganges, Bhagalpur, with its population of 84,000 inhabitants, was less affected.[28] In Patna and its suburb Dinapur, with nearly 200,000 inhabitants and 40,000 houses spread along the Ganges, many buildings were ruined in the earthquake, but only in Monghyr did the GSI record an isoseismal reading of 10 (Map 2.1).[29]

The earthquake's effect on all forms of communication—the telegraph system, roads and the railways—and the landscape of the region both played a significant role in explaining the relief response of the local government. In the government's narrative, the pre-existing environmental conditions in north Bihar, especially the rivers, were factors contributing to slow communication and delays in sending relief from south to north Bihar.[30] North Bihar was, and still is, one of the most flood-prone areas of the region.[31] The branches of the river Kosi, known for its troubled history of floods,[32] were described as dominating the area. The north-eastern earthquake zone between Supaul in the north and Purnea in the east was, according to the local government, 'a tract entirely devoid of roads'.[33] The railway network connecting Tirhut with Patna had gradually expanded via Muzaffarpur and Motihari to reach Bettiah but the lines mainly catered to

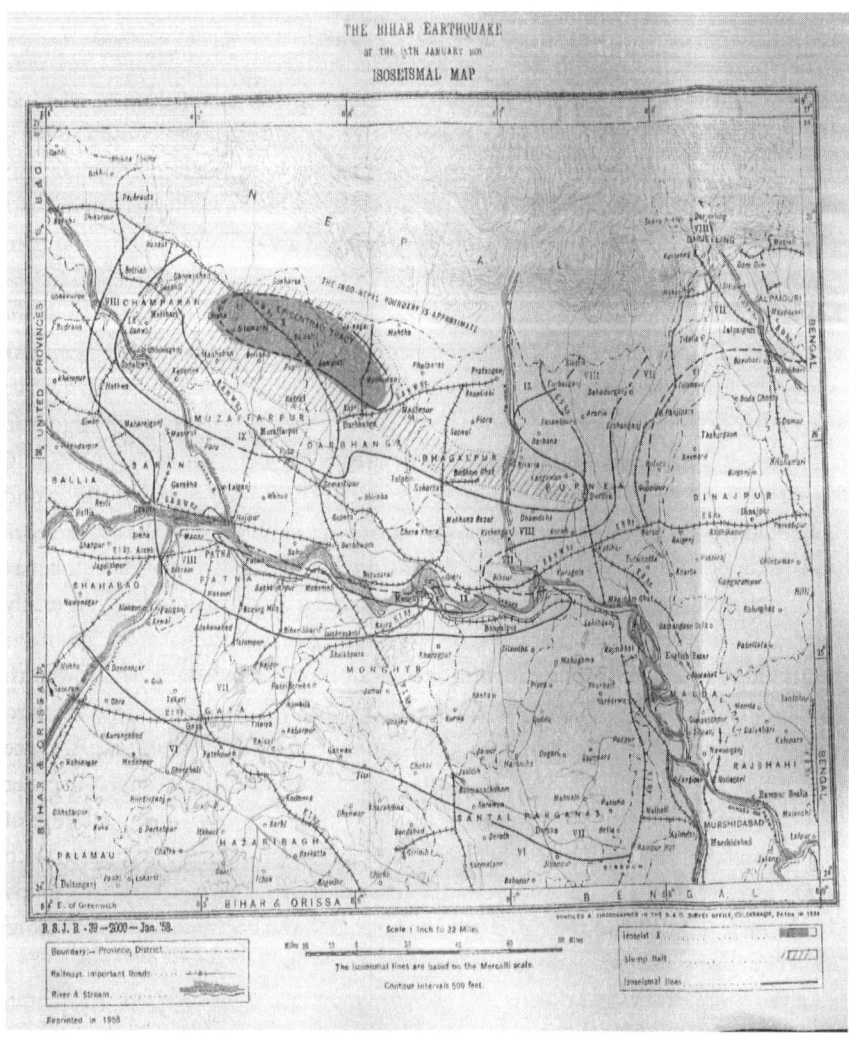

Map 2.1 Isoseismal map of the epicentre tract and Bihar by the Geological Survey of India. The shaded oval shape in the northern part of Bihar demarcates the worst affected area (isoseismal 10 area). Monghyr, situated to the east of Patna, on the south bank of the Ganges, is also marked isoseismal 10.* The striped area demarcates the so-called slump belt, which was badly affected by the earthquake in terms of damages but experienced less shaking.

* On isoseismals, see Chapter 1, note 12.

Source: Dunn et al. 'The Bihar–Nepal Earthquake of 1934', pl. 2 (reprinted map from 1958 with blue and red colours; also in Brett, A Report on the Bihar Earthquake and on the Measures Taken in Consequence thereof up to the 31st December 1934 [1935]).

professional trade and the rural north remained accessible by cart roads and rivers until the early twentieth century.[34] Much of the communication with the districts and outlying areas normally took place via Muzaffarpur; however, since the town's communication with Patna via road, rail and telegraph was cut off, it meant in effect that contact with the whole division initially was disrupted, according to a government communiqué published a week after the earthquake. Since Motihari was located in the division's north-western corner towards the border of Nepal, it was difficult to access even before the earthquake.[35] According to the local government's yearly report, communication across the region 'had always been bad' due to the lack of infrastructure, which could be explained by the province's environment, for instance, the Ganges remained unabridged for a stretch of 200 miles. The 35-mile journey from Patna to Muzaffarpur usually lasted for over four hours, and in order to reach the northern parts, the report lamented how 'even more tedious' travel was required.[36] Notably, the government viewed pre-existing environmental conditions as the reason for a vulnerable communication network that contributed to a delay in sending relief and rescue teams. In the government's narrative, its success or failure in providing relief depended on access by roads, railways or telegraph and knowledge gathering about the situation. The breakdown in road and telegraph communication left Patna unaware of the earthquake's scope until the morning of 16 January 1934. The first reports from Muzaffarpur, in a letter 'sent down by hand', reached the local government in Patna at approximately the same time as a much-delayed telegram from Bhagalpur arrived. It had been sent on behalf of Monghyr, requesting help, in the afternoon of 15 January but had remained undelivered until the morning of 16 January 1934.[37] The local government upgraded the earthquake from 'serious' to 'very serious' in a telegram to the Secretary of State in New Delhi after having received more extensive information about damages, and most importantly, after realizing that information could not be obtained from several places:

> Further reports received show very serious situation created by earthquake. Sixty-one deaths hitherto officially reported from Patna district, ten from Gaya town. Not detailed report from Arrah but known that buildings have suffered severely. Bhagalpur reports six deaths in town and extensive damage to buildings including Central Jail. Damage more serious at Monghyr and Jamalpur but details not available. Police assistance has been sent and medical assistance is being sent to Monghyr. Communications cut with north of river [Ganges] and aeroplanes summoned from Calcutta. Much loss of life reported from Muzaffarpur. No reports from other districts in Tirhut

or Purnea. Earthquake felt in Chota Nagpur and Orissa but such reports as received suggest less heavy damage than in Bihar.[38]

The news of not much being known—'no detailed report from Arrah', 'details not available', 'communications cut', 'no reports'—communicated a lack of information about the situation in many places. What was known, however, was the gravity of the earthquake—'[a] very serious situation', towns and people had 'suffered severely', 'much loss of life', 'less heavy damage', 'bill for repairs will run to lakhs of rupees'—and although described in vague terms such rough estimates of its impact confirmed the event of the disaster. As the solution to the breakdown in communication with north Bihar, the local government in the same telegram requested two aeroplanes from Calcutta for reconnaissance of the area north of the Ganges at midday of 16 January 1934, almost 22 hours after the earthquake had hit.[39] To its surprise, however, within hours of having sent the request, a private aeroplane from Captain Barnard's Air Circus arrived at Patna at 5 p.m. with news from Muzaffarpur and Tirhut.[40] As the earthquake happened, Captain Barnard and his India Air Pageants were on an air circus tour with 92 shows, including parachute performances, aerobatic displays and stunts with a number of aeroplanes, in north and central India in 1933–34.[41] The aeroplane had by chance flown over Muzaffarpur on its way to Calcutta, and in response to the message 'Earthquake Take Care'[42] chalked in white across the ground, it had landed among the fissures at Sikandar maidan. Mr W. Fairweather, a manager of an engineer company and resident of Muzaffarpur, had before the sight of an aeroplane assisted the district administration in preparing a landing ground with the message.[43] Mr Fairweather and not a government official was on the same day (16 January) taken on an air reconnaissance towards the subdivision Sitamarhi in Muzaffarpur district and Motihari in Champaran district (Image 2.1), and afterwards continued with the crew of the aeroplane to Patna.[44]

The same day, the local government at Patna perceived the situation in Tirhut as 'far worse than anticipated' after hearing the aeroplane crew's descriptions of collapsed bridges, water standing over large tracts of land usually dry, ground fissures with grey mud forced through in many places, large buildings in ruins, including parts of the Imperial Agricultural Research Institute at Pusa, destroyed sugar factories and heavy death tolls.[45] The damage to the grand buildings of the Imperial Agricultural Research Institute at Pusa was taken as a sign of total destruction in the area, so severely damaged was the institute that it had to be transferred to Delhi after the earthquake.[46] This first air reconnaissance on 16 January 1934 was in the district gazetteer wrongly accredited to the

Image 2.1 Aerial view of Muzaffarpur town. The crew of an aeroplane flying over Muzaffarpur on 16 January 1934 was among the first to report the scope of the earthquake's destruction in north Bihar.

Source: 'The Indian Earthquake: An Aerial View—Taken by the Air Survey Co., Ltd—of the City of Muzaffarpur, Bihar State, Showing Many of the Buildings in Ruins', *Flight*, no. 1311 (8 February 1934): 119.

government, whose survey was not conducted until one day later.[47] According to the GSI, the magnitude of the disaster in north Bihar 'became known as a result of aerial surveys undertaken by the Bihar Government and by private enterprise'.[48] BCRC also gave credit to the local government's air reconnaissance for being 'the very first act of the government in connection with the earthquake'.[49] Like the government, the BCRC's account claims that the lack of communication left the residents of Patna unaware of the earthquake's scope in Tirhut until the day after the earthquake when the aeroplane crew broke the news,[50] but this was a private initiative. Two days after the earthquake, on 17 January, the government administration in Patna, for the first time, accessed the area by using the aeroplane of Captain Barnard's Circus for an official air reconnaissance over Bettiah and Motihari.[51]

In Calcutta, the press had no consistent news from north Bihar until *The Statesman* reported the eyewitness accounts by the members of Captain Barnard's Circus two days after the earthquake.[52] For the inhabitants of Calcutta, the pilot's impression from the air published on 17 January 1934 was, like for the government administration in Patna, the first indication of the disaster's scope in north Bihar. News had, until 17 January, been confined to death and destruction in other areas, mainly Patna, Jamalpur and Gaya, with reports from various locations in northern and north-eastern India of damages to houses and large buildings such as temples in Assam, Lucknow, Allahabad and Benares.[53] In Calcutta, the earthquake caused cracks in buildings of masonry and important government buildings, and larger structures such as churches had sustained damages that would need repairs, but no heavy collapses involving casualties had been reported.[54] The government's official narrative—that the breakdown in communication was the major obstacle in receiving information and sending aid—was supported by the fact that the disrupted information flow between Tirhut and Patna or Calcutta clearly influenced reports on the earthquake damages. On 17 January, the focus of *The Statesman* in Calcutta shifted to the scope of the disaster in north Bihar from having so far reported damages on tea estates managed by Europeans in Darjeeling, the death of 'coolie women' and 'extensive damages', as well as destruction in Calcutta, Gaya and Jamalpur on 16 January 1934.[55] Initial reporting had also focused on Jamalpur,[56] an important town and well-connected railway hub next to Monghyr, geographically close to and financially connected with Calcutta.[57] The strong presence of Bengalis and Europeans in the railway workshops[58] damaged in the earthquake held considerable news value to Calcutta's urban Bengali and European readership, reflected in the separate counts of destruction and deaths for the railway colony and the bazaar.[59] The importance of a functional communication network for information about the disaster was underlined by the newspaper's reporting of the earthquake through eyewitness accounts of survivors, received by telegram or in person after having arrived in Calcutta by train.[60]

The lack of news in Calcutta about Tirhut immediately after the earthquake was lamented by the Maharajadhiraja of Darbhanga who at his residence in the city anxiously awaited information. The Darbhanga Raj was the largest of three major estates affected by the earthquake, the others being the Bettiah Estate in Champaran and the Hathwa estate in Saran. The Bettiah Estate, with 1,800 square miles yielding a rental of almost 2 million rupees, was as the second-largest *zamindari* in north Bihar after the richer and larger Darbhanga Raj which possessed more than 2,400 square miles of land and had an annual income of approximately 4 million rupees.[61] About two hours after the earthquake, the Maharajadhiraja learned that Jamalpur had 'suffered very badly',[62] but the 'gruesome tale that the airmen had reported to the press about Muzaffarpur' was the first news of the earthquake's magnitude in north Bihar.[63] Overall, the dramatic description of 'the streets strewn with corpses' and 'hundreds left buried under the debris' was an apparent eyewitness account of the disaster unfolding in front of the pilot.[64] After reading the news the Maharajadhiraja sent an aeroplane to Darbhanga on the evening of 17 January, but upon returning from the town's polo grounds, one of its wheel got stuck in a crevice and the plane was stranded.[65] Consequently, extensive information about the situation was not obtained until five days after the earthquake when a brother-in-law of the Maharajadhiraja arrived from Darbhanga.[66]

Judging from the content of initial telegram correspondences and narratives of the aftermath, 24 hours elapsed before the government in Patna realised the gravity of the earthquake with the help of Captain Barnard's aeroplane. In the afternoon of 16 January, the local administration in Patna knew of serious damages in the Tirhut division from an air reconnaissance by the same aeroplane, which was again used on 17 January by government officials to review the situation in Bettiah and Motihari in Champaran. Once the requested aeroplane arrived, officials from Patna also visited Muzaffarpur in the afternoon of 17 January.[67]

Facing severe restrictions in communication by land and telegraph, the use of aeroplanes became an important mode of communication with Tirhut, which was considered a distinctively modern force deployed by the government. The Indian Red Cross described aeroplanes as 'a striking feature' in the aftermath; by 24 January aeroplanes were still the only means of communication as well as carriers of newspapers, medical stores and urgent communications from anxious relatives to several towns in north Bihar. Daily flights between Patna and Muzaffarpur served to transport correspondence and government officials as well as medicine, distributed to Darbhanga, Motihari and Sitamarhi by light motorcars.[68] The very limited number of aeroplanes, at most three, as well as the lack of landing grounds due to land damages, restricted air traffic. Once the first aeroplane requested by the local government had arrived in the afternoon of 17 January, from the Indian Air Survey and Transport Company in Calcutta, it left for Muzaffarpur and Tirhut.[69] Captain Barnard's aeroplane left for Calcutta the next day, and on 19 January, the second aeroplane requested by the government arrived; a private aeroplane from Cossipore close to Calcutta was also placed at the disposal of the government.[70] Aeroplanes were also important as the means for the Revenue Department to conduct an initial survey of damages to agricultural land in Tirhut, born out of concern for the sugar cane harvest and the consequences of the earthquake on agricultural production in the division considered most populous and fertile.[71] An aeroplane, a D. H. Moth from the Royal Air Force, was stationed in Patna and used for morning and afternoon flights to Muzaffarpur, carrying official correspondence and government officials from 25 January 1934 until 11 February 1934 when it was wrecked while taking off from Darbhanga.[72] In this way, aeroplanes served to support correspondence and communication when roads and telegraphs failed in the aftermath of the earthquake. Patna's General Post and Telegraph Office suffered cracks in the earthquake yet remained functional until an aftershock badly damaged the building.[73] Although Muzaffarpur's telegraph line was reopened relatively soon—at 10 a.m. on 16 January—the local government could not manage to get telegrams through to Muzaffarpur.[74] The town's telegraph office normally connected outlying districts in north Bihar with Patna and Calcutta via certain nodes, which meant that once the Muzaffarpur telegraph line was out of function, the outlying districts remained isolated. The office first became dysfunctional due to electricity failure and the staff being 'panic-stricken' or absent while looking for their family members. The main line and important side-lines were reopened once batteries and additional staff had arrived after a couple of days, but by then the huge backlog of telegrams and current traffic was far beyond the office's capacity.[75] Apart from outgoing messages, a 'flood of messages' overburdened Muzaffarpur's telegraph office after anxious relatives in Calcutta had read about the destruction in the newspapers on 17 January 1934, resulting in the suspension of all normal telegraph traffic between Calcutta and north Bihar.[76] In order to speed up the transmission of the 3,000 express and 4,000 ordinary messages waiting in the morning of 25 January 1934, the government's aeroplane transported the backlog of outward telegrams from Tirhut to Patna. Ten days after the earthquake, all telegraph lines from Darbhanga to Jayanagar were still cut off, as were several other towns. The telegraph line between Patna and Monghyr appears to have been re-established on 17 January, and so were the connections between Muzaffarpur and Motihari and with Darbhanga on 19 January. Less affected was the post office's main services that continued, although irregularly and with delays, by means of lorries, *ekkas* (a two-wheel light buggy pulled by a pony) and runners.[77]

As the accidents of the government's aeroplane in Darbhanga on 11 February and of the Darbhanga Raj's aeroplane on 17 January proved, using aeroplanes in the damaged polo grounds or cracked fields was a risky undertaking.[78] Many open spaces, such as the landing grounds in Patna, were covered with people camping out in the open, escaping their ruined or damaged houses.[79] The lack of even grounds, mainly being restricted to the polo grounds at Muzaffarpur, Motihari, Bettiah and Bhagalpur, hampered access by aeroplane, and at the end of January, it would take a minimum of another week to arrange for access, if at all possible, in selected towns. To use aeroplanes for the transport of the large quantities of supplies was not possible by practical or economical means, according to a lieutenant in charge of transporting a limited amount of medical supplies, in addition to correspondence and government officers. The sole aeroplane in use was appreciated as sufficient for the transport of medicines and vaccines in case of 'abnormal outbreaks' of a disease.[80]

'Delayed Relief Is Denied Relief'

The way that the earthquake had severed roads and railway lines and cut off communication with the Tirhut division in the north as compared to the relatively less destructive effect it had on the southern bank of the Ganges, with the tragic exception of Monghyr, had a geological explanation. The geological investigations by the GSI recorded 'slumping' and severe fissuring to the ground in the worst affected area in the Tirhut division. The so-called slump belt area that recorded an isoseismal reading of 10 in Tirhut was 20 miles in width and stretched for 80 miles in the east-south-eastern direction from Motihari through Sitamarhi and Madhubani (Images 2.2 and 2.3). Wholesale sinking and tilting of large areas made houses slump rather than tumble down, and ruined waterways, embankments and roads. What further aggravated the situation was the fact that fissures in the ground had emitted sand that covered the floors of houses, streets and choked drains and wells. Land damages, which caused severe disruptions to the roads and railway lines in north Bihar, were by the GSI explained by proximity to the epicentre and the alluvial soil base of the land, composed mainly of loam and layers of water-bearing sand of unknown depth. In the slump belt area, embankments had sunk from an elevation of 6 feet to ground level and houses in general tilted and slumped. South of the Ganges, the alluvium was chiefly made up of clay and to some extent mixed with rocks. As a result, many buildings collapsed with devastating effects in Monhgyr.[81]

The extraordinary scenery of the damages to the landscape and flooding in north Bihar were iterated in eyewitness accounts by prominent persons. The Governor of Bihar gave a first-hand account of damages and how the earthquake had destroyed and 'actually obliterated' some roads, rendering Tirhut 'largely impassable'.[82] The Viceroy visited the area 18 days after the earthquake and recounted a story about a peasant getting his thighs crushed in a fissure only to be shot up onto the roof of his house the next second by a gush of water as 'easily credible'.[83] The staff of Captain Barnard's Circus had first reported the

J. A. Dunn, Photos.

FIG. 1. A FISSURE, SITAMARHI, LOOKING N.W.

Image 2.2 A fissure in Sitamarhi documented by the Geological Survey of India officer J. A. Dunn. A woman is standing with a parasol in the fissure to illustrate its depth.

Source: Fig. 1, 'A Fissure, Sitamarhi, Looking N. W.', in Dunn et al, 'The Bihar–Nepal Earthquake of 1934'.

Image 2.3 Slumping of the ground along the lake in Motihari documented by the Geological Survey of India officer J. B. Auden.

Source: Fig. 1, 'Motihari. Slumping along Margin of the Lake', in Dunn et al., 'The Bihar–Nepal Earthquake of 1934'.

large fissures in the ground out of which water 'spouted out in terrifying fashion, inundating whole areas'.[84] According to Nehru's observations from a tour of the area at the beginning of February, the towns were impressive in their extensive ruins but even more so, 'the garden of Bihar', as the plains of north Bihar was called, 'had desolation and destruction stamped upon them'.[85] The author Rahul Sankrityayan (1893–1963), who had experienced the earthquake in Allahabad and had gone to Patna to join relief work in north Bihar, testified to the trials of travelling across the ruined landscape and broken bridges to Muzaffarpur.[86]

Considering the extensive damages to infrastructure, one of the first actions of the local government was to authorise the District Boards in Tirhut to overdraw to the extent of Rs 600,000 in order to start work on the damaged roads. About a week after the earthquake, the government apprehended that it would take another month to regain road access to many areas in north Bihar. A damaged road was the only accessible land route to Muzaffarpur until the government restored the railway-line connection with the town by the end of January.[87] Out of the 2,100 miles of rail comprising the Bengal and north-western and Tirhut system, 900

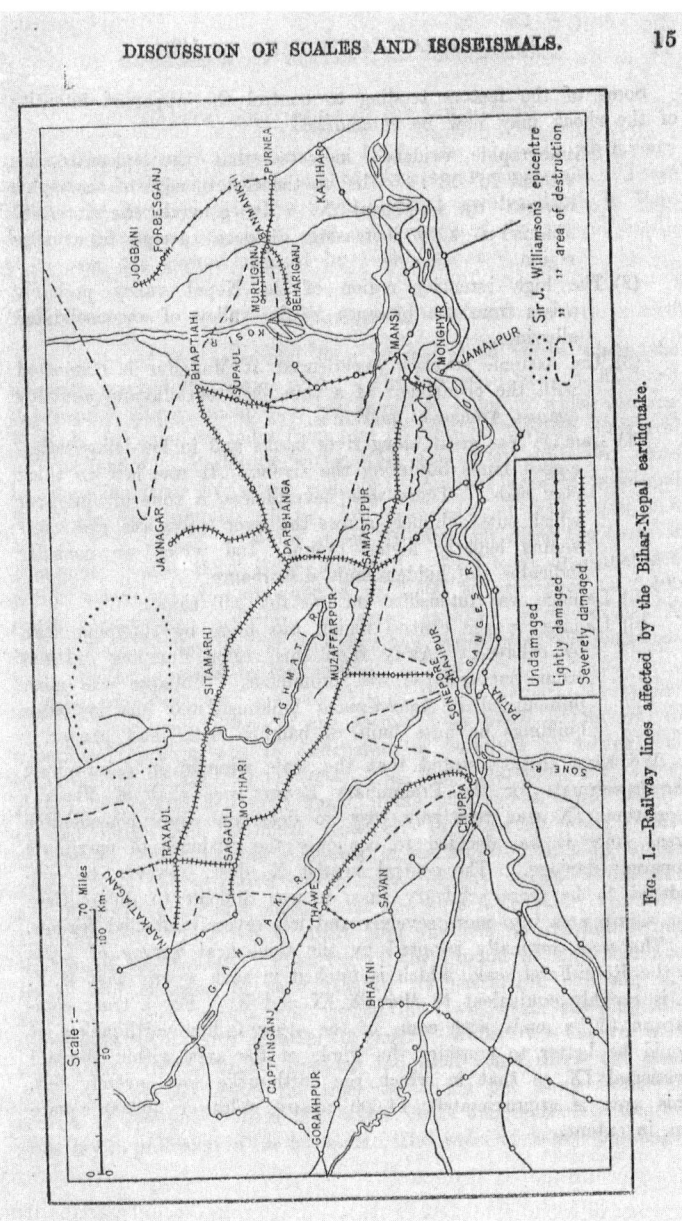

Fig. 1.—Railway lines affected by the Bihar-Nepal earthquake.

Map 2.2 Railway lines affected. Based on data by the GSI and J. Williamson, Agent of the Bengal and North-Western Railway. The map shows damages to the railways accurately, but the isoseismals and the epicentre marked by Williamson were based on 'arbitrarily selected localities' according to GSI.

Source: Fig. 1, 'Railway lines affected by the Bihar–Nepal earthquake', in Dunn et al., 'The Bihar–Nepal Earthquake of 1934', 15.

miles traversed north Bihar and the eastern United Provinces and hardly a mile of track out of those 900 miles was undisturbed (Map 2.2).[88] Tirhut remained isolated by rail from the neighbouring province since all trains to the east of Gorakhpur, a railway town located approximately 140 kilometres west of Tirhut, stopped running after the earthquake and a number of trains remained stranded between stations for days.[89] In Brett's report, the interruption of communication between Patna and the affected areas, via land and across the Bagmati and the Bur Gandak basin, was a 'central difficulty' in the immediate relief operations. The delayed dispatch of medical relief to Monghyr and Tirhut was also explained in the same report by the breakdown of telegraph communication, resulting in the government having difficulties in finding accurate information.[90]

While the local government explained disrupted communication as the main obstacle in assessing the scope of the disaster, it was at the same time able to mobilise the police and military to the affected areas. Significantly, the police would, in addition to acting as a force of security, be the central actor in the government's relief response. According to the local government's reports, the police was readily available to move at notice. In Monghyr, the administrative stronghold in the area, and perhaps the worst-affected town due to the intense collapse of buildings in the Chowk area of the bazaar, the police arrived from nearby Bhagalpur within hours, and about 250 police officers arrived in the emergency phase. It would take three days for 200 policemen to move across the Ganges into Tirhut. Even if communication with Muzaffarpur town had been severed in the earthquake, its geographical location and its strategic importance as the administrative headquarters in north Bihar meant that the police, as well as relief and rescue teams, arrived sooner than in Darbhanga, Motihari and at the sub-divisional headquarters. Muzaffarpur was, however, difficult to access and neighbouring towns had been severely affected, unlike in the case of Monghyr, where the fast arrival of medical relief, goods and staff were facilitated by communication with nearby areas and access by rail from both Patna and Bhagalpur, since damages to connecting railways lines could be repaired relatively soon. Besides, Bhagalpur, Jamshedpur and Jamalpur had valuable resources at hand. The Tata Iron and Steel Company Ltd in Jamshedpur sent medical relief, workers, technical staff and a sanitation unit as well as materials and food by a special train in the immediate aftermath.[91] Bhagalpur was considered 'lucky' with a final number of eight recorded deaths,[92] and private relief parties from the town reached Monghyr already on 16 January and during the first crucial days of rescue work. Overall, the district administration's response in Monghyr became more efficient thanks to functional communication and access to nearby resourceful areas unaffected by the earthquake, clearly facilitating the erection of shelters for hospital patients, arrangement of relief centres, arrival of medical aid and distribution of food and blankets among other things. Access to Monghyr via road and availability of manpower led to more resources reaching the town, for instance, there was help that came in the form of coolies from nearby Jhajha, Dumka and Jamui, and workers, staff and tools from the East Indian Railway workshops in Jamalpur, which also supplied electricity for three days after the earthquake. Additionally, a lorry and officers with 270 men arrived to help with the clearance of debris from the Imperial Tobacco Company's factory.[93] At the instance of the first shock, the whistle in the railway workshops in Jamalpur had blown and 'all the workers rushed out', a measure that was thought to have saved many lives.[94] The functional roads and rail, coupled with Monghyr's proximity to places that were relatively less damaged and in a position to supply equipment and workers, explained the fast inflow of assistance from nearby stationed police, relief societies and industries.

Even if Monghyr was the town best facilitated by a steady inflow of help from neighbouring areas, the district administration's difficulties in clearing the bazaar of debris in the immediate aftermath resulted in the local government's call on the military to help. It was difficult to find workers willing to participate in the rescue work in the bazaar: according to Brett's report 'labour was frightened' after the death of a coolie, who was killed by a collapsing building in an aftershock one day after the earthquake, and on top of it a fire raged in the ruins, yet fortunately, Monghyr's water tower was undamaged. Also, after the second tremor (10.30 a.m. on 16 January), the workers continued working until dark. Notably, the 200 coolies available were not enough and only after 300 coolies 'had been collected' did the work progress under the supervision of the Superintendent of Police.[95] Since the workers hesitated to enter the bazaar, the district administration had to ask for assistance[96] and consequently the local government requested the Government of India to send the 'expert help' of Sappers and Miners to clear debris on 17 January 1934. In Muzaffarpur, too, Brett's report acknowledged 'a shortage of coolies' to have delayed clearing debris.[97] Apart from requesting Sappers and Miners from the military, the government administration did not specify how the difficulties in finding labour were addressed, but a narrative of the earthquake aftermath by Reginald Reynolds, a vocal criticizer of British imperialism, claimed that the military used force in order to coerce people to clear debris.[98] In general, it is unclear how the police responsible for counting bodies found volunteers or workers for the often hazardous undertaking of clearing the sites and removing bodies. For instance, no information revealed if the 'posse of

Santals', members of a regional tribal group, whom a Member of the Legislative Council 'collected ... and took to Monghyr' to help in clearing debris,[99] received compensation, or whether they had volunteered or been coerced to help. The task of removing dead bodies was described by local relief workers as one that 'even paid labourers would not touch for love or money', necessitating volunteers to bring the bodies to the burning *ghat* in Monghyr.[100] The local branch of the BCRC claimed to have removed more than 2,000 bodies with the help of volunteers.[101]

Like in the case of the arrival of the police in the earthquake-affected towns, the military's arrival at Monghyr four days after the earthquake depended on geographical location, accessibility and the urgency to commence work, while the inaccessibility and location of Muzaffarpur and Darbhanga delayed the clearing of debris which did not happen until the sixth and seventh days after the earthquake, respectively.[102] The military brought lorries and carried tents, which were used as shelters for the homeless and injured, and, according to the local government's request to the major garrisons, such equipment was considered the first and most urgent requirement.[103] Functional communication and road networks evidently played a role in efficiently mobilising aid, but equally important if not more crucial in the arrival of help, whether by police, military, medical relief or relief societies, were the towns' geographical locations and proximity to unaffected areas.

According to accounts by eyewitnesses and by organisations, both in the immediate aftermath as well as in later publications, the delay in calling on the military to help in clearing debris was the primary fault in the government's response since it allegedly resulted in a number of deaths that could have been avoided if assistance had arrived sooner. If the difficulties caused by the breakdown of communication played a decisive role in the government's narrative of the aftermath, the nationalist press criticised the local government for the delayed call on the military. An article in the nationalist Bengali newspaper *Bande Mataram*[104] pinpointed recurring criticisms regarding the local government's organisation of rescue, and questioned why it had not despatched the army:

> Though the Government of Bihar have not been inactive it does not appear that they have been able to make necessary arrangements. It would not be too much to say that we have been disappointed in our hope of seeing prompt action taken by the Government of Bihar. Why are not the soldiers being called upon to give relief and clear away debris? In any civilised country the soldiers would have been entrusted first of all with such work. The Government of Bihar are only busy with making police arrangements. However preoccupied the Viceroy and the Commander-in-Chief might be,

their duty was to dispatch the soldiers and Sappers and Miners under them to the affected areas without delay. It will not do to depend on the police alone. The police cannot be expected to attend to all the various duties they are called upon to perform in view of the situation.[105]

Bande Mataram accused the government of lacking organisational capacity, and highlighted its inability to handle the situation by providing manpower in clearing debris. At the same time, it also acknowledged the police's multifunctional role in conducting relief tasks, which it was insufficiently equipped to perform. A call for the military to take action and a similar critique of the government's response was provided with the example of Japan after the 1923 Kanto earthquake when sappers and miners had been released from the army to help in clearing debris.[106] Ironically perhaps, the military and police in Japan were, according to secondary sources, not called on for the purpose of clearing debris but to quench disorder and restore order before relief and rescue work could begin.[107] Another critical voice in *Amrita Bazar Patrika* claimed that the government's insufficient organisation was to blame for letting poorer people die under the debris in Muzaffarpur since only a 'fortunate few' could afford to hire coolies for three rupees per day.[108] This was a large amount compared to the agricultural wage labour rate for adult males of approximately 4 annas per day in the area in the early 1930s.[109] Like the article in *Bande Mataram*, the newspaper criticised the government's arrangements for clearing debris which started only on 21 January in Muzaffarpur as the chance of finding survivors decreased with each day that passed. It questioned why the local government, one week after the earthquake, had stated communication as the main obstacle in providing relief according to two recent communiqués but was yet to despatch the military. Rather than disrupted communication, the newspaper blamed negligence on behalf of the government for the delay.[110] It agreed with Rajendra Prasad that 'delayed relief is denied relief' and urged for concerted action by the government.[111] The local government's organisation of rescue operations in Monghyr was subject to harsh criticism in nationalist eyewitness accounts that ascribed 'martyrs' death' to victims who were trapped under the debris crying for help but left to die due to the insufficient number of workers available.[112] Supporting criticism of the slow-paced work in the bazaars, the Marwari Relief Society in its report from 1935, claimed more people could have been saved had the clearing of debris and rescue efforts in Monghyr been more efficiently organised.[113] Several dramatic and tragic eyewitness accounts in *Bhūkamp pīḍitoṃ kī karuna-kahāniyāṃ: Bihār ke bhūkamp-pīḍitoṃ kī param āścarya-janak aur karunāpūrṇ saccī ātma-kathāeṃ* (Hindi, Stories of the Victims of the Earthquake: Bihar's Earthquake Victims' Most Astonishing and Pitiful True Narrations) from May 1934, testified to a lack of assistance in often futile attempts at digging out family members in Muzaffarpur, Sitamarhi, Motihari and Monghyr.[114] This publication may, however, have highlighted, if not exaggerated, the particularly tragic circumstances in view of its reliance upon a dramatic narrative rather than images. Published by the leader of the Akhil Bhartiya Goshala Sammelan (All India Cow Shelter Conference), the sale proceeds went towards the reconstruction of cow shelters damaged in the earthquake.[115]

Such stories of suffering and the Marwari Relief Society's report were still relatively modest in their criticism of the government's relief effort compared to Jawaharlal Nehru, who decried its lack of effort in mobilising help by, for instance, calling on the army, labourers or railway workers from Jamalpur.[116] His slim book based on a tour of the area was sold in direct support of the BCRC: its sale proceeds went towards the BCRC, and it was edited by Mohanlal Saksena (alt. Saxena), a Congressman based in Patna who would later become the president of the Provincial Congress Committee.[117] Even thirteen days after the earthquake, living persons were rescued from the debris according to Nehru, and many bodies were also recovered of people who, the doctors testified, must have died a day or two earlier. Nehru had, according to his retrospective account, criticised the local government in Patna for inactivity especially in Monghyr where he noticed debris still lying untouched on his second visit to the town in February 1934. While castigating the government, Nehru at the same time offered one of the harshest criticisms against the local population, both in villages and towns, who, he said, had waited for help from the government and relief organisations rather than taking action. Among those who did take part, he blamed foremost a group of urban residents who 'thought that work meant ordering people about'. [118]

A look at the resources and organisation available in the Darbhanga Raj throws further light on the local government's response. In Darbhanga, the presence of the Darbhanga Raj and the colonial government administration provided two sets of parallel and partly collaborative relief operations. The colonial government administration's delay in organising workers for clearing the bazaar is mentioned in its report by Brett as well as in *The Bihar Earthquake and the Darbhanga Raj* by Kumar Ganganand Sinha, a semi-official account of the aftermath authored with 'help' from the central administrative office of the Darbhanga Raj.[119] Contrary to the government's response, the Raj is described to have immediately mobilised about 1,000 coolies to clear debris and tear down dangerous and damaged buildings, while the colonial government administration issued proclamations calling for labour to clear debris only after two days had passed.

While waiting for the government's organisation of labour, the men hired by the Darbhanga Raj worked 'not only in the Raj area but also in the bazars for about a week, after which the Government could get their own men to work outside the Raj lands'.[120] Despite its hagiographic approach to the Darbhanga Raj's organisational expediency, the account gives an idea of the actions undertaken and the resources available to the Raj administration, partly also the Raj's role in assisting the local government's relief response which it also acknowledged. The delay by the government administration in Patna in mobilising labour for the removal of debris was, in its report, explained by the District Officer's absence until 17 January.[121] Not until on 22 January 1934, did the Sappers and Miners from Samastipur arrive in lorries borrowed from the Raj administration. The Raj administration also assisted the government hospital in Laheriasarai with medical equipment and lent the first tent to be set up for hospital patients at the polo ground.[122] In comparison with the Raj's administrative capacities, the local government's response appeared disorganised and limited in scope in terms of material resources and manpower.

Medical Relief: The Official Organisation of Volunteer Societies

The police was the government's principal organisation for providing relief according to its own report of the earthquake's aftermath. The police, a force of control and at the same time rescuer in the local government's narrative, was, however, inadequately equipped for the task. The police was responsible for counting bodies, the organisation of medical relief, sanitation and food control, and later in charge of the 'special organisation' of transport via alternative routes to the northern parts in cooperation with the railways. Far from a domain of the government, as subsequent appeals in newspapers and the yearly report by the Indian Red Cross showed, medical relief depended on resources of cooperating organisations and mobilisation of medical volunteers. Even if damages to the communication system created delays in delivering aid to the affected areas, the local government did not despatch medical relief to Muzaffarpur, the nodal point for Tirhut Division, until 17 January—approximately 24 hours after the first news of destruction in the area had reached Patna. A message delivered by hand had arrived at Patna from Muzaffarpur on the morning of 16 January 1934 and the government sent seven public health doctors on 17 January. In Monghyr, the Civil Surgeon's request for medical supplies on 16 January resulted in a party of four doctors and five senior medical students from Patna being sent there.[123] This scant provision of medical relief should be seen in the light of the local government's call on philanthropic organisations to carry out emergency relief, as will be discussed later. The total or partial collapse of hospitals complicated medical care as both equipment and facilities were left buried or ruined, and patients needed alternative accommodation in all the affected areas. The General Hospital in Patna was shattered; the Sadr Hospital in Motihari was ruined, and in Monghyr patients had to be accommodated in shelters.[124] In Sitamarhi, 'every patient' was killed in the collapse of the hospital, except for one who was left with both legs broken and a fractured skull, afterwards cared for in one of the temporary sheds of bamboo for the injured organised by the sub-divisional officer.[125] The Darbhanga Raj hospital was in ruins[126] and about 34 patients and staff had died.[127] Another source claimed 200 patients had been killed in the collapse of the same hospital and another that 200 patients had succumbed in the ruins of the government hospital at Laheriasarai.[128] As a result, first-aid stations were opened at the police lines and on the Darbhanga Raj maidan, and camp hospitals set up on the polo ground at Laheriasarai and in the Darbhanga Raj's football ground. A private individual in Calcutta (Messrs. B. K. Paul) sent an ambulant 'relief hospital' to work together with the Darbhanga Raj hospital. As a general relief measure to address both the damaged hospitals and the need for medical relief, the government's immediate response, according to its own report, was to authorise civil surgeons to order additional medical stores at their discretion and to provide 6,000 rupees for emergency relief to each district magistrate in the affected areas.[129]

If damages to hospitals to a certain extent explain the lack of medical relief provided by the government, it must be noted that the government at the same time did not perceive a great need of doctors. The local government in a message to the Home Department and the Secretary of State on 17 January 1934 clearly stated that medical relief was sufficiently provided for as doctors despatched to the affected areas 'were in excess of the requests by local officers' and more doctors were 'standing by' in Patna. In Champaran, 'isolated and largely destroyed', the District Magistrate of Motihari by telegram communicated 'no doctors required' two days after the earthquake.[130] According to the official death toll, 455 people were killed in the district Champaran.[131] When, from the air, the Commissioner of Tirhut estimated damages to land and crops one week after the earthquake, he did not regard damages to water supplies or houses as grave enough to address or call for medical assistance to rural areas.[132] At the end of January, the same lack of a need for more doctors was reiterated in a confidential report to the central government: 'The measures taken for relief are proceeding satisfactorily. Confidence is returning. No epidemic has occurred. There are more doctors than are required (...)'.[133] At that point, for example, the qualified extra medical staff sent to Darbhanga was restricted to three public health doctors who had arrived from Patna via Muzaffarpur on the evening of 18 January, out of whom two continued to Samastipur and Madhubani.[134] A month later, a confidential report claimed unofficial reports of epidemics to be 'highly inaccurate' and that there was 'nothing in the nature of an epidemic'.[135] However, the situation in Motihari changed in early March when plague broke out in Bettiah town and the Public Health Department in Patna sent two doctors and 'plague vaccine' by aeroplane in order to bring the epidemic, with only fourteen cases reported, under control.[136] Again in August, the earthquake was seen as the cause of another outbreak of an epidemic in Darbhanga, and the local government sent vaccines from Patna.[137]

Medical relief was to a considerable extent carried out by medical associations, a provision of philanthropic activities encouraged and appealed for by the local government. The Bihar and Orissa branch of the Indian Red Cross Society worked with the local government, as well as independently, to provide medical relief and humanitarian assistance. The close cooperation with the local government was facilitated by the philanthropic engagement by Sir James Sifton, Governor of Bihar and Orissa, who acted as President of the Bihar and Orissa Red Cross Society Branch, and his wife, Lady Sifton, Chairman on its Executive Committee, along with the principal of the Medical College, the Director of Public Health and the Secretary of the Local Self Government Department on its sub-committee.[138] The local Red Cross branch distributed its entire Epidemic Relief Fund to the District Boards in the most severely affected areas for prevention of epidemics.[139] The fund provided a convenient reserve since the local Indian Red Cross societies normally depended on public appeals every time a disaster occurred. At the same time, the resort to the Epidemic Relief Fund served to justify the establishment of a disaster relief fund. The need for an actor to provide emergency relief expanded the domain of the Indian Red Cross to also cover disaster relief. According to its President, the earthquake showed that the society 'badly needs a Disaster Relief Fund which can be drawn upon at once without waiting for the result of a public appeal'. The proposal to establish such a fund with the St John Ambulance Association was announced in the Annual General Meeting in 1935 and was realised with the help of contributions to King George's Silver Jubilee Fund, the Patron of the British Red Cross Society. Before that, in April 1934, cooperation between the St John Ambulance Association and the Indian Red Cross was formalised in an agreement where the former, in exchange for financial support, was to handle all ambulance responsibilities that the Red Cross had agreed to under the Geneva Convention. The agreement was seen as a more structured and professional approach towards disaster relief for both organisations, with St John Ambulance as the provider of trained personnel for the Red Cross disaster relief programme.[140] In total, the local Red Cross branch spent 76,529 rupees on earthquake relief and collected 'more than a lakh' in cash and 'thousands of bales of stores'. The society's yearly report mentions the sum of 34,000 rupees to the Commissioners of Bhagalpur, Tirhut and Patna for medical comforts, plus an additional 14,000 rupees at the disposal of a sub-committee for purchasing medical comforts unavailable locally,[141] but these sums may partially have been taken from the epidemic fund. In view of the 6,000 rupees granted by the government to each district magistrate for medical relief, the amounts provided by the local Red Cross were substantial.

The Bihar and Orissa branch of the Indian Red Cross Society became the most prominent actor among the medical organisations, a position encouraged and gained by its close cooperation with not only the local government, but also the Patna Medical Association[142] and the Indian Medical Association (IMA) from Calcutta that participated with staff and equipment. By 20 January, the IMA, alongside the Red Cross and St John Ambulance, had begun giving medical assistance in Muzaffarpur, Darbhanga and Monghyr.[143] In Calcutta, the IMA's appeal for a range of trained medical staff and in particular the need for 'medical men with administrative experience' indicated a shortage of qualified senior medical staff.[144] Similarly, appeals by pharmacists and companies in Calcutta indicate a need for medicine.[145] These philanthropic initiatives were welcomed by the local government in communiqués appealing for so-called self-contained units, medical units or field hospitals.[146] The District Magistrate in Monghyr appealed through public announcements in newspapers for 25 volunteers to carry out ambulance work, and for stretchers, tents and tarpaulins to shelter the wounded in hundreds.[147] 'Self-contained' meant that the respective organisations provided resources and staff while the practical provision of medical care remained under the supervision of the District Magistrates. This type of relief and philanthropy was greatly in need according to communiqués in the newspapers.[148] The Bengal Red Cross in cooperation with the Bengal branch of the St John Ambulance Association received special recognition for sending a 'fully equipped medical unit',[149] which included tents, medical stores, rations and a team of more than 30 medical professionals, to Monghyr (Image 2.4).[150] The Bengal Branch gave substantial financial support with a 'special contribution' of 10,000 rupees distributed at the relief centres.[151]

St. John Ambulance party under Lt.-Col. K. K. Chatterjee (second from right) at work among the ruins at Monghyr.

Image 2.4 St John Ambulance and a Red Cross relief party at work in Monghyr.

Source: Moore (ed.), *Record of the Great Indian Earthquake*, 44.

The local Red Cross held a central function in managing the collection and distribution of charitable relief goods at a depot in Patna from 21 January. Small and large provisions sent from around India arrived in response to appeals by the local government,[152] as well as by Indian Red Cross branches, for blankets, clothing, food, bandages, tents and medical stores.[153] The most urgent relief provision, according to an emergency meeting, was blankets for the homeless who had been left stranded in the winter cold. This resulted in 20,000 blankets being collected and distributed. In addition to this act of humanitarian relief, Lady Sifton organised 'work parties' to roll bandages and make dressings and pneumonia jackets for the injured.[154] The local government facilitated transport to the districts' distribution centres, to Monghyr or to the northern regional depot in Muzaffarpur by providing free tickets and free carriage for relief materials and the transport of staff, tents and medical supplies.[155] The local government ensured that travel concessions were also granted to the St John Ambulance, the IMA[156] and a few other relief societies.[157] The governments of the United Provinces and Punjab were especially prolific at contributing by sending blankets, clothes and tents, so much so that they had to be approached twice in order to stop sending supplies when the depot at Patna closed down at the end of March in 1934.[158]

Transports to north Bihar remained limited until 22 January 1934 after which the amount of emergency and provisional relief increased considerably. Not until then could the IMA in Calcutta send heavier medical equipment[159] and relief teams of trained staff to the affected towns.[160] By 24 January, the local government had sent doctors and medical students to Muzaffarpur, Darbhanga and Motihari but not yet to rural areas and small towns outside the district headquarters—again explained by a breakdown in communication.[161] By this time relief societies such as the Indian Red Cross Society, St John Ambulance, the local government and companies sent staff and resources in the form of provisions for medical relief, food, blankets and iron sheets to build temporary shelters.[162] On 27 January, the IMA sent two self-contained medical units equipped with X-ray machines to Sitamarhi and Motihari.[163] One of its units carried out surgeries on behalf of the BCRC in north Bihar in February.[164]

Official Death Toll: Contested Data

The number of people dead or injured was contested in the aftermath of the earthquake and until today the final death count varies between the official government figure of 7,253 deaths[165] and the approximate number of 20,000 deaths claimed by the BCRC.[166] The latter is closer to the accepted figure among historians,[167] while recent scientific publications rely on the official data.[168] The BCRC's considerably higher estimates of the number of deaths challenged the official narrative. The committee estimated 3,000 deaths in Muzaffarpur town, three times more than the official figure of 956 deaths; and 6,000 in Muzaffarpur district, while the government recorded 1,583 deaths.[169] The starkest discrepancy was recorded in Monghyr town where the BCRC questioned the government's official number of 1,260 deaths with an estimate of 10,000 deaths.[170] The local government's report claimed the final official figure to be a rough estimate, but did not concede to the general appreciation that it was too low; instead, the government described it as 'surprisingly small'.[171] Adding to the confusion, deaths in Nepal were sometimes included in the final figures, as, for example, in the case of the GSI publication from 1936.[172] The same publications fail to mention an appreciation of the number of injured,[173] except for approximate numbers in a few areas.[174] An indication of the large number of injured people can be inferred from the treatment of 4,500 cases by 30 medical professionals in the medical unit sent to Monghyr by the Bengal Red Cross and the Bengal branch of the St John Ambulance Association. The total number of people in need of treatment, or those who were fatally injured, may have been much larger, in particular considering that patients left Monghyr to seek medical care in nearby relatively undamaged towns or Calcutta.[175]

The government's underestimates of the death toll were in the press perceived as attempts to downplay the severity of the disaster, thereby reducing a need for relief and financial assistance. The first official number of 2,500 deaths was regarded as a 'gross underestimate' which 'un-official' reports countered with statements by anonymous eye-witnesses and newspaper correspondents of 'far larger' numbers.[176] *Amrita Bazar Patrika* reported that 'non-official reports were unanimous' about the death toll to exceed the government's estimates at Muzaffarpur, Monghyr and Darbhanga.[177] Government communiqués cautiously added numbers to the districts of Darbhanga, Muzaffarpur and Champaran in Tirhut until the end of January. For instance, the official figure in Muzaffarpur changed from 'about' 600 deaths by 18 January[178] to 'about' 800 deaths four days later.[179] The yearly report of the Indian Red Cross Society noted how the number of deaths multiplied with each government communiqué: 'the first estimates of the number killed was 2,000, then 4,000, then 6,000 and the last figure mentioned officially was between 7,000 and 8,000'. As the death toll had increased from 2,500 to 4,000 in the 10 days following the earthquake, the government recognised the official figures as incomplete and the number of dead was expected to increase after the debris had been removed.[180] On the last day of January, two weeks after the earthquake, a government communiqué reported 6,041 deaths[181] and the final official number of 7,253 deaths was almost three times the initial official estimate of 2,500,[182] which the Government of Bihar and Orissa repeated in the first week after the earthquake.[183]

If the government's official number of deaths was an underestimate, the unofficial numbers were disparate and exaggerated, provided scant information about data collection and often appeared in connection with a critique of the government's relief and rescue work. For instance, the official death toll was 600 to 800 in Muzaffarpur town on 20 January, while the unofficial figure quoted in the press stated 3,100 deaths.[184] Several eyewitness accounts came from Congress leaders such as Rajendra Prasad who said the official figure underestimated the disaster and instead claimed the earthquake to have killed 20,000,[185] a statement supported by Jawaharlal Nehru who said that the government deliberately 'tried to minimise the loss'.[186] Although 'unofficial' reports may have contained exaggerated data in terms of deaths and destruction, an editorial in *Amrita Bazar Patrika* pointed out that the government at the same time ignored eyewitness accounts from Europeans and people with no interest in falsified accounts,[187] indicating a general perception of relief and rescue operations as insufficient in relation to injuries and people buried in debris. Despite these persistent reports of widespread damages, the local government did not perceive a need for any larger mobilisation of rescue. Its response resembled an 'information panic' in the sense that it trusted neither the information provided by nor the intentions of the local society.

In Monghyr, the number of deaths remained contested and unofficial estimates of 10,000 deaths[188] stood in sharp contrast to the final official figures of 1,260 deaths.[189] As in other towns, 'unofficial' eyewitness accounts gave disparate numbers without details regarding the data, and the discrepancies were large: 5,563 deaths recorded on 21 January or 1,700 bodies disposed of by 22 January,[190] compared to the official figure of between 400 and 500 dead reported by 23 January 1934.[191] Most of the deaths were supposed to have happened in the lanes of the two old bazaars, Chowk bazaar and Madhupura bazaar, where approximately 3,000–4,000 people resided,[192] though the actual numbers of residents were unknown, according to the municipality, since many holdings held two families.[193] Satish Chandra Das Gupta, a member of the Congress party from Bengal and part of a relief team, apprehended that one-fourth of the population were dead or buried under debris,[194] thereby insinuating a much larger death toll of around 12,000–13,000.[195] This number is close to the 'unofficial' figure of 10,000 deaths out of the town's more than 50,000 residents, as mentioned in Jawaharlal Nehru's personal account, and the same figure as quoted in *Devastated Bihar* by the BCRC.[196] The accusation of downplaying the number of deaths in Monghyr bazaar resulted in a house-to-house enquiry by the government that in the end confirmed the official number. The official number was, like in the other areas, based on data collected by the police who was responsible for recording bodies and subsequently burnt them at the *ghat* under the supervision of a gazetted officer.[197] As two newspapers pointed out, the official number represented bodies registered, a procedure that not everyone followed in the exceptional circumstances of the aftermath.[198]

According to Tirthankar Roy, the victims formed a 'selective group' of women, city-dwellers, Indians and merchants, who lost more lives than men, villagers and Europeans.[199] Initially, injuries and deaths among the Indian public were reported separately from the European, Anglo-Indian and Indians employed in official positions in the press and government correspondence.[200] The 'Indian death-roll' was estimated to exceed a thousand while 'no European had been killed' in Muzaffarpur.[201] Planters of European descent, residing in north Bihar, and European and Anglo-Indian staff in Jamalpur made *The Statesman* assume it for 'certain that Europeans must have been among those who have perished' and kept a record of the 'Indian death-roll' separately,[202] which in the end proved to be a pointless practice since Ms Francis Christian, a resident of Monghyr, was the only officially recorded 'European' victim of the earthquake.[203]

One explanation for why more women[204] than men had succumbed, claimed that the practice of purdah kept women indoors and made them victims of collapsing buildings.[205] If not the practice of purdah, household work and child-rearing made it more likely for women than men to be indoors at the time of the earthquake. As research on gendered vulnerability in disasters has shown, class, financial means and religion, among other variables, intersect with gender, and it is therefore problematic to apply the practice of purdah to the female population as a group.[206] Since demographic data of the fatalities is missing, one can only conclude that many of the female victims lived in towns and in houses of bricks that belonged to merchant, trader or professional communities which, judging from causalities in the bazaars, formed a sizeable group among the victims.

In general, the occurrence of the earthquake in the afternoon, when people were awake, and its slow onset, reaching peak intensity after about two and a half minutes, helped many take refuge in the open.[207] The number of deaths was more than expected in Monghyr since in the afternoon, when the earthquake happened, the Chowk bazaar was unusually full of visitors shopping for the occasion of observing the new moon, Mauni Amavasya. Adding to the crowd, many Muslims were making purchases in the bazaar for the festival of Eid al-Fitr on the following day.[208] While the narrow lanes in the bazaars became a death trap for consumers as well as residents and traders, like in the bazaars of Muzaffarpur and Darbhanga, the wide roads in Motihari saved people from getting crushed under falling debris, which was given as an explanation for the relatively few deaths there.[209] Similarly, Jamalpur's less congested buildings and lower population density probably saved lives, considering that 130 houses out of the railways' 150 houses had been completely ruined.[210] In the reconstruction of the bazaars in Darbhanga, Muzaffarpur and Monghyr, widening of roads was a measure promoted with earthquake safety in mind (discussed in Chapter 6).

Conclusion: Communication Panic

This chapter has examined how the disruption of information and communication in the earthquake shaped the government's narrative of the aftermath as well as its immediate response. The earthquake caused a severe disruption of the transport and communication system, cutting off the affected areas from the reach of the local government headquarters in every possible way. While the conventional means of communication by road, rail and telegraph were dysfunctional, the local government had to rely on a limited number of aeroplanes for communication with north Bihar, a method that had obvious limits and constraints regarding access and frequency of correspondence. As discussed in this chapter, there is ample data on deaths in the press and in government communiqués that show how the local colonial government's initial estimates of the death toll severely misjudged the impact of the earthquake by ignoring information available in reports from the public and civil society.

Although it should be recognised that the disrupted infrastructure and a lack of information caused obvious problems for the government in providing aid, its communication panic resulted in a security-oriented response that increased vulnerability. Compared to the 'information panic' persuasively argued by Bayly,[211] the physical destruction resulted in a 'communication panic' as the established infrastructure of communication was destroyed. While the government's master narrative of the aftermath explained the delayed response with the breakdown in communication and lack of information about the scope of the disaster, the disrupted communication infrastructure per se made the government prioritise security before emergency relief. In the official narrative of Relief Commissioner Brett's report, however, the earthquake became the cause of potential disorder and looting. According to his narrative, the earthquake was used to justify the local government's security-oriented response as well as blamed for disrupting communication, and thereby indirectly held responsible for the failure of the local colonial government in making a rapid impact assessment of the need for relief.[212] The local government's perception of technical advances, that is, roads, telegrams and railways, as essential for an adequate response reflected a misplaced faith in the capabilities of infrastructure. If we recall Ulrich Beck's argument that modernisation contributed to institutionalised scientific knowledge and technical expertise that exacerbate vulnerability,[213] a colonial perception of communication infrastructure as integral to governance shaped its risk perception and thereby how it responded to the earthquake. The ineptitude of the colonial government in dealing with the aftermath resulted from its perception of risk: its agency to govern was circumscribed by failing infrastructure, a technological breakdown caused by the earthquake.

As pointed out in Brett's report and corroborated by the report of BCRC, the function of the police in the immediate aftermath was first to ensure that law and order were upheld, and second, to provide assistance in the relief work and organisation of medical relief. In this dual role, its traditional responsibility to act as the long arm of the law took priority over its extraordinary duties as rescuer and relief organiser. For the provision of emergency medical relief, the government cooperated closely with the Indian Red Cross Society and encouraged medical relief teams like the St John Ambulance and medical staff from nearby Calcutta to help. The role of high government officials as patrons of the Bihar and Orissa Red Cross Society was likely to have been instrumental in decisions to tap the society's fund meant for epidemics and hand it over to the government administration to use for emergency relief. Medical relief and emergency relief in the form of food and shelters were in this way sourced from philanthropic organisations while the government's contribution to relief operations was first represented by the police forces, which formed the core of the local government's relief apparatus in the immediate aftermath. As the primary emergency force of the local government, its role was to coordinate the crucial resources and participation of local and regional companies and relief associations in rescue operations. Such private contributions in the aftermath played a major role in the implementation of the local colonial government's relief operations, as seen, for instance, in Monghyr. The inability to respond according to the needs of the citizens' well-being in the face of disaster reflected not only a lack in infrastructure to deal with the earthquake, but above all an over-reliance on communication and information as essential factors in responding to the disaster.

Notes

1. Yi Lu and Jiuping Xu, 'The Progress of Emergency Response and Rescue in China: A Comparative Analysis of Wenchuan and Lushan Earthquakes', *Natural Hazards* 74, no. 2 (2014): 421–44, 422.
2. Mukherjee, 'Afterword', 191–92.
3. Papiya Ghosh, *The Civil Disobedience Movement in Bihar, 1930–1934* (New Delhi: Manak Publications, 2008).
4. Roy, 'State, Society and Market', 278. The BCRC criticised the government's lack of organisation in clearing debris and saving lives. BCRC, *Devastated Bihar*, 52.
5. 'No. 2628-P. R.', untitled report (printed), 15 pp., P. C. Tallents to the Sec. to the GOI (Home Dept, Simla), Political Department, Ranchi, 17 August 1934, File: 'Bihar and Orissa Earthquake 1934. Publicity, Relief and Reconstruction Measures in Connection Therewith. Accounts of the Bihar Central Relief Committee's Fund', NAI HP 34/1/1934. The same report is also found in 'Report of the B&O Government on the Earthquake Which Occurred in Bihar in January 1934', NAI Dept of Education, Health and Lands, Agricultural Section, 17/28/1934-A.

6. A longer communiqué of eighteen pages about damages and plans for reconstruction of infrastructure and buildings has been used extensively in Brett's report. 'Communiqué', R. D., Patna, 8 February 1934, forwarded to Home Dept, GOI, by the Governor of B&O, NAI HP 34/1(B)/1934.

7. Wilcock, *Bihar and Orissa in 1933–34*, 13. P. C. Roy Chaudhury, *Monghyr* (Bihar District Gazetteers, Bihar, Patna: Superintendent Secretariat Press, 1960), 544–45.

8. Brett, *A Report on the Bihar Earthquake*, 19.

9. The days of 18 and 20 January 1934 were notified holidays for Eid ul-Fitr and Basant Panchami, respectively. Tallents, 'No. 2628-P. R.', 17 August 1934, NAI HP 34/1/1934.

10. Brett, *A Report on the Bihar Earthquake*, quote from 11, 13.

11. Henry W. Fischer, III, *Response to Disaster: Fact versus Fiction and Its Perpetuation: The Sociology of Disaster* (Lanham, MA: University Press of America, 1988), 20–21.

12. Robert A. Stallings, 'Methodological Issues', in *Handbook of Disaster Research*, ed. H. Rodriguez, E. L. Quarantelli and R. R. Dynes, 55–82 (New York: Springer, 2006), 65.

13. Dawn Brancati, 'Political Aftershocks: The Impact of Earthquakes on Intrastate Conflict', *Journal of Conflict Resolution* 51, no. 15 (2007): 715–43, 737.

14. Brett, *A Report on the Bihar Earthquake*, 16, 19.

15. Interview with the Manager of the Darbhanga Circle, four days after the earthquake in Calcutta. 'At Darbhanga', *ABP*, 20 January 1934.

16. BCRC, *Devastated Bihar*, 26–27.

17. Michael Guggenheim, 'Introduction: Disasters and Politics—Politics as Disasters', in *Disasters and Politics: Materials, Experiments, Preparedness*, ed. Torini, Rodriguez-Giralt and Guggenheim, 1–16 (Oxford; West Sussex: Wiley Blackwell, 2014), 10 (originally published in *The Sociological Review* 62, S1 [2014]: 1–16).

18. For a compelling account of cultural politics, or the culture and politics of disasters, see Mark D. Anderson, *Disaster Writing: The Cultural Politics of Catastrophe in Latin America* (ProQuest Ebook Central; Charlottesville and London: University of Virginia Press, 2011).

19. On the role of colonialism and communication in Bihar, see Nitin Sinha, *Communication and Colonialism in Eastern India: Bihar, 1760s–1880s*, Anthem Modern South Asian History (London: Anthem Press, 2012). The English East India Company Trade increased its regional influence by trade and transport along the Ganga. Murari Kumar Jha, 'The Political Economy of the Ganga River: Highway of State Formation in Mughal India, c.1600–1800', doctoral thesis, Leiden University, Institute for History, 2013.

20. Christopher Bayly, *Empire and Information: Intelligence Gathering and Social Communication in India, 1780–1870* (Cambridge: Cambridge University Press, 1996), 174.

21. Eleonor Marcussen, 'Explaining the 1934 Bihar-Nepal Earthquake: The Role of Science, Astrology, and "Rumours"', in *Historical Disaster Experiences: Towards a Comparative and Transcultural History of Disasters Across Asia and Europe*, ed. G. J. Schenk, Transcultural Research—Heidelberg Studies on Asia and Europe in a Global Context, 241–66 (Heidelberg: Springer, 2017).

22. Geneviève Massard-Guilbaud, 'Introduction: the Urban Catastrophe— Challenge to the Social, Economic, and Cultural Order of the City', in *Cities and Catastrophes: Coping with Emergency in European History*, ed. G. Massard-Guilbaud, Harold L. Platt and Dieter Schott, 9–42 (Frankfurt am Main: Lang, 2002), 23–25. Kitao Abe, 'Levels of Trust and Reactions to Various Sources of Information in Catastrophic Situations', in *Disasters: Theory and Research*, ed. E. L. Quarantelli, 147–58 (Beverly Hills, California: SAGE Publications, 1978).

23. Mukherjee, *Natural Disasters and Victorian Empire*, 43.

24. Beck, *Risk Society: Towards a New Modernity*, 26–27.

25. Disaster response can also include mitigating the impact of further hazardous events, such as aftershocks and secondary infectious diseases. Alpaslan Oezerdem and Tim Jacoby, *Disaster Management and Civil Society: Earthquake Relief in Japan, Turkey and India* (New York: I. B. Tauris & Co. Ltd, 2006), 11.

26. Telegram from the Govt of B&O to Sec. of State (London), and Home Dept (New Delhi), Patna, 15 January 1934, File: 'Report of Earthquake to Secretary of State', BSA RE 500/1934.

27. Brett, *A Report on the Bihar Earthquake*, 3.

28. Population of Tirhut Division, 10,739,274, and 830 persons to the square mile (Table III); Darbhanga town, 60,676; Purnea, 15,474; Katihar, 15,864 (Table V); Monghyr, 52,863; Bhagalpur, 83,847; Muzaffarpur town, 42,812; Motihari, 17,545 (Table IV). W. G. Lacey, Census of India, 1931, vol. VII, *Bihar and Orissa Part II– Tables* (Patna: Superintendent, Govt Printing, 1932).

29. Dunn et al., 'The Bihar–Nepal Earthquake of 1934', 216–19.

30. Brett, *A Report on the Bihar Earthquake*, 1–4; Wilcock, *Bihar and Orissa in 1933–34*, 13–14.

31. See introduction in Singh, '"Colonising the Rivers": Colonial Technology, Irrigation and Flood Control in North Bihar, 1850–1950'.

32. Hill, *River of Sorrow*.

33. Brett, *A Report on the Bihar Earthquake*, 3.

34. Jacques Pouchepadass, *Land, Power and Market: A Bihar District under Colonial Rule, 1860–1947* (New Delhi: Sage, 2000), 386.

35. 'Communqué', *ABP*, 23 January 1934.

36. Wilcock, *Bihar and Orissa in 1933–34*, 13–14. The journey was about 25 miles according to BCRC, *Devastated Bihar*, 26.

37. Tallents, 'No. 2628-P. R.', 17 August 1934, NAI HP 34/1/1934.

38. 'Telegram', Govt of Bihar and Orissa to Sec. of State, New Delhi, 16 January 1934, BSA RE 500/1934.

39. Ibid.

40. Tallents, 'No. 2628-P. R.', 17 August 1934, NAI HP 34/1/1934. Brett, *A Report on the Bihar Earthquake*, 18.

41. Captain Charles Douglas (C.D.) Barnard (8 December 1895–7 August 1971). Lord Sempill, 'Private Flying: Developments in India', *Flight*, no. 1360 (17 January 1935): 75. The aeroplane carried A. Auden, Captain A. H. Dalton, and Palmer, the two latter were partners of Barnard. 'Ruined Muzaffarpur', *The Statesman*, 18 January 1934. 'Capt. C.D. Barnard for India', *Flight*, no. 1298 (9 November 1933): 1130–31. 'The Barnard Tour' (Correspondence), *Flight*, no. 1323 (3 May 1934): 448; 'The "Jupiter" in India', *Flight*, no. 1334 (19 July 1934): 754.

42. Captain Dalton's account in 'Ruined Muzaffarpur', *The Statesman*, 18 January 1934.

43. Tallents, 'No. 2628-P. R.', 17 August 1934, NAI HP 34/1/1934. Mr Fairweather's experience was accounted in 'Muzaffarpur's Night of Terror', *The Statesman*, 18 January 1934. Reproduced as 'A Night of Terror: Earthquake in Muzaffarpur', *The Leader*, 20 January 1934.

44. Tallents, 'No. 2628-P. R.', 17 August 1934, NAI HP 34/1/1934. Contrary to Tallents, Brett omits Fairweather's role.

45. Telegram from the Government of B&O ('Draft, corrected with notes included'), to Sec. of State, and Home Dept (New Delhi), Patna, 16 January 1934, BSA RE 500/1934.

46. David Arnold, *Science Technology and Medicine in Colonial India* (Cambridge: Cambridge University Press, 2004 [2000]), 137, 151–3.

47. P. C. Roy Chaudhury, *Muzaffarpur*, Bihar District Gazetteers (Patna: Superintendent Secretariat Press, 1958), 183.

48. Dunn et al., 'The Bihar–Nepal Earthquake of 1934', 3.

49. See BCRC, *Devastated Bihar*, 26.

50. Ibid.

51. From Muzaffarpur over Bettiah, the crew were accompanied by E. L. Marriott, Deputy Inspector-General (D.I.G.) of Police (Northern Range), 'Rescue Work by Plane [aeroplane]', *ABP*, 19 January 1934. Brett, *A Report on the Bihar Earthquake*, 15.

52. 'Hundreds Perish in Earthquake; Floods Ravage Districts in North Bihar: Houses Swept Away; Bodies Strewn in the Streets of Muzzafarpore; Thousands Dead in Ruined Town: Railways Destroyed; Mounting Death-Roll in Patna and Jamalpur', *The Statesman*, 17 January 1934. Captain Dalton interviewed in *The Statesman*, 16 January 1934. 'Scenes of Stark Desolation', *The Statesman*, 17 January 1934.

53. 'India Earthquake Kills Many, Deaths in Patna, Gaya and Jamalpore; Station Collapses on Goods Train; Severe Damage in Darjeeling District', *The Statesman*, 16 January 1934.

54. 'Calcutta's Big Shake; Damage Done to Buildings; Citizens Rush into Streets; Shocks Last for 8 Minutes', *The Statesman*, 16 January 1934.

55. 'India Earthquake Kills Many...', *The Statesman*, 16 January 1934.

56. '17 Dead: 48 Injured' (referring to Jamalpur); 'Howrah Station Scene; Mrs. Majumdar's Dead Body Brought to Calcutta', *ABP*, 17 January 1934. 'India Earthquake Kills Many...', *The Statesman*, 16 January 1934. A series of photos, 'the first to reach Bombay' from Jamalpur, were published four days after the earthquake. 'Exclusive Pictures of Jamalpur Earthquake Havoc', *Times of India*, 19 January 1934.

57. For a brief history of Jamalpur, see Nitin Sinha, '*Entering the Black Hole*: Between "Mini-England" and "Smell-Like Rotten Potato", the Railway Workshop Town of Jamalpur, 1860s–1940s', *South Asian History and Culture* 3, no. 3 (2012): 317–47.

58. So-called home-born Europeans made up as many as 20 per cent of the subordinate posts in the Indian railways by 1934. Sarmistha Dey, *Marginal Europeans in Colonial India: 1860–1920* (Kolkata: Thema, 2008), 4.

59. 'Jamalpore', *ABP*, 20 January 1934.

60. '17 Dead: 48 Injured'; 'Howrah Station Scene; Mrs. Majumdar's Dead Body Brought to Calcutta', *ABP*, 17 January 1934.

61. Kumkum Chatterjee, *Merchants, Politics, and Society in Early Modern India: Bihar, 1733–1820* (Leiden: E.J. Brill, 1996), 216–17. Anand A. Yang, *Bazaar India: Markets, Society, and the Colonial State in Gangetic Bihar* (Berkeley: University of California Press, 1998), 69. Henningham, 'Bureaucracy and Control', 43, 47, 53.

62. Narrated by the Maharajadhiraja in the newspaper *National Call*, Delhi, in March 1934, mentioned in Kumar Ganganand Sinha, *The Bihar Earthquake and the Darbhanga Raj* (Calcutta: Thacker's Press and Directories, Ltd and published by the Darbhanga Raj, 1936), 5.

63. Sinha, *The Bihar Earthquake and the Darbhanga Raj*, 5–6. The Government of Bengal also appears to have been informed about the scope of the earthquake in Tirhut in the morning of 18 January 1934, 'Magnitude of Disaster: Messages of Sympathy from Secretary of State', *ABP*, 20 January 1934.

64. 'Scenes of Stark Desolation', *The Statesman*, 17 January 1934.
65. Sinha, *The Bihar Earthquake and the Darbhanga Raj*, 5. R. D. Bilimoria, 'Bombay Parsi's Thrilling Experiences; Eye-Witness of Earthquake at Darbhanga Relates Story of Terrible Happenings on Fateful Monday', in Syed Abdullah Brelvi and B. G. Horniman (eds.), *Earthquake Number: Which Hand Is Yours*, special issue by *Chronicle-Sentinel*, Bombay, March 1934.
66. Sinha, *The Bihar Earthquake and the Darbhanga Raj*, 7.
67. Tallents, 'No. 2628-P. R.', 17 August 1934, NAI HP 34/1/1934.
68. Press Communiqué from the Organizing Secretary, Indian Red Cross Society, temporarily at Patna, enclosed with letter from the Indian Red Cross Society, New Delhi, to the Chief Sec., St John Ambulance Association (St John's Gate, Clerkenwell, London, E. C. 1), 24 January 1934 (copy), Museum and Library of St John, Clerkenwell, London.
69. Tallents, 'No. 2628-P. R.', 17 August 1934, NAI HP 34/1/1934.
70. The private aeroplane, which was used until 28 January, was provided by H. I. Matthews, M. C., Superintendent of the Gun and Shell Factory, Cossipore, who offered both the aeroplane and his own services to the government. He was a member of the Bengal Flying Club in Calcutta. 'The Bengal Flying Club', *Flight*, no. 1318 (29 March 1934): 302. The club had 359 members and altogether six aeroplanes at its disposal by the end of January 1934. 'Bengal Flying Club', *Flight*, no. 1309 (25 January 1934): 78.
71. The first report contains the Commissioner's observations from an aeroplane survey made from 8:40 a.m. to 1:45 p.m. on 21 and/or 22 January 1934: D.O. J-297, 'Notes of Reconnaissance by Aeroplane from Muzaffarpur to Bettiah and back via Raxaul and Sitamarhi' (6 pp.), J. E. Scott to P. C. Tallents, Muzaffarpur, 21–22 January 1934, File: 'Sugarcane Situation and General Economic Condition in Tirhut', BSA RE 23/1934. Unpublished government report by the Director of Industries, S. Lal [alt. Lall] and Director of Agriculture D. R. Sethi, submitted 26 January 1934 (21 pp.), in D. O. 223, P. C. Tallents to J. E. Scott, Patna, 9 February 1934. File: 'Staff-allotments of Grants Required for Relief Engineers of Town Engineers', BSA RE 76/1934.
72. V. E. Groom, Flight Lieutenant, Royal Air Force, to Headquarters, Royal Air Force (New Delhi), Patna, 28 January 1934, NAI HP 34/1/1934. John Tarlton (J. T.) Whitty, member of Legislative Council, was seriously injured in the accident. Tallents, 'No. 2628-P.R.', 17 August 1934, NAI HP 34/1/1934.
73. Several aftershocks around midnight, 3 a.m. and 10 a.m. were reported by eyewitness on 16 January in Patna. 'More Earthquake Shocks', *The Statesman*, 18 January 1934. The aftershock taken into consideration in the seismometric

study appeared on 19 January 1934. Roy, 'Seismometric Study', in 'The Bihar–Nepal Earthquake of 1934', ed. Dunn et al., ch. 4, 64–67.

74. Brett, *A Report on the Bihar Earthquake*, 3, 18. 'The destruction of communications was one of the principal obstacles the local Government had to meet in their relief operations' (Wilcock, *Bihar and Orissa in 1933–34*, 14).

75. 'Information regarding the present state of telegraph and postal communication in the region principally affected by the earthquake', Dept of Industries and Labour, no. 423/34, 25 January 1934, NAI HP 34/1/1934.

76. 'Telegraph Office Queues; Anxious Relatives; Flood of Messages in Calcutta', *The Statesman*, 18 January 1934. 'Telegrams Stopped; Only Express Messages to Muzaffarpur', *The Statesman*, 18 January 1934. Another newspaper cites 17 January, 'North Behar' (editorial), *ABP*, 18 January 1934.

77. Public announcement by the Postmaster-General, Patna: 'Booking Traffic for N. Bihar Suspended'; 'Information regarding the Present State of Telegraph and Postal Communication in the Region Principally Affected by the Earthquake', Dept of Industries and Labour, no. 423/34, 25 January 1934, NAI HP 34/1/1934.

78. V. E. Groom, Flight Lieutenant, Royal Air Force, to Headquarters, Royal Air Force (New Delhi), Patna, 28 January 1934, NAI HP 34/1/1934.

79. *Illustrated Weekly* in Bombay commissioned an aeroplane with a pilot who was also a photographer (N. Vincent, manager of Tata Sons Aviation Dept) to fly back and forth to Bihar from Bombay. M. H. B. 'On the Trail of the Earthquake', *Illustrated Weekly of India*, 28 January 1934.

80. V. E. Groom, Flight Lieutenant, Royal Air Force, to The Headquarters, Royal Air Force, New Delhi, dated Patna, 28 January 1934, NAI HP 34/1/1934.

81. Dunn et al., 'The Bihar–Nepal Earthquake of 1934', 17–19, 38–39.

82. 'Note on the Bihar Earthquake by Sir James Sifton', 2, enclosed in telegram from Viceroy to Sec. of State, New Delhi, 21 January 1934, File: 'Short Notice Question in the Legislative Assembly Regarding the Recent Terrible Earthquake in North Bihar', NAI HP 1/3/1934.

83. Telegram R. No. 258 (Immediate), Viceroy to Sec. of State for India (London), New Delhi, 4 February 1934, NAI HP 34/1/1934.

84. 'Scenes of Stark Desolation', *The Statesman*, 17 January 1934.

85. Jawaharlal Nehru, *An Autobiography: With Musings on Recent Events in India* (London: The Bodley Head, 1949 [1936]), 487.

86. Rahul Sankrityayan wrote under the pseudonym Rahul Vangmaya. Rahul Vangmaya, *Jīvan Yātrā*, Pt I, 4 Vols (New Delhi: Radhakrishna Prakashan Private Limited, 1994), 5.

87. District Boards in the province were responsible for maintaining roads, bridges, dispensaries, schools, ferries and *ghats*, public health provisions such as vaccinations and the maintenance of a number of wells. The work was financed by taxes and road cess. Roy, *Monghyr*, 339, 341–42. 'Communiqué', *ABP*, 23 January 1934. The railway to Muzaffarpur was restored by 27 January 1934. Brett, *A Report on the Bihar Earthquake*, 21.

88. 'Extracts from a Report by Sir J. Williamson', in Dunn et al., 'The Bihar–Nepal Earthquake of 1934', 14, 192–96. Photos documenting damages to the railways are found in Satow Collection: 'B. & N.W. Railway. Views of the Great Behar Earthquake of 15th January 1934', Mss Eur F290, Photo 1082/6. Collection by Jonathon Satow; East India Railway, *Report on the Earthquake on 15th January 1934* (Calcutta, 1934), 36; D. W. Ravenhill and G. Wilson, 'The Reconstruction of the Inchcape Bridge, Bengal and North Western Railway', *Journal of the ICE 7*, no. 1 (1 November 1937): 49–56. Dunn et al., 'The Bihar–Nepal Earthquake of 1934', 193.

89. Dunn et al., 'The Bihar–Nepal Earthquake of 1934', 192.

90. Brett, *A Report on the Bihar Earthquake*, 3, 18.

91. Brett, *A Report on the Bihar Earthquake*, 11–14, 19–20, 75. Tallents, 'No. 2628-P. R.', 17 August 1934, NAI HP 34/1/1934. The Hazaribagh armed police was sent to Bettiah, the large estate in Champaran close to Motihari. 'Communiqué', *ABP*, 23 January 1934.

92. BCRC, *Devastated Bihar*, 22.

93. Brett, *A Report on the Bihar Earthquake*, 8, 11–12, 16. Medical staff mentioned in 'Communiqué', *ABP*, 20 January 1934.

94. 'Jamalpore', *ABP*, 20 January 1934. Brett, *A Report on the Bihar Earthquake*, 8.

95. Brett, *A Report on the Bihar Earthquake*, 11–13. The fire was in the Halwaipatty Mohalla part of the bazaar and, according to *ABP*, had not yet been brought under control five days after the earthquake. 'Deadbodies [*sic*] Decomposing; Incalculable Loss of Lives and Property', *ABP*, 21 January 1934.

96. Tallents, 'No. 2628-P. R.', 17 August 1934, NAI HP 34/1/1934.

97. Brett, *A Report on the Bihar Earthquake*, 13, 19.

98. Although Reynolds confused the Bihar earthquake with the 1935 Quetta earthquake, where the government used more overt force and the military, the source he cites refers to the aftermath in Bihar and was published 17 February 1934. According to a passage quoted from a newspaper, a Second Lieutenant in the 'East Yorks Regiment' in Muzaffarpur had stopped 'every native' on the road and forced him to work with clearing debris for '10 minutes': if he refused 'a bayonet is stuck into him'. Reginald Reynolds, *The White Sahibs in India* (London: M. Secker and Warburg, 1937), 339.

99. Correspondence from W. B. Brett to Mainwaring, 20 February 1934; J. T. Whitty to W. B. Brett, 19 February 1934, File: 'Publicity in the matter of relief given by Govt to the sufferers (clearing debris by Santals in the district of Monghyr)', BSA RE 2/1934.

100. The document of eight pages (carbon copies) is likely to have been written by a person in charge of the local BCRC branch office in early February 1934. It describes the local BCRC's work, cooperation with other relief parties and rates paid for goods and materials. Last date mentioned is 22 January 1934. 'Monghyr', Anonymous, s.l., s.d., s.a., in BCUL PC 1028.

101. BCRC, *Devastated Bihar*, 20.

102. Tallents, 'No. 2628-P. R.', 17 August 1934, NAI HP 34/1/1934. Brett, *A Report on the Bihar Earthquake*, 13, 19–20. 'Quick! Quick!! Quick!!!' (editorial), *ABP*, 23 January 1934. Sinha, *The Bihar Earthquake and the Darbhanga Raj*, 19.

103. 'Request Sent to Allahabad, Rawalpindi, Lahore and Fort William, Calcutta, for Help', N.N. (Private and Personal, General Staff) to M. G. Hallett, Sec. Home Dept, GOI, 'Copy of telegram dated 19 January 1934 from the M. G. O. in India to Ordnance, Allahabad, Fort William, Calcutta, etc. and Chief Sec., Patna', New Delhi, 19 January 1934, NAI HP 34/1/1934.

104. *Bande Mataram*, branded an 'extremist' newspaper, displayed 'extremism though mostly softened' in political matters in 1934. Its circulation was relatively modest (2,000) in 1934. Government of Bengal, *Annual Report on Indian Papers Printed or Published in the Bengal Presidency: For the Year 1934*, 1, 5, 10.

105. Extract from article number 28 'The Earthquake and the Duty of the Army', *Bande Mataram* (Calcutta), 22 January 1934. Government of Bengal, *Report on Newspapers and Periodicals in Bengal 1934* (Superintendent, Government printing, Bengal Government Press: Alipore, Bengal, 1935).

106. Two articles comparing the government's response with that of the Japanese government were published in *ABP*: 'What Japan Did', 21 January, and 'Quick! Quick!! Quick!!!' (editorial), 23 January 1934.

107. J. Charles Schenking, '1923 Tokyo as a Devastated War and Occupation Zone: The Catastrophe One Confronted in Post-Earthquake Japan', *Japanese Studies* 29, no. 1 (May 2009): 111–29, 115–19.

108. Three rupees per day as the rate for hiring coolies was also quoted in another article by the correspondent at Patna, 'Stark Desolation: Numberless Deadbodies [*sic*] Still under Debris; Difficulties in Rescue Work; What People Immediately Need Is Food and Shelter', *ABP*, 21 January 1934.

109. This estimate is based on nominal agricultural wages in Champaran, which according to Pouchepadass was 4 annas and 6 pice in 1924, after which it 'decreased somewhat during the 1930s' as an effect of the Great Depression, and stood at

4 annas in 1935–39 (1 rupee equals to 16 annas and 64 pice). Pouchepadass, *Land, Power and Market*, 494. As a further indication of the real value of the salary, the purchasing power of the rupee according to the yearly local government report stated the price of rice as 15.04 seers in the rupee in February 1934, that is, about 14 kilos. Samuel Solomon, *Bihar and Orissa in 1934–35* (Patna: Superintendent, Government Printing, 1937), 18. These figures should, however, only be seen as rough indicators of earnings and food costs since cheaper grains of less nutritional value were available locally. Tirthankar Roy, *Rethinking Economic Change in India: Labour and Livelihood* (London and New York: Routledge, 2005), 87.

110. 'Stark Desolation; Numberless Deadbodies [*sic*] Still Under Debris', *ABP*, 21 January 1934. 'More about the Earthquake' (editorial), *ABP*, 23 January 1934.

111. Rajendra Prasad quoted in 'Appeal', *ABP*, 23 January 1934.

112. 'Wanted More Sappers and Miners', *ABP*, 2 February 1934.

113. The Marwari Relief Society, *Report of the Behar Earthquake Relief Work* (Calcutta: March 1935), 18.

114. For instance, in Monghyr, a man recounted how family members struggled to dig out the living and dead for at least four to five days after the earthquake. Ramchandra Varma (ed.), *Bhūkamp pīḍitoṃ kī karuna-kahāniyāṃ: Bihār ke bhūkamp-pīḍitoṃ kī param āścarya-janak aur karunāpūrṇ saccī ātma-kathāem* [Stories of the Victims of the Earthquake: Bihar's Earthquake Victims' Most Astonishing and Pitiful True Narrations], Compiler, Radhanath Mishra (Kashi [Varanasi], Rajmandir: Chunnilal Malviya, May 1934], 74–5.

115. Varma (ed.), *Bhūkamp pīḍitoṃ kī karuna-kahāniyāṃ*, 2, and cover page.

116. In Mohanlal Saksena, *Devastated Bihar through Jawaharlal's Lenses/Bihār-bhūkamp Javāhar lāl ke citroṃ dvārā* (Lucknow: Mohanlal Saksena; Allahabad: Mahendra Nath Pandey, Allahabad Law Journal Press, 1934), 32–34. Nehru first visited Patna and Muzaffarpur on 21 and 22 January 1934, respectively, after which he travelled to Allahabad where he issued press statements and appealed for funds for the Allahabad Earthquake Relief Committee. He again toured the earthquake area from the Nepal border to Monghyr in order to document the relief activities of the Allahabad Earthquake Relief Committee from 3 to 11 February 1934. Nehru was arrested at Allahabad on 12 February 1934 for 'seditious speeches' made in Calcutta on 17 and 18 January 1934. Anonymous, 'Trial and Imprisonment of Pandit Jawaharlal Nehru', *The Modern Review (A Monthly Review and Miscellany)* Ramananda Chatterjee (ed.) 55, no. 3, whole no. 327, March 1934: 351–53, Calcutta. Nehru, *An Autobiography*, 487–92.

117. B. R. Tomlinson, *The Indian National Congress and the Raj, 1929–1942: The Penultimate Phase* (London; Basingstoke: The MacMillan Press, 1976), 39, 94.

118. Nehru, *An Autobiography*, 484–85, quote in 488.

119. Sinha, *The Bihar Earthquake and the Darbhanga Raj*, 4. 'Sreenagar Ruined by Earthquake; Kumar Leaving Calcutta in Hurry', *ABP*, 19 January 1934. Kumar Ganganand Singha (alt. spelling of Sinha) was president of Bihar Provincial Hindu Sabha. Henningham, *A Great Estate and Its Landlords in Colonial India*, 132.

120. Sinha, *The Bihar Earthquake and the Darbhanga Raj*, 2, 4, 19.

121. Brett, *A Report on the Bihar Earthquake*, 14.

122. Copy of telegram, Govt of B&O, Political Dept, to India Office, London and to Sec. to the GOI, Home Dept, 22 January 1934, NAI HP 34/1/1934.

123. Brett, *A Report on the Bihar Earthquake*, 16, 18, 20–21. 'Nine extra medical men' mentioned in 'Communiqué', *ABP*, 20 January 1934. According to another account, the government had sent nine additional doctors 'at once' from Patna to Monghyr, three of them soon went to Darbhanga and three doctors with six senior medical students were sent to Muzaffarpur. J. W. Houlton, Patna, 26 January 1934, in 'Indian People's Famine Trust Fund', NAI F&P Foreign 302-P/1934.

124. Brett, *A Report on the Bihar Earthquake*, 12, 15. 'Patna Advocate; Succumbs to Quake-Injuries', *Behar Herald*, 20 January 1934.

125. According to the General Manager of the Sursand Raj, C. H. Gordon, who arrived in Sitamarhi on the afternoon 16 January, he counted 200 'dead and dying' dug out from the debris, and final non-official estimates for Sitamarhi sub-division amounted to 1,000 deaths. Gordon's account of the earthquake from 'Chapter XII: Some Reports by Eye-Witnesses', Dunn et al., 'The Bihar–Nepal Earthquake of 1934', 185–87, quote from 186. Speaker Chandreshvar Prashad Narayan Sinha, Muzaffarpur, 14 February 1934, *BOLCP* 30, no. 1, 107. BCRC, *Devastated Bihar*, 12. The hospital and some other government buildings later had to be re-erected half a mile away because of damages and fissures in the ground. J. A. Dunn, 'Advisory Observations on Reconstruction', ch. X (161–81) in Dunn et al., 'The Bihar–Nepal Earthquake of 1934', 164.

126. Sinha, *The Bihar Earthquake and the Darbhanga Raj*, 10–12.

127. 'At Darbhanga', *ABP*, 20 January 1934.

128. 'Patients under Debris; Two Hospitals Collapse in Darbhanga: Id Bazar Tragedy', *ABP*, 20 January 1934.

129. Brett, *A Report on the Bihar Earthquake*, 14, 21.

130. 'Cable' (Telegram), Govt of B&O to Sec. of State, London, and Home Dept (New Delhi), Patna, midnight 17 January 1934, BSA RE 500/1934.

131. Brett, *A Report on the Bihar Earthquake*, 15.

132. D.O. J-297, 'Notes of reconnaissance by aeroplane', Scott to Tallents, Muzaffarpur, 21–22 January 1934, BSA RE 23/1934.

133. 'Fortnightly Report for the Second-Half of January 1934' (Confidential), Public and Judicial (P&J) (S) Department, B&O Local Government's Reports, Patna 1934, IOR/L/P.J/12/743.

134. Tallents, 'No. 2628-P. R.', 17 August 1934, NAI HP 34/1/1934.

135. 'Fortnightly Report for the Second-Half of February 1934' (Confidential), P&J (S) Dept, B&O Local Government's Reports, Patna, 1934, IOR/L/P.J/12/743.

136. 'Progress Report for the Week Ending 1 March 1934', District officer S. L. Marwood to J. E. Scott, Commissioner of Tirhut, Motihari, 2 March 1934, BSA RE 13/1934.

137. File: 'Vaccination in Darbhanga Epidemic Caused by Earthquake', BSA LSG Dept, Sanitation branch S/IV/7/1934.

138. Indian Red Cross Society, *Annual Report 1934* (Delhi: Government Printing at the Delhi Printing Works, 1934), 20–21, 73. 'Lady Sifton's Lead; Help from Bihar Red Cross Committee', *ABP*, 23 January 1934; Indian Red Cross Society, *Annual Report 1934*, 21; Brett, *A Report on the Bihar Earthquake*, Appendix II: List of Officers; Tallents, 'No. 2628-P. R.', 17 August 1934, NAI HP 34/1/1934.

139. Indian Red Cross Society, *Annual Report 1934*, 21. Rupees 4,500 was distributed to the District Boards in Muzaffarpur, Darbhanga, Monghyr and Champaran. Indian Red Cross Society, *Annual Report 1934*, 21, 73. Also mentioned in 'Lady Sifton's Lead; Help from Bihar Red Cross Committee', *ABP*, 23 January 1934.

140. Indian Red Cross Society, *Proceedings of the Annual General Meeting 1935* (New Delhi. Delhi: Thakur Das and Sons, Government Printing at the Delhi Printing Works, 1935), 9. Indian Red Cross Society, *Proceedings of Annual General Meeting 1936* (Delhi: Thakur Das and Sons, Government Printing at the Delhi Printing Works, 1936), 1.

141. The headquarters in Delhi could not provide exact figures in the yearly report since collections had been sent directly. Indian Red Cross Society, *Annual Report 1934*, 20–21, 73–74.

142. 'I. M. A. Undertake Relief Fund', *Behar Herald*, 24 January 1934.

143. 'Earthquake Havoc: Appeal for *Medical* Relief', *ABP*, 20 January 1934.

144. Dr H. Ghosh, Honorary Sec., IMA, Bengal Branch, 67, Dharamatala Street, Calcutta. *ABP*, 23 January 1934.

145. For example, Ayurveda Pharmacy (Dacca), Bengal Immunity Ltd, Great Asiatic Medicine and Stores. *ABP*, 20 January 1934.

146. The Secretary of the IMA, Dr K. S. Ray, appealed for such units to work under the district administration, in *ABP*, 20 January 1934.

147. The appeal to the public mention the names of two persons authorised to collect donations at Naraingunj and Dacca: Sj. Rajendra Kumar Das and Sj. Phanibhusan Sarkar. 'Appeal', *ABP*, 23 January 1934.

148. 'Communiqué', *ABP*, 23 January 1934.

149. Indian Red Cross Society, *Proceedings of the Annual General Meeting 1934*, 1. 'Medical Relief Work in Bihar', in Moore (ed.), *Record of the Great Indian Earthquake*, 44.

150. Brett, *A Report on the Bihar Earthquake*, 12. J. W. Houlton, Patna, 26 January 1934, in 'Indian People's Famine Trust Fund', NAI F&P Foreign 302-P/1934. Indian Red Cross Society, *Proceedings of the Annual General Meeting 1934*, 1. Indian Red Cross Society, *Annual Report 1934*, 20. A total of 61 men had worked in the unit between 22 January and 19 February 1934. 'Medical Relief Work in Bihar', in Moore (ed.), *Record of the Great Indian Earthquake*, 44.

151. Indian Red Cross Society, *Annual Report 1934*, 73.

152. P. C. Tallents, Chief Sec. to the Govt of Bihar and Orissa, to J. M. Clay, Chief Sec. to the Govt of the United Provinces (U.P.), and C. C. Garbett, Chief Sec. to the Govt of the Punjab, Patna/Ranchi, 22 March 1934, File 'Articles for Relief Purposes Sent from Other Provinces to the Red Cross Depot at Patna', BSA RE 485/1934.

153. Indian Red Cross Society, *Annual Report 1934*, 21, 73–74. The depot and distribution centre distributed over 40,000 blankets, 546 tents and 4,840 bags of *atta* (whole wheat flour) and other articles received in response to the society's and the government's appeals. Brett, *A Report on the Bihar Earthquake*, 20–21. Appeal for 'blankets, bed sheets, tinned milk, Horlick's malted milk, barley, sago, petdomax [*sic*] lamps, primus stoves, waterproof sheets, tea, sugar, brandy and towels'. 'Communiqué', *ABP*, 23 January 1934.

154. Indian Red Cross Society, *Annual Report 1934*, 20–21.

155. W. G. Lacey, Sec., LSG, to Finance Sec., 22 January 1934, File: 'Railway Concessions on Occasion of Earthquake', BSA RE 33 I/1934.

156. Note by H. C. Prior, Finance Sec., Govt B&O, 22 January 1934, BSA RE 33/1934.

157. Note by J. W. Sinha, 23 January 1934, BSA RE 33 I/1934.

158. D. O. 2919–20 P, 22 March 1934; D. O. 267 P. R., N. N. to H. Bomford, Chief Sec. to the Govt of the U.P., Ranchi, 25 April 1934, BSA RE 485/1934.

159. Notice by Dr H. Ghosh, Honorary Sec., IMA, Bengal Branch, 67, Dharamatala Street, Calcutta. *ABP*, 23 January 1934.

160. 'I. M. A. Undertake Relief Fund', *Behar Herald*, 24 January 1934.

161. Enclosure no. 2, *Hindustan Times*, 25 January 1934. Sir Harry Haig's statement in the Assembly on the recent earthquake disaster in reply to G. P. Singh's question

on 24 January 1934. In letter from M. G. Hallett to GOI, Home Dept (New Delhi), 25 January 1934, NAI HP 34/1/1934.

162. 'Communiqué', *ABP*, 23 January 1934.

163. 'Motihari Situation: Medical Relief Units Start', *ABP*, 28 January 1934.

164. BCRC, *Report for the Period Ending 30th June 1934*, 8.

165. Brett, *A Report on the Bihar Earthquake*, 7.

166. Twenty thousand dead according to the BCRC, *Devastated Bihar*, 2.

167. Ghosh proposes a rough figure of 25,000 deaths. Ghosh, *The Civil Disobedience Movement*, 245. Mukherjee, 'Afterword', 190–91. According to a short note on 'Destructive Earthquakes in 1935', the science magazine *Nature* claims the number of 2,000 deaths is 'too low' (quoting M. Bois, *Nature*, 136, 472, 21 September 1935), while an unnamed 'official report' claimed the number to be 'more than 10,000'. 'Destructive Earthquakes in 1935', *Nature* 136 (1935), 639.

168. Sapkota, Bollinger and Perrier, 'Fatality Rates of the Mw ~8.2, 1934, Bihar–Nepal Earthquake', 1–2.

169. The highest death toll was found in Muzaffarpur town (956), Muzaffarpur district (1,583), Darbhanga district (1,839) and Monghyr town (1,260). Brett, *A Report on the Bihar Earthquake*, 8.

170. Stark differences in numbers were also recorded in Darbhanga town and Laheriasarai and Darbhanga district where the BCRC recorded altogether 4,000 deaths and Brett only 1,839 for the whole district. BCRC, *Devastated Bihar*, 12, 16, 18, 20. Brett, *A Report on the Bihar Earthquake*, 8.

171. Brett, *A Report on the Bihar Earthquake*, 7.

172. More than 10,000 people were killed in India and Nepal according to L. L. Fermor, 'General Report of the Geological Survey of India for the year 1934', 1–108, in *Records of the Geological Survey of India*, vol. 69 (Calcutta: Geological Survey of India, 1936), 24–25. According to the final GSI report from 1939, 3,400 deaths resulted directly from the earthquake in the Nepal valley, while people who had died in rock falls indirectly caused by the earthquake in other parts of the country were not included in the figures. Dunn et al., 'The Bihar–Nepal Earthquake of 1934', 3.

173. The present author was unable to locate files on medical relief in the BSA, which may contain valuable sources.

174. Saran district, 'over a thousand' injured; 48 injured in Jamalpur; 11 persons had died in the bazaar and 200 were injured in the small town of Khagaria, close to Monghyr; Patna, 'a few hundred injured'. BCRC, *Devastated Bihar*, 19, 21, 23.

175. Indian Red Cross Society, *Proceedings of the Annual General Meeting 1934*, 1. Indian Red Cross Society, *Annual Report 1934*, 20.

176. 'More Serious than Believed: Earthquake Havoc in Bihar: Official Figure', *The Leader*, Allahabad, 20 January 1934.

177. 'The Death-Roll', *ABP*, 20 January 1934. The same type of critique surfaced in the weeks following the earthquake, see 'Monghyr Situation. Slow Progress of Clearing Debris: Epidemic Apprehended', *ABP*, 2 February 1934.

178. 'Official Figures: 2,500 Deaths in Behar Province', *ABP*, 19 January 1934.

179. 'Communiqué', *ABP*, 23 January 1934.

180. Indian Red Cross Society, *Annual Report 1934*, 19.

181. 'Mounting Death-Roll', *The Statesman*, 31 January 1934.

182. 'Fortnightly Report for the Second-Half of January 1934' (Confidential), P&J (S) Department, Bihar and Orissa Local Government's Reports, Patna, 1934, IOR/L/ P.J/12/743.

183. 'Note on the Bihar Earthquake by Sir James Sifton', 2 pp., enclosed in Telegram from Viceroy to Sec. of State, New Delhi, 21 January 1934, NAI HP 1/3/1934.

184. '3,100 Deaths; Muzaffarpur Practically in Ruins', *ABP*, 20 January 1934. Another similar eyewitness account claimed the loss of life to have exceeded 50,000. 'The Earthquake', *Behar Herald*, 20 January 1934.

185. 'Bihar Leader's Estimate: 20,000 Dead in Earthquake', *The Englishman*, 5 February 1934. The statement was mentioned in the British press. 'New India Tremor: 20,000 Dead in Former Quake', *Daily Telegraph*, 12 February 1934.

186. Saksena, *Devastated Bihar through Jawaharlal's Lenses*, 32–33.

187. The 'Europeans' mentioned were Mr Fairweather and the European crew that took part in the air survey of Tirhut by Captain Barnard's Circus. 'The Government's Responsibility', *ABP*, 19 January 1934.

188. 'Non-official estimates' taken from BCRC, *Devastated Bihar*, 20.

189. An additional 237 deaths were recorded in Monghyr district. Brett, *A Report on the Bihar Earthquake*, 8.

190. A 'special correspondent' for *The Leader* suggested a similar figure according to an unnamed relief party at work. '1,700 dead at Monghyr?' *The Leader*, 23 January 1934. Such an account was given by 'a Pundit Bindanand Jha' who claimed to have counted the bodies extracted from the ruins. Another anonymous report provided the number of 2,315 excavated bodies. 'Monghyr', report by BCRC's Monghyr branch until end of June [July–August] 1934, BCUL PC 1028.

191. 'Communiqué', *ABP*, 23 January 1934.

192. Brett, *A Report on the Bihar Earthquake*, 11–12, 72.

193. Officially there were 700 holdings in Madhupura and Chowk bazaars together. Brett, *A Report on the Bihar Earthquake*, 8. The municipality counted that in 500 holdings in the Chowk bazaar, two families lived in half of them, thereby

counting 750 families. See section titled 'Improving Slums': Planning Bazaars' in Chapter 6.

194. 'At Monghyr', *ABP*, 23 January 1934.

195. The last census recorded a population of 52,863 (Table IV). Lacey, *Census of India, 1931*, vol. VII, part II.

196. Saksena, *Devastated Bihar through Jawaharlal's Lenses*, 23–24. BCRC, *Devastated Bihar*, 20.

197. Brett, *A Report on the Bihar Earthquake*, 8, 12, 14.

198. 'Behar's Hour of Need; Organise Relief; Babu Rajendra's Appeal', *ABP*, 19 January 1934. '1,100 Corpses Disposed of by Police', *The Leader*, 21 January 1934.

199. Roy, 'State, Society and Market', 278–79.

200. 'No European and no Indian of note killed or wounded', Telegram, Govt of U.P., Lucknow, to Home Dept, New Delhi, 24 January 1934, NAI HP 34/1/1934. 'No European or Anglo-Indian has been killed', and lists of details with deaths of Indian officials and their relatives were mentioned. In Motihari, 'no European or Indian official has been injured'. 'Deadbodies [*sic*] Decomposing; Incalculable Loss of Lives and Property', *ABP*, 21 January 1934.

201. 'Scenes of Stark Desolation', *The Statesman*, 17 January 1934.

202. 'Hundreds Perish in Earthquake ...', *The Statesman*, 17 January 1934.

203. 'Cable' (Telegram), Govt of B&O to Sec. of State, London, and Home Dept (New Delhi), Patna, midnight 17 January 1934, BSA RE 500/1934. 'European Woman Killed in Saving Dog', *The Statesman*, 19 January 1934. 'Destruction in Bihar: Fourth Press Communiqué', *The Leader*, 21 January 1934.

204. BCRC, *Devastated Bihar*, 20.

205. Brett, *A Report on the Bihar Earthquake*, 8.

206. Elaine Enarson, Alice Fothergill and Lori Peek, 'Gender and Disaster: Foundations and Directions', in *Handbook of Disaster Research*, ed. H. Rodriguez, E. L. Quarantelli and R. R. Dynes, 130–46 (New York: Springer, 2006), 132–33.

207. Dunn et al., 'The Bihar–Nepal Earthquake of 1934', 3.

208. BCRC, *Devastated Bihar*, 20. According to the calendar, Eid was on the 17 January, not 16 January, in 1934.

209. BCRC, *Report for the Period Ending 30th June 1934*, 50.

210. Rai Bahadur Harendra Nath Banarji, Jamalpur, 14 February 1934, *BOLCP* 30, no. 1, 167–68.

211. Bayly, *Empire and Information*, 174.

212. Brett, *A Report on the Bihar Earthquake*.

213. Beck, *Risk Society: Towards a New Modernity*, 26–27.

3

From Local to National Politics of Relief

Natural disasters occur in a political space.[1]

Introduction: The Use and Abuse of Aid

According to the official narrative of the aftermath, as discussed in the previous chapter, the government's ability to act swiftly was partly hampered by destroyed infrastructure and administrative chaos. Under these circumstances, the colonial government focused on security rather than mobilising personnel for rescue operations. As a result, the government's organisational goals, preparedness and leadership in terms of organising disaster relief appeared limited and inadequate. It is in this space of weakened governance that Rajendra Prasad, with support from other leading INC members, began organising relief operations, resulting in the formation of the BCRC, a committee formed with the purpose of collecting funds and organising relief.

Disasters as exogenous shocks to which a political system must respond become political in their aftermath. The politicisation of the event tends to increase, rather than decrease, as the affected society moves from emergency response through recovery and reconstruction phases.[2] As a part of the politicisation of the relief process, new organisational patterns often form to deal with the sudden disruption of a disaster.[3] The BCRC was formed in response to the need for relief and built upon established networks of local politicians and relief organisations. This chapter addresses how political space and relief after natural disasters can be used for meeting political ends, arguing that for the INC, the BCRC served as a tool for nation-building and a practice in state formation where the Congress proved its ability to take on governance—even under extreme circumstances. The criticism of the colonial government was not directed at its incompetence and failure in disaster management, but at the systemic failure of the colonial governance in the Indian state. The BCRC, as a 'non-political' relief committee, carried out relief in the name of the nation, largely achieved by coordinating the work of a number of local, regional and national relief associations. In order to collect funds, as well as to coordinate and provide relief, the BCRC invoked a language of the nation that served its purpose to efficiently unite local relief associations with the wider networks of socially and politically active groups sympathetic towards the INC.

Research on disasters as sites for nation-building finds politics at the core of relief programmes and aid as a political tool.[4] Carey A. Watt has demonstrated how relief and social service was one site for nation-building by civil society organisations and among them the INC. Relief programmes and social service organisations functioned as sites for nation-building activities and fostered nationalism among an increasingly nation-conscious civil society in early twentieth-century India. Social service organisations, among them many Congress-affiliated organisations, associations and committees such as the Gandhi Seva Sangh and the Servants of India Society engaged in nation-building activities of education, health and relief provisions through local societies and provincial associations.[5] Philanthropy, charity and relief work came to be practiced in the name of the nation. Focusing on the formation of the state rather than of the nation, William Kuracina argues that the INC by the 1920s was involved in a process of state formation by using what he refers to as parallelism in governance. Since Britain's dominance of the subcontinent obstructed Indians from establishing indigenous governmentality as a logical outcome of politicisation, the INC 'artificially constructed parallel institutions and practices of governance'.[6] Although not an official policy, this political development took off in 1934 and was marked by 'the construction of an extra-constitutional bureaucracy that ambiguously cooperated with, and opposed, the Raj'.[7] Interestingly, Kuracina gives the example of disaster relief as a mode of parallelism in governance inspired by 'oppositional discourse', where Congress operations complemented and mimicked the government's relief efforts, only to point out shortcomings and responsibilities of the state. The implications of oppositional rhetoric meant that the Congress was able to safeguard the people, while the government had failed, as illustrated in public allegations of the government's inadequate response to natural disasters.[8] Kokila Dang has further expanded on the ability of the INC to 'gain credibility' by way of both criticising the government's relief policies and by organising relief for the victims after the Quetta earthquake.[9] The methods to do so, described by Dang, are next to identical to the political modes described by Kuracina as parallelism and oppositional discourse in governance. Dang's analysis expands Kuracina's example of how disaster relief by the INC became incorporated into its larger political work. By the time the Quetta earthquake happened in 1935, the Bihar 1934 earthquake had already gained retrospective significance: the Congress used the 'success' in Bihar in its open criticism of the government's relief operation. Seen in the context of relief activities conducted by the INC, Bihar and Quetta became sites where authority was contested by the colonial state and by 'an emerging nationalism'.[10]

In the field of disaster research, how and why governance in the aftermath of a disaster is politicised for certain ends and to various degrees is debated.[11] When the disaster is seen as a 'tipping point', the event itself is an accumulation of unsustainable social practices and processes that can motivate reform of governance in the aftermath.[12] Accordingly, a disaster entails both political causes and consequences. But a reordering of society might not take place; politics in the aftermath does not necessarily reflect learning and the opportunity to 'focus' disaster policy in terms of prevention or responses.[13] The 1934 earthquake's sudden and physical devastation in towns, on the communication infrastructure and on human lives (see Chapter 2) was a massive disaster that opened up a space for political transformations. In order to understand how and why disaster relief changed governance, this chapter provides an analysis of the political and social context of the earthquake. Disaster relief reveals how political discourse can be put into practice.

The Congress occupied a space of fundamental importance in the organisational set-up of a parallel disaster administration by using networks and established infrastructural facilities. As this chapter argues, the BCRC was used by the Congress to criticise the colonial government's approach to governance and exemplify its own political philosophy through governance. At the same time, the BCRC represented an organisation larger than the Congress: it made a point out of uniting, cooperating with and coordinating relief associations and funds from across the subcontinent. The administrative apparatus for disaster relief developed by the BCRC was an appropriation of certain government functions. By establishing physical infrastructure, the Congress could practice political rhetoric in terms of rendering assistance to people depicted as 'poor' and neglected by the colonial government. The development described by Kuracina stresses the importance of state-building practices rather than nation-building exercises by the Congress at this point in history, an argument that this chapter supports in the case of relief efforts organised after the earthquake. However, the idea of a nation in the BCRC's and Congress leaders' rhetoric cannot be dismissed as it served the purpose to unite organisations, mobilise relief workers as well as encourage financial contributions towards the BCRC. As such, the committee was a practice in governance that called for national unity in relief.

The intense response by INC and multiple civil society associations and organisations in relief work was cautiously watched by the local government. In reports and correspondence, an apprehension of the Congress's involvement in the relief work manifested itself in three kinds of suspicions against the BCRC as an organisation. Throughout the chapter, the government's stance towards civil society's relief work will be discussed according to three themes. First, the government feared that the BCRC would gain 'political capital' on behalf of the Congress by outdoing the government in relief provisions through parallelism. Second, even if the BCRC vowed to keep political questions out of relief work, the government was apprehensive that Congressmen, from Bihar and outside the province, would not follow the relief committee's official line and make 'political capital' by starting a political campaign. Third, government officials and other organisations encountered and accused the BCRC of corruption and misuse of funds. According to the government, this was supposedly done either by using funds to finance political activities or by handing out grants and charitable relief as a method of overtly or covertly buying support for the Congress. Compounded, these uses of aid by the BCRC helped the Congress gain political capital.

To begin with, this chapter charts the developments leading up to the INC emerging as a viable relief organiser in Bihar in 1934 and to the formation of the BCRC. The larger part of the chapter discusses how the BCRC conceptualised its relief programme and organised itself as a coordinative relief committee. This process partly took shape in relation to the government's relief organisation and, not the least, the government's approach towards civil society's participation in disaster relief. Building upon previous research discussed earlier, about disaster relief and nation-building, this chapter stresses the importance of cooperating relief organisation in order to collect funds as well as carry out tasks. Though the Congress's organisational networks and workers constituted an integral part of the committee, the cooperating relief organisations provided local contacts and contributed with experiences gained from previous disaster operations. The chapter's central theme revolves around the politics of relief, arguing that the committee's control of fund collections, the display of a political philosophy in practice, its coordinative function and parallelism in governance became political tools that served to prove the ability of the INC to supersede the colonial government. In order to prove its authority and legitimacy in carrying out relief operations, it stressed the government's lack of initiative and organisational power in aiding the victims.

The Indian National Congress and Politicised Relief

Rajendra Prasad, later the first President of India, experienced the earthquake as a prisoner under guard in Patna Hospital where he was being treated for various health problems.[14] According to official sources conveyed to Prasad, the medical board had recommended his release prior to the earthquake but the notice was delayed in the administrative chaos caused due to the partial collapse of the Civil Secretariat in Patna, hence he was not released until 17 January 1934.[15] The newspapers speculated that the need for relief workers or a leader for the organisation of relief motivated his release.[16] It was perhaps not a far-fetched idea since political prisoners in Patna, serving a sentence less than a year and belonging to Tirhut, were released on 19 January 1934 'in view of the earthquake'.[17] Pandit Prajapati Misra, one of the Congress members released from Camp Jail in Patna, proceeded to Motihari where he took charge of the local relief committee.[18] The government denied any connection between the earthquake and Prasad's release; it was done upon the doctors' recommendation due to his seriously deteriorating health.[19] That the earthquake relief work had no bearing on his release is also substantiated by confidential reports prior to the earthquake which stated that 'the release was ordered as the local Government were satisfied that Babu Rajendra Prashad [Prasad] will require medical treatment for some time to come', implying that in his medical condition he would anyhow circumscribe his movements.[20]

'The un-crowned king of Bihar', as the nationalist friendly newspaper *Amrita Bazar Patrika* ordained Prasad in an editorial praising his efforts in organising relief,[21] descended from a landed family in north Bihar and was well connected throughout the earthquake area. He had previously acted as a key figure in the organisation of relief work after floods.[22] His political work had begun with M. K. Gandhi and the Champaran movement in 1917–18[23] in the same area of the Tirhut division where the earthquake had caused severe damages. In 1917–18, the enquiries into the conditions of the impoverished peasantry under the oppressive indigo planters not only helped to establish Gandhi as a political force on the national scene but also to bind together a network of intellectual leaders in Patna and north Bihar.[24] Lawyers and politically active persons who gathered around Gandhi in 1917–18 now became engaged in relief work after the earthquake.[25] When Prasad met Gandhi for the first time in 1917 he was a young lawyer; in 1934 he had risen to become a leading Congressman and would act as a central figure in the BCRC.

Firmly rooted in Bihar and active in the INC at national and local levels, the reason for Prasad's imprisonment was, like for most political prisoners at that time, his participation in the Civil Disobedience movement. The first year of the decade, 1930–31 was marked by the successful spread of the movement. Demonstrations, volunteers going to prison en masse, non-payment of the *chaukidari* tax and boycott of foreign cloth and liquor stores took place throughout the districts of the state.[26] However, the imprisonment of Congress leaders and the counter actions of the government in the form of attachment of property made many small landholders pay the *chaukidari* tax again, and the campaign was brought to an end in March 1931. In January 1932, following M. K. Gandhi's Round Table Conference in London, the Civil Disobedience campaign was taken up again. This time it lasted effectively for only three months and 6,000 Biharis and all of the 'prominent' Congress leaders were in jail by March 1932.[27] The Civil Disobedience movement wore off in mid-1933 and finally by April 1934 it was called off, but Bihar, being a stronghold for Congress action, was continuously monitored by the government for any possible flare-up of sympathy.[28] The earthquake preceded the elections to the central legislative assembly that were to be held in the autumn of 1934. It was the first elections in which the Congress once more participated after three years of agitational campaigns and where the Congress candidates were very successful and emerged as spokesmen for a national economic policy.[29]

The lay of the political landscape and the role of the Congress in the wake of the earthquake are captured in the notes of William George Archer (1907–79), a young sub-divisional officer stationed in Madhubani during the time of the earthquake.[30] Having taken into consideration the physical damages and psychological effects of the earthquake experience, he perceived its political ramification for the Congress to be of greater importance 'historically':

From being dormant, if not as good as dead, Congress has suddenly come to life. Congressmen who were in prison have been released and under the leadership of B. [Babu] Rajendra Prasad, have formed the [Bihar] Central Relief Committee. This dominates every newspaper, except the 'Statesman.' (...) Its [BCRC's] cooperation with Government has been offered and accepted. Thus, from being lost in prison, Congress is again in the position of telling Government what to do, (for this is the meaning of cooperation) and Government is in the position of having to listen. (for cooperation cannot be rejected) Consequently, while the [Bihar] Central Relief Committee sits prudently on its funds, waiting for Government to exhaust its finances, the *Searchlight* prints tales of the earthquake area, Government money mis-used [*sic*], suffering unrelieved, no adequate steps taken. In eighteen months time, the Council elections will be ripe, Government re-construction will be finished, and with a Relief Fund still of ample size, Congress will distribute relief. With the whole press more or less Congress, no counter-propaganda is possible. Congress will receive all the credit and Government all the criticism. Whatever else the earthquake has done, it has jerked Congress into future power.[31]

In his autobiography, Prasad describes how the organisation of relief work started from his hospital bed.[32] First, he appealed to 'non-official agencies' and 'all Congressmen and women' to join the relief work on 18 January,[33] and two days later he founded the committee of four people, followed by more appeals.[34] Prasad notified the local government that he had started a 'non-official organisation ... formed under the name of the Bihar Central Relief Committee',[35] promising to 'assist and cooperate with other organisations, official or non-official, working for relief'.[36] Prasad made it plain that in this regard, 'in humanitarian work of relief', he, in his role as the committee's president, intended to cooperate with any other organisation engaged in relief.[37] The Chief Secretary to the Government of Bihar and Orissa welcomed the initiative and forwarded a copy of Prasad's letter to the Commissioners of the affected districts, assuring his approval, 'provided it [BCRC] works in consultation and cooperation'.[38]

The BCRC was, however, not the first attempt by the INC to organise relief for people in distress. The Congress had extensive experience in setting up relief funds in various regions of the subcontinent; however, nation-wide appeals for relief in instances of natural disasters did not appear until the 1934 Bihar earthquake and after the 1935 Quetta earthquake.[39] The Congress' relief collections covered a wide range of activities in the 1920s to the 1940s. At the beginning of the 1920s, the Congress founded several local committees and expanded its relief activities to also include relief and financial compensation to political sufferers.[40] The Tilak Swaraj Fund was most prominent and served several purposes for the Congress, spanning from compensation to 'victims of natural disasters, support to families of political prisoners, to propaganda, organization, khaddar production', and funding education. The vast amounts collected by this fund also served as an eye-opener for the government which, by 1922, put forward a proposal for an audit of all public funds raised by way of subscriptions for charitable, religious, political and educational purposes.[41] The result of Congress's larger organisational scope and growing significance enabled it to include all forms of activities under the term 'relief', from overtly political objectives of the Congress to seemingly non-political support in disaster relief.[42]

It was perhaps no wonder then that the government's stance towards potential Congress involvement in relief was cautious. Preceding the earthquake, in the aftermath of a severe flood in Orissa in September 1933, the government suspected that the situation would be used for 'Congress propaganda' and it instructed the local administration 'to anticipate Congress action in connection with movements in themselves unobjectionable, e.g. relief in calamities, legitimate grievances, assistance to depressed classes, etc., by direct action taken by Government'.[43] In accordance with directives, the government supervised the administration of funds collected by 'Congress agents' through regular Flood Committees in order 'to prevent the establishment of a definite Congress organisation'.[44] More than a year after the Bihar earthquake, in the aftermath of the Quetta earthquake on 31 May 1935, the imposition of martial law closed the city for outsiders and only a selected number of relief organisations could enter. The government twice declined Prasad's request on behalf of the Congress to send relief teams. The Bombay Provincial Congress Committee prompted Prasad to start the All India Non-official Relief Committee for relief of the victims, and the majority of its funds came from provincial Congress collections.[45] If the committee was allowed to enter Quetta, Prasad promised 'not to take to any kind of political propaganda',[46] a promise he did not need to honour since he remained confined to helping refugees evacuated in nearby states.[47] The government was explicitly against the involvement of Congress in relief work and 'deliberately refrained from suggesting that they should collect funds as it would mean encouraging another Congress Earthquake Fund'.[48] The government's attitude towards Congress' involvement in relief was defensive at best and was directed at preventing the formation of a fund of BCRC's proportions.

As the president of the BCRC, Prasad cooperated with the local government in relief work, a decision many Congressmen supported according to his autobiography.[49] Despite Prasad's claim of having the support of other Congress members, police intelligence reported loud disagreements in the Congress regarding cooperation that foremost rested on the will of M. K. Gandhi, Prasad and 'other elderly people'.[50] Nehru, who until his arrest on 12 February 1934 was an important person with regard to appeals for funds and someone who had been accredited with giving the first donation towards the BCRC,[51] disagreed with Prasad and others willing to cooperate with the government.[52] His arrest was based on political content in three speeches, but several 'extremist papers' in Bombay claimed the government's disapproval of his reluctant attitude towards cooperation in relief work as the actual reason.[53] His approval of any kind of cooperation with the colonial government appeared as unlikely in view of one of his articles published two days before his arrest, in which the earthquake and the relief response posed as an allegory of current political developments:

> We have stood up bravely to face the unthinking cruelty of nature and have tried to fight it and lessen its tragic effects. Nature is often pitiless and cruel. We feel helpless and bow to it, or we try to control it, according to our temperaments and the measure of strength and will within us. But there are other earthquakes which are not caused by unthinking nature but by thinking man. Human masses, when their lot becomes unbearable, rise up and smash the order that enslaves them. And there are political earthquakes when a government, fearful of its existence, loses all self-control, all sense of perspective, all dignity and begins to behave as a mob that has no clear purpose except that of destruction and the desire to revenge itself on its adversaries.[54]

Nehru's stance in the matter of relief work was to continue a firm political non-cooperation policy with the government and, contrary to Prasad, making no exception for cooperation in relief work. According to an intercepted telegram, he encouraged relief organisations to 'co-operate with everybody except government'.[55] His official attitude against cooperation with the government in disaster relief swayed as police and local administration mapped his whereabouts and conversations with the press and officials in the area. Subsequently, he ensured in an article in *The Searchlight* 'that the Congress organisation would co-operate provided it was allowed to work in its own way', yet he soon made 'an attack' on the local government published in a local newspaper.[56] Contrary to Prasad, he took a political stance in the relief work by calling for a suspension of taxes and rents based on the damages.[57]

Though the BCRC agreed to cooperate with the government, the fear of non-cooperation might have been fuelled by the released political prisoners in Patna. Even if a non-cooperation campaign was not on the agenda, former political prisoners from outside the province and Congress workers from Patna showed a symbolic display of the capacity of the Congress. These relief workers were described as '[a] much-needed army of workers for relief work' according to the nationalist *Amrita Bazar Patrika*.[58] M. K. Gandhi mentioned, in particular, the mobilisation of male Congressmen who had suspended their civil resistance.[59] Although, as Gandhi pointed out, the political programme of civil disobedience was cancelled in the context of the disaster relief work, to spend time and personal resources on volunteer work in Bihar was perceived as political mobilisation.

The BCRC carrying out 'manual labour' in the form of relief work was in 1935 recognised as 'valid manual labour' under the Congress Constitution.[60] The active participation in relief work under the leadership of the BCRC in 1934 qualified participants for political participation.

As the workforce of the BCRC's organisation was reinforced by Congress members from outside the province, the government was kept on its toes by the fear of the Congress trying to 'make capital' out of including the politically charged question of rent remission for the peasantry and revenue, or tax, remission for the *zamindars* into the relief programme. Any concession by the government in these questions would possibly appear as giving in to political demands of a no-rent campaign, a feature of political turbulences preceding the earthquake. The beginning of civil disobedience in 1930 coincided with an agrarian crisis in Bihar and the Great Depression of 1929.[61] It was difficult for tenants to pay their rents,[62] and unlike prior downturns such as the post-1918 inflation, this depression did not strike the poorest the hardest but enhanced the burdens of revenue, rent and interests for the 'middle' peasants with a surplus to sell. The economic situation for these classes resulted in a mobilisation, mainly led by the Congress and the Kisan Sabhas, so-called Peasant Committees, for reduction of revenue, irrigation charges, rent and debt burdens, and the abolition of *zamindari*.[63]

Hence after the earthquake, attempts by the politically active to argue or send petitions for remission of rents, *chaukidari* taxes and revenue were closely watched in the districts.[64] In the Tirhut division, the local government officers reported Congressmen who raised the issue of rent payments, intervened by intercepting telegrams and issued warnings to 'Congress leaders' that 'any attempt to make capital out of the calamity by exaggerations or false reports, or by inciting tenants to withhold rents and taxes will be promptly dealt with by Government'.[65] Police reports from the end of February 1934 recorded talks in the districts about how the BCRC would 'move the authorities to remit rents'.[66] According to the government, Congress members were eager to regain political support among the peasantry by drawing attention to a lack of relief measures for the rural population:

> It seems certain that Congress have given up the idea of making capital out of charges of supine and apathy on the part of the Government officials, and are now going to concentrate upon the slogan of rent and tax remission in order to win back popularity. Intercepted telegrams this morning bear this cut. The *raiyat* [a peasant paying land revenue directly to the government] is to be represented as totally ruined and with a hard-hearted Government

and landlords pressing him for full payment of rent, cess, and taxes. It is imperative that steps be taken to counter this propaganda.[67]

Significantly, however, the local colonial government perceived the Congress members from outside the province as central in spreading such propaganda. The intercepted telegrams referred to before were sent by 'two leading Congressmen' from Bombay,[68] one described as 'of the blatantly military and un-reasonable type' and the other as 'utterly un-reliable' to the nationalist newspaper the *Bombay Chronicle*.[69] It was stories like theirs—of 'want starvation nakedness and death' and 'harassment of peasants by government and *zamindars*'—that the government wanted to stop before catching fire in national papers. It was in this context, in February until towards the end of March, that the issue of rent and revenue was repeatedly argued for by Swami Sahajanand Saraswati,[70] the founder of the Bihar Kisan Sabha (Bihar Peasant Association/Movement) and the All India Kisan Sabha.[71] By March, the police reported instances of Congressmen encouraging or instigating peasants not to pay rent to *zamindars*. Throughout Tirhut and Champaran there was widespread interest in the remission of rent and revenue, resulting in, for example, a collection of thumb impressions and signatures for a petition for remission of rent to the Darbhanga Raj.[72] Sahajanand Saraswati wanted the BCRC to raise the issue for the peasantry and the *zamindars*; Prasad, however, in the formative meeting of the BCRC in March 1934, threatened to resign if they were going to 'bring politics of any kind into this organisation'.[73] Their difference of opinion reflects their general positions at that time when the Congress in Bihar nurtured a close relationship with the landholding classes, while Sahajanand worked for the improvement of peasants' conditions.[74] The form of 'cooperation' with the local government in relief entered by Prasad, and thereby the BCRC, should be seen in the context of non-cooperation used as a political tool by the Civil Disobedience movement. Cooperation in relief meant that the BCRC intended *not* to non-cooperate with the local government. The promise to leave political questions out of the relief work by central leaders such as Rajendra Prasad did manage to convince the local government that although the BCRC was a Congress organisation in terms of leadership and support, yet not on paper, the committee would stick to disaster relief. The political stance of Prasad in this specific context reflected his relationship with the Kisan Sabhas and the agrarian power relations in Bihar. It was clear that his loyalties lay with the land-owning classes who also formed a strong political base for the Congress in the region.[75] Sahajanand continued to propagate non-payment of rent in the press as well as in person in Tirhut, but only with sporadic support by Congress members whose official stance was to fully cooperate with the government.[76] Later in 1934 when floods worsened the conditions in the countryside, the very cautious and selective critique of landowners' privileges by the Congress played a decisive role in Sahajanand's disassociation from the party.[77] These conflicting stances within the Congress and BCRC reflected political undercurrents in prioritising certain groups in the distribution of relief. The local government was, however, certain of Prasad's and M. K. Gandhi's commitments to keep political questions such as a no-rent campaign out of the relief work.

The BCRC's cooperation with the government to a large extent appeared to be based on an agreement with Prasad, or as a government official wrote, 'the pact made by Rajendra Prasad'.[78] The government endorsed BCRC's work (Map 3.1) and welcomed its cooperation in providing relief while keeping a constant eye on the undertakings of the committee and the political figures involved in the relief work. According to the local government, its objective was to maintain cooperation with the BCRC in order to prevent overlapping of the relief programme and thereby potential competition. Even if Prasad claimed and to a large extent appeared responsible for sustaining a smooth cooperation with the government, the local government remained suspicious regarding the Congress's use of relief operations for broadening its political support. Per se, the BCRC's official disassociation from the Congress was rhetorical, though Prasad may have, as noted in the aforementioned quote, sensed a need to call on a larger audience than the Congress due to organisational issues. Although the BCRC had pronounced its work to be detached from a political agenda, the government and the public regarded it an extension of the Congress's political work, an image that members and supporters of the BCRC did not do much to dissuade. Both in the eyes of the public and the government, the BCRC's association with the Congress was evident from references to 'the Congress fund' and 'Babu Rajendra Prasad's fund'.[79] The 'apolitical' and at the same time political image of the committee was an enduring duality which could be negotiated according to the situation.

Towards 'National' Relief

The BCRC grew as the result of its expanding networks as well as persistent appeals for contributions to the committee. In the initial phase, the committee and a modest mobilisation of relief efforts essentially relied on participation by established relief organisations from outside the affected area. The idea of national support was further articulated in the rhetoric of the committee as it became

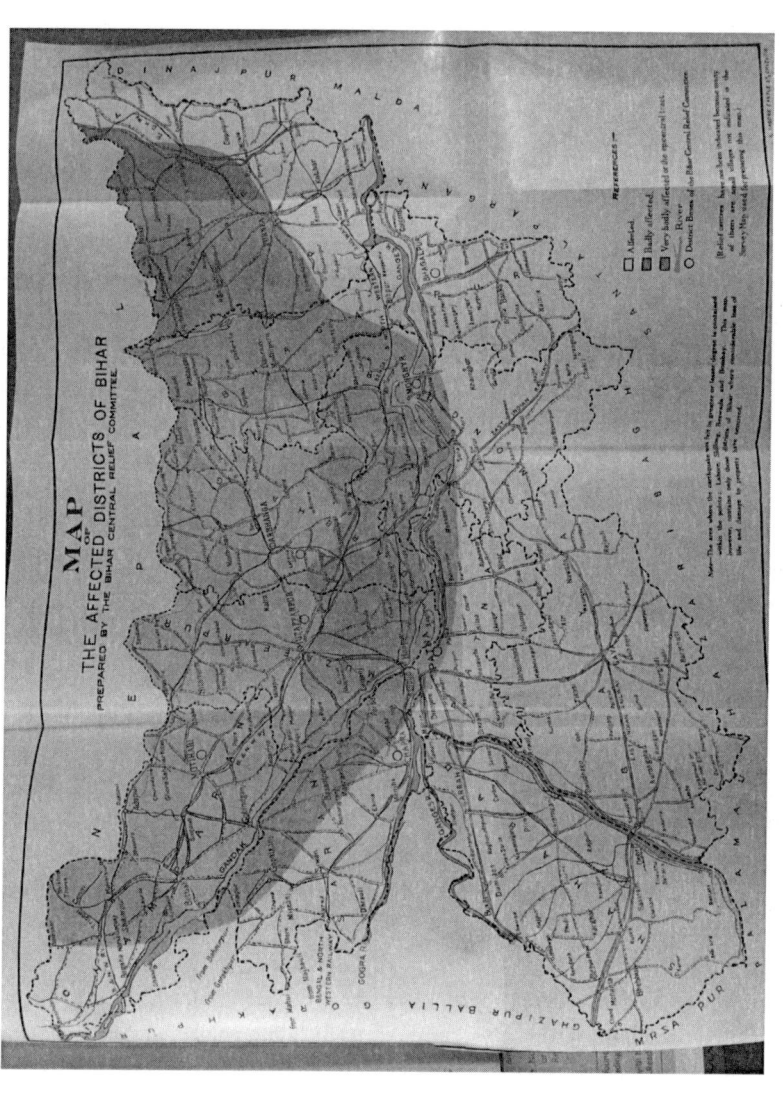

Map 3.1 Map of affected districts in Bihar. BCRC's map of the area with the district bases of the committee marked.

Source: Map from BCRC, *Devastated Bihar.*

increasingly institutionalised in the period leading up to its reconstitution in March 1934. A vision of 'national' relief was realised by including a network of leaders for social service associations and committees from other parts of India.

Outside agencies are often the first to take on emergency measures after a sudden catastrophe[80] and in Bihar many associations from outside the worst-affected area arrived soon after the earthquake. Nehru, on his tour of the area, noticed the 'energy and capacity' of the large number of relief workers who had arrived at Monghyr to be in contrast with 'a very painful absence of self-help among the residents'.[81] The BCRC listed 74 organisations and associations carrying out relief work in the earthquake area, many of them from Bihar and Bengal such as the established larger organisations—the Ramakrishna Mission[82] and the Marwari Relief Society.[83] The government recorded 36 'non-official' relief organisations at work in Muzaffarpur, out of which only one had been formed locally,[84] while the BCRC claimed that 'more than 35' came from outside Muzaffarpur and 'some' had a local origin and, in addition, 'individual philanthropists' and 'private parties' took part 'without much fuss and went away silently'.[85] The *Indian Nation*, the Maharaja of Darbhanga's newspaper, wrote that as many as 45 relief organisations started working in Muzaffarpur within two weeks of the earthquake.[86]

Among the first relief societies to arrive from outside the earthquake area were the Marwari Relief Society, the Ramakrishna Mission and the Vivekananda Mission from Calcutta whose teams arrived in north Bihar on 18 January 1934.[87] In the newspapers, from 20 January 1934, several appeals from regional relief organisations of all sizes filled the pages asking for contributions to carry out relief operation in north Bihar, Jamalpur and Monghyr. The Vivekananda Mission financed the first team with remains from an old relief fund and appealed for further funds, as well as medical students, blankets, money, food-stuffs and medicines, according to the standard format used by many relief associations: a list of names of the office bearers, details of the transactions and a promise of acknowledgement in public print as well as a receipt for every contribution. The Hindu Mission in Calcutta sent relief teams to Monghyr and Muzaffarpur and appealed to individuals to start fund collections and volunteer.[88] The Bengal Hindu Sabha, or the Bengal Provincial Hindu Sabha, also collected funds and encouraged 'all *Hindu Sabhas* in Bengal, Orissa and Assam' to send contributions to the secretary in Calcutta.[89] These organisations, like the Ramakrishna Mission Association from Calcutta, had established regional experience in relief work, foremost famine relief,[90] and the Marwari Relief Society, the Bharat Sewak Sangh and the Hindu Mahasabha would again take part in relief work in Midnapore and Calcutta in the Bengal famine of 1943–44.[91] Their previous record in relief work facilitated the participation of these relief societies as the Government of Bihar and Orissa gave concession on railway freight only to the Marwari Relief Society and the Seva Samaj societies. Together with the St John Ambulance Association and the Indian Red Cross Societies,[92] they counted as established relief organisations.[93] This policy was unfavourable to the many smaller associations and emerging relief organisations. Other large organisations entertaining a good relationship with government officials were the Memon Relief Society, the party of Baba Gurdit Singh, the Indian Medical Association (IMA) and the Sankat Tran Samiti under Satish Chandra Dasgupta, all of which made prominent contributions according to Prasad.[94] The Seva Samitis and the Sankat Tran Samiti were fundamental in providing initial funding and regional support to the BCRC. One of the first to mobilise funds and relief workers for BCRC, Madan Mohan Malaviya, a prominent person in the INC, founder of the Banaras Hindu University and the Allahabad and Akhil Bharatiya Seva Samiti (the All-India Service Committee/Society), was known as a major force behind organised social service initiatives in northern India.[95] By 18 January 1934, Malaviya had initiated an earthquake fund in Benares and used the local Benares Seva Samiti as well as the national organisation, the Akhil Bharatiya Seva Samiti, to organise relief work and raise an advance of 5,000 rupees to the newly initiated earthquake fund.[96] Even though earthquake relief was a departure from the Seva Samitis' regular function to provide social services such as education, 'unofficial policing' during melas, disposal of corpses and distribution of medicines, the organisational capacities deployed in emergency relief during epidemics and famines proved useful.[97] The support of Malaviya and the Seva Samiti ensured funds and manpower from both the local and 'national' branches of the established social service organisations.

The Sankat Tran Samiti of Bengal in Calcutta,[98] a relief society started by Congressman Subhas Chandra Bose[99] for flood relief in north Bengal in September 1922, initially held a similar function as the BCRC: it aimed to unify relief societies on a working committee in order to agree on an agenda for the relief programme and prevent overlaps.[100] With its previous experience and organisational network between relief organisations in Calcutta, it was quick to appeal for donations, calling on students to donate money rather than spend it on Saraswati puja, and holding a meeting to organise the collection of funds which would be disbursed in collaboration with the BCRC.[101] These initial contributions by established organisations relied on local networks outside the earthquake area and helped to portray the BCRC as a national committee.

The second phase of the BCRC's existence, a rebirth in terms of constitution, began in early February with a wider mobilisation of funds and workers, which meant an expansion of the organisation in terms of size and numbers. The reconstitution made the committee 'more efficient and business-like' according to its own account. A constitution of the committee was adopted after the resignation and re-election of the office-bearers in a meeting on 18 March 1934, presided over by M. K. Gandhi. It was registered under the Societies Registration Act of 1860 (Act 21 of 1860).[102] Since 1860, the act regulated charitable endeavours for public benefit, including the relief of poverty to the advancement of education and religion.[103] The BCRC was founded with the aim: a) to raise funds for the relief of the distressed; b) to organise and distribute relief; c) to take such steps as may be necessary for the purpose of achieving the aforesaid objects and d) to work in cooperation with other organisations with similar objects. In total, 29 members represented donors and relief societies from all over India.[104] Organisations and individuals became members of the committee by contributing 5,000 rupees towards its relief programme. Its composition, it claimed, represented 'all shades of public opinion and all communities' and it willingly cooperated with all organisations.[105] According to Charles Freer Andrews, who campaigned nationally and internationally for the donation of funds to the BCRC and published the book *The Indian Earthquake*, the committee's office-bearers were meant to represent the two major religious communities of Hindus and Muslims in the province.[106]

Preceding the reconstitution of the BCRC, the governing committee's members had all come from Bihar. In preparation for the re-election, the committee took help from the nationalist press that published appeals across the subcontinent.[107] The purpose was to invite 'leading individuals from other provinces' in order to mobilise the 'resources and energies of the whole country', according to the committee's own account.[108] People regarded as leaders were wanted as members on the 'All-India Committee' in order to strengthen its 'All-India character'.[109] The process of including persons of public importance was a strategy of the BCRC to establish 'national' cooperation, in order to develop into a relief organisation 'representative of the people of India', thereby expanding its scope to incorporate the 'nation'.[110] The transformation from a local gathering into a national organisation was accredited to Nehru who initially encouraged the local committee of 'Gentlemen of Bihar only' to form an 'All-India Committee'.[111] He described BCRC as 'by no means a purely Congress organisation', but rather an 'all-India body'.[112] The committee's members and work were portrayed by him as surpassing the political aims of the political party. Yet such claims may largely be seen as attempts to portray the BCRC as a 'national' organisation. Even if its relief programme was supposedly 'free' from Congress politics according to its leaders, the political organisation was integral to its organisation and work, and further strengthened as the work progressed.

Local Networks in Aid

The INC was significant in terms of leadership and in collecting funds for the BCRC. Yet the cooperation of relief societies and associations proved essential in order for the committee to substantiate its claim to embrace 'the nation'. Even though the growth of the BCRC into a larger body was an organic development resulting from cooperation between the numerous organisations joining in the relief and reconstruction phase, its relief programme and institutionalisation was the outcome of political aims. Nevertheless, relief societies carried out work according to their own relief programmes and in cooperation with other members of BCRC by taking on certain tasks or carrying out relief in areas according to wards.[113] They thereby continued to collect and distribute aid partly independently and partly in agreement with the decisions taken by the BCRC. The BCRC's report, however, highlights the committee's role in the organisation of relief as central.[114]

In order to reach local communities, the BCRC to a large extent relied on an established network of member societies and associations. The most evident example can be found in the networks of the well-established Marwari Relief Society from Calcutta, founded in 1913 by reformist Marwaris for volunteerism in public health.[115] Its cooperation with other societies in the region facilitated relief work and the distribution of aid collected in Calcutta. Even though a great number of relief societies initially flocked to the earthquake area, sources indicate that they, to a great extent, carried out relief tasks in close cooperation with local 'earthquake-born' or established organisations already engaged in social welfare work or relief work. Such locally initiated relief tends to have better survival chances in terms of sustainability and catering to the grassroots of the communities affected.[116] Considering the ability of the Marwari Relief Society to establish local cooperation partners, source urban funding as well as maintain a relationship with other relief organisations, the BCRC's role as a provider of relief appeared marginal. The Marwari Relief Society's ability to work both with networks of local relief organisations and the newly founded BCRC appeared to have been based on civic networks among Marwaris, facilitated by personal acquaintances and trust.

As mentioned earlier, the Marwari Relief Society was among the first to establish relief centres in Muzaffarpur, Monghyr and Darbhanga[117] where a large number of the merchant community had died in the bazaars.[118] An observer visiting the earthquake area described the Marwari Relief Society as 'purely Indian', most likely referring to the absence of Europeans on its managing committee and among its major donors.[119] The 'reputable Birla Family and the Calcutta Corporation' provided 'very liberal and generous support' according to its own account,[120] and in a list of funds contributors in a newspaper the 'Birla Brothers' from Calcutta had given 27,000 rupees out of the 200,000 rupees collected in February.[121] In 1934–35, the president of the Marwari Relief Society was Braj Mohan Birla, the brother of the wealthy industrialist G. D. Birla, a contemporary well-known supporter and financer of the INC. Marwaris were generally sympathetic towards the political position of the INC and, since the 1920s, leading Marwari businessmen and industrialists such as G. D. Birla, Prabhu Dayal Himmatsinka (also known as P. D. Himatsingka) and Jamnalal Bajaj had become involved in nationalist politics.[122] In 1934, both P. D. Himatsingka and Jwala Prasad Kanoria (the Marwari Relief Society's Honorary General Secretary) actively participated in BCRC's 'Cheap Shops Sub-Committee' under Jamnalal Bajaj, treasurer of the INC, Gandhian and president of the Marwari Agarwal Sabha.[123] The close relationship between leaders of the Marwari Relief Society and the INC was an obvious advantage in cooperation that facilitated interaction with other service organisations. For instance, Sriram Bajpai was in charge of the Servants of India Society's relief work in Bihar in 1934, and represented the society as a member of the BCRC, while simultaneously assisted the Marwari Relief Society's centre at Muzaffarpur.[124] According to Dang's research on the organisation of relief work by the INC in the same period, the overlapping commitments between relief-oriented associations and political work was common; for instance, the Servants of India Society and the Indian Mahasabha shared leaders and workers with the Congress committees and helped with the organisation of its political activities.[125] Relief work was a form of social service for the country, described by the founder of the Servants of India Society as 'nation-building through active citizenship'.[126]

The inflow of resources from urban centres and wealthy patrons appears to have been a valuable strength of the Marwari associations from outside the earthquake area. As Ritu Birla has noted, making a gift for *dharma*, whether to a local temple or social welfare, was a way to negotiate the mobile commercial community's entry as immigrants into a new social world. The practice of gifting did not claim wide political authority but served to display local market dominance and 'a kind of localized sovereignty'. Gifting was an important social function among Marwaris where 'the community's economic ethics' was emphasised as a method to achieve social progress, thereby disciplining expenditure and excess.[127] The Marwari Relief Society received funds from other Marwari associations based outside the earthquake area, such as the Oswal Navyuwak Samity from Calcutta, which helped with both funds and volunteers in Minapur and Muzaffarpur, and the Marwari Sahayak Samiti in Ranchi which also contributed to the fund.[128] In appeals to residents of Calcutta, the Marwari Relief Society collected funds towards the mentioned towns, often stressing local affinity to 'their brethren of Bihar' and providing dramatic eye-witness accounts of the devastation encountered by the relief workers,[129] for instance, the death of 25 schoolboys in the local Marwari *pathshala* (school).[130] The link between the Marwaris in Calcutta and the bazaars across north Bihar turned out to be vital for the inflow of resources and funds.[131] Marwaris in Bihar had strong links to Marwari businesses in Calcutta, their principal trades in Bihar and Bengal being cloth, jute and moneylending.[132] Gifts in kind consisting of jute, a well-known Marwari trade in the area, featured on the long list of donations and to a certain extent reflected the business network of the Marwari community. Hessian, in particular, which is a jute or hemp fabric that the Marwaris generally acted as brokers for, was widely distributed in the relief centres. The Oswal Marwaris were especially prominent in the jute trade,[133] and the same name featured in the Oswal Navyuvak Samity from Calcutta and Assam, and the Oswal Earthquake Relief Fund, all of which donated substantial amounts towards the relief society. A large share, 203,615 rupees out of 216,762 rupees, of the Marwari Relief Society's collection came from Calcutta through these networks.[134] Urban funding and the established social and financial ties between Marwari businessmen and members of the INC appear to have facilitated a close cooperation between the society and the BCRC. Though this cooperation contributed to increasing both the committee's and the society's scope, the latter's reach in the earthquake area depended on cooperation with local Marwari organisations. The ability to develop cooperation locally was fundamental in establishing the society as an important actor in the relief work.[135] The society in general upheld a good relationship with local government officials, partly maintained by providing unofficial reports regarding its relief programme.[136] To some extent the relief society appeared to take charge of the work begun by smaller local associations, for instance, clearing debris in Monghyr,[137] a task initiated by the Bhagalpur Marwari Sudhar Samiti.[138] The society's negotiation into cooperation with local associations is not always clear as in Muzaffarpur, where it jointly headed the Marwari Earthquake Relief Fund together with the local Marwari Panchayat Seva Samiti, and even though the two associations cooperated in running and setting up relief centres, financial accounts and tasks were managed separately. The local Marwari associations played a central role in the distribution of relief, for instance, the relief centres opened by the Marwari Relief Society were in the course of time taken over by the local Marwari Panchayat Seva Samiti in Darbhanga and Samastipur, and the Marwari association, the Arya Pratinidhi Sabha, was deputed to handle the relief centre in Rampurhari.[139] Notably, local Marwari relief organisations could organise and manage relief centres of their own accord: the main function of the Marwari Relief Society was to bring in manpower and funds. The society perhaps worked under ideal conditions for carrying out relief. Based in a metro unaffected by the earthquake, it had readily available finances, access to necessary equipment and cooperation partners in local and regional Marwari associations which may have shared similar organisational structures, as well as leading members who had important roles in cooperating relief organisations such as the Servants of India Society and the BCRC.

Adding to the established relief providers at ease in cooperation with local networks and political actors in the BCRC, emergent relief providers like the Memon Relief Society in Calcutta expanded its scope in the aftermath.[140] The society's founder, Adamji Haji Dawood (1880–1948) of the Adamjis, belonged to the Memon community, often referred to as a Muslim mercantile community hailing from western India. The community had traded in Calcutta since the late eighteenth century, specifically in Burma rice, and in the 1920s they started investing in the jute and match industries.[141] Before 1934, the society had operated in flood relief in Gujarat in 1928, and could send, relatively swiftly, about 70 volunteers to north Bihar within the first five days after the earthquake. Its activities were to repair and build *pucca* and *kuccha* houses, that is, houses of bricks and those of lighter materials such as grass, straw and mud,[142] including schools and mosques, set up grain shops, and distribute food and clothing worth 60,375 rupees in 344 towns and villages in a span of five months. The BCRC had a say about where it carried out work, for instance, rebuilding in Muzaffarpur, Motihari and Olai (alt. Aurai, Awrai or Orai) in particular had been assigned to the society by the committee.[143] At the same time, its work clearly extended beyond these areas, as the society approached the local government to address rural distress in Katra and the need for additional funds to provide relief, as well as to rebuild huts for homeless village people.[144] Though few sources provide data of the Memon Relief Society's contribution in Bihar 1934, the mention of it repairing *kuccha* houses indicates that it also directed its relief work towards people of lesser means, a task rarely mentioned in connection with other relief societies. The BCRC recognised, in particular, its ability to construct and repair houses 'at incredibly cheap cost' in Muzaffarpur.[145] Building upon its experience in organising flood relief, the society's expansion in operations and organisational set-up appears to have emerged as a consequence of the earthquake.[146] After the 1934 earthquake, the society organised relief operations and reconstruction work after the Quetta earthquake in 1935, as well as during the riots in Rangoon and at the refugee camps for Indian Muslims from Rangoon in Calcutta in the 1940s.[147]

Relief societies based on community, such as the Marwari Relief Society and the Memon Relief Society, did not appear to have attracted criticism for being communal. At least in official publications, relief societies distributed relief independently of religious identity and communalism gave way to seamless cooperation with other relief societies according to eye-witnesses involved in the distribution of relief.[148] One exception would be the care of '[one] hundred' Muslim orphans organised by the Memon Relief Society at two Muslim orphanages in Kanpur[149] and Calcutta.[150] The local government initially claimed that local institutions had taken care of the 'very few cases' of orphans in the earthquake,[151] but later appears to have supported private initiatives by granting 7,500 rupees from the Viceroy's Earthquake Relief Fund (henceforth VERF) in order to provide for an undisclosed number of orphans at the Muslim orphanage in Kanpur.[152] Rather than giving preference to Muslims, the Memon Relief Society was, according to a government official, prioritising the 'middle classes' by distributing cash and providing temporary quarters.[153] The claim was substantiated by the relief society's own report until 15 March 1934, according to which it had distributed 24,005 rupees in cash to 'thousands' of middle class people in villages and towns while the reconstruction of three mosques had been granted only 1,500 rupees.[154] The BCRC, however, accepted donations earmarked for 'Hindu Relief', 'Khathari Sufferers', 'Kayastha Relief', 'Hindu Temple Repair', 'Guru Nanak Langar' (a Sikh relief association providing food), and though these amounts were minimal as part of the collection, it was relief set aside according to communal belonging.[155] The local government accused local workers from the BCRC in Muzaffarpur of 'misappropriating money and clothes', 'peculation, favouritism and inactivity' and instigating communal tensions by giving old clothes to Muslims and new clothes to Hindus.[156] The editorial of *Amrita Bazar Patrika*, a newspaper with a predominantly Bengali readership, questioned the accusations of communalism among relief societies as perhaps being based on personal grievances rather than biases in distribution.[157] Accusations had been raised against relief operations conducted by 'Benarees, Mahomedans and Marwaris' in the government administration, including a Muslim Deputy Magistrate, who were said to have conducted the distribution of relief along 'strictly and bitterly communal lines'. The editorial in *Amrita Bazar Patrika* described the treatment as expressions of 'anti-Hindu' and 'anti-Bengali' sentiments, the former community a majority in the area and the latter considered a privileged minority. Bengalis in the area reported what they perceived as a grudge against them among their Bihari neighbours, according to the editorial, perhaps due to the presence of Bengali relief organisations which may have favoured their 'own' according to regional ties.[158] Discontent regarding the government's preferences in relief communities lingered as questions were raised regarding the distribution of loans and gratuitous relief to Muslims as opposed to other religious denominations in Muzaffarpur.[159] The government was not prepared to undertake the task of collecting the statistics and the questions came to an end.

Invoking the Nation through Images: Devastated Women, Devastated Bihar

As mentioned in the Introduction to this chapter, a way of collecting funds for earthquake relief was by selling special newspaper issues or reports of the earthquake. Two publications that sold in support of the BCRC relied on imagery and language which depicted Bihar as a suffering woman in what is analysed as a personification, localisation and feminisation of the disaster. Their imagery was in stark contrast to publications by the colonial loyalist press that used photographs of ruined buildings, town landscapes of bricks and spectacular land damages side by side with advertisements of goods and materials for reconstruction such as the *Statesman's* special issue, *Record of the Great Indian Earthquake*, sold for 6 annas 'to help the earthquake relief work' through the VERF.[160]

A number of nationalist publications also described the disaster through imagery that relied on material destruction, but at the same time connected it to the experience of individual suffering. A book-length publication in Hindi with a collection of often tragic stories by survivors who had barely made it out of their crumbling houses such as *Stories of the Victims of the Earthquake: Bihar's Earthquake Victims' Most Astonishing and Pitiful True Own Narrations*,[161] and articles in the Hindi press,[162] as well as the eye-witness account of the aftermath by Nehru, *Devastated Bihar through Jawaharlal's Lenses*,[163] all focused on material destruction, yet individual losses and tragedies featured as examples. In particular,

Image 3.1 Cover of *Devastated Bihar* by BCRC.

Source: BCRC, *Devastated Bihar*.

Image 3.2 Cover of *Earthquake Number: Which Hand Is Yours*, published jointly by *Bombay Chronicle* and *Bombay Sentinel* under the name *Chronicle-Sentinel*.

Source: Cover of Syed Abdullah Brelvi and B. G. Horniman (eds.), *Earthquake Number: Which Hand Is Yours*, special issue by *Chronicle-Sentinel*, Bombay, March 1934.

Nehru's brief narrative relied to a great extent on spectacular photographs accompanied by texts describing the destruction. Notably, it was one of three publications which used 'Devastated Bihar' in the main title, the other two being Rajendra Prasad's *Devastated Behar: The Problem of Reconstruction*, and BCRC's *Devastated Bihar: An Account of Havoc Caused by the Earthquake of the 15th January 1934 and Relief Operation Conducted by the Committee.*

Two major publications by the nationalist press, *Devastated Bihar* published by BCRC and the special *Earthquake Number: Which Hand Is Yours* by Chronicle-Sentinel,[164] a collaboration between the two newspapers *Bombay Chronicle* and *Bombay Sentinel*, paired images of women in distress with images and text depicting a ruined Bihar in their call on 'the nation'. The publication *Devastated Bihar* was sold after BCRC's reconstitution in March 1934.[165] The sales proceeds from the report that was sold for 1 rupee went towards the fund of the BCRC.[166] The cover (Image 3.1) appealed for contributions with an image of a dejected woman's face in profile, literally shedding tears over Bihar's ruined landscape. The woman appeared devastated, just as Bihar was 'devastated' according to the title of the report. In the frame of small squares around the central image, a number of scenes contrast life before and after the earthquake. One line of images depicts everyday life scenes: a farmer ploughing his field, students attending class, and the next line showed flooded land, a ravaged landscape, towns in ruins and peasants struggling to get water. The images constructed a narrative of a prosperous life in towns and rural areas before the earthquake and the destruction in its aftermath. Central to this narrative of destruction was the devastation of Bihar.

The *Chronicle-Sentinel's* special issue *Earthquake Number: Which Hand Is Yours* (Image 3.2) was a Bombay publication; the number appealed especially to people of western India and the metropolis, portrayed as a centre for wealth and power as opposed to Bihar's helplessness after the earthquake.[167] The issue was published in March 1934 by the editors of two important nationalist newspapers in Bombay, B. G. Horniman of the *Bombay Sentinel* and Syed Abdullah Brelvi of the *Bombay Chronicle*—the latter was a member of BCRC by way of having donated 5,000 rupees to the committee.[168] The issue's cover used dramatic imagery depicting human bodies, dead livestock, a naked youngster and women in torn saris kneeling and sitting in the ruins of what was once a town. Above the scene of destruction hangs a collection urn into which hands are depicted giving money ('Which Hand Is Yours') that is simultaneously being distributed over the landscape and ruins. As will be discussed later, the issue called on specifically 'Congressmen' to act, and its content was to a large extent written by Congress members repeatedly invoking the nation as the rescuer. These images of Bihar left in ruins, 'devastated' women in agony and in need of rescue, dressed in torn saris and bent in dejected poses called for funds from the nation, an entity united and embodied in the largely male leadership of the BCRC. Bihar, or the woman, needed rescue by the nation, which was represented by the BCRC.

Both *Devastated Bihar* by the BCRC and the *Chronicle-Sentinel's Earthquake Number: Which Hand Is Yours* invoked a paternalistic language to elicit gifting from the general public. Women and children were used in images and the province Bihar was portrayed as a female in need of help. Images communicate culture-specific values and, at the same time, children and women in need are well-known universal themes for aid agencies to arouse generous gifting or paternal funding.[169] The publications, in turning Bihar into a feminine object, borrowed rhetoric from nationalist depictions of the 'nation' in the form of a female figure, as a 'Motherland'. *Bhārat Mātā* (Mother India) as a nationalist symbol in literature and political writings became popular in nationalist discourse during the late nineteenth century, as Manu Goswami has lucidly analysed.[170] The modern nation of India was imagined as an ancient goddess, *Bhārat Mātā* who embodied ideas and values and served to arouse reverence 'among her citizen-devotees'.[171] As Ramaswamy notes, during the late nineteenth and early twentieth centuries, the vision of *Bhārat Mātā* was accepted by 'secularists' as an embodiment of the geopolitical space India. She was often depicted as a mother situated in a globe, with the Indian tricolour or a map delineating the borders of India, thereby turning her devotee–citizens into 'geopiety'.[172] The image of Bharat as a goddess or national space was not infrequently depicted as invaded, raped and assaulted by foreign rulers and in need of rescue by specifically masculine and upper-caste Hindu political agency.[173] Similarly, disaster imagery and imagination in the two nationalist publications after the earthquake alluded to a woman in need of rescue, an embodiment of the province Bihar 'devastated' by the earthquake.[174]

The portrayal of Bihar as a female was further reinforced by the use of nationalist language in the *Earthquake Number*. Sarojini Naidu, the first female president of the INC in 1925 and a prominent politician of the 1930s, in a short introductory note titled 'Our Supreme Duty' depicted Bihar as a physically and emotionally hurt female in need of the nation's help:

It is not enough that on the first poignancy of Bihar's anguish and affliction the whole country was moved to render her instant succour and solace.

Every hour brings fresh revelation of the magnitude of her disaster and the magnitude of her need. Does it not, therefore, behove us all to make Bihar the central burden of our daily thought and duty and offer her our love and consolation transmuted into unstinted and unceasing service for her redemption from the sorrows and perils that beset her.[175]

The devotional ('offer her our love and consolation transmuted into unstinted and unceasing service for her redemption') and at the same time patriotic language ('central burden of our daily thought and duty') coupled with ascribing Bihar human emotions ('Bihar's anguish and affliction') and a physical state ('her need') that could be remedied ('redemption from the sorrows and perils') served to encourage contributions to the fund based on the same nationalist language as depicted in the images. Naidu's introductory note was followed by a string of short notes and articles calling on the nation for support in the relief work. Headings such as 'Rajen Babu [Rajendra Prasad] Appeals for Funds: Task Ahead of Bihar Is of Tremendous Magnitude, but God Willing We Shall Face It with Backing of Our Nation', 'A National Disaster', 'A Calamity Code: All Natural Disasters of a Major Kind in Whatever Province Should Be Viewed by the State as National Burdens', and 'Country's Response Still Inadequate: Bihar Minister Urges Further Nation-Wide Effort to Aid Stricken Province'[176] left no one in doubt that the rescue of Bihar necessitated a 'national' response.

A print of a woman juxtaposed with a ruined town appeared inside the issue as well (Image 3.3), notably the same components as on the cover as well as on the BCRC's publication *Devastated Bihar* (Images 3.1 and 3.2). The drawing by Palin Bihari Dutt was made in aid of BCRC's fund collection. Again the nation was called on to rescue Bihar: 'The Agony of Bihar: The Nation's Call'. The relief providers, the embodiment of 'the nation' had legitimate grounds to act as 'the agony of Bihar is a nation's agony' and they, as the embodiment of 'the nation', were the saviours of the 'woman', or Bihar. However, the physical and mental appearance of the woman in this drawing is remarkably different from the dejected pose of the devastated women on the cover. The woman, a young mother holding a baby on her shoulder, has an almost triumphant posture as she towers over the ruined town. In her determined outlook, the woman with her head raised high appears to look beyond the damaged town as she protectively holds her baby and looks into the future. The imagery may here have communicated a vision of the resurrected mother, a young nation with a bright future.

Image 3.3 'The Agony of Bihar: The Nation's Call'.

Source: Illustration by Palin Bihari Dutt, in Brelvi and Horniman, *Earthquake Number: Which Hand Is Yours.*

Relief Programme: Administration, Distribution and Priorities

The experience of leading Congress members and the INC's institutional organisation and networks helped the committee to collect funds, outline a relief programme and set up an administration for the distribution and management of relief. In all, the committee created an administrative apparatus that paralleled the government administration in providing relief. The Viceroy noted that the Congress held considerable sums and feared 'that Gandhi and his friends are going to make a desperate effort to restore their position by being extremely active, if they can, in the devastated areas'.[177] According to the local police reports, the BCRC, and thereby the Congress, threatened to gain 'parallel control' in relief work.[178] At the same time, a personal account from a government official claimed BCRC to have worked 'side by side with the officers of Government', stressing a cooperative spirit rather than the running of two separate organisations.[179]

As the BCRC was reconstituted in March it formalised its relief programme and closed the 'immediate relief' programme.[180] The reconstruction phase, in comparison to the immediate aftermath, involved much larger funds. Reconstruction, beginning in April, included repairs of houses and infrastructure, agricultural land restoration, building wells and tanks outside the towns, as well as other types of aid such as grants to small traders and artisans as well as training of volunteers in first aid in case of epidemics.[181] By June 1934, the BCRC Head Office, located on Exhibition Road in Patna, coordinated and served as storage for the considerable national and also international contributions pouring in from purse collections, charity organisations and private persons before being sent to the districts.[182] In addition to a publicity department, the office contained 15 departments, including a medical, an agricultural and an engineering department and seven branch offices in the districts. The BCRC's costs for administration by the end of June 1934, amounted to 1,33,423 rupees, covering the costs for travelling, volunteers and office equipment, huts, cars and cycles. The amount spent on administration reflected the set-up of a fairly large organisation for relief which included 258 centres and 2,277 workers by June 1934.[183] Administratively experienced politicians such as Jawaharlal Nehru advised in the organisation of the Head Office, and J. C. Kumarappa, a chartered accountant, was sent by M. K. Gandhi.[184]

According to official data, the BCRC, in the end, collected almost 3 million rupees and a large number of donations in kind.[185] Initial government reports acknowledged the committee's active participation in relief work and noted, in particular, its 'large reserves of money' received from the public.[186] Appeals by M. K. Gandhi, Rabindranath Tagore and Sarojini Naidu helped to collect national and international funds, supported especially by C. F. Andrews who was urged by Rajendra Prasad to appeal for relief in Europe and Africa.[187] Contributions from abroad were added to by private initiatives such as the Indian Earthquake Relief Fund in Great Britain.[188] Foreign collections were modest compared to the large domestic collections from Bengal, Bombay and Gujarat, as illustrated in Table 3.1.[189] Confidential reports by the local governments described the administrative organisation of the INC provincial offices as the base for the BCRC in collecting funds.[190] Papers by the All-India Congress Committee confirm the active involvement of the Desh Sevika Sangh and the Gandhi Seva Sena in collecting funds on behalf of 'the national relief committee' BCRC. Since these organs of the INC financed political work, such as an INC session,[191] the BCRC was supported by collections meant for both overtly political purposes and humanitarian relief. The BCRC's report until June 1934 supports the government's perception of the INC's regional offices as the backbone in collecting funds. In particular, the larger collections from Bombay and Ahmedabad (Table 3.1) were substantial and may have been facilitated by the fact of them being strongholds of the INC as well as the strong presence of business communities in these two cities. The Congress shared close ties with Gujarati merchants in particular—a regional and community tie which has been explained by Gandhi's personal connection with Gujarati merchant communities.[192] Many merchants, in general, supported Gandhian movements, often generously, without themselves engaging too openly with the activities.[193] The good relationship between the Congress and the Marwari merchants in particular formed the foundation for BCRC's cooperation with the Marwari Relief Society from Calcutta, an influential relief provider with a far-reaching local network that will be examined in the following section of this chapter.

In the reconstructive phase, the committee prioritised clearing wells and tanks in order to address the problem of clean drinking water. M. K. Gandhi, who suggested to the committee to focus on water-related issues, claimed the BCRC to know 'better than any other agency' the needs of the rural population and the necessity of water to sustain livelihoods.[194] The space carved out by the committee in the relief programme stressed its ability to provide relief in a better way than the government and also proved it to be more attuned to the needs of the people. According to Nehru, no other agency but the BCRC, 'not even the Government', had the same ability to provide relief among the peasants. The reason, according to Nehru's retrospective account, was the availability of the

Table 3.1 Donations from the provinces and abroad to BCRC:
20 January–30 June 1934 (in rupees)

	20 January to 31 March 1934	1 April to 30 June 1934
Bihar & Orissa	65,044	11,329
Bengal	247,112	31,983
Burma	57,527	9,124
Assam	9,004	865
Bombay	782,771	85,918
Bombay city	723,435	74,341
Gujarat	346,133	66,003
Ahmedabad	229,082	51,634
Kathiawad	76,881	13,794
Khandesh	14,392	1,205
Central Provinces	53,470	5,074
Central India	32,198	7,046
Sindh	63,073	14,727
Rajputana	30,373	5,212
Baluchistan	1,031	190
Madras*	173,165	31,105
Canara	3,598	-
The Punjab	166,835	12,779
N.W.F.P.	6,936	3,365
Kashmere State	4,583	218
United Provinces	196,545	46,301
Foreign	42,615	76,889
Total	**2,308,247**	**423,128**

Source: Based on 'Summary of Annex A: Donations Received from 20 January to 31 March 1934' and 'Summary of Annex B: Donations Received from 1 April to 30 June 1934', in BCRC, *Report for the Period Ending 30th June 1934*, 112, 126. All data are in round numbers.

Note: *Data on Madras includes donations from Mysore, Hyderabad and Malabar.

Congress' organisation and its workers being at its disposal, many of whom hailed from a peasant background.[195]

In practice, the task of securing water sources proved difficult to implement. According to the proceedings from the committee's second general meeting in August 1934, 484,000 rupees were allotted to solve issues related to water, which included reconstruction of wells, re-excavation of tanks, repair of embankments and water channels and drainage of water-logged areas. By the end of June, the committee had constructed 3,519 new wells, repaired 2,781 wells and re-excavated 552 tanks, and some 700 tanks were to be completed by early 1935 (Table 3.3).[196] It may have looked like a large figure, but considering that the number of wells and tanks damaged or destroyed amounted to 'anything between 75,000 and one lakh [100,000]' according to the BCRC, the effort was in the committee's own words 'poor'.[197] BCRC started boring tube-wells but found it a waste of time since it could only be used by one person at a time, apart from the fact that they were difficult to maintain. Instead, the construction of masonry wells was favoured since it could be used by several people at a time and the villagers could be employed in the construction work rather than engaging contractors from outside, as in the case of the bore wells.[198] Repairs of embankments and roads provided an opportunity for so-called unemployment relief in order to help the rural population. The 44,192 rupees spent on unemployment relief reflected a relatively modest undertaking considering the allotment of 167,000 rupees by the end of June 1934 (see Tables 3.2 and 3.3). Still, water issues, huts and building materials, and unemployment relief were the three main categories of aid in the period until the end of June (Tables 3.2 and 3.3).

The large sums for so-called middle-class relief mainly constituted grants for rebuilding houses and were distributed in September, after the rains, when reconstruction could be initiated in north Bihar. Even though middle-class relief as a category was not initially given priority in the relief programme, a sub-committee of eight members dedicated to this type of relief was an evident sign of the classes' presence in the relief programme in a longer perspective. Like the local government's relief programme, the BCRC, too, equalled house grants or assistance in reconstruction with middle-class relief: 'the particular form of relief which can be given to this class is in rebuilding houses'.[199] Out of the allotted 500,000 rupees towards middle-class relief largely concentrated in the towns of Muzaffarpur, Darbhanga and Monghyr, only 23,471 rupees had been spent by June 1934.[200] Similar to how the local government defined the middle classes as a relief category based on foremost property (Chapter 5). Until June, the committee had prioritised securing water supplies for the cost of 379,285 rupees. Although

Table 3.2 BCRC budget allotments: 1 April–30 June 1934 (in rupees)

District	Wells, tanks, etc.	Huts, etc.	Doles and un-employment	Seeds	Debris	Middle-class relief	Famine	Total
Muzaffarpur	170,000	25,000	10,000	10,000	3,000	113,000	6,000	331,000
Champaran	91,000	30,000	73,000	10,000	1,000	65,000	-	276,000
Darbhanga	100,000	25,000	50,000	10,000	1,000	112,000	-	298,000
Monghyr	36,000	40,000	15,000	2,000	5,000	90,000	-	188,000
Bhagalpur	40,000	10,000	9,000	-	-	25,000	-	84,000
Saran	27,000	10,000	10,000	-	-	32,000	-	79,000
Patna	-	20,000	-	-	-	35,000	-	55,000
Gaya	-	-	-	-	-	6,000	-	6,000
Shahabad	-	-	-	-	-	6,000	-	6,000
Purnea	20,000	-	-	-	-	16,000	-	36,000
Total	484,000	160,000	167,000	32,000	10,000	500,000	6,000	1,359,000

Source: Based on 'Budget Allotments: Since 1st April 1934', in 'Proceedings from the Second General Meeting', in BCRC, *Report for the Period Ending 30th June 1934*, 135–36 and unnumbered pages after 129.

Table 3.3 BCRC relief from 20 January to 30 June 1934: main heads for payments (in rupees)

	Audited 20 January– 31 March 1934	Preliminary Audit 1 April– 30 June 1934	Total
Water supply	11,382	367,903	379,285
Huts, semi-permanent buildings and building material	97,277	98,602	195,879
Immediate aid	26,702	38,385	65,087
Unemployment	14,366	29,825	44,192
Stores and freight	20,764	20,116	40,881
Aid to middle classes	-	23,471	23,471
Total	170,491	578,302	748,795

Source: 'Bihar Central Relief Committee. Receipts and Payments Accounts from 20 January to 30 June 1934'. See 'Proceedings from the Second General Meeting', in BCRC, *Report for the Period Ending 30th June 1934*, 135–36.

water was the priority to begin with, 'Middle-Class Relief' was granted an almost equal amount in aid as water-related issues (Table 3.2). The initial modest expenditure on middle-class relief was explained by three factors: immediate relief needs such as water issues were prioritised; second, the committee's strategy was to wait for the government to act first since it was a larger expense than the committee could cover; and last, the beginning of the rains in the summer made it practically difficult to rebuild houses.[201] Although the committee, judging from allocations, readily provided substantial funds to the middle classes for the reconstruction of private property, its relief programme stressed broader support of public goods in the form of water and livelihoods in rural areas.

The BCRC's success in organising relief work should also be viewed against the government's partial failure to carry out the same task. For instance, in Muzaffarpur, the government attempted to coordinate relief organisation after BCRC had already started the same task. Five days after the BCRC had started work,[202] the district administration attempted to set up 'The Central Relief Committee' (*not* the BCRC) to coordinate relief work in Muzaffarpur. However, relief organisations turned out to be reluctant to participate as evidenced by the fact that only 15 leaders of 36 'non-official' relief organisations joined and only a few submitted reports.[203] The BCRC could claim legitimacy as a relief provider and coordinator based partly on a general unwillingness on behalf of the relief associations to recognise the government as a partner in relief work. The government records of the district administration's failure in organising relief associations locally show that descriptions in the nationalist press of the BCRC and not the government as the central provider of relief was not merely part of a rhetoric.

Rhetoric, however, served as an efficient tool. The nationalist friendly press helped in advertising the BCRC as practically oriented and efficient compared to the government's attempts. Implicit criticism of inadequate government efforts emerged in articles mentioning the work of the respective fund collections of the BCRC and the VERF. While giving marginal space to a visit by the Governor of Bihar and Orissa in the earthquake area, and providing 'examples of self-help' by government officials who with 'spades and baskets' would repair a *bund* in a village, a writer described how 'non-official relief agencies' made efforts to get support on an 'All-India basis' and to find 'the best technical skill available in the country'.[204] The government's attempt at reconstruction with basic labour appeared less skilled in comparison with the relief organisations' focus on technical expertise. The press helped in making prominent the presence of Congress leaders in the worst-affected areas known. Muzaffarpur, which had turned into a 'place of pilgrimage' for 'great men', mentioned Nehru, Santosh Kumar Basu, Mayor of Calcutta, and Rajendra Prasad among the first to visit, only to be followed by the Viceroy, the Governor of Bihar and Orissa and M. K. Gandhi.[205] The accounts emphasised the presence of a 'national' spirit in the work of relief organisations, which was portrayed as being faster and more able than the government's response. The importance of the BCRC's contribution in the relief work was strengthened by the wide acclaim it received in the nationalist friendly press for its relief programmes, hailed as more generous and successful than the government's efforts.

Despite clearly favouring the BCRC and a variety of relief societies, the nationalist press was careful while delivering criticism of the government's operations at a local level. The press in Bihar was in the local government's yearly report of the political situation for 1934 described as having 'displayed a distinctly helpful attitude and refrained from the bitter and immoderate criticism which generally characterises their remarks on every activity of the local Government'.[206] The local government administration in Bihar acknowledged leading members of the BCRC for upholding a cordial relation. The change in the attitude of *The Searchlight* and the other 'more extremist papers' was ascribed by the government to 'the improvement in political feeling which was manifest during the relief operations'. In the case of *The Searchlight*, it remained a 'bitter critic' of the central government throughout the year, though the withdrawal of civil disobedience had diminished the use of 'violent language'.[207] While the government appeared content with a relatively cooperative ambience in the relief work locally, Congress members in other parts of the country were accused of using the nation-wide press to launch verbal 'attacks' against the government's lack of engagement in the relief work.[208] In February, the government deputed a publicity officer to Bihar whose primary responsibility was to secure more space for approving articles of the local government in the press. The articles were based on 'old material' and material obtained from persons whom the officer had met with in Bihar. He used the signatures 'An Earthquake Sufferer' and a 'Visitor' in the newspaper articles he published.[209] It was not considered propaganda against the Congress but an attempt 'to create a more favourable and accurate impression outside Bihar of what this Government really has done and is doing'.[210] Lauding the government's relief effort served to counter reports featured in the 'advanced nationalist newspapers' in Calcutta and Bombay, while the local press remained comparatively cooperative in reporting the government's work mainly through communiqués.[211]

Corruption and Aid as 'Political Capital'

A major concern of the government was the committee's large fund collection of 3 million rupees out of which half was still undistributed by the end of 1935. In the second general meeting held by the BCRC in early August 1934, the committee claimed to have spent 2.2 million rupees out of the 2.7 million rupees collected by then, leaving a balance of 500,000 rupees.[212] According to the government's calculations, however, the BCRC had at the end of 1934 a balance of about 1.4 million rupees.[213] In the early months of the aftermath, the government feared embezzlement of funds for private use or for political work, the latter a concern that grew with the large balance left unspent by the end of the year. Suspicions were almost exclusively directed towards distribution and the local organisation of relief while the management, mainly Prasad, remained in good faith regarding his intentions among the government officials in Bihar.

The central government feared that money collected by the BCRC would 'stick' and instead of being used for relief, it would be used for political ends;[214] it feared that Congressmen engaged in 'filling their own pockets', either for their personal gain or perhaps for the Congress, which would be more worrisome.[215] The government suspected first of all the BCRC's co-opted workers and so-called unorganised volunteer helpers from across India to have come for the 'very large sum of money' collected by the BCRC. Among these 'undesirables', the members of the Hindustan Seva Dal were prominent. The centre of activities was first Patna, but by the end of the first week of February, Muzaffarpur had become a hub for relief workers.[216] Police reports claimed Bihar to be 'flooded with questionable characters since the earthquake (…) some with a revolutionary taint (…)'.[217] In Madhubani district, the BCRC distrusted its local workers and a vigilance committee of mostly pleaders in Muzaffarpur accused it of discriminating 'in favour of their own servants and sympathisers',[218] and 'extensive corruption', particularly in Champaran, was observed by the local government.[219] Suspicions of corruption surfaced regularly regarding the relief workers' distribution locally as well as regarding a more widespread systematic use of aid as a form of bribe.

Brett, throughout 1934, remained assured that Prasad showed little interest in using the inflow of INC members and financial resources against the government.[220] He dismissed the Home Department's concerns with the charges of corruption against BCRC and disagreed with the *Indian Nation*, described as the mouthpiece of Darbhanga Raj, which claimed that the BCRC workers used relief money to buy votes,[221] presumably referring to the elections to the Central Legislative Assembly in 1934. The local colonial government administration, in general, had a positive image of Prasad's leadership and showed concern that he would increasingly dedicate his time to politics, as he was expected to become President of the INC in October 1934 and thereby have a diminishing influence on the committee. The government feared his absence further escalated the misuse of funds driven by political ambitions and corruption.[222] In the elections for the constituencies to the Legislative Assembly, the INC made a clean sweep of the non-reserved seats,[223] and it had been 'freely suggested' according to the local government that the BCRC fund came in useful.[224] The Congress was perceived to have revived itself with the help of relief funds; from having been under embargo just a few months earlier, with no funds to spend, it had emerged as the only political party that could be counted on in the province.[225]

After the government report *India in 1933–34* caused a public outcry early in 1936,[226] with its insinuations of corruption or mismanagement by the BCRC,[227] Brett revisited his experience during 1934. According to Brett, the BCRC was regarded as incapable of distributing considerable sums in house grants without being 'abused', because it lacked organisation and was at a risk of corruption at the local level. The level of cooperation between the Congress and government officials varied; in Champaran and Muzaffarpur, some of the leading members were described as 'extremely helpful' in cooperating with district officers, while BCRC workers in other areas obstructed the government's work.[228] Brett unofficially confirmed that Rajendra Prasad and M. K. Gandhi had themselves been concerned with the waste of money.[229]

Some substance to the suspicions of corruption may have been there since in the same month, early in June 1934, M. K. Gandhi sent a letter to J. C. Kumarappa regarding the management of funds, sharply criticising the Managing Committee and Prasad for giving 'blank cheques to officers in charge' and for the neglect of the committee's work.[230] The problems with alleged corruption in distribution were addressed by Gandhi who recognised 'the absolute control and discretion vested in the officers in charge at the districts' as the 'weak point' of the BCRC.[231] Such suspicions were supported by an intercepted letter from Kumarappa who confirmed the misuse of funds by workers of the BCRC and unofficially called for the complete reorganisation of the committee's work.[232] The first audit of BCRC accounts by end of August 1934 did not directly address accusations of embezzlement, though the last point of the auditor urged for the adjustment of 'debit balances of long standing' in 'some of the personal accounts, which are said to be for expenses', perhaps hinting at misuse of funds. To this point, Prasad could only confirm that the Managing Committee was 'quite alive', and had already taken steps to call in the advances.[233]

However, as Brett's retrospective account of the alleged corruption also discloses, the local government had in September 1934 pressurised the BCRC's management to allocate further sums to middle-class relief. According to Brett, Rajendra Prasad discussed plans for the BCRC to distribute its remaining funds as house-building grants in cooperation with the government, a plan that eventually did not materialise since it was turned down by 'the more extremist elements' in BCRC, or in other words, a number of unidentified persons who opposed the committee's cooperation with the government in terms of sharing funds.[234] The pressure to steer more funds towards middle-class relief did, however, also come from the districts and BCRC's own workers. Preceding the proposal, the district workers of the BCRC demanded more house-building grants in its second general meeting in August 1934.[235] They claimed to have insufficient funds for middle-class relief, describing it as 'very inadequate' and mentioning that 'at least' four times the amount was needed.[236] At this point, the government saw a need for as large funds as possible for the reconstruction of houses while the BCRC's diversion of funds towards flood relief was viewed as a means of 'getting more money to spend on vague forms of so-called "relief"'.[237] The need for additional funds to middle-class relief, expressed by both the BCRC and the local government, resulted in an attempt by the latter to make Prasad hand over the committee's relief fund for middle-class relief to the local government to cooperate with it in its distribution. Prasad provided a plan for such cooperation in distributing grants but the local government did not find it 'workable'[238] and Brett instead proposed three schemes by which one million rupees from the BCRC would be distributed by the government through the collectors, none of them acceptable to the committee.[239] All three schemes were designed to use the funds for grants to persons who had insufficient security to raise a house loan, or who, in addition to a loan, needed an extra grant, as these were the needs for relief according to the local government at that time.[240]

The BCRC emerged as an opportunity for INC, not only for political action but also for material gain and possibly broadened popular support in the province through the distribution of relief. Relief work was not only the display of good governance in practice, but also a distribution of help, or aid as a 'gift' that entitled the giver to initiate a reciprocal relation to the aid-takers.

Conclusion: From the Local to the National

Relief work after the Bihar earthquake offered a space for political organisations as well as associations to fill a void in the provision of relief. For the INC, Rajendra Prasad and other politically active persons in Bihar, relief carried out through the BCRC became a way of showing a political ability to take on responsibilities that the state may be expected to carry out. In the formation of the BCRC, the contemporary political climate and Bihar being an important seat for the INC shaped its success. While the committee claimed to be a separate organisation 'free from Congress politics', it, to a large extent, relied on contributions and manpower from the INC and at the same time, gained further popular legitimacy by coordinating the work and fund collections of other relief societies. The language of nationalism in the images of publications collecting funds on behalf of the BCRC and in the rhetoric of Congress leaders ('Towards National Relief' in this chapter) strengthened the idea that the disaster was a 'national' concern taken care of by the BCRC. The nationalist imagery and participation by organisations from across India served to project an image of the BCRC, and thereby the INC, as the legitimate provider of relief for the nation.

The committee's legitimacy rested upon local and national support: by combining local and national resources it managed to collect information, manpower and funds that created an aid apparatus running parallel to the government's relief programme. While Congress offices in the provinces functioned as a foundation for collecting funds, the local and national links of the committee were strengthened by the participation of cooperating relief associations that upheld offices in localities of the earthquake area and secured funds from the cities of their origin, for instance, the Marwari relief organisations. Though relief funds sometimes appeared to represent communities, such as in the case of the Marwari Relief Society, the cooperation with the BCRC showed their wider scope. At the same time, community identity made the Marwari Relief Society cooperate with other Marwari societies in Bihar, and local networks facilitated the BCRC's work and scope. Such a concerted effort in relief work among Marwaris and between the relief societies and the BCRC seems largely to have built upon existing networks.

While the government controlled relief work by setting priorities in relief and by legislation, the agency and organisational skills of Congress workers and cooperating relief organisations were integral to the committee. The conceptualisation of the committee should be understood in relation to the government's response and regulations circumscribing aid; both the government and the networks of civil society, running parallel to or separate from the Congress, patterned the committee's activities. In this way, the committee's organisation of relief reflected a state formation 'from below' in the sense that political opposition, civil society organisations and, not to forget, the victims of the earthquake were central to its existence.[241] Early on, however, the representatives of peasant interests were to a great extent marginalised in the process as Swami Sahajanand's concern to demand relief for the poorer agricultural classes was considered to border on political agitation. Instead, representatives of the BCRC and collaborating relief societies had closer ties to the interests of the urban middle classes and the affluent landholding classes of the zamindars. The BCRC's success was to a large extent based on its ability to capitalise on social networks, especially the trust established among communities by local organisations, which efficiently made its scope wide and localised. This ability of the committee to address earthquake relief by social capital rather than technical or financial resources represented a form of community resilience that helped to create a coordinated response.[242] Although there is little that indicates that the committee and cooperating organisations represented the interests of the poor or marginal groups,[243] the local roots of some of the cooperating partners may have provided platforms to consider local needs. At the same time, the participation of the numerous small and large organisations and associations, local as well as from cities such as Bombay and Calcutta, served to create an identity of the committee as representing the nation. It, to a large degree, justified its existence with the need to coordinate the relief efforts to prevent an overlap of the activities of the numerous organisations involved. Such an explanation of the committee's formation primarily served to justify its purpose while it continued to encourage leaders and organisations to join in the relief work, further expanding its organisational branches. While the committee's administrative infrastructure and scope expanded beyond that of the co-opted organisations, its work was partly conceptualised based on their organisational skills. With their established ability to provide help by carrying out tasks such as collecting funds, mobilising volunteers and relief materials in previous instances of floods, famine or social relief, the committee's core function was to coordinate and invite more relief organisations to take part. Such proven organisational abilities, sociological research on disaster argues, are important for the organisation not only in carrying out its tasks, but also for its public image as it gains credibility by performance.[244] The establishment of a larger relief fund, as compared to numerous small ones headed by individual organisations, held significance as a political 'tool' in the hands of civil society. In the next chapter, I will discuss the colonial government's collection of relief funds and how it aimed to appropriate subscriptions from the public.

Notes

1. Charles Cohen and Eric D. Werker, 'The Political Economy of "Natural" Disasters', *Journal of Conflict Resolution* 52, no. 6 (2008): 795–819, 795.
2. Richard Stuart Olson, 'Towards a Politics of Disaster: Losses, Values, Agendas, and Blame', *International Journal of Mass Emergencies and Disasters* 18, no. 2 (August, 2000): 265–87, 266.
3. Russell R. Dynes, 'Interorganizational Relations in Communities under Stress', in *Disasters: Theory and Research*, ed. E. L. Quarantelli, 49–64 (London: Sage Publications, 1978), 60–61.
4. Famine relief as part of the nation-building project in Andrea Janku, 'From Natural to National Disaster: The Chinese Famine of 1928–1930', in *Historical Disasters in Context: Science, Religion, and Politics*, ed. Andrea Janku, Gerrit J. Schenk and Franz Mauelshagen, 227–60 (New York: Routledge, 2012). For a similar discussion, see Kathryn Jean Edgerton-Tarpley, 'From "Nourish the People" to "Sacrifice for the Nation": Changing Responses to Disaster in Late Imperial and Modern China', *The Journal of Asian Studies* 73, no. 2 (May 2014): 447–69. For Indian famine relief, see

Georgina Brewis, "'Fill Full the Mouth of Famine": Voluntary Action in Famine Relief in India 1896–1901', *Modern Asian Studies* 44, no. 4 (2010): 887–918. The links between volunterism, association and nationalism on an everyday basis and times of crisis are discussed in Watt, *Serving the Nation*.

5. Watt, *Serving the Nation*, 173–76. Seva, or service, as a concept has changed and keeps changing depending on the sociopolitical context, R. Srivatsan, 'Concept of "Seva" and "Sevak" in the Freedom Movement', *Economic and Political Weekly* 41, no. 5 (Feb. 4–10, 2006): 427–38.

6. Kuracina, *The State and Governance in India*, 4.

7. Ibid., 25.

8. Ibid., 21, 25–26.

9. Dang, 'The Congress and the Politics of Relief: 1920–1940', 110.

10. Ibid., 108.

11. Borland, 'Capitalising on Catastrophe', 875.

12. Mark Pelling and Kathleen Dill, 'Disaster Politics: Tipping Points for Change in the Adaptation of Sociopolitical Regimes', *Progress in Human Geography* 34, no. 1 (2010): 21–37, 34.

13. Thomas Birkland, 'Natural Disasters as Focusing Events: Policy Communities and Political Response', *International Journal of Mass Emergencies and Disasters* 14, no. 2 (1996): 221–43. Thomas Birkland, *Lessons of Disaster: Policy Change after Catastrophic Events* (Georgetown University Press, 2006). Also see Butler, 'Focusing Events in the Early Twentieth Century'.

14. Prasad had been sentenced to 15 months of 'rigorous' imprisonment in January 1933. 'Fortnightly Report for the First Half of January', B&O Local Government's Reports, 1934, IOR/L/P.J/12/59.

15. Prasad, *Autobiography*, 351. Prasad was released on the evening of 17 January 1934. 'Babu Rajendra Prasad Released', *Behar Herald*, 20 January 1934.

16. 'Release of Political Prisoners' (Comments section), *The Behar Herald*, 24 January 1934. 'Medical Grounds; Why Babu Rajendra Has Been Released', *ABP*, 18 January 1934. Prasad, *Autobiography*, 349–50.

17. 'Political Prisoners Released; In View of the Earthquake Disaster', *The Leader* (Allahabad), 22 January 1934.

18. The Bihar Central Relief Committee, *Report for the Period Ending 30th June 1934 as Adopted by the Managing Committee*, vol. I, Patna: s.d. [probably issued July or later in 1934], 51; henceforth referred to as BCRC, *Report for the Period Ending 30th June 1934*. Mathura Prasad and Satyanarain Sinha from Hazaribagh Jail joined the relief work. Prasad, *Autobiography*, 355.

19. Prasad, *Autobiography*, 350–51.

20. 'Fortnightly Report', B&O Local Government's Reports.

21. 'Bihar Relief Work: A Warning' (editorial), *ABP*, 1 February 1934.

22. Prasad was involved in flood relief for Bihar as a student in Calcutta in 1914, and organised relief in the district of Chapra in 1921. Prasad, *Autobiography*, 144–45.

23. See chs. 7 and 8 in Jacques Pouchepadass, *Champaran and Gandhi: Planters, Peasants and Gandhian Politics* (French Studies in South Asian Culture and Society) (New Delhi: Oxford University Press, 1999), 167–229. Gandhi had in the years between the Champaran movement and the earthquake in 1934 risen to being the Congress's major leader and driving force behind the Civil Disobedience campaign launched in 1930. Brown, *Gandhi: Prisoner of Hope*, 214–15; Sarkar, *Modern India*, 183.

24. Pouchepadass, *Champaran and Gandhi*, 190–91, cf. chs. 7 and 8.

25. Dharanidhar, J. B. Kripalani and Anugraha Narayan Sinha. BCRC, *Devastated Bihar*, 60–61 and Appendix A, 'Members and Office Bearers of the Bihar Central Relief Committee' in ibid.; Pouchepadass, *Champaran and Gandhi*, 168–69; Sarkar, *Modern India*, 183.

26. G. McDonald, 'Unity on Trial: Congress in Bihar, 1929–39', in *Congress and the Raj: Facets of the Indian Struggle 1917–47*, ed. Donald A. Low, 289–314 (New Delhi: Oxford University Press, 2004 [1977]), 295–96; Ghosh, *The Civil Disobedience Movement*.

27. McDonald, 'Unity on Trial', 297. Henningham, *Peasant Movements in Colonial India*, 134.

28. Ghosh, *The Civil Disobedience Movement*, 58, 257–58.

29. Dietmar Rothermund, *An Economic History of India: From Pre-Colonial Times to 1991* (New York; London: Routledge 1993 [1988]), 104.

30. Stuart Cary Welch and Diane M. Nelson, 'William G. Archer (1907–1979)', *Archives of Asian Art* 33 (1980): 109–11; William G. Archer and Mildred Archer, *India Served and Observed* (London: BACSA, 1994).

31. W. G. Archer, 'The Bihar Earthquake', [s.l.] February 1934, Mss Eur F236/1, Papers of William G. Archer and Mildred Archer.

32. Prasad, *Autobiography*, 355.

33. 'Behar's Hour of Need; Organise Relief; Babu Rajendra's Appeal', *ABP*, 19 January 1934. 'Babu Rajendra's Statement', *The Leader* (Allahabad) 19 January 1934.

34. The committee members were Rajendra Prasad (President), Baldeva Sahay and Syed Mohammed Hafeez (Secretaries), R. C. Pandit (Treasurer). BCRC, *Devastated Bihar*, 27.

35. 'Copy of letter dated the 22nd January 1934, from Babu Rajendra Prasad, Patna, to the Chief Sec. to the Govt of B&O', NAI HP 34/1/1934. The letter and reply by

Chief Secretary P. C. Tallents enclosed in Appendix C in BCRC, *Devastated Bihar*, 63–64.

36. Prasad to Chief Sec., in letter dated 22 January 1934, see ibid.

37. BCRC, *Devastated Bihar*, 27.

38. 'Copy of letter dated the 23rd January 1934 from the Chief Sec. to the Government of B&O, to Babu Rajendra Prasad, Patna', NAI HP 34/1/1934.

39. Dang, 'The Congress and the Politics of Relief', 48.

40. Dang, 'Colonial Ideology', 305–06; Dang, 'The Congress and the Politics of Relief', 3, 25–26.

41. Dang, 'The Congress and the Politics of Relief: 1920–1940', 19–23, 30–31.

42. Ibid., 2–3.

43. Confidential D.O. No. S.6624/33-Poll, M. G. Hallett, Home Dept., to W. B. Brett, Chief Sec. to the Govt of B&O, Shimla, 29 September 1933, BSA PS KW 178/1933.

44. Confidential D.O. 3502, W. B. Brett to M. G. Hallett, Ranchi, 4 October 1933, BSA PS KW 178/1933.

45. Dang, 'The Congress and the Politics of Relief', 98–100. Dang, 'Colonial Ideology', 313.

46. Rajendra Prasad, quoted from Rajendra Prasad Papers, Roll no. 8 (NMML) and NAI Home Dept 34/4-(3)/1935, in Dang, 'Colonial Ideology', 287, 289.

47. Dang, 'The Congress and the Politics of Relief', 109.

48. M. [G.] Hallett, 6 June 1935, HP NAI 34/4-(4)/1935, cited in Dang, 'The Congress and the Politics of Relief', 106.

49. As Prasad emphasised in his autobiography, 'we would be always willing to *cooperate with the government. There was no question of competing with the government*, I assured them. My friends approved of my stand.' There was 'no room for conflict' (353) and 'the atmosphere had completely changed after the earthquake' (Prasad, *Autobiography*, 363).

50. Police report of the BCRC meeting in Sinha Hall, Patna, 18 March 1934. Enclosed with D.O. No. 1080-C, to M. G. Hallett, Patna, 22 March 1934. File: 'Proceedings of the Meeting of the Bihar Central Relief Committee on an All-India Basis', BSA PS 33 VII /1934.

51. BCRC, *Report for the Period Ending 30th June 1934*, 24.

52. See foreword by Jawaharlal Nehru in Saksena, *Devastated Bihar: Through Jawaharlal's Lenses*.

53. '1–6th March 1934', Bombay to Home Dept, File: 'Fortnightly Reports on the Political Situation in India for the Month of February 1934', NAI H. Pol. 18/2/1934. Nehru was sentenced based on three speeches held in Calcutta after the earthquake (Nehru, *An Autobiography*, 483).

54. Jawaharlal Nehru, 'The Humiliation of India', *The Nation* 138, no. 358 (April 1934): 410–11.

55. Memo. 'Confidential: Position in Bihar' by A. A. L. Parson, 8 February 1934. in 'Financial Assistance to the Govt of B&O in connection with the Earthquake', NAI Finance Dept, Budget Branch, File 3 (2), Budget, Serial nos. 1–52/1934.

56. 'Fortnightly Report for the Second Half of January', B&O Local Government's Reports, 1934, IOR/L/P.J/12/59.

57. 'Fortnightly Report for the First Half of February', B&O Local Government's Reports, 1934, IOR/L/P.J/12/59.

58. 'Appeal', *ABP*, 20 January 1934.

59. 'Letter to Agatha Harrison, 1 February 1934' (from a Photostat: G. N. 1477), *Collected Works of Mahatma Gandhi (CWMG)* 57: 76–78.

60. 'Manual labour' had been adopted in 1934 by the Congress as a qualification for membership of Congress committees. Gyanendra Pandey, *The Ascendency of Congress in Uttar Pradesh: Class Community and Nation in Northern India, 1920–1940* (London: Anthem Press, 2002), 27, 56.

61. McDonald, 'Unity on Trial', 297. Dietmar Rothermund, *India in the Great Depression: 1929–1939* (New Delhi: Manohar, 1992).

62. The situation was perhaps also further aggravated by the increase in population; the 1931 Census noted a 10 per cent increase in population since the 1921 Census. With a largely rural population, it was the agrarian sector of the economy which most felt the impact of the transition and increased pressure on the land. McDonald, 'Unity on Trial', 297–98.

63. Sarkar, *Modern India*, 257–58.

64. 'Weekly Earthquake Report for the Week Ending 3 March 1934' (Muzaffarpur), and 'Week Ending 17 March 1934' (Darbhanga), by DIG to McDowell, Inspector General, CID, BSA PS 33 III/1934.

65. 'Weekly Earthquake Report for the Week Ending 3 March 1934' (Muzaffarpur), in ibid.

66. 'Weekly Earthquake Report for the Week Ending 23 February 1934' (Darbhanga), in ibid.

67. Confidential, J. E. Scott to all District Officers (Tirhut), Tirhut Division, Muzaffarpur, 13 February 1934, BSA PS 33 VI/1934.

68. 'Press Telegram', from Abidali Jafferbhai and G. Vishwanath, Behar [Bihar] Central Relief Committe [sic] Muzaffarpur, to *Bombay Chronicle*, Bombay, Muzaffarpur, 12 February 1934, BSA PS 33 VI/1934.

69. J. E. Scott to P. C. Tallents, Muzaffarpur, 14 February 1934, Patna, BSA PS 33 VI/1934.

70. 'Weekly Earthquake Report for the Week Ending 3 March 1934' (Muzaffarpur), by DIG to McDowell, Inspector General, CID, BSA PS 33 III/1934.

71. Swami Sahajanand Saraswati (1889–1950), see introduction to *Sahajanand on Agricultural Labour and the Rural Poor*, ed. Walter Hauser, xxiii (New Delhi: Manohar Publishers and Distributors, 2005 [1994]).

72. 'Weekly Earthquake Report for the Week Ending 3 March 1934' (Muzaffarpur) and 'Weekly Earthquake Report for the Week Ending 10 March 1934' (Darbhanga), by DIG to McDowell, Inspector General, CID, BSA PS 33 III/1934. However, in Champaran the District Magistrate, reporting on the progress of earthquake relief, mentioned, 'there were no signs of a no rent campaign'. 'Progress Report for the Week Ending 1st March, 1934', enclosed in D.O. 2935/VIII-E-7, S. L. Marwood, Champaran District Office, to J. E. Scott (Muzaffarpur), Motihari, 2 March 1934, BSA RE 13/1934.

73. Copy of police report from the meeting of BCRC, 18 March 1934, 5, attached with D.O. 1018, 22 March 1934, BSA PS 33 VII/1934.

74. Walter Hauser, 'The Indian National Congress and Land Policy in the Twentieth Century', *Indian Economic and Social History Review* 1, no. 1 (1964): 57–65, 61–63.

75. 'The Bihar Provincial Kisan Sabha and the Congress' in Walter Hauser, *The Provincial Kisan Sabha 1929–1942: A Study of an Indian Peasant Movement*, ch. 4 ([PhD dissertation, University of Chicago, 1960] New York: Routledge, 2019), 142–65. Swami Shahajanand Saraswati, *Mera Jivan Sangharsh* (Hindi, Autobiography) (Patna: Sitaram Ashram, Bihta, 1985 [1950]).

76. Swami Sahajanand Saraswati, 'Terrible Plight of the Kisans [peasants], Relentless Machine of Landlordism, Remission of Rent the Only Remedy', 18 March 1934; 'Relief to Agriculturalists' (editorial) *The Searchlight* 18 March 1934; Extract from the DIG's report, 21 March 1934, 'II – Agitation, C. Kisan Sabha and Agrarian Agitation', BSA PS 33 VI/1934.

77. In Tirumal Mundargi, 'Congress and Zamindars: Collaboration and Consultation in Bihar, 1915–36', *Economic and Political Weekly* 25, no. 22 (June 2, 1990): 1217–22, 1220.

78. J. E. Scott to P. C. Tallents, Muzaffarpur, 14 February 1934. File: 'Question of Remission of Land Revenue and Other Tariffs and Grant of Loans in Earthquake Areas. Letters of Earthquake Intercepted. Activities of Swami Sahajanand', BSA PS 33 VI/1934.

79. '*Ullekhaniya phand*' (Hindi, 'Significant Fund') *Yugantara* (Hindi newspaper), 12 February 1934. Another name of the fund was 'The People's Fund'. C. F. Andrews in *The Friend*, 2 November 1934: 1019–20.

80. Massard-Guilbaud, 'Introduction: The Urban Catastrophe', 25.

81. Nehru, *An Autobiography*, 489.

82. BCRC, *Devastated Bihar*, 62; The Ramakrishna Mission, *The Eighth General Report of the Ramakrishna Mission (1934–35)* (Kolkata, Belur Math: Ramakrishna Mission, s.d.).

83. Marwari Relief Society, *Report of the Behar Earthquake Relief Work*. A 'Marwari' is technically speaking a person hailing from the district Marwar in Rajasthan, more specifically it is used for the trader and merchant castes hailing from that area or neighbouring areas in Rajasthan and Gujarat. Thomas A. Timberg, *Marwaris: From Traders to Industrialists* (New Delhi: Vikas Publishing House Pvt Ltd, 1978), 9–11. In eastern India, Marwaris had generally retained a separate identity while at the same time reaching a certain level of integration with local society. Claude Markovits, *Merchants, Traders, Entrepreneurs: Indian Business in the Colonial Era* (Ranikhet: Permanent Black, 2008), 204, 207.

84. D.O. G1221, District Officer R. E. Swanzy, Muzaffarpur, 2 March 1934; Enclosed 'Note by the Honorary Sec. of the Central Relief Committee', BSA RE 13/1934.

85. BCRC, *Report for the Period Ending 30th June 1934*, 34.

86. 'Province Day by Day; News from the Mofussil; Earthquake Relief; Muzaffarpur', *Indian Nation*, 25 March 1934.

87. The Vivekanda Mission's relief organisation appeared to have been acting detached from the Ramakrishna Mission's relief party which was financed separately. 'Vivekananda Mission', *ABP*, 20 January 1934. Vivekananda, the disciple of Ramakrishna, set up organised famine relief in India in 1897. See ch. 4, '"First of All Comes the Gift of Food": Swami Vivekananda's Response to the Problem of Famine', in Gwilym Beckerlegge, *The Ramakrishna Mission: The Making of a Modern Hindu Movement* (New Delhi: Oxford University Press, 2000), 79–95. On major institutional reforms within the association in 1926, see G. Beckerlegge, *Swami Vivekananda's Legacy of Service: A Study of the Ramakrishna Math and Mission* (New Delhi: Oxford University Press, 2006), 28, 35.

88. 'Appeal' by Swami Satyananda, President, The Hindu Mission, Calcutta. *ABP*, 20 January 1934.

89. Bengal Hindu Sabha, Bhutnath Mukerjea, Secretary, Relief Committee, Bengal Provincial Hindu Sabha, Calcutta. *ABP*, 21 January 1934; Raj Ballav Para Bayam Samity in Calcutta held a meeting to 'devise ways and means to contribute money etc.' *ABP*, 23 January 1934.

90. The Ramakrishna Mission Association first became involved in famine relief in Murshidabad in 1897 and flood relief in Bhagalpur and Midnapore in 1899, and after 1926 it shifted towards maintenance of permanent, institutional provisions of

service such as outdoor dispensaries. Beckerlegge, *Swami Vivekananda's Legacy of Service*, 29–31, 35.

91. Lance Brennan, 'Government Famine Relief in Bengal, 1943', *Journal of Asian Studies* 47, no. 3 (1988): 542–67. Anindya Sen, *Ramakrishna Mission and Community Service in Eastern India, 1922–1962: A Qualitative and Quantitative Analysis* (Kolkata: Readers Service, 2005), 205–07; Rakesh Batabyal, *Communalism in Bengal: From Famine to Noakhali, 1943–47* (New Delhi: Sage Publications, 2005), 101–64. The Marwari Relief Society, Calcutta, conducted cyclone relief in Contai in 1942 and opened relief centres in 1943–44. Paul Robert Greenough, *Prosperity and Misery in Modern Bengal: The Famine of 1943–1944* (New York: Oxford University Press, 1982), 131.

92. Telegram from B. N. W. Railways to Patna, 27 January 1934; note by J. W. Sinha, 23 January 1934, BSA RE 33 I/1934.

93. Govt of B&O to Colonel J. A. S. Philips, Director of Public Health, with note to the Chief Sec. added by Col. Philips, 27 January 1934, BSA RE 33 I/1934.

94. Prasad, *Autobiography*, 356.

95. Watt, *Serving the Nation*, 102. About the Seva Samiti movements, see Carey Watt, '"No Showy Muscles": The Boy Scouts and the Global Dimensions of Physical Culture and Bodily Health in Britain and Colonial India', in *Scouting Frontiers: Youth and the Scout Movement's First Century*, ed. Nelson R. Block and Tammy M. Proctor, 121–42 (Newcastle: Cambridge Scholars Publishing, 2009), 135.

96. 'Pt. Malaviya's Appeal', *ABP*, 19 January 1934.

97. Watt, *Serving the Nation*, 109.

98. Sankat Tran Samiti, 'Aid-to-the-Afflicted Committee', also referred to as *Bangiya Sankat Tran Samity* 'Bengal Calamity Relief Committee', or 'Bengal Relief Committee'. Prafulla Chandra Ray, *Life and Experiences of a Bengali Chemist* (Calcutta: Chuckervertty, Chatterjee & Co., Ltd, 1932), 249. P. C. Ray (1861–1944), renowned chemist and founder of Bengal Chemicals Factory, was elected as its president. Ibid., 239. Bipan Chandra, Mridula Mukherjee, Aditya Mukherjee, Sucheta Mahajan and K. N. Panikkar, *India's Struggle for Independence 1857–1947* (New Delhi: Penguin Books, 1988), 131.

99. Subhas Chandra Bose (1897–1945), Congress leader from Bengal of a left radical stance. Sugata Bose, *His Majesty's Opponent: Subhas Chandra Bose and India's Struggle against Empire* (New Delhi: Penguin Books, 2011).

100. Bidyut Chakrabarti, *Subhas Chandra Bose and Middle Class Radicalism, 1928–40* (London: I. B. Tauris & Co. Ltd., 1990), 122–23; Ray, *Life and Experiences of a Bengali Chemist*, 238, 249.

101. 'Bangiya Sankat-Tran', *ABP*, 20 January 1934; 'Relief to Sufferers', *ABP*, 21 January 1934. The society collected about 20,000 rupees. *'Funds'* [Hindi], *Yugantara*, 12 February 1934.

102. BCRC, *Devastated Bihar*, 5, cf. 4–5.

103. Ritu Birla, *Stages of Capital: Law, Culture, and Market Governance in Late Colonial India* (Durham: Duke University Press, 2009), 78–79.

104. BCRC, *Devastated Bihar*, 27, 61–62.

105. 'Appendix D', a statement from BCRC meeting 3 February 1934 in BCRC, *Devastated Bihar*, 64. BCRC, *Report for the Period Ending 30th June 1934*, 4. BCRC, *Report for the Period Ending 30th June 1934*, 4.

106. C. F. Andrews, *The Indian Earthquake* (London: George Allen and Unwin Ltd., 1935), 5, 57.

107. 'Country-wide Response to Babu Rajendra's Appeal', *ABP*, 27 January 1934.

108. BCRC, *Devastated Bihar*, 29.

109. 'Reconstruction Work in Bihar. Governor Visits "Quake Area"', *Times of India* (1861–current), 24 February 1934.

110. 'Appendix D' in BCRC, *Devastated Bihar*, 64.

111. BCRC, *Report for the Period Ending 30th June 1934*, 4.

112. Nehru, *An Autobiography*, 488.

113. BCRC, *Devastated Bihar*, 32–34.

114. BCRC, *Report for the Period Ending 30th June 1934*, 34.

115. Timberg, *Marwaris: From Traders to Industrialists*, 72–75. See also Birla, *Stages of Capital*, 213. According to Hardgrove's ethno-historic study of Marwaris in Calcutta, the Marwari Relief Society was born as the successor to the *Marwari Sahayak Samiti* in 1914, after the government had curbed its increasingly political work of trying to stop forced labour migration. See sub-chapter 'Indentured Emigration and Beginnings of Marwari Political Action', in Anne Hardgrove, *Community and Public Culture: The Marwaris in Calcutta* (New Delhi: Oxford University Press, 2004).

116. About the longevity of 'earthquake-born' organisations after the 1995 Kobe earthquake, see Rajib Shaw and Katsuihciro Goda, 'From Disaster to Sustainable Civil Society: The Kobe Experience', *Disasters* 28, no. 1 (2004): 16–40, 17.

117. The mobilisation of a relief team from Calcutta to north Bihar started 40 hours after the earthquake, as soon as the news had reached. Marwari Relief Society, *Report of the Behar Earthquake Relief Work*, 4–5. It was the first relief society from outside the province to arrive in Muzaffarpur on 19 January. BCRC, *Report for the Period Ending 30th June 1934*, 24.

118. BCRC, *Devastated Bihar*, 20.

119. Cornelia Sorabji, 'Earthquake in Bihar', *Nineteenth Century and After* 115 (May, 1934): 535–47, 542.

120. Marwari Relief Society, *Report of the Behar Earthquake Relief Work*, 7.

121. 'Sahāyatā mil bhī rahī hai' (Assistance Is Also Being Provided), *Yugantara*, 12 February 1934.

122. Markovits, *Merchants, Traders, Entrepreneurs*, 203. Claude Markovits, *Indian Business and Nationalist Politics 1931–1939: The Indigenous Capitalist Class and the Rise of the Congress Party* (London: Cambridge University Press, 1985). See sub-chapter 'Gandhi's Shadows: Marwari Reformists and the Nationalist Movement', Hardgrove, *Community and Public Culture*.

123. BCRC, *Devastated Bihar*, 61; BCRC, *Report for the Period Ending 30th June 1934*, 82, 88. For Jamnalal Bajaj and the INC, see Birla, *Stages of Capital*, 214.

124. Sriram Bajpai, alternatively spelt 'Shri Ram' or 'Sri Ram' Bajpai, started the Balchar-Mandal (Boy Scouts Association) in Shahjahanpur in 1913. Watt, *Serving the Nation*, 114–16, n127. Contributions were collected by H. N. Kunzru, Vice-President, Servants of India Society, Allahabad. 'Servindia ['Servants of India'] Earthquake Relief', Editor, P. Kodanda Rao, Poona, *Servants of India* 27, no. 9 (1 March 1934), 97; Marwari Relief Society, *Report of the Behar Earthquake Relief Work*, 12, 52–53, 56. BCRC, *Report for the Period Ending 30th June 1934*, 86.

125. 'Appendix: The Congress's Relationship with Other Organizations' in Dang, 'The Congress and the Politics of Relief', 119–25.

126. Gopal Krishna Gokhale, founder of the Servants of India Society, in a speech 1910, cited in Watt, *Serving the Nation*, 171, 107–08.

127. Birla, *Stages of Capital*, 73–75. See also Claude Markovits' dense ch. 8, 'Merchant Circulation in South Asia (Eighteenth to Twentieth Centuries)' about Marwaris and their role as traders across northern and east India. Markovits, *Merchants, Traders, Entrepreneurs*.

128. Agrawal Jatiya Kosh in Bombay, and private persons such as Ramnath Goenka in Madras, contributed and collaborated. Marwari Relief Society, *Report of the Behar Earthquake Relief Work*, 14, 16, 64. Another Marwari association did not, however, feature as a cooperation partner—Marwari Seva Samiti, Kushtia, or Kushtia Marwari Seva Samiti, Calcutta. D.O. G1221, Swanzy, Muzaffarpur, 2 March 1934, BSA RE 13/1934.

129. 'Appeal by the Marwari Relief Society', Jwalaprasad Kanoria, Marwari Relief Society, *ABP*, 20 January 1934.

130. Marwari Relief Society, *Report of the Behar Earthquake Relief Work*, image with text, 32–33. Announcement by the Secretary of the Marwari Relief Society of 7-1, Jugomohan Mullick Lane, Calcutta, in *ABP*, 23 January 1934.

131. 'Marwari Relief Society: Acknowledgement of Contributors', *ABP*, 27 January 1934.

132. Yang, *Bazaar India*, 254–56; Markovits, *Merchants, Traders, Entrepreneurs*, 203.

133. Marwaris and the jute trade in Bengal, see Timberg, *Marwaris: From Traders to Industrialists*, 57–58, 190–93.

134. Data in round numbers. The Oswal Earthquake Relief Fund donated 2,000 rupees and collected 5,668 rupees. The jute dealer the Calcutta Hessian Exchange contributed 1,000 rupees. Marwari Relief Society, *Report of the Behar Earthquake Relief Work*, 14, 16, 64.

135. In Muzaffarpur, it cooperated with the 'Muzaffarpur Navyuvak Samity' and the Seva Samiti society. Marwari Relief Society, *Report of the Behar Earthquake Relief Work*, 12. 'Relief Work at Muzaffarpur; Marwari Relief Society's Splendid Activities', *The Behar Herald*, 31 January 1934.

136. For instance, to the district office in Muzaffarpur the society reported distribution of relief to 498 families and clearing 1,386 houses of debris. D.O. G1221, R. E. Swanzy, Muzaffarpur, 2 March 1934, with enclosed 'Note by the Honorary Sec. of the Central Relief Committee', BSA RE 13/1934,

137. Bihar, Marwari Relief Society, *Report of the Behar Earthquake Relief Work*, 49.

138. Brett, *A Report on the Bihar Earthquake*, 8.

139. Out of the 55,000 rupees collected, the Marwari Relief Society spent 20,000 rupees and the Marwari Panchayat Seva Samiti spent 35,000 rupees. Marwari Relief Society, *Report of the Behar Earthquake Relief Work*, 5, 7, 61.

140. An 'authentic account', a hagiographic biography commissioned by the 'Trustees of the Adamjee Foundation', focuses on the foundation of the Memon Relief Society and Sir Adamji Haji Dawood's (30 June 1880–27 January 1948) philanthropic work. Daleara Jamasji-Hirjikaka and Yasmin Quereshi, *The Merchant-Knight, Adamjee Haji Dawood* (Karachi: Adamjee Foundation, 2008 [2004]), 42–53.

141. Markovits, *Merchant, Traders, Entrepreneurs*.

142. *Pucca* (lit. 'solid', anglicised from Hindi *pakkā*): houses generally referred to buildings made of bricks or stone with mortar, or constructed of concrete. Village houses made of mud and grass are referred to as *kuccha* houses (lit. 'raw' as in unfired brick unslaked lime, anglicised from Hindi *kaccā*).

143. Jamasji-Hirjikaka and Quereshi, *The Merchant-Knight*, 43–46.

144. Officer-in-charge (unreadable sign.) Calcutta Memon Relief Society, to Relief Commissioner (Patna), Muzaffarpur, 31 March 1934; 920 R.D., W. B. Brett, to the Sec. of Calcutta Memon Relief Society (Muzaffarpur). Patna, 1 April 1934, File: 'Request from the Menon Relief Society for Allotment of Funds from the Viceroy's Earthquake Fund', BSA RE 132/1934.

145. BCRC, *Report for the Period Ending 30th June 1934*, vi.

146. E. L. Quarantelli, 'Emergent Behaviors and Groups in the Crisis Time Period of Disasters', Preliminary Paper No. 206 (Newark, DE: Disaster Research Center, University of Delaware, 1994), 5–6.

147. Jamasji-Hirjikaka and Quereshi, *The Merchant-Knight*, 48–50; see also Markovits, *Merchant, Traders, Entrepreneurs*, 115, 148.

148. In Monghyr, Vivekananda Mission lauded the work of the 'Monghyr Muslim camp', see 'Monghyr. Muslim Relief Committee', *The Nation*, 15 April 1934.

149. Jamasji-Hirjikaka and Quereshi, *The Merchant-Knight*, 45.

150. By 10 March 1934, six orphans had been sent from north Bihar to the Calcutta Muslim Orphanage, Syed Salley Lane, and three orphans were in the society's care in Muzaffarpur. 'The Calcutta Memon Relief Society's Report of Relief until 15th of March, 1934', 5, Muzaffarpur, 18 March 1934, BSA RE 132/1934.

151. W. B. Brett, 'Weekly Bulletin' (for the week ending 9 March 1934), Reconstruction Office, Patna, to M. G. Hallett, Sec. to the GOI, Home Dept., NAI 34/1B/1934.

152. From data provided until October 1934, in 'Allotment from the Bihar and Orissa VERF', File: 'Grants Sanctioned from the V.E.R.F. (Muzaffarpur District)', BSA RE 43 IV/1934.

153. 'Note by the Honorary Sec. of the Central Relief Committee', enclosed with D.O. G1221, Swanzy Muzaffarpur, 2 March 1934, BSA RE 13/1934.

154. 'The Calcutta Memon Relief Society's Report of Relief until 15th of March, 1934', Muzaffarpur, 18 March 1934, BSA RE 132/1934.

155. Only 23 rupees had been given earmarked for 'Hindu Relief' until 31 March. From April to the end of June, the BCRC received 37 rupees earmarked for 'Hindu Widows and Children' etc. BCRC, *Devastated Bihar*, 119, 129.

156. 'Weekly Earthquake Report for the Week Ending 17 March 1934' (Muzaffarpur), DIG to McDowell, Inspector General, CID, BSA PS 33 III/1934; 'Weekly Earthquake Report for the Week Ending 10 March 1934' (Muzaffarpur), DIG to McDowell, Inspector General, CID.

157. 'Bihar Relief Work: A Warning' (editorial), *ABP*, 1 February 1934.

158. 'Note by the Honorary Sec. of the Central Relief Committee', with D.O. G1221, Swanzy Muzaffarpur, 2 March 1934, BSA RE 13/1934.

159. 'Amounts of Gratuity and Loan Given to Musalmans and Non-Musalmans in the District of Muzaffarpur out of the Funds at the Disposal of the Local Government in Connection with the Earthquake', 13 February 1935, BOLCP 32, no. 4, 259.

160. Moore (ed.), *Record of the Great Indian Earthquake*.

161. *Bhūkamp pīḍitoṃ kī karuna-kahāniyāṃ: Bihār ke bhūkamp-pīḍitoṃ kī param āścarya-janak aur karunāpūrṇ saccī ātma-kathāeṃ* (Hindi).

162. Sriram Sharma, 'Bhūkamp-Pīḍit Bihār' (Hindi, 'Earthquake-Plagued Bihar'), *Vishāl Bhārat, bhāg* 13, *ank* 2 (February, 1934): 129–40. Established in 1928, the magazine was a miscellany known for publishing images and contemporary Hindi literature, but also as an organ of nationalism and progressivism. Bhatnagar, *The Rise and Growth of Hindi Journalism (1826–1945)*, 360, 368.

163. Saksena, *Devastated Bihar*.

164. Brelvi and Horniman, *Earthquake Number*, 3.

165. See preface in BCRC, *Devastated Bihar*.

166. According to an advertisement in *ABP*, 22 March 1934.

167. By co-editor B. G. Horniman, 'The Living Grave of Bihar' in Brelvi and Horniman, *Earthquake Number: Which Hand Is Yours*, 4. In the same issue, see also Nagindas T. Master, 'The Rich and the High Have Not Responded Adequately' (no page number) and M. C. Joshi 'Bombay Must Make Still Greater Effort: Mayor Suggests New Ways of Raising Funds for Relief', 6; N. S. Hardikar, 'Thousands Are Hungry and Homeless: Bombay Must Continue Good Work of Relieving Bihar's Suffering' (no page number).

168. BCRC, *Devastated Bihar*, 62. Prashant Kidambi, *The Making of an Indian Metropolis: Colonial Governance and Public Culture in Bombay, 1890–1920* (Historical Urban Studies. Aldershot, U.K.: Ashgate Publishing, 2007), 198–99.

169. Jonathan Benthall, *Disasters, Relief and the Media* (Wantage, UK: Sean Kingston Publishing, 2010 [1993]), 176–77.

170. See sub-chapter 'The Gendering of National Space-Time: Envisioning Bharat Mata', in Manu Goswami, *Producing India: From Colonial Economy to National Space* (Chicago; London: The University of Chicago Press, 2004), 199–206.

171. Sumathi Ramaswamy notes the hymn '*Bande Mātaram*, (Homage to [the] Mother)', first published in 1875, soon became 'the rallying cry for an emergent patriotic cult of Bharat Mata' from the beginning of the twentieth century in the context of the Swadeshi movement. Sumathi Ramaswamy, 'The Goddess and the Nation: Subterfuges of Antiquity, the Cunning of Modernity', in *The Blackwell Companion to Hinduism*, ed. Gavin Flood, 551–68 (Oxford: Blackwell Publishing, 2003), 551, 558.

172. Ibid., 556–57.

173. Goswami, *Producing India*, 200–03, cf. ch. 6.

174. For a discussion on feminisation of natural environments, see Liz Bondi and Joyce Davidson, 'Troubling the Place of Gender', in *Handbook of Cultural Geography*, ed. Kay Anderson, Mona Domosh, Steve Pile and Nigel Thrift, 325–44 (London: SAGE, 2003), 329–30.

175. Sarojini Naidu, 'Our Supreme Duty', in Brelvi and Horniman, *Earthquake Number*, 3.

176. Ibid.

177. Willingdon to Hoare, 13 March 1934, 484, in Papers of Sir Samuel Hoare, Sec. of State for India 1931–35. Mss Eur E240/7.

178. 'Weekly Earthquake Report for the Week Ending 3 March 1934' (Muzaffarpur), by DIG to A. E. J. C. McDowell, Inspector General of Police, CID, March 1934. File: 'Weekly Reports on Earthquake by D.I.G., C.I.D.' BSA PS 33 III/1934.

179. Archer, 'The Bihar Earthquake', Mss Eur F236/1.

180. Immediate relief was removing debris, rescuing of buried persons, disposing of dead bodies, providing food and clothing, cattle relief, providing shelter to sufferers, and organising water supplies that had suffered considerably due to the choking of wells by sand and the dislocation of the waterworks in towns. Proceedings of the Second General Meeting of the Bihar Central Relief Committee, ii, in BCRC, *Report for the Period Ending 30th June 1934*, 3. 'Report of the Distressed Cattle Relief Committee. Summary of Cattle Relief in Bihar', in ibid., 104–06.

181. 'Central Relief Committee's Activity', *Behar Herald*, 11 April 1934. BCRC, *Report for the Period Ending 30th June 1934*, 3.

182. BCRC, *Devastated Bihar*, 18. '300 money orders a day' and 'hundreds of parcels', according to Prasad, *Autobiography*, 354.

183. Accounts for 1 April–30 June were not audited by August 1934, hence the sums mentioned in the report are preliminary. BCRC, *Report for the Period Ending 30th June 1934*, 92, 136.

184. BCRC, *Devastated Bihar*, 27–30. Abdul Aziz, Jayaprakash Narayan and Anugrah Narain Sinha also held central roles. Prasad, *Autobiography*, 355.

185. Rupees 2.8 million, donations worth 300,000 rupees. Solomon, *Bihar and Orissa in 1934–35*, 11.

186. *RPER*, 1.

187. 'Appeal for Help', *The Times*, 22 February 1934, IOR/20/165 (L/I/2/57); BCRC, *Report for the Period Ending 30th June 1934*, 5. Andrews, *The Indian Earthquake*; 'Copy of cable to C. F. Andrews from Babu Rajendra Prasad', Patna, 6 February 1934. Mss Eur D1113/5, folio 8–9.

188. 'The Indian Earthquakes', appeal by V. K. Krishna Menon (Chairman), Indian Earthquake Relief Fund, 165 Strand, W.C.2. *New Statesman* and *Nation*, 3 March 1934.

189. International donations increased in the period April to June, probably a delayed increase due to being remitted from abroad. Foreign donations were: 42,615 rupees, 20 January–31 March 1934, and 76,889 rupees, 1 April–30 June 1934. See Table 3.1.

190. 'First Half of February 1934' (U.P.), 'First Half of February 1934' (North Western Provinces), '16–21 February 1934' (Bombay) to Home Dept., NAI H. Pol. 18/1/1934.

191. All-India Congress Committee: Papers on the Desh Sevika Sangh and the Gandhi Seva Sena: AICC file G-8/1929, parts 1 and 2. 'Appendix 10, Funds Collected by the Desh Sevika Sangh and the Gandhi Seva Sena on Behalf of the Congress and Other National Relief Committees'. Undated, last date mentioned is December 1934. Mss Eur F 341/167.

192. 'Table 3: Major International Trading Networks Operating from India', in Markovits, *Merchants, Traders, Entrepreneurs*, 5–6, 237. On Gandhi's 'hold' over the business community in Ahmedabad, see Judith M. Brown, *Gandhi's Rise to Power: Indian Politics 1915–1922* (New York: Cambridge University Press, 1972), 120.

193. Claude Markovits, 'What about the Merchants? A Mercantile Perspective on the Middle Class of Colonial India', in *The Middle Class in Colonial India*, Oxford in India Readings: Themes in Indian History, ed. Sanjay Joshi, 118–31 (New Delhi: Oxford University Press, 2010), 128.

194. '314. Speech at Bihar Central Relief Committee Meeting, Patna, 3 August 1934', *The Searchlight*, 5 August 1934, CWMG 64, 267–69.

195. Nehru, *An Autobiography*, 489.

196. Meeting on Friday 3 August 1934, Wheeler Senate Hall, Patna, in 'Proceedings of the Second General Meeting of the Bihar Central Relief Committee', in BCRC, *Report for the Period Ending 30th June 1934*, ii.

197. The recorded number of wells and tanks damaged or destroyed in Muzaffarpur, Darbhanga, Champaran, Saran and Monghyr were 65,938; data for north Bhagalpur and Purnea missing. 'Approximate figures of damage done by earthquake on 15th January, 1934, in the Districts of North Bihar and Monghyr', ibid., iii, 93.

198. Prasad, *Autobiography*, 358.

199. BCRC, *Report for the Period Ending 30th June 1934*, 84.

200. 'Appendix: Proceedings of the Second General Meeting of the Committee' in BCRC, *Report for the Period Ending 30th June 1934*, vi. BCRC, *Devastated Bihar*, 54.

201. 'Appendix: Proceedings of the Second General Meeting of the Committee' in BCRC, *Report for the Period Ending 30th June 1934*, vi–vii.

202. BCRC began to work 'formally' in Muzaffarpur on 21 January 1934. BCRC, *Report up to 30 June 1934*, 24.

203. D.O. G1221, District Officer R. E. Swanzy, Muzaffarpur, 2 March 1934; Enclosed 'Note by the Honorary Sec. of the Central Relief Committee', BSA RE 13/1934. The inception of the BCRC at Muzaffarpur was mentioned in 'Relief in Muzaffarpur: Central Committee Formed', *ABP*, 28 January 1934.

204. 'Ways and Means of Relief', *ABP*, 23 January 1934.

205. 'Province Day by Day; News from the Mofussil; Earthquake Relief; Muzaffarpur', *Indian Nation*, 25 March 1934.

206. 'Notes' by PS, 15, BSA PS 1/1935.

207. Ibid., 4, 15.

208. Telegrams sent from Muzaffarpur by two 'leading Congress-men' from Bombay, Moulvi Abi Ali Zaffery and Babu G. Vishwanath, and the local Babu Ramdayalu Singh to the *Bombay Chronicle* had been intercepted. J. E. Scott to P. C. Tallents, Muzaffarpur, 14 February 1934, BSA PS 33 VI/1934.

209. S. N. A. Jafri, deputed to the Govt of B&O for about two months, was normally Deputy Director, Information Dept D.O. 2090, personal letter with a copy of a 'rough note' prepared for Jafri. I. M. Stephens, DPI, to M. G. Hallett, New Delhi, 31 March 1934; 'Personal', S. N. A. Jafri to I. M. Stephens, Director of Public Information (DPI), Home Dept (New Delhi), Patna, 3 April 1934, enclosed with D.O. 2235, I. M. Stephens to M. G. Hallett, 6 April 1934; D.O. 1799 R.D., W. B. Brett to M. G. Hallett, Patna, 24 May 1934. HP NAI 34/1/1934.

210. D.O. 132, P. C. Tallents to Commissioners of Patna, Tirhut, Bhagalpur; District officers of Patna, Muzaffarpur, Champaran and Saran, Monghyr, Bhagalpur and Purnea, Patna, 28 March 1934, File: 'Deputation of the Deputy Director of Information (GOI), Mr Jafri, to Work as Press or Publicity Officer in Connection with the Earthquake', BSA PS 33 VIII/1934.

211. D.O. 2090, I. M. Stephens to M. G. Hallett, New Delhi, 31 March 1934, NAI HP 34/1/1934.

212. Collector's House, Bankipore, Patna to P. C. Tallents, 11 August 1934, D.O. No. C.1248, BSA PS 33(B)/1934.

213. Accounts until end of September, audited and published in end of December 1934, in a note by publicity officer Samuel Solomon, enclosed with Brett, NAI H. Pol. 22/21/1936.

214. Memo, M. G. Hallett, New Delhi, 3 February 1934. NAI HP 34/1/1934.

215. 'Weekly Earthquake Report for the Week Ending 3 March 1934' (Muzaffarpur) DIG to McDowell, Inspector General, CID, BSA PS 33 III/1934.

216. 'Fortnightly Report for the First Half of February', B&O Local Govt Reports, 1934, IOR/L/P.J/12/59.

217. 'Extract from Movements of Political Suspects from the Superintendent of Police, Muzaffarpur', Muzaffarpur, 20 June 1934, File: 'Report of Arrival and Departure of Important Congress Relief Workers of Other Provinces', BSA PS 33 IV/1934.

218. 'Weekly Earthquake Report for the Week Ending 17 March 1934' (Muzaffarpur), DIG to McDowell, Inspector General, CID, in ibid.

219. 'First Half of December 1934', B&O Local Government's Reports, IOR/L/P.J/12/59.

220. 'Weekly Earthquake Report for the Week Ending 3 March 1934' (Muzaffarpur), DIG to McDowell, Inspector General, CID, BSA PS 33 III/1934. Also in 'Fortnightly Report for the First Half of September 1934', B&O Local Government's Reports, 1934, IOR/L/P.J/12/59.

221. Confidential D.O. 2047 R. D., Brett to Hallett, Patna, 13 June 1934. NAI HP 34/1/1934.

222. 'Fortnightly Report for the First Half of September 1934', B&O Local Government's Reports, 1934, IOR/L/P.J/12/59.

223. 'Second-Half of November 1934', B&O Local Government's Reports, IOR/L/P.J/12/59. The polling ended 14 November 1934, 'First Half of November 1934', in ibid.

224. 'Second-Half of November 1934', B&O Local Government's Reports, IOR/L/P.J/12/59.

225. Ibid. 'Second Half of September, 1934', B&O Local Government's Reports, IOR/L/P.J/12/59.

226. Bureau of Public Information, GoI, *India in 1933–34* (New Delhi: Manager of Publications, 1935). The *Bombay Sentinel* labelled the report 'stale and malicious', 'a scurrilous pamphlet' in its accusations of corruption against INC, Jawaharlal Nehru and M. K. Gandhi. 'Stale and malicious', *Bombay Sentinel*, 22 January 1936 (newspaper clipping enclosed with file). Confidential D.O. 4430-C, Brett to Hallett, Patna 23 December 1935; 'Confidential', D.O. Brett to Hallett, Patna, 1 February 1936, NAI H. Pol. 22/21/1936.

227. D.O. from DPI to Home Dept, 1 February 1936, NAI H. Pol. 22/21/1936. GOI (ed.) *India in 1934–35* (Simla/Delhi: The Manager of Publications, GOI Press, 1937). The information came from Solomon's *Bihar and Orissa in 1934–35*, publicity officer of the Government of B&O.

228. 'Confidential', Brett to Hallett, Patna, 1 February 1936; notes with BCRC accounts until 30 September 1934, NAI H. Pol. 22/21/1936.

229. Confidential Letter, W. B. Brett to Hallett, Patna, 1 February 1936. BSA, Foreign-Pol., 22/21 1936 and H. Pol. 3/EQ 1935.

230. '76. Letter to J. C. Kumarappa', (8 June 1934) from Photostat: G. N. 10105. *CWMG*, vol. 64, p. 53.

231. Ibid.

232. Intercepted letter from J. C. Kumarappa to A. N. Singh (Sadaqat Ashram, Patna) 28 June 1935, cited in Dang, 'Colonial Ideology', 283.

233. Contrary to a resolution passed by the Managing Committee, that all articles for relief should have been purchased from 'local traders as far as practicable', Rangoon rice had been purchased from Calcutta, partly through dealers and agents from outside the province. Bihar Central Relief Committee: [Internal] Auditor's Report. B. Gupta & Co., Incorporated Accountants, Registered Accountants, Bankipore, 31 August 1934. Appendix in BCRC, *Report for the Period Ending 30th June 1934*.

234. 'Confidential', Brett to Hallett, Patna, 1 February 1936, File: 'Bihar Earthquake', NAI H. Pol. 22/21/1936.

235. Patna Collector's House, Bankipore, to P. C. Tallents, 11 August 1934. D.O. No. C.1248, BSA PS 33(B)/1934.

236. BCRC, *Report for the Period Ending 30th June 1934*, vii, 48.

237. 'Fortnightly Report for the First Half of September 1934', B&O Local Government's Reports, 1934, IOR/L/P.J/12/59.

238. Letter 12668, Rajendra Prasad to W. B. Brett, 7 September 1934; D.O. 3656 R. D., Brett to Prasad, Ranchi 17 September 1934; letter 12956, 18 September 1934, NAI H. Pol. 22/21/1936.

239. See previous note, 'Brett to Prasad, 17 September 1934'.

240. 'Confidential', Brett to Hallett, Patna, 1 February 1936, NAI H. Pol. 22/21/1936.

241. In understanding state building 'from below', social conflicts, popular protests and resistance provide one perspective for understanding the process of state building that cannot be regarded as without consequences, even if they were often suppressed. See André Holenstein, 'Introduction: Empowering Interactions: Looking at Statebuilding from Below', in *Empowering Interactions: Political Cultures and the Emergence of the State in Europe 1300–1900*, ed. Wim Blockmans, André Holenstein and Jon Mathieu, 1–31 (Farnham (UK): Ashgate, 2009), 12–14.

242. For a discussion on the role of communities and social capital in building resilience, see 328–29 in Greg Bankoff, 'Dangers to Going It Alone: Social Capital in the Origins of Community Resilience in the Philippines', *Continuity and Change 22*, no. 2 (2007): 327–35.

243. Bankoff finds community resilience built upon social capital to be an asset benefiting 'the most vulnerable', the poor and marginal. Ibid., 328.

244. Dynes, 'Interorganizational Relations', 51.

4

Colonial Relations in Aid

In faith and hope the world will disagree,
But all mankind's concern is charity.[1]

Introduction: The Viceroy's Earthquake Relief Fund and 'State-Aided' Charity

After having discussed the ways in which political agendas and local, regional and national networks shaped the organisation of relief funds and relief associations, this chapter examines the colonial government's position towards charitable relief and the role of so-called colonial, imperial or state-aided relief funds as a part of the government's relief and rehabilitation response. The colonial government indirectly or directly controlled these funds created with the purpose of providing the main source of funding for charitable relief and managed to collect a large amount by relying on networks surrounding elites, the government administration and emerging institutionalised international cooperation.

The colonial government played a central role in collecting public charity by facilitating collections of the Viceroy's Earthquake Relief Fund (VERF), founded by the Viceroy and Governor-General of India after the earthquake.[2] It is interesting to note in this context that although Lady Countess of Willingdon first intended to organise a relief fund, it was her husband the Viceroy who became the fund's front figure.[3] At the time of the earthquake the couple was about to leave Calcutta from Howrah station and Lady Willingdon remarked 'Well, we left Madras in a cyclone, and now we leave Calcutta during an earthquake.'[4] In India the VERF received public subscriptions and collections organised by government officials. The Governor of Bihar and Orissa, James Sifton, soon followed the Viceroy's announcement with a speech and appeal for the fund, and diverted the provincial relief fund under him to the VERF.[5] In London a Mansion House fund collected international subscriptions on behalf of the VERF. In addition to using established networks in order to collect charity, the government managed to pool funds into the VERF from two other large fund collections—a collection made in an international appeal by the International Relief Union and by the Mayor of Calcutta, Santosh Kumar Basu, for the Mayor's Earthquake Relief Fund, commonly referred to as the Mayor of Calcutta's fund.

While the VERF was closely associated with the government and framed as the earthquake fund for 'India', two supporting urban funds, a Mansion House fund, also known as the Lord Mayor of London's fund or the Indian Earthquake Fund or Lord Mayor's/Mayor fund,[6] and the Mayor of Calcutta's fund[7] acted as intermediaries based on their relationship with urban audiences. The Mayor of Calcutta started a fund collection in his city by asking for the support of 'the leading citizens representing the landed aristocracy, trade and commerce, and leaders of public opinion'.[8] Among the Europeans in Calcutta, a group of Germans and William Arthur Moore, editor of *The Statesman*, had been the first to contribute to the Mayor's fund in an inaugural public meeting.[9] The director of the Reserve Bank of India for the Calcutta register, Sir Edward Benthall, expressed support with the claim that 'in all national disasters the Europeans had always stood with their fellow citizens and would always do'.[10] The Europeans held a noticeable presence in the meeting where they portrayed themselves as a community of benevolent givers. A group of 'Muslim merchants',[11] prominent citizens and industries of the city, for example, the Bengal Chamber of Commerce and members of the East India Jute Association, supported the fund or promised donations, as announced in the newspapers.[12] For all funds, public gifting was important to elicit gifting: it attracted subscriptions and positioned them in the spectre of relief. Perhaps this important feature of the funds was even more pronounced in the two 'Mayor funds' as gifting became embedded in a local context where the contributor's social act was on display. In the case of the two Mayor funds, public gifting served as a bond between the audience and the patron of the fund. The identity of the fund, based on the patron and his rhetoric, elicited gifting from the local audiences.

This chapter begins with a discussion on the role of the VERF and charitable relief within the financial plan for aid and reconstruction. Next follows a discussion on how patronage influenced methods for collecting subscriptions and the VERF's public image in comparison with other relief societies and funds. Building upon the inferences drawn, the next section argues that the government's cautious stance towards other large-scale fund collections, and in particular the BCRC's fund and international relief funds, was mainly based on its interest in the VERF as a source of charitable relief controlled by the government. Other fund collections were seen by the state as challenging its authority as the main source of charitable relief.

Governance of Public Aid

A fund headed by a viceroy was a known concept. Prior to 1934, the Viceroy had opened a relief fund after the Kangra earthquake in 1905[13] and again, after the Quetta earthquake in 1935, a fund under his patronage was founded.[14] Tirthankar Roy suggests that the history of 'state-aided' charity in the Indian subcontinent goes back to the time when the East India Company administration was socially close to prominent commercial classes of Calcutta, giving the example of relief organised by the Governor-General after a tidal wave in south-eastern Bengal in 1822.[15] Roy notes how a standard response of the state in emergencies during the nineteenth century was revenue remission and charity in the form of a subscribed fund, which he refers to as state-aided charity.[16] The management and structure of VERF in 1934 bear close resemblance to the two Indian Famine Charitable Relief Funds from 1897 and 1900 in terms of being 'mainly imperial', as Georgina Brewis calls the two famine funds.[17] The Viceroy presided over the inaugural meeting in 1900, the central committee in Calcutta received international funds collected by the Mayor of London, by other mayors around the country, and by governor-generals in the colonies.[18] These two famine funds collected substantial sums in India, Great Britain and from around the empire through fundraising, volunteering and cooperation between relief agencies. The fund of 1897 received 1.7 million pounds, 'the largest amount that ever had been collected anywhere' according to the Lord Mayor of London, and the fund of 1900 received more than 1 million pounds out of which 627,000 pounds were collected in Great Britain.[19] Contrary to the voluntary efforts in the committees and in the local management of the famine funds, as Brewis' article highlights, the government closely controlled the VERF of 1934 in terms of distribution and collections, even though it claimed the VERF to be a private fund.[20] Very similar to the Indian Famine Charitable Relief Funds, it was managed by committees at central, regional and local levels, with the Viceroy and the fund's central committee in Delhi deciding 'major questions of policy'[21] and the Governor of Bihar and Orissa directing expenditure in consultation with a local committee of high-ranking officials and 'non-officials' of prominent positions.[22] The committees, however, held peripheral roles as advisers as the decision-making power for how the fund was to be distributed rested with the Viceroy and the Governor. While the government of Bihar and Orissa was excluded from taking decisions regarding allocations, its officers disbursed the fund as gratuitous relief at police stations or other official buildings,[23] in accordance with the promise that the fund would 'remain in the hands of officers of Government'.[24] In practice, the high government officials' influence over the fund and the local government's responsibility for distribution made it into a government fund. The fund was promoted by the government and distributed by government officials, yet it was described as one of the private relief funds by the government.

Out of 10 million rupees distributed by charitable funds in earthquake relief, the VERF collected 7 million rupees.[25] By the middle of March the VERF had received almost 3.2 million rupees.[26] Around the same time the Viceroy estimated that a total of 350,000 pounds, a collection of about 4.5 million rupees in his fund would be 'satisfactory' to cover the needs for charitable relief on behalf of the government.[27] According to the press, VERF's committee received 20,000 rupees every day by the end of April 1934.[28] The amount seems exaggerated, or the subscriptions declined gradually, as by the end of May 1934 the total collection was almost 3.7 million rupees[29] and in July 1934, the VERF had received slightly more than 5.4 million rupees.[30] The fund reached the sum of more than 6.1 million rupees by end of October 1934[31] and amounted to 7 million rupees when it closed in March 1935.[32] Almost 4.1 million rupees were contributions from the public to the VERF, an achievement close to the estimate of the needed 4.5 million rupees provided by the Viceroy.[33]

The VERF was from the beginning part of the government's plan for collecting charitable relief to cover the 'wide scope for private charity' as the Secretary of State phrased it.[34] While discussing the financial plan for reconstruction, Alan A. L. Parsons, Secretary to the Government of India, Finance Department, recommended public charity as a source of funds.[35] He advised to withhold the announcement of a contribution by the Government of India towards charitable relief until private charity had 'dried up':

> So far as grants are concerned, I think that these should be a charge on the funds raised by private subscription, but that if, as is probable, insufficient money is raised from private charity, the Government of India should consider making a direct grant to His Excellency's fund [the VERF]. It would not of course be desirable to make this grant or announce any intention of doing so until private charity has dried up.[36]

In effect, he recommended the government to first exhaust public charity as far as possible, before providing a government grant to the relief fund, which in turn would distribute it as charitable relief. His stance was supported by the Governor of Bihar and Orissa, who recommended the central government to withhold an announcement of making a complimentary grant 'to supplement' the relief funds since he feared that such news would adversely affect charitable subscriptions from the public to the VERF.[37] According to the political plan for financing relief and reconstruction, publicly subscribed funds would cover reconstruction of private property for 'the poorest classes' and 'if necessary' a grant by the central government would cover the remaining balance.[38] The dependence upon public charity for the reconstruction of private property instead of government grants was, however, challenged in a resolution in the Council of State, suggesting the Governor-General donate a million rupees specifically with regard to the large numbers of houses in need of reconstruction.[39] From the position of the government, it was important to encourage subscriptions and not to give the impression that the government would be willing to provide funds for charitable relief.

Once the initial hurry to arrange emergency relief had subsided and the scope of the disaster started to sink in, amounts needed for the different heads of disaster relief became a topic of speculation. Compounded, the financial expenditure required to rebuild to a semblance of normality was expected to be huge.[40] Government officials had provided widely disparate estimates, probably due to inclusion of different heads, ranging from 50 million rupees mentioned by the Secretary of State for India to 300 million rupees by the Governor of Bihar.[41] The unofficial 'very rough estimate' of 50 million rupees was often repeated as the amount of funds needed for relief and reconstruction, out of which 20 million were estimated for urban reconstruction, 10 million for relief in rural areas and 20 million for the reconstruction of Government and Local Board buildings.[42] The budget for reconstruction announced to the public by the end of February presented a proposed division of costs financed with loans and grants from the central and local governments and with charity collected from the public.[43] The central government would cover half the costs of reconstruction and extend a loan to the local government for its share of the cost. Local bodies managed by the District Boards, such as schools, dispensaries, hospitals and so-called aided schools, private institutions run with the support of grants, were regarded as unable to repay loans considering that they had little resources at hand and had lost their main source of income since many houses and roads had been ruined. Therefore the government allocated free grants to these institutions for 7.5 million rupees, to be taken from a fund created by the surplus of the central revenues. The total of this fund was 12.9 million rupees. The central and local government carried the cost of reconstruction for official buildings and infrastructure up to the estimated cost of 20 million rupees. At this stage, the VERF was promoted as a fund for charitable relief towards reconstruction of private property and to the poorer classes, for all those unable to take loans. While the government used the Provincial Famine Relief Fund to partially cover agricultural charitable relief, the budget for reconstruction counted on the VERF and other publicly subscribed relief funds for 'many of the poorest sufferers'.[44]

In spite of claims that the VERF was a private fund, the Government of India directly worked to secure the substantial contribution of 800,000 rupees from the Indian People's Famine Relief Trust to the fund.[45] The large amount and relatively fast transfer were indicative of how the government played a decisive role in boosting the VERF. The Indian People's Famine Trust had been created by the Maharaja of Jaipur in 1900 for charitable relief during famines and soon received substantial contributions by wealthy nobilities across the country as well as general public subscriptions.[46] Although the fund was private in the sense that it collected subscriptions from the public for charitable relief to private individuals, its board's operation depended on the Government of India, making its actual administration no different than state assistance, according to Kokila Dang.[47] Even though famine relief was the initial purpose of the trust, it provided grants after great calamities and not only famines. An important criterion for grants was the factual occurrence of disaster, for instance, in the 1906 Darbhanga famine the Government of India declined assistance to the Government of Bengal with the argument that the distress was managed by local efforts and neither perceived as 'general' nor widespread enough to qualify for a grant.[48] Dang notes how the fund served the Government of India's interests in the sense that it made government relief or grants into a supplement while the trust was used as the primary source for gratuitous relief.[49] The purpose of the VERF resembled the trust in terms of serving as a provider of gratuitous relief according to the Government of India's wishes. However, in 1934 the Government of India arranged a transfer of a grant from the trust to the VERF, although the local Government of Bihar and Orissa featured as the applicant. The initial application at the end of January 1934 requested a grant of 200,000 rupees 'for the special purpose of reconstruction of the houses of impoverished persons'.[50] Already within a week, a revised application stated the considerably higher sum of 800,000 rupees as 'most urgently' necessary.[51] According to the board of management of the trust, the local government would receive the amount, provided it would utilise the amount according to the 'general scheme' agreed on with the central government for repairing damages caused by the earthquake.[52] The local government was thereby relatively free to dictate how the grant would be used, and not necessarily 'for the special purpose of reconstruction of the houses of impoverished persons' as the initial application had stated.[53] According to a government communiqué in October 1934, the donation was earmarked for reconstruction of houses in rural areas,[54] but according to Brett's report, government officials distributed the fund as 'free grants' of 'a few rupees' while on tour in rural areas[55] which may have paid some consideration to the initial purpose to rebuild houses of 'impoverished persons'. The VERF received the grant from the trust according to its balance sheet,[56] even though the application and allocation of the grant were between the local government and the trust.[57] As the grant of 800,000 rupees to the VERF showed, the local and central governments' active involvement gave the VERF a good start. Perhaps the move was a strategy to avoid a prolonged wait for public subscriptions to trickle in, often an issue in the management of publicly subscribed relief funds as John Hutchinson points out in his article on international relief in the interwar period.[58] The prompt transfer of a large amount from the famine trust to the VERF within two weeks after the earthquake solved the uncertain wait for funds.

The VERF from the very beginning served as a convenient resource for the government until the allocation of grants and government funds had been cleared. The VERF balance sheet contains two large 'reimbursements' received from the central and local governments respectively for expenditure on the sugar cane harvest in north Bihar and costs for sand clearance of agricultural land.[59] These two heads were subsequently covered by the budget for relief and charged to revenue in due course of time. The VERF initially covered the full cost of sand removal with 355,000 rupees but would in the end only use 100,000 rupees[60] since the local government provided the amount from the Bihar and Orissa Provincial Famine Relief Fund by June 1934.[61] Both the central and the local governments' ability to rely on the fund for charitable relief, even if only temporarily, underlined that the fund served to support the relief operations by the government. Once reimbursed, the VERF spent the amount on other heads, though the sources omit how this was negotiated. Although the government claimed the fund to be private and support charitable relief for the poor—from the public to the public—it bore large expenses until it figured out how to source the unexpected expenses.

Publicity and Public Gifting

The VERF appealed for contributions from the Indian public, first of all from its most affluent layers, the British administration, as well as an international public mainly based in Great Britain. Industrialists, government officials and local rulers were of special importance in its appeals and subscription lists. In order to attract public attention, the government made considerable efforts by using publicity and propaganda. It was a premeditated strategy by the Home Department in New Delhi to portray the VERF as 'the really substantial fund for the relief of distress'.[62] Publicity work started with publications and articles based on facts provided in public speeches and appeals by high officials.[63] In connection with the inception of the fund, the government deployed its administration throughout India to ensure publicity and collect funds. The government administration was not new to the idea of encouraging fund collections; it had previous records of urging wealthier citizens to donate towards public projects of importance to the government.[64] The central government requested all local governments to give the appeal by the Governor of Bihar and Orissa[65] 'wide publicity', and to translate it into the vernaculars in order to raise funds from the public.[66] The government increased pressure on its local governments to collect funds by requesting active participation in the organisation of subscriptions and list names of donors in order to prompt donations. In Bombay, all government officers were requested to cooperate 'fully' with the public in raising funds and assist those who collected money for the VERF.[67] Published lists in the newspapers of donors did not only display contributors favourably, they also served to tell who had not contributed. The public display of gifting could have the function to both attract as well as coax givers.

The government's keen pursuit of amassing public charity resulted in collections by government officials towards the VERF from around India. In the district of Burdwan in Bengal, high-ranking officials engaged in setting up and collecting money for the Burdwan Relief Fund and subsequently announced that the whole collection would be given to the VERF.[68] When the Commissioner of Lucknow division closed the city's fund in support of the VERF, it had collected more than 50,000 rupees with the help of the administration[69] and in Aden, the Chief Commissioner despatched funds on behalf of the British settlement.[70] Personal sacrifice and individual gifting by offering a part of one's salary to the fund was another way to gain the approval of superiors among the government officials in Motihari: the deputy magistrates and veterinaries gave 2 to 5 per cent of their salaries for six months, while the magistrate gave a one-time amount of

250 rupees.[71] The Bihar and Orissa Police had collected 7,450 rupees, a sum that earned special attention according to the Relief Commissioner.[72] The VERF, with the use of government propaganda and under the direct patronage of high government officials, managed to secure subscriptions from the government administration, Indian local rulers, Europeans and industrialists.

Like individual contributions that were often announced in public, the current balances of the fund collections were published in the newspapers almost on a daily basis. As if contending over which fund could amass the largest amount, substantial contributions by important people and the current balances of funds were published side by side.[73] The VERF became known as a recipient of donations by government officials and nobilities, while the BCRC represented the common people. As Carl Heath, the British Quaker leader who later got involved in the reconstruction of villages in north Bihar wrote to his friend:

> Actually, in India there are two funds, the Viceroy's and a more popular one
> (…). The only real difference between them is that Maharajas, Nawabs and
> Nizams will naturally send their money to the Viceroy, whilst the rank and
> file are afraid, often, of contributing even to a Government fund.[74]

The sharp division between the 'more popular one', the BCRC fund as representing 'the people', and the VERF that held the support of 'the nobilities' was an exaggeration with some truth to it. Many local rulers had contributed to the VERF, yet both funds had the support of the elites. Odd articles in *The Statesman* described donations to the VERF as 'genuine cases of the poor helping the poor'.[75] Such well-composed stories of the fund as recipient of subscriptions from 'poor' persons, the aged, unemployed and 'villages schools in Bihar' giving 14 rupees appeared unlikely and may have been composed as part of a strategy to attract collections from common people as well. The VERF's close association with the government gave rise to suspicions regarding the fund's intended purpose. When disbursements of grants from the VERF began, an officer reported 'wild rumours' afloat concerning the fund being used for the reconstruction of government buildings, and recommended that the government publish details on the fund's disbursements.[76] The government subsequently published a communiqué to counter the allegation that the VERF was being used for repairing government buildings instead of housing for 'the poor'.[77]

The public display of gifting in the newspapers served as material for the *Amrita Bazar Patrika*'s editorial to criticise government officials' contributions as they were less than expected.[78] The publication of relatively modest amounts donated by the King and Queen of England and the lack of contributions by other officials to the VERF served as negative publicity in the hands of the nationalist press. Upon launching the VERF, *Amrita Bazar Patrika*'s editorial had applauded the Viceroy for starting a fund and hoped to see contributions from 'officials and non-officials and from our Rajas and Maharajas'.[79] Soon the newspaper criticised the amount given by the British monarchs and singled out the Secretary of State, Sir Samuel Hoare, for having made 'no personal donation yet', in contrast with the response after the Kanto earthquake in 1923 when the prime minister of Japan had made a private donation and allocated money from the state treasury, while the Viceroy and Lady Willingdon were commended for at least having started the VERF.[80]

The two 'Mayor funds' by the Mayor of Calcutta and the Lord Mayor of London followed similar patterns with foundational meetings where the business communities, prominent persons and wealthier sections of the two metropolises presented donations, fundraising from charity events and smaller amounts collected through subscription lists from the public. An important difference between the funds was, however, the colonial government's direct support in the organisation and publicity on behalf of the Lord Mayor fund.[81] The opening of a Mansion House fund in London, in direct support of the VERF, was motivated by the need for a large collection already a few days after the VERF had been launched. The Viceroy notified the Secretary of State of the situation being far more grave than first expected, quoting damages amounting to 'several' *crores* [one crore is 10,000,000]. The Mansion House fund in England, headed by the Mayor of London, presumably could increase international subscriptions substantially.[82] According to Hutchinson, the Mansion House fund was the British government's preferred means for collecting emergency relief funds from the public in the 1920s and 1930s.[83] The Mayor's funds served as a system of national as well as international fund collections in times of disaster. In 1861, the Mayor of London announced the first international appeal for Indian famine relief.[84] Similarly, the Titanic Relief Fund 1912–59 served to provide funds, especially for British victims, and offered long-term financial relief in support of survivors and relatives of the deceased,[85] while a number of relief funds from the Mansion House supported miners' families in Great Britain during the second half of the nineteenth century.[86] Besides aiding disaster victims within the British Empire, these type of funds collected substantial sums for disaster relief in foreign countries, including 6,600,000 gold francs given to Japan after the 1923 Kanto earthquake.[87]

The India Office was responsible for the organisation of publicity work in order to stimulate especially international contributions to the Lord Mayor Fund.[88] The India Office kept a close watch on the sums collected and the progress of the fund for weeks after the inaugural meeting.[89] The meeting at the Mansion House in London presided over by the Secretary of State for India and the High Commissioner for India[90] was anticipated as a popular event for the financial urban elite where the 'wealthy City people, including the bankers' would prefer to give to their Mayor's fund rather than to the VERF, partly because the meeting provided an opportunity to display their contributions.[91] The public display of gifting in the company of powerful patrons was an essential part of the fund's ability to attract contributions. At the same time contributions by, for instance, the Bank of England, and a string of affluent public figures such as the Lord Chancellor and Lord Archbishop of Canterbury also presented instances of public gifting available to a wider audience via lists published in newspapers.[92]

The fund continued collecting grants by appealing to churches, universities, schools, local authorities and various organisations and institutions throughout the country, in other words, all institutions expected to amass large funds with the help of their considerable organisational capacities and established networks.[93] The Mayors of Sheffield and Manchester pooled their fund collections into the VERF.[94] Overall, the fund followed a similar organisational pattern in collecting and managing contributions as did other funds such as the Mansion House fund and the Titanic Relief Fund, which also received funds from mayors across the country. [95] The Mayors and donors, often wealthy private individuals and corporations, were 'rewarded' with the amount and their name publicly announced in the newspapers.[96] Whether contributing with a smaller sum in a box outside the Mansion House or by a cheque marked 'Indian Earthquake Fund',[97] subscriptions from the public were performed in public where subscribers received recognition for the act (Image 4.1).

Contrary to the Mayor of London's fund, whose purpose was to solely support the VERF, the Mayor of Calcutta's fund was at first profiled as a supplement to and collaborator with not just the VERF but also a range of established organisations. However, it was restricted to be distributed by 'non-political organisations' engaged in 'purely social work' and 'commended by officials and non-officials alike'.[98] The Mayor of Calcutta, in spite of the fund's 'non-political' stance, later in January 1934 became a member of the All-India-Committee of BCRC, and was one of its fifty-four 'distinguished leaders and publicmen [sic] of India' among whom M. K. Gandhi was listed first.[99] This was hardly surprising as Mayor Basu himself was perceived as 'a staunch Congressman'.[100] The ambiguous political profiling of the Mayor's fund

Image 4.1 Lists of donations to Indian earthquake funds.

Source: *The Times* (London), 22 February 1934.

may, however, have been important considering the motley crew of subscribers. Douglas E. Haynes suggests that 'gift giving' and philanthropy in the colonial period can be seen as 'statements' by businessmen and commercial magnates in the absence of rare written statements regarding their political positions.[101] The political stance of prominent subscribers was not uniform, ranging from the nationalist newspaper *Amrita Bazar Patrika* to the director of the State Bank of India for the Calcutta register, the Bengal Chamber of Commerce and several established European corporations in the region.[102] Interpreting commitments towards the Mayor's funds as political statements may be doubtful since the fund at the outset held an ambiguous political position by being outspokenly apolitical, favouring the VERF and government relief, and a recipient of donations by Congress supporters. Its politically uncertain stance, at least officially, may have contributed to its popularity among those reluctant to take a political position in public.

Financial support to the BCRC from the Mayor of Calcutta's fund was fractional compared to the amounts provided to the government and the VERF in the reconstruction phase, and even compared to a number of relief organisations based in Calcutta.[103] The Ramakrishna Mission received an initial grant of 20,000 rupees from the Mayor's Fund, and another 30,000 rupees later, in April or May.[104] The fund financed immediate relief carried out by relief societies operating in the area, while funds given to the government and the VERF were earmarked for reconstruction.[105] According to Brett's report, the Mayor of Calcutta's fund was 'spent in consultation with Government and largely by Government officers'.[106] The Mayor's fund allotted sums for erection of temporary buildings constructed by the local government, sinking tube-wells and middle-class relief.[107] As the Mayor closed the fund at 475,000 rupees, the VERF received the remaining amount and spent it on temporary houses and huts.[108]

Collecting International Funds

In the light of a political plan for aid that encouraged public subscriptions for charitable relief, the government's rejection of an appeal for international relief by the International Relief Union (IRU) may at first glance appear contradictory as it encouraged international relief. According to Hutchinson, who has written two in-depth articles on the IRU,[109] the reliance on the Mansion House funds was partly the reason for Great Britain's reluctance towards international cooperation between governments in disaster relief,[110] a relatively novel endeavour that took root in the climate of international cooperation in the inter-war period.[111] Great Britain was one of the strongest opponents of the IRU mainly because of its institutionalisation of private charity.[112] The British foreign office showed contempt, ridiculed its idealism and made a point out of not joining a project 'proposed by the Italians'. From Great Britain's perspective, joining the IRU meant introducing 'action by the state' in times of disasters, which would lead to 'the end of action by the individual', according to the British delegate to the League of Nations.[113] Despite such scepticism towards institutionalised disaster relief, the British government had acceded to the IRU's convention in 1929, and the Indian Government ratified the convention in 1931.

The IRU, founded by the League of Nations members for the organisation of international government cooperation in disaster relief,[114] did not take part in relief work in Bihar 1934 'in accordance with the wishes of the Indian

Government', as explained by Camille Gorgé, member of the Board of Governors of the Swiss Red Cross and of the Executive Committee of the IRU, in 1938. The Bihar earthquake in 1934 and the Quetta earthquake in 1935 are cited by Gorgé as the two initial attempts to provide coordinated international disaster relief by the IRU; the first was deemed a failure and the latter was regarded as its first successful operation, although modest in scope.[115]

The rejection of the IRU's international appeal was partly motivated by its competition over funds with the Mayor's Mansion House fund. After the earthquake, the IRU contacted its cooperation partner, the League of Red Cross Societies in Paris, which offered 1,000 pounds to the Indian Red Cross for first-aid expenses,[116] as also acknowledged by the Viceroy on 23 January 1934.[117] The same day, the IRU launched an international appeal in telegrams to all 26 member states of the IRU. Barely had the telegrams been sent, when the IRU heard from the India Office that India did not wish for a public appeal for funds and the appeal was called off.[118] According to the Secretary of State and the Viceroy, they had never approved an international appeal. The Secretary of State was particularly disturbed by the international appeal of the IRU since he had just discussed a Mansion House fund aimed at attracting international contributions to the VERF. The IRU's international appeal had preceded the colonial government's launch of an international fund and posed a possible threat to the VERF's international subscription. An indignant Secretary of State demanded to know who had sent an international appeal without prior consultation. In view of the appeal for funds in Great Britain, he cautioned the Viceroy's office that an international appeal by the IRU 'might prove very embarrassing'.[119] The Viceroy's office conducted a small inquiry, which suggested that the League of Red Cross Societies in Paris was 'the origin of the rumour' for the international appeal,[120] perhaps executed after the Indian Red Cross Society had welcomed assistance.[121]

All the funds collected by the IRU were transferred to the Indian Red Cross and subsequently to the VERF. The union's initial donation of 1,000 pounds to the Indian Red Cross Society, as well as the subsequent Red Cross donations from the international appeal by the IRU, were transferred to the VERF,[122] although secondary literature claims the Red Cross to have benefited from the IRU's appeal. The yearly report by the Indian Red Cross Society mentioned the IRU's appeal to the 26 IRU member states on 23 January 1934 and the IRU's contribution of 1,000 pounds. Even though the IRU's appeal was limited and soon revoked, the initial round of telegrams to member states resulted in donations of substantial amounts which the Indian Red Cross forwarded to the VERF. As a result of the IRU's appeal, the Indian Red Cross received 74,980 rupees from national

Red Cross Societies. These sums were immediately deposited with the VERF.[123] A contribution of 26,450 rupees from the American Red Cross Society arrived within a week of the appeal.[124] The IRU's contribution did only receive evasive recognition—it was, as Hutchinson noted, not even mentioned in an article about the relief work in the *Bulletin of the League of Red Cross Societies* later in 1934.[125] Similarly, the Indian Red Cross Society credited the International Red Cross for taking action by appealing to the National Red Cross Societies for funds.[126]

With the transaction of funds from the Indian Red Cross to the VERF, the purpose of the appeal was lost. The IRU had appealed for emergency funds, while VERF, according to its audited accounts, spent the larger part of the collection on reconstruction of various kinds. In the end, the IRU received evasive official recognition for its role in collecting funds for the VERF, and the Secretary of State's push for international contributions to the Mansion House fund was unintentionally accomplished by the IRU's appeal.

Framing Disaster for Local Audiences

As the name of the VERF gave away, the fund appealed for contributions towards 'earthquake relief' under the patronage of the Viceroy.[127] Although 'India' evaded its name, the VERF appealed for contributions towards a general group of sufferers in the 'Indian earthquake'. The distance from the disaster and the 'distant suffering' of the earthquake victims were articulated in the delocalisation of the earthquake and the homogenisation of victims. Luc Boltanski's book *Distant Suffering: Morality, Media and Politics* shows how the framing of victims as local or distant play a role in evoking feelings or relation to victims.[128] As opposed to a local disaster, where the presence of victims is felt in order to invoke compassion or sympathy, victims of distant disasters are often framed as a general group of unfortunates. In the 'politics of pity' the distant sufferers cannot be questioned and the urgency of action prompts gifting.[129]

The cursory commitment among the public towards contributing to the VERF during the first two months of the aftermath was explained by the frontmen of the fund as the result of a lack of media attention. Already ten days after the Viceroy's initial appeal, the Director of Public Information reviewed subscriptions as 'none too good', in particular contributions from Indian local rulers had been disappointing.[130] Consequently, a propaganda strategy was devised with the help of the Department of Public Information in order to stimulate contributions. While an initial appeal had stressed the difficulties in giving 'proper appreciation of the catastrophe', the Director of Public Information asked to have it referred to as one of the 'biggest and most extensive earthquakes in history' with the aim to increase public charity.[131] Conveniently, the Publicity Department's efforts to revive interest in the earthquake preceded the launch of the Mayor's fund in London and appeared as a deliberate move to prompt donations from among the British public. The Director of Public Information had contacted the General Manager of Reuters and the API in India who, like their colleagues at the London office, did not want to publish anything on the earthquake 'unless sensational'.[132] Less than two weeks after the earthquake, the press saw little news value in the earthquake except as a spectacular and destructive event. The remainders of the spectacle—numbers of deaths, material losses and general stories of suffering—had no appeal as news. When, as expected, the Indian press took a cursory interest in the VERF appeal by the Governor of Bihar and Orissa, the Government of India tried to publish news reports in Great Britain since it was 'very desirable that the Viceroy's Fund should reach a very large figure'.[133] The relatively fast fading out of the news of the earthquake in the British press was, according to the government, one reason for the less-than-expected amounts being donated even to the Lord Mayor fund, the other reason being the economic crisis.[134]

The VERF and the Mansion House fund appealed for relief to a homogenised group of sufferers in the 'Indian earthquake', from the general public in England as well as from bankers and nobilities, who were also persons of substantial financial means, high social standing and associated with the British government. The politics of pity partly failed in the sense that the British public did not respond as generously as the government expected, in spite of considerable efforts to enhance publicity and organise collections. As it became apparent that it was difficult to raise the needed funds from the public, Hallett at the Home Ministry in New Delhi even pondered whether it was time for the British government to consider a grant to the VERF for charitable relief as 'a gesture of sympathy which would appeal to the Indian imagination'. A similar act of sympathy which public subscriptions had failed to display could be manifested in a grant from the British government. As a political act, Hallett suggested, such a grant for gratuitous relief would have had 'a very good political effect in India'.[135] The India Office recognised that the live news of the earthquake had gone but in order to uphold interest in the VERF it encouraged leading newspapers in London to have correspondents in India to telegraph 'a little more freely than perhaps the economic circumstances and interest value justify'.[136] However, even after the government and officials had pushed the newspapers to step up reporting on the havoc wrought by the earthquake, contributions did not amount to their expectations. Rather than media exposure, the framing of the unfortunates resulted in a failure to elicit a relationship between the audience of givers and the recipients of relief.

After the newspapers, visual media in the form of public film screenings served to collect funds. In cinemas across India and London, the screening of an earthquake film, a short news film of the devastation, offered spectacular views from the air and walk-through perspectives from the ruined towns in a Calcutta cinema less than two weeks after the earthquake.[137] A few days later, an earthquake film was included on the newsreel on view in England. The film was made by a cameraman stationed in India who had by aeroplane hurried to the earthquake area. The film had been sent with the Imperial Airways and eight days after leaving India it was included on the newsreel on view in England.[138] The screening coincided with the opening of the fund by the Lord Mayor of London. Starring himself in the earthquake film,[139] he used it in an appeal shown all over Great Britain, in a matinee screening attended by the Queen[140] and other publicity events that attracted funds by wealthier sections of society as well as the philanthropic engagement by a committee of ladies from the upper classes.[141] As in the news reporting, the destruction caused by the earthquake rather than the suffering of the victims was the theme of the images. Buildings in ruins, material losses and spectacular damages painted scenes of spectacular destruction while individual suffering remained a peripheral topic, if at all addressed.

Notably, the VERF was slow in using visual media in the initial appeals where the images of the Viceroy and the Governor of Bihar and Orissa instead appeared in print alongside the text. By mid-March, two months after the earthquake, the Viceroy issued a film with an appeal for funds in India.[142] The novelty in using the medium of films, not only in the context of a relief appeal, transpires from the Viceroy's excitement: '(...) I have, for the first time in my life, become a Hollywood Star!'[143] Preceding the launch of the appeals, the businessman H. E. Ormerod, an editor of the *Indian Concrete Journal*, showed photos of the destruction in Monghyr to the Governor of Bihar and Orissa and suggested that images to a far greater extent could be used in order to convey to the public its 'duty' of subscribing to the VERF.[144] For this purpose, he tried to sell his experience in marketing by suggesting a committee for propaganda work with the editors of *The Statesman* and the *Times of India*. He was, the governor remarked, 'no doubt combining business with philanthropy' as he offered his services on such a committee.[145] The managing director of the *Times of India* agreed to the idea of a propaganda committee in order to increase contributions, as he thought that 'so much more could be done to elicit the sympathy of the public'.[146] The Governor declined, partly since he thought such a committee 'could not be directly connected with the local government',[147] and partly since it was perceived as too late: the government's priority gradually shifted towards publicity work on the progress of relief and reconstruction where images did not have the same effect.[148] Considering the government's efforts to distribute written propaganda, use of images in raising support was surprisingly modest.

The *Times of India* and *The Statesman* subsequently published special illustrated earthquake issues later in March 1934. The monthly journal edited by the businessman Ormerod in Bombay, *The Indian Concrete Journal*, published on behalf of the Cement Marketing Company of India Ltd published a special issue on the earthquake in October 1934;[149] some of the photos in the issue were reused in the local government's official report on the earthquake.[150] The earthquake special issue in the *Illustrated Weekly of India*, featured eight pages with photographs by Ormerod and an appeal for the VERF.[151] The photographs were arranged according to themes and under the title 'An Appeal to World Humanity', the pages ingeniously linked by headings that formed a poem in what can be seen as an attempt at an emotive as well as a descriptive portrayal of people's suffering:

The World has not yet Realised the terrific Havoc,
The Destruction of Uninsured Homes of the People, and
The Suffering Through Damaged Road and Rail Arteries,
Nor the Human Stories of Fear, Courage, Loyalty
And the Queer Tricks of Fate the Earthquake Played,
The Terrifying Phenomena when Cities Rocked and Fields Gaped:
Now see the Courage of Victims who Still Carry on,
And Realise the Pressing Need for Reconstruction and Relief

Although the poem acknowledged people's suffering, it evaded themes such as individual tragedies or death, by instead focusing on material and economic suffering. 'Uninsured homes' implied that homeowners, the middle classes in towns, were affected and alive to claim insurance money, rather than mentioning the people crushed as the roofs fell in. 'The suffering through damaged roads and rail arteries' turned an eye to the impact the destruction had on trade and commerce, while the last line accentuated the 'pressing need' for rebuilding and assistance. *The Statesman's* special issue, *Record of the Great Indian Earthquake*, contained appeals by the Governor and Viceroy for the VERF and part of the sales proceeds went to the fund.[152] Before it was published in April,[153] subscriptions to the colonial funds were low and it was apprehended that it would add only small amounts since the earthquake had lost its news value.[154] It was published rather late and as an afterthought rather than as part of a strategy to raise funds. The issue had first been published by *The Statesman* in Calcutta, and it was printed on art paper and sold in England for one shilling to an intended audience of 'people who had lived in India or who have relatives or business interests there'.[155] *The Statesman's* London Manager, while marketing the publication in England, promised 'amazing pictures of the earthquake' as 'a pictorial record of one of the greatest disasters in Indian history'.[156] The earthquake in the form of an event and the spectacular destruction it offered, rather than the suffering of those affected, served to sell numbers and thereby collect funds on behalf of the VERF.

In a few instances, the VERF appeals connected the audience with the victims of the earthquake, but unlike publications that addressed the 'suffering' of specifically Bihar and its population, as discussed in Chapter 3, and in the context of the Mayor of Calcutta's appeal, these appeals relied upon themes and groups of 'sufferers' with whom the British audience could identify. An appeal by the Viceroy in *Record of the Great Indian Earthquake* spoke directly to an intended British audience by comparing the destruction in Bihar with that of towns on the West Front in World War I.[157] The material destruction, whether caused by war or earthquake, was known to the audience in Great Britain and created a visualisation shared between the earthquake sufferers and the audience. In order to elicit a commitment to help, the effect of disaster was communicated in a manner which made the suffering familiar to the intended audience. The commitment to help was framed as based on affinity with suffering.[158] Another way of directly invoking help from Great Britain in the special issue on the earthquake was to emphasise the financial troubles of the sugar cane growers, a large European community in north Bihar whose factories had suffered damages.[159] Planters formed a well-known community of Europeans in India, and through descriptions of their hardships as a group they formed a distinct object for sympathy with whom the readers in Great Britain could identify.

With regard to the less-than-expected contributions to the VERF, the Government of India noted that the British public was 'frequently' accused of giving more liberally to a foreign country (that is, Japan) than to 'their own dependency', India.[160] The government initially expressed high hopes that the earthquake would attract donations comparable to the 1923 Kanto earthquake when Japan had received 25 million rupees (or two million pounds sterling) from the international community.[161] After the 1905 Kangra earthquake, which had far less devastating effects compared to the scenario in

Bihar, the VERF received about 20,000 rupees from Japan, and 1.5 million rupees from London as well as donations from Ceylon.[162] Donations from the British public 'in aid of the fellow citizens of the Empire' as *The Statesman* put it,[163] disappointed those who may have expected more sympathy from the British public than what was displayed through fund contributions. By mentioning the 'dependency' as the receiver, the government had implied a hierarchical relationship between the British public and the subjects in the colony that was expected to elicit gifting.[164] As Boltanski puts it: 'Pre-existing conventions establish a precommitment that only has to be actualized when needed.'[165] Contrary to expectations, the relationship had not elicited more 'pity' transformed into charity than in other disasters. Charity based on a communitarian bond or sense of commitment among the British public towards the dependency did not manifest.

As we move from the VERF and the Mayor of London's fund to the Mayor of Calcutta's fund, the depiction of the sufferers becomes more specific and familiar. Instead of speaking about the 'Indian earthquake', the Mayor's appeal reflected Calcutta's geographical proximity to the earthquake area and close relations with its population by referring to them in a far more affective language. The Mayor referred to Calcutta's 'providential escape' from the earthquake, a statement that probably had resonance considering that the city had felt the earthquake. The Mayor of Calcutta used the geographically close position of Calcutta to the earthquake area as a means to evoke sympathy. Calcutta was described as having been 'spared the calamity that had overtaken the sister province Bihar'[166] and it was a sign 'to fulfil God's great purpose by affording relief to the sufferers in a spirit of absolute unanimity, inspired by one common desire to serve the afflicted'.[167] The definition of the victims depended on the audience: if the earthquake and sufferers had been generalised in appeals by the VERF, the Mayor emphasised the particulars of the disaster to raise subscriptions. Markedly in the Mayor's appeal, altruistic gifting was partly encouraged based on the idea of Calcutta having by chance been saved from the same destiny as Bihar and as a fortunate survivor alive to help its neighbour. Contrary to the VERF and the Mayor of London's earthquake fund, which generalised the target of relief as earthquake sufferers in 'India', the appeal in Calcutta spoke of 'Bihar' and expressed affinity with the victims. The geographical position of Calcutta and its citizens' socio-economic status were in the Mayor's appeal transformed into a commitment to help, which positioned the audience as prospective good Samaritans, to use the example raised by Boltanski.[168] To a certain extent, the audience had already committed to the cause by attending the foundational meeting; some of them had, in addition, publicly promised or given donations. The opportunity to act as good Samaritans involved further action by committing goods and money, particular strengths of the business people, merchants and public figures present in the meeting.

The bond between Calcutta and the earthquake area was demonstrated in business ties and communal networks of some donors. The Marwari-dominated East India Jute Association[169] earmarked a substantial sum for the Marwari Relief Society,[170] indicating that communal and, or, business ties served to motivate aid. Common business interests and networks sometimes overrode differences, such as the collection by the Indian Jute Mills Association, which although ridden with fractions between European and Indian mills[171] included donations by 'non-member' mills as well as two mills excluded from the Association in its collection.[172] Even though corporate fund collections were given ample space for publicity, smaller fund collections based on professional status, nationality, clubs, associations and shops—for instance, students and staff of several colleges, interpreters at the Calcutta High Court, several bar associations, customers of Bengal stores, the Rotary Club, the Young Ladies of Bengal Telephone Corporation[173]—served to make the Mayor's fund representative of the city. Similar to the Mansion House fund in London, the Mayor's fund paid notice to smaller contributions and individual efforts to collect funds in public spaces, such as students giving 25 rupees out of their Saraswati puja fund, 'girl-students' setting up plays, 'charity shows', staging performances and dances,[174] and the Governor of Bengal for setting up a 'benefit show' in aid of the fund.[175] Public fundraising on the streets and door-to-door collections was a domain in which middle-class women of Calcutta participated. The Women's Association in Calcutta collected 10,000 rupees for earthquake relief. Similarly, in Patna the Aghore Nari Samiti (Women Association) mobilised to help earthquake victims.[176] The working committee of the Mayor of Calcutta's fund decided to observe flag-day on Saturday, 28 January 1934 in order to collect funds from the public in aid of the relief fund. Women wearing badges (see Image 4.2) and carrying sealed boxes collected money in public spaces and offices such as banks, railway stations and the New Market area, and the Bengal Stores.[177] The flag-day appeared to have been organised independently of the 'Behar Relief Day' organised by Madan Mohan Malaviya in his country-wide appeal to make house collections on behalf of the BCRC, a call that did not specifically gender the participation in collecting funds.[178] Further afar, members of the participating constituencies

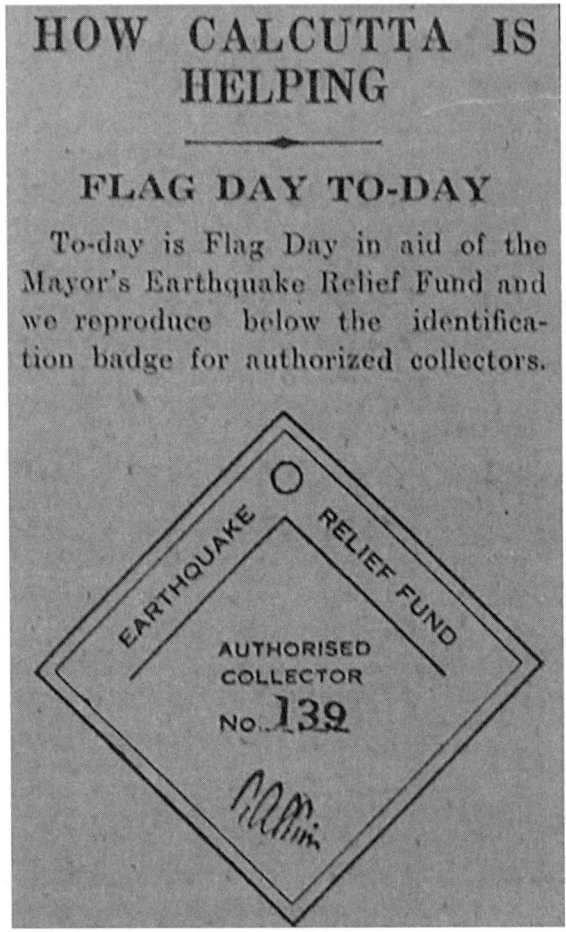

Image 4.2 Identification badge: 'Earthquake Relief Fund: Authorised Collector No. 139'. Reproduction of badge for authorised collectors on the flag-day for the Mayor of Calcutta's Earthquake Relief Fund in *The Statesman* (Calcutta), 28 January 1934.

in the All India Women's Conference in Karachi organised a flag-day at the end of December 1934 and more than 30,000 rupees was raised in total.[179] Women appeared to have had a noticeable presence in fundraising among the public and not only in restricted spaces of performances, schools and workplaces. Even if affluent sections had a prominent role as patrons of the fund, the fund represented above all relief from the city of Calcutta, a place populated by a diverse urban citizenry according to its official profile.

Conclusion: Controlled Charity

Against the backdrop of the larger question regarding the colonial state's involvement in relief in times of disaster, the response in 1934 represented an instance of tightening control over domestic as well as international relief funds.

As this chapter has discussed, the state was directly involved in collecting funds by using publicity campaigns and propaganda, the established networks of the wealthy and publicly known patrons and the government administration in India as well as in the UK in order to maximise public contributions. The public was but one source of donation towards the VERF, considering the importance government patronage played in ensuring the large initial grant by the Indian People's Famine Trust and collections made by the IRU and the international Red Cross societies towards the VERF. International relief cooperation through the IRU was seen by the colonial government as potentially competing with the collections of the VERF. Imperial as well as international subscriptions were effectively pooled into the fund by the colonial administration. These two developments together indicate not so much a growing involvement in disaster relief by the government and the collaborating fundraisers but rather the government's increased control over charitable relief and its preference for centralised funds.

Considering the government officials' involvement in the collection of contributions towards the VERF, the degree to which the government was involved in the fund leaned more towards control of, than in 'aid' of, subscriptions to the fund. Through the VERF, the government shaped the spectre of relief by strengthening its control over publicly subscribed relief. Even though the VERF had a semi-official status by means of its high-ranking patrons, it was explicitly referred to as 'private' by the government.[180] This conundrum of calling it private, when in practice it was thoroughly managed by state officials, can be explained by the government's view of the fund as outside the official budget, that is, it was a fund for donations from private individuals, as well as from non-governmental bodies such as other relief funds towards charitable relief to the public.

The publicity of the disaster and that of the relief funds became intrinsically linked in the collection of subscriptions. Focusing on the funds and subscribers, this chapter highlights the extent to which public display of gifting invoked the earthquake or the victims according to the audiences addressed. As the chapter shows, the publicity surrounding the earthquake appealed to audiences depending on geographical location and presumed relationship with the affected region. The earthquake was the 'Indian earthquake' or the 'Bihar earthquake', respectively, in appeals for funds. In the case of Calcutta an imagery of sympathy and the audience's obligation to offer relief were invoked based on regional bonds which portrayed closeness to the victims and strong feelings of the city having been saved by luck from the earthquake. Framing the local specificities of the earthquake created affinity with victims. In the case of the Mayor of London fund, donating to it offered an opportunity for a local display of gifting in London. As an intermediary, the established networks surrounding the Mayor's funds appeared to have increased the importance of the local aspect of giving. The sense of closeness or remoteness to the victims hence mattered less in giving to the Lord Mayor of London's fund, compared to the VERF, as the Mayor's fund created an arena to display gifting towards an important patron of the city.

The colonial government supported and participated in collecting charity from the public to the VERF in order to use it for distributing charitable relief. In terms of allocations and distribution according to needs, the government regarded charitable relief as a domain that needed not only to be controlled by the government, but preferably be under the direct administration of the government. Contrary to methods followed by the Indian Famine Charitable Relief Funds, which extensively relied on 'un-official' contacts such as local nobilities and men in high positions outside government service for grant distribution in the provinces and districts, the control over the VERF remained within the government administration (discussed in Chapter 5). The centralisation of charitable relief at the government's discretion increased as the government ensured the VERF's support by fashioning it as the principal fund for charitable subscriptions towards earthquake relief.

As we move on to the next chapter, the categories of victims, long-term reconstruction and allocation of charitable relief will be discussed.

Notes

1. Alexander Pope (1688–1744) quoted in Sachchidananda Sinha, 'The Devastation of Behar and the Problem of Reconstruction', *Hindustan Review* LVX [*sic* 60], nos. 350–52 (January 1934): 151–57.
2. Lord Willingdon, Major Freeman Freeman-Thomas, 1st Marquess of Willingdon (b. 1866–d. 1941) and Viceroy of India 1931–36. D. A. Low, 'Thomas, Freeman

Freeman, first marquess of Willingdon (1866–1941)', *Oxford Dictionary of National Biography* (Oxford University Press, 2004, online edition, January 2008, http://www.oxforddnb.com.ubproxy.ub.uni-heidelberg.de/view/article/33266, accessed 13 May 2015).

3. 'The Viceroy's Fund', *ABP*, 19 January 1934. 'Government's Relief Fund Measures', *The Statesman*, 19 January 1934.

4. 'A Shocking Farewell', *The Statesman*, 17 January 1934.

5. 'Appeals', *ABP*, 23 January 1934. Brett, *A Report on the Bihar Earthquake*, 21.

6. Also referred to in sources as 'the Lord Mayor fund'. 'Appeal for Help at Mansion House', *News Chronicle*, 31 January 1934; 'Letter to the Editor', *Morning Post*, 1 February 1934; 'Lord Mayor and Indian Earthquake', *Morning Post*, 7 February 1934; 'The Indian Earthquake', *Near East and India*, 8 February 1934.

7. 'The Mayor's Earthquake Relief Fund', often referred to as 'the Mayor's Fund' (and sometimes confused with 'the Lord Mayor Fund', 'the Mansion House Fund' by the Lord Mayor in London). 'Mayor's Fund; Total Reaches Rs. 1,77,389', *ABP*, 28 January 1934.

8. 'Scheme for Relief; Mayor to Convene a Public Meeting', *The Statesman*, 18 January 1934; 'Calcutta Fund; Steps for Relief of Sufferers', *The Statesman*, 20 January 1934; 'Mayor's Appeal for Fund' (appeal by Santosh Kumar Basu), 22 January 1933 [*sic* 1934], *ABP*, 24 January 1934; 'Earthquake in Behar: Public Meeting at Town Hall To-Day', *ABP*, 23 January 1934.

9. 'Government's Relief Fund Measures', *The Statesman*, 19 January 1934.

10. Ibid.; 'Earthquake in Behar: Public Meeting at Town Hall To-Day', *ABP*, 23 January 1934.

11. 'The Bihar Disaster; Contributions to Mayor's Fund', *Behar Herald*, 20 January 1934.

12. 'Earthquake Relief; Mayor's Fund over Rs. 2,86,000; Flag Day Success; Rs. 54,140 from Jute Mills Association', *The Statesman*, 31 January 1934. 'National Cataclysm; Bengal's Profound Sympathy for Behar; Mayor's Earthquake Relief Fund; "Service and Sacrifice-The Supreme Need of the Moment"', *ABP*, 24 January 1934.
To mention a few names among the first contributors: Jamnadas Brothers Rs 250, ABP Rs 250, J. S. Henderson Rs 200, Mrs. Henderson Rs 100, Mrs. Z. Sinclair Rs 100, Lord Sinha Rs 250, Asutosh Dutt Rs 25, S. C. Mitter, Barrister Rs 50, *The Statesman* Rs 1,000, Rai Bahadur Motilal Chamaria Rs 4,000. 'Earthquake Fund', *ABP*, 20 January 1934.

13. Roy, 'State, Society and Market', 282n65.

14. Ch. XIV, 'The Viceroy's Quetta Earthquake Relief Fund', in Louis Alexander Gordon Pinhey, *Report on the Quetta Earthquake on the 31st of May 1935* (Delhi: Manager of Publications, 1938), 46–50.

15. Roy, 'State, Society and Market', 268.

16. Ibid., 268.

17. Brewis, 'Fill Full the Mouth of Famine', 898–900. *Report of the Central Executive Committee, Indian Famine Charitable Relief Fund, 1900, With Complete Accounts and Proceedings, Including the Reports of the Provincial Committees* (Calcutta: Office of the Superintendent of Government Printing, 1901).

18. *Report of the Central Executive Committee, Indian Famine Charitable Relief Fund, 1900*, 4–5.

19. Brewis, 'Fill Full the Mouth of Famine', 899.

20. George Schuster (Finance member), 14 February 1934, in GOI, *Legislative Assembly Debates* (Official report), vol. I, 1934 (24 January–16 February 1934), 830–31.

21. Advisory Committee members H. L. Mitter, Frank Noyce, Shanmukham Chetty, E. [Ernest] Burdon, Alan Parsons [A. A. L. Parsons], M. G. Hallett, B. J. Glancy, H. A. F. Metcalfe, U. N. Sen, E. C. Mieville, Maneckji Byramji Dadabhoy, 'Viceroy's Fund; Advisory Committee Set up in Delhi', *The Statesman*, 26 January 1934.

22. J. T. Whitty, Vice-President, Executive Council and J. A. Hubback, Member Board of Revenue, were the two government officials, and the 'non-officials' were Rajandhari Sinha, President Legislative Council, Kulwant Sahay, retired High Court Judge and Sir S. Sultan Ahmed. 'Articles for press other than Official', note, s.n., s.l., s.a., in BSA RE 484/1934. 'Some Political and Other Aspects of Earthquake Relief in Bihar' (17 pp.), M. G. Hallett, 31 March 1934, NAI HP 34/1/1934.

23. No. 3365 R. D. [Letter], W. B. Brett to Under Sec. to the GOI, Home Dept, Ranchi, 23 August 1934. NAI HP 1/41/1934. 'Progress Report for the Week Ending 1 March 1934', District officer S. L. Marwood to J. E. Scott, Commissioner of Tirhut, Motihari, 2 March 1934, BSA RE 13/1934.

24. Brett, *A Report on the Bihar Earthquake*, 80.

25. Solomon, *Bihar and Orissa in 1934–35*, 10–11.

26. Notes by M. G. Hallett, 12 March 1934, File: 'Questions in the Council of State Regarding Earthquake', NAI H. Pol. 3/2/1934.

27. Lord Willingdon to Samuel Hoare, 13 March 1934, Papers of Sir Samuel Hoare, Secretary of State for India 1931–35, Mss Eur E240/7, 484.

28. 'Statement from a Meeting in New Delhi', *Behar Herald*, 21 April 1934.

29. Rupees 3,659,488. *REPR*, 18.

30. 'His Excellency the Viceroy's Earthquake Relief Fund, Bihar and Orissa Branch, Balance Sheet', 31 July 1934, in NAI, HP 1/41/1934

31. The total appears to have included contributions from the Mayor of Calcutta's fund of 50,000 rupees, and 800,000 rupees from the Indian People's Famine Trust Fund. Appendix 3', in Brett, *A Report on the Bihar Earthquake*, 26.

32. An amount of 200,000 rupees remained in balance. Solomon, *Bihar and Orissa in 1934–35*, 10–11.

33. Appendix 3, in Brett, *A Report on the Bihar Earthquake*.

34. Sec. of State for India, Samuel Hoare, on required relief measurement, in 'Earthquake (Relief Measures)', House of Commons Debates 19 February 1934, vol. 286 cc.3–4, available at http://hansard.millbanksystems.com/commons/1934/feb/19/earthquake-relief-measures#column_3, accessed 12 January 2010.

35. Untitled summary of finances for relief and reconstruction in preparation for a visit to Patna in order to discuss a financial plan for the aftermath by A. A. L. Parsons [Sir Alfred Alan Lethbridge Parsons], submitted to Home Department, GOI, 31 January 1934, NAI HP 34/1/1934, 9.

36. Ibid.

37. Quoted in 'Confidential: Position in Bihar', note/correspondence by A. A. L. Parsons, 8 February 1934. File: 'Financial Assistance to the Govt of B&O in connection with the earthquake', NAI Finance Department, Budget Branch, File: 3 (2), 'Budget, Serial nos. 1–52/1934.

38. 'Earthquake. Method of Financing Assistance to Bihar', Financial Department, Reg F. 1030/34, Draft telegram, 13 February 1934 (dispatched 14 February 1934), IOR/L/F/7/913.

39. The motion 'Resolution *RE* Donation to Bihar Earthquake Relief Fund' was declined. Introduced by Rai Bahadur Lala Ram Saran Das (Punjab), 7 March 1934, in *The Council of State Debates*, vol. 1, 1934 (8 February–27 April, 1934) (Delhi: Published by Manager of Publications, 1934): 411–21.

40. D.O. F/34/1/34, M. G. Hallett, Sec. to the GOI, to All Local Governments and Administrations (except Bihar and Orissa), New Delhi, 5 February 1934, NAI HP 34/1/1934. See also 'Question in the Council of State Regarding Earthquake', Sec. of State for India, Sir S. Hoare, on required relief measures for Bihar after the earthquake. 'Earthquake (Relief Measures)', in House of Commons Debates, 19 February 1934, vol. 286 cc3–4, available at http://hansard.millbanksystems.com/commons/1934/feb/19/earthquake-relief-measures#S5CV0286P0_19340219_HOC_17, accessed 11 February 2021.

41. 'Earthquake (Relief Measures)', in House of Commons Debates, 19 February 1934, vol. 286 cc3–4, available at http://hansard.millbanksystems.com/commons/1934/feb/19/earthquake-relief-measures#S5CV0286P0_19340219_HOC_17, accessed 11 February 2021. 'The Reconstruction Problem; Mr. Mookerjea's Suggestions in Bihar Council' (Patna, 20 February 1934), *ABP*, 23 February 1934.

42. D.O. 7 34/1/34 Pub., Air Mail by M. G. Hallett, GOI, Home Dept, New Delhi, to R.T. Peel, Sec., P&J Department, India Office, Whitehall, London, 30 January

1934, NAI HP 34/1/1934. These figures were further debated in the Legislative Assembly, 14 February 1934, GOI, *Legislative Assembly Debates*, vol. I, 1934, 822, cf.

43. The budget was announced by the Finance Member Sir George Schuster on 27 February 1934. 'Appendix 1: Extracts from the Speech by the Hon'ble Finance Member of the GOI in Introducing the Budget Proposals for 1934–35', in Brett, *A Report on the Bihar Earthquake*, 91–94.

44. Ibid., 92.

45. 'Relief to the People of Bihar Who Have Been Affected by the Earthquake', J. W. Houlton, Officiating Sec., Revenue Dept, Govt of B&O, to Sec. of the Board of Management, Indian People's Famine Trust Fund (New Delhi), Patna, 26 January 1934, in File: 'Indian People's Famine Trust Fund. Proceedings of the Meeting of the Board of Management of the Indian People's Famine Trust 1934. Sanction of the sum of Rs 8 lacs towards relief of distress caused by the earthquake in the province of Bihar and Orissa', NAI F&P Foreign 302-P/1934.

46. Also referred to as 'The Indian People's Famine Trust Fund' or 'The Indian People's Famine Relief Fund'. *Report of the Central Executive Committee, Indian Famine Charitable Relief Fund, 1900*, 4, 9.

47. Dang, 'Colonial Ideology, Nationalist Politics and the Social Organization of Relief', 157.

48. Ibid., 160–61. The trust was approached in an unsuccessful attempt at diverting funds to aid the distribution of quinine to prevent malaria in 1903. Rohan Deb Roy, 'Quinine, Mosquitoes and Empire: Reassembling Malaria in British India 1890–1910', *South Asian History and Culture* 4, no. 1 (2013): 65–86, 4. After 1934, the trust again granted 25,000 rupees for famine relief in Madras Presidency and 50,000 rupees to the Quetta Earthquake Relief Fund in the summer of 1935. 'Indian People's Famine Trust. Board of Management Meets', *The Searchlight*, 19 July 1935.

49. Dang, 'Colonial Ideology, Nationalist Politics and the Social Organization of Relief', 155.

50. 'Relief to the People of Bihar Who Have Been Affected by the Earthquake', J. W. Houlton, Officiating Sec., Revenue Dept, Govt of B&O, to Sec. of the Board of Management, Indian People's Famine Trust Fund, New Delhi, Patna, 26 January 1934, NAI F&P Foreign 302-P/1934.

51. Telegram from Bihar Revenue to Sir Ernest Burdon [Honorary Sec. of Board of Management for the Indian People's Famine Trust], 1 February 1934, NAI F&P 301-P/1934.

52. 'Minutes of the Meeting of the Board of Management Held in the Honourable Sir George Schuster's Room in the Council House', New Delhi, 15 February 1934, NAI F&P 301-P/1934.

53. 'Relief to the People of Bihar Who Have Been Affected by the Earthquake', J. W. Houlton, Officiating Sec., Revenue Dept, Govt of B&O, to Sec. of the Board of Management, Indian People's Famine Trust Fund, New Delhi, Patna, 26 January 1934, NAI F&P Foreign 302-P/1934.

54. '42nd Communiqué', R.D., Govt of B&O, Ranchi, 11 October 1934, NAI 1/41/1934.

55. Brett, *A Report on the Bihar Earthquake*, 61.

56. Appendix 3, in Brett, *A Report on the Bihar Earthquake*, 100–01.

57. 'Minutes of the Meeting of the Board of Management', New Delhi, 15 February 1934, NAI F&P 301-P/1934.

58. John F. Hutchinson, 'Disasters and the International Order. II: The International Relief Union', *International History Review* 23, no. 2 (2001): 253–98, 254.

59. The government was thereby given a prolonged period to estimate totals and discuss budget allocations. For the provision of sugar mills the VERF disbursed 232,528 rupees and the GOI 'reimbursed' the VERF by transfer of 198,632 rupees. 'His Excellency the Viceroy's Earthquake Relief Fund, Bihar and Orissa Branch, Balance Sheet, 31 July 1934'. For 'Sand clearance' the VERF disbursed 354,091 rupees and the Govt of B&O 'reimbursed' the fund with 300,000 rupees. Appendix 3, in Brett, *A Report on the Bihar Earthquake*.

60. *RPER*, 18.

61. 'Expenditure during the year 1934–35 on sand clearance grants', No. 1490, F[inance] R[evenue], Govt of B&O, Finance Dept, H. C. Prior to the Accountant General, B&O, Ranchi 11 June 1934, File: 'Allotment for free grants in connection with sand clearance in North Bihar', BSA R-L II 7/13/1935. Also Appendix 3, in Brett, *A Report on the Bihar Earthquake*.

62. Memo, M. G. Hallett, New Delhi, 3 February 1934, NAI HP 34/1/1934.

63. For instance, a request to use the governor's public speech for publicity purposes in, 'Telegram "R"', from Home Dept, New Delhi to P.S.G. [Private Sec. to the Governor], Bihar and Orissa, 25 January 1934, NAI HP 34/1/1934.

64. Douglas E. Haynes, *Rhetoric and Ritual in Colonial India: The Shaping of Public Culture in Surat City, 1852–1928* (Berkeley; Los Angeles: University of California Press, 1991), 121–22.

65. 'Speech Delivered by H. E. the Governor of Bihar and Orissa on the 22nd January 1934', enclosed as copy from P. T. Clarke, Private Sec. to H. E. the Governor of B&O, Patna, to the Sec. to the GOI, 26 January 1934, NAI HP 34/1/1934.

66. D.O. F. 34/1/34, M. G. Hallett to All Local Governments and Administrations, New Delhi, 25 January 1934, NAI HP 34/1/1934.

67. 'Confidential, Government of Bombay, Political and Reforms Department, Circular no. 734/33-F (Fin.)', C. W. A. Turner, Chief Sec. to Government, circulated to Aden Residency; Sind; Commissioners of Divisions; Commissioner of Excise; The High Court Bombay; All Collectors, Including the Deputy Commissioner, Upper Sind Frontier; All Departments of the Secretariat', Bombay Castle, 30 January 1934, File: '1113 Earthquake relief: H. E. the Viceroy's Fund. Co-operation by Government Officers', IOR/R/20/A/3607.

68. Minister Sir Bejay Prasad Singh Roy donated 200 rupees and 1,000 rupees was collected in a meeting presided over by M. M. Stuart, I. C. S. District Magistrate. Notices in *ABP*, 21 and 23 January 1934.

69. 'Viceroy's Relief Fund', *ABP*, 5 October 1934.

70. Telegram to P.S.V., Simla. No. 77, 20 August 1934. Subject: 'Subscription collected in Aden for the Earthquake Relief Refund', IOR/R/20/A/3658.

71. 'Flying visit to Motihari Town', *ABP*, 28 March 1934

72. W. B. Brett, 'Weekly Bulletin' (for the week ending 9 March 1934), Patna, to M. G. Hallett, Sec. to the GOI, Home Dept NAI HP 34/1B/1934.

73. The following contributors to the VERF are mentioned in the *ABP*: 'The Nizam's Government Rs 15,000; Sir Cowasjee Jehangir, senior and junior Rs 7,500; the Maharaja of Jind Rs 10,000; The Maharaja of Baroda Rs 5,000', *ABP*, 24 January 1934; 'Notable donors' were the trustees of the Dorab Tata's Fund (50,000 rupees), Lady Ratan Tata (10,000), the Dumrao Raj (10,000 rupees), Sir Thomas Smith of Cawnpore (5,000 rupees) and the Governor of Bombay (1,000 rupees), *ABP*, 23 January 1934. In *The Statesman* four funds were displayed next to each other; the Mayor of Calcutta's fund and the VERF were given prominent headings while the Marwari Relief Society and Muslim Relief Committee appeared within the text. 'Earthquake Relief; Viceroy's Fund Now Rs. 6 ½ Lakhs; Response from Poor'; and 'Earthquake Relief; Mayor's Fund over Rs. 2,86,000; (...)', *The Statesman*, 31 January 1934.

74. Carl Heath (London), to Bertram Pickard (Geneva), 12 March 1934, BCUL PC 903:1.

75. 'Earthquake Relief; Viceroy's Fund Now Rs. 6 ½ Lakhs; Response from Poor'; and 'Children Pay', *The Statesman*, 31 January 1934.

76. 'Confidential, D.O. 42 T. C.', Commissioner's Office, Ranchi, to P. C. Tallents, 12 February 1934, in 'Fortnightly Reports–Chota Nagpur', BSA PS KW 14/1934. A report of similar content soon followed. 'Confidential D.O. 78 T. C.', Commissioner's office, Ranchi, to P. C. Tallents, 25 February 1934, BSA PS KW 14/1934.

77. 'Confidential', by I. M. Stephens, New Delhi, 7 May 1934, NAI HP 34/1/1934.

78. A few days after the opening of the fund, the collected total amount of the VERF was 100,291 rupees and 1,158 pounds. *ABP*, 23 January 1934.

79. 'Viceroy's Appeal for Funds' (by Lord Willingdon, New Delhi, 19 January 1934), *ABP*, 20 January 1934.

80. 'Relief to Sufferers', *ABP*, 21 January 1934; 'Quick! Quick!! Quick!!!' (editorial), *ABP*, 23 January 1934.

81. Samuel Hoare to Lord Willingdon, London, 25 January 1934, Mss Eur E240/4, 958–65.

82. Lord Willingdon to Samuel Hoare, New Delhi, 22 January 1934, Mss Eur E240/7, 447, in ibid.

83. Hutchinson, 'Disasters and the International Order. II', 255.

84. Brewis, '"Fill Full the Mouth of Famine"', 894.

85. Sarah Gregson, '"Women and Children First?" The Administration of Titanic Relief in Southampton, 1912–59', *English Historical Review* 127, no. 524 (February 2012): 83–109.

86. John Benson, 'Colliery Disaster Funds, 1860–1897', *International Review of Social History* 19, no. 1 (1974): 73–85.

87. Hutchinson, 'Disasters and the International Order. II', 254–55.

88. Copy of letter no. 68/34, A. H. Joyce, Information Officer, India Office, to I. M. Stephens, DPI, 4 February 1934, NAI HP 34/1/1934.

89. Copy of a letter from A. H. Joyce, Information Office, India Office, to I. M. Stephens, DPI, No. 129/34, London, 8 February 1934, NAI HP 34/1/1934. Copy, Infn. Offr. No. 160/34. Air mail by A. H. Joyce Information Officer's Department, India Office, to I. M. Stephens, DPI, Home Dept (New Delhi), London, 22 February 1934, NAI HP 34/1/1934. The fund had reached 46,000 pounds by 1 March 1934. Air Mail 'Infn. Offr. 185/34', Joyce to Stephens, London, 1 March 1934, ibid.

90. Lord Mayor, Sir Charles Collett, announced the appeal on 31 January and held the inaugural meeting at the Mansion House on 8 February 1934. 'Appeal for Help at Mansion House', *News Chronicle*, 31 January 1934.

91. Copy of letter no. 68/34, A. H. Joyce, Information Officer, India Office, to I. M. Stephens, DPI, London, 4 February 1934, NAI HP 34/1/1934.

92. In addition to the mentioned contributors, the Mayor acknowledged Lord Reading, Lord Hardinge, Lord Linlithgow and several other 'Lords'. 'Lord Mayor's Fund', 'The Horners' company; 'Lord Mayor and Indian Earthquakes', *The Times*, 31 January 1934.

93. Copy, Infn. Offr. No. 160/34. Air mail by A. H. Joyce, Information Officer, India Office, to I. M. Stephens, DPI, Home Dept (New Delhi), London, 22 February 1934, NAI HP 34/1/1934.

94. 'Indian Earthquake Funds', *The Times*, 2 March 1934.

95. Gregson, '"Women and Children First?"', 95–96.

96. 'The Indian Earthquake. Further Donations to the Lord Mayor's Fund', *The Times*, 16 February 1934; 'Charities and Appeals. Lord Mayor's Indian Earthquake Fund. Second List of Donations, 20 February, 1934', *The Times*, 22 February 1934.

97. 'Indian Earthquake Fund', *Daily Telegraph*, 15 February 1934; 'Ever Open Doors', *Daily Telegraph*, 7 February 1934. The Lord Mayor was at that time Sir Charles Collett. 'Lord Mayor's India Earthquake Fund. Appeal Broadcast', *Daily Telegraph*, 7 February 1934.

98. 'Mayor's Appeal for Fund' (appeal by Santosh Kumar Basu), 22 January 1933 [*sic* 1934], *ABP*, 24 January 1934.

99. 'Distribution of Funds; Relief Measures; Support to Babu Rajendra Prosad's [Prasad's] Committee' (Patna), *ABP*, 29 January 1934. A second instalment of 10,000 rupees mentioned in 'Mayor's Fund; Working Committee Meeting', *ABP*, 30 January 1934. BCRC, *Devastated Bihar*, 61, 64.

100. Notes by M. G. Hallett, 3 February 1936. NAI H. Pol. 22/21/1936. Santosh Kumar Basu's political affiliation to the Congress, in Rajat Kanta Ray, *Urban Roots of Indian Nationalism: Pressure Groups and Conflict of Interests in Calcutta City Politics, 1875–1939* (New Delhi: Vikas, 1979), 112.

101. Douglas E. Haynes, 'From Tribute to Philanthropy: The Politics of Gift Giving in a Western Indian City', *Journal of Asian Studies* 46, no. 2 (May, 1987): 339–60, 339–40.

102. See note 12 for a list of contributors.

103. 'Mayor's Fund; Working Committee Meeting', *ABP*, 30 January 1934.

104. *Prabuddha Bharata*, May 1934, no. 5, 260. The total sum from the Mayor's fund was 60,470 rupees according to 'The Eighth General Report of the Ramakrishna Mission (1934–1935)' received at Ramakrishna Mission, Belur Math, October 2011.

105. Marwari Relief Society 25,000 rupees, Indian Red Cross Society 15,000 rupees, Babu Rajendra Prosad [*sic* Prasad] (President, Bihar Central Relief Committee) 10,000 rupees, Ramakrishna Mission 7,500 rupees, IMA 5,000 rupees, Vivekananda Mission 2,500 rupees, Salvation Army 2,500 rupees, Bengal Provincial Hindu Sabha 1,000 rupees, and Central Khadem-ul Ensan Society 1,000 rupees. 'Earthquake Relief; Mayor's Fund over Two Lakhs', *The Statesman*, 30 January 1934.

106. Brett, *A Report on the Bihar Earthquake*, 26–27.

107. The respective amounts were 75,000 rupees, 50,000 rupees and 20,000 rupees. BCRC, *Devastated Bihar*, 46.

108. Letter by M. G. Hallett, Patna, 3 February 1936. BSA, Foreign-Pol. 22/21 1936. The final amount appeared as less, considering that as per 28 February 1934, a newspaper notice declared the collection to be 441,618 rupees. 'Mayor's Fund', *ABP*, 28 February 1934.

109. John F. Hutchinson, 'Disasters and the International Order: Earthquakes, Humanitarians, and the Ciraolo Project', *International History Review* 22, no. 1 (2000): 1–36. Hutchinson, 'Disasters and the International Order. II'.

110. Hutchinson, 'Disasters and the International Order. II', 255.

111. John Hannigan, *Disasters without Borders: The International Politics of Natural Disasters* (Cambridge, UK: Polity, 2012), 46–47.

112. Hutchinson, 'Disasters and the International Order. II', 253–54.

113. Austen Chamberlain quoted in Hutchinson, 'Disasters and the International Order. II', 254–55, 288.

114. Camille Gorgé, *The International Relief Union: Its Origin, Aims, Means and Future* (Geneva: International Relief Union, 1938).

115. Gorgé, *The International Relief Union*, 37–38.

116. Hutchinson, 'Disasters and the International Order. II', 291. Peter Macalister-Smith, 'The International Relief Union of 1932', *Disasters* 5, no. 2 (1981): 147–54, 151.

117. Hutchinson, 'Disasters and the International Order. II', 291. *ABP* reported that the IRU had decided to give 1,000 pounds for first aid to the Indian Red Cross and that the India Office had accepted the money. 'Relief to Sufferers', *ABP*, 21 January 1934. According to Gorgé, IRU gave 1,000 pounds for first aid after the Bihar earthquake, without providing further details of how the money was distributed. Gorgé, *The International Relief Union*, 37–38.

118. Hutchinson, 'Disasters and the International Order. II', 291.

119. The same day as Hutchinson mentioned that the Viceroy's office had acknowledged the appeal, the Secretary of State for India Samuel Hoare asked the Viceroy's office for the origin of the appeal in an urgent telegram. Telegram XX No. 189, Immediate, Sec. of State for India, London, to Viceroy (Home Dept.), New Delhi, 23 (recd 24th) January 1934; P.S.V.O. Secy. & Dept, NAI HP 34/1/1934.

120. Telegram from Sec. of State no. 1568, 18 January 1934; Williams to Sec. of State, regarding telegram no 189, 24 January 1934; Telegram XX No. 168, Immediate, Viceroy (Home Dept) to Sec. of State for India (London), New Delhi 24 January 1934; P.S.V. [Private Sec. to the Viceroy], P.S.V.O. [Private Sec. to the Viceroy Office] Dept, NAI HP 34/1/1934.

121. A telegram from the IRU office in Paris to Secretary of State, however, claimed that the appeal had been issued 'from Delhi' which he presumed must have been of 'the unofficial kind' from the Indian Red Cross. Telegram XX No. 189, Immediate, Sec. of State for India, London, to Viceroy (Home Dept), New Delhi, 23 (recd 24th) January 1934; Williams to Sec. of State, regarding telegram no 189, 24 January 1934, NAI HP 34/1/1934.

122. The decision to transfer the sum to the VERF is mentioned in Notes, M. G. Hallett to Secretary of State for India, New Delhi, 22 January 1934, NAI HP 34/1/1934. Indian Red Cross Society, *Annual Report 1934*, 19. The donation from IRU to VERF is mentioned in 'Enclosure no. 1: Viceroy's Appeal for 'Quake Sufferers. Relief Fund Opened: £1,000 from International Union. The King's Sympathy. Heavy Darbhanga Casualties: Hospital Collapses'. Extract from *The Statesman*, 20 January 1934, NAI HP 34/1/1934.

123. Indian Red Cross Society, *Annual Report 1934*, 19–20.

124. 'Viceroy's Fund; Advisory Committee Set up in Delhi', *The Statesman*, 26 January 1934.

125. 'After the Indian Earthquake', *Bulletin of the League of Red Cross Societies*, XV (1934), 53–54, in Hutchinson, 'Disasters and the International Order. II', 291.

126. Indian Red Cross Society, *Annual Report 1934*, 19.

127. 'An Appeal to Our Readers throughout the World by His Excellency the Governor of Bihar and Orissa' (Sir James Sifton), 'An Appeal by the Viceroy', in Moore (ed.), *Record of the Great Indian Earthquake*, 3–7, 21.

128. Luc Boltanski, *Distant Suffering: Morality, Media and Politics*, trans. Graham Burchell (Cambridge: Cambridge University Press, 2004 [French edition 1993]).

129. Ibid., 4–6.

130. Correspondence of I. M. Stephens, DPI, to E.C. Mieville, P.S.V., New Delhi, 30 January 1934, NAI HP 34/1/1934.

131. Extract in 'Associated Press of India (Inland News Telegrams)', Patna, 2 February 1934, NAI HP 34/1/1934.

132. According to correspondence, I. M. Stephens, DPI, to E. C. Mieville, P.S.V., New Delhi, 30 January 1934, NAI HP 34/1/1934.

133. D.O. 7 34/1/34 Pub., Air Mail by M. G. Hallett, GOI, Home Dept, to R. T. Peel, Sec., P&J Department, India Office (London), New Delhi, 30 January 1934, NAI HP 34/1/1934.

134. Conf. letter, M. G. Hallett to P. C. Tallents, New Delhi, 24 February 1934, NAI HP 34/1/1934.

135. Conf. letter, Hallett to P. C. Tallents, 24 February 1934. NAI HP 34/1/1934.

136. Air Mail 'Infn. Offr. 185/34', A. H. Joyce, Information Officer, India Office, to I. M. Stephens, DPI (New Delhi), London, 1 March 1934, NAI HP 34/1/1934.

137. 'The Devastations by the Earthquake', production 'our own' according to advertisement of "The New Cinema"', 171, Dharamtala Street, Calcutta, *ABP*, 27 January 1934.

138. 'Lord Mayor Sees Earthquake Film', *Daily Telegraph*, 2 February 1934.

139. 'Earthquake Film: Lord Mayor of London Impressed' (London, 2 February 1934), *The Statesman*, 3 February 1934.

140. 'Indian Earthquake Fund: The Queen to Attend Special Matinee', *The Times*, 5 April 1934. Copy of letter no. 68/34, A. H. Joyce, Information Officer, India Office, to I. M. Stephens, DPI (New Delhi), London, 4 February 1934, NAI HP 34/1/1934.

141. Indian Earthquake Fund: Drury Lane Matinee', *Daily Telegraph*, 26 April 1934.

142. The Imperial Film Company of Bombay produced the film and provided free copies for the fund. Commentary was by A. G. A. Norman, member of editorial staff of the *Illustrated Weekly of India*. 'Viceroy's "Quake Film"', *Illustrated Weekly of India*, 18 March 1934. 'A Special Behar Earthquake Film with a Personal Appeal by His Excellency Lord Willingdon', Pathe – The Finest Cinema in Bombay, *The Englishman*, 17 March 1934. One version of the 'earthquake film' issued by Universal newsreel footage can be viewed at http://www.harappa.com/mom/dec98.html (accessed 12 September 2012).

143. Lord Willingdon to Hoare, New Delhi, 30 January 1934, Mss Eur E240/7, 453.

144. J. D. Sifton to the Earl of Willingdon, Patna, 11 March 1934, NAI HP 34/1/1934.

145. William Arthur Moore was the editor of *The Statesman* and Pearson the managing director of the *Times of India*. J. D. Sifton to the Earl of Willingdon, Patna, 11 March 1934, NAI HP 34/1/1934.

146. Extract from Pearson, *Times of India*, to J. D. Sifton, in J. D. Sifton to the Earl of Willingdon, Patna, 11 March 1934, NAI HP 34/1/1934.

147. J. D. Sifton to the Earl of Willingdon, Patna, 11 March 1934, NAI HP 34/1/1934.

148. D.O. 2090, personal letter a 'rough note' prepared for Jafri in connection with his deputation to the Govt of B&O, I. M. Stephens, DPI, to M. G. Hallett, New Delhi, 31 March 1934, NAI HP 34/1/1934.

149. Ormerod appeared to have been the owner or chairman. W. J. Turnbull and H. E. Ormerod, 'The Great Indian Earthquake', special issue of the *Indian Concrete Journal* 8, no. 10 (15 October 1934): xix.

150. See Preface in Brett, *A Report on the Bihar Earthquake*.

151. Photos 'by courtesy of H. E. Ormerod, of the Cement Marketing Company Co. of India, Ltd', *Illustrated Weekly of India* (Bombay), 18 March 1934.

152. Cover and 'An Appeal by the Viceroy', in Moore (ed.), *Record of the Great Indian Earthquake*, 21.

153. Brett, *A Report on the Bihar Earthquake*, 88.

154. 'Some Political and Other Aspects of Earthquake Relief in Bihar' (17 pp.), M .G. Hallett, 31 March 1934, NAI HP 34/1/1934.

155. The VERF is here referred to as 'the Indian Earthquake Fund'. C. R. C. Nixon, 'The Indian Earthquake', *Journal of the Royal Society of Arts* 82, no. 4142 (9 March 1934): 486.

156. Ibid.

157. 'An Appeal by the Viceroy', in Moore (ed.), *Record of the Great Indian Earthquake*, 21.

158. Boltanski makes a difference between the 'natural' helper, the 'contractual' (professional and specialised helpers), and a category which has no obligation to help. Boltanski, *Distant Suffering*, 11, 14.

159. 'An Appeal by the Viceroy', in Moore (ed.), *Record of the Great Indian Earthquake*, 21. Wilcock, *Bihar and Orissa in 1933–34*, 17.

160. 'Some Political and Other Aspects of Earthquake Relief in Bihar' (17 pp.), M. G. Hallett, 31 March 1934, NAI HP 34/1/1934.

161. Sir James Sifton, 'An Appeal to Our Readers throughout the World by His Excellency the Governor of Bihar and Orissa', Patna, 18 February 1934, in Moore (ed.), *Record of the Great Indian Earthquake*, 3.

162. Notes by M. G. Hallett, 12 March 1934, NAI H. Pol. 3/2/1934. The Viceroy's fund after the 1905 Kangra earthquake collected 1.35 million rupees according to a statement in *The Council of State Debates* vol. 1, 7 March 1934, 412. Kangra had a population of 400,000 while north Bihar, which had a population of 13 million, raised 4.7 million rupees according to Roy, 'State, Society and Market', 282n65.

163. 'Earthquake Relief; London Assistance for Viceroy's Fund', *The Statesman*, 27 January 1934.

164. For a discussion on hierarchies of aid within the British Empire, see Christina Twomey and Andrew J. May, 'Australian Responses to the Indian Famine, 1876–78: Sympathy, Photography and the British Empire', *Australian Historical Studies* 43, no. 2 (2012): 233–252.

165. Boltanski, *Distant Suffering*, 11.

166. 'Scheme for Relief; Mayor to Convene a Public Meeting', *The Statesman*, 18 January 1934.

167. 'Mayor's Appeal for Fund' (appeal by Santosh Kumar Basu), 22 January 1933 [*sic* 1934], *ABP*, 24 January 1934.

168. Boltanski, *Distant Suffering*, 8.

169. On the East India Jute Association, Marwaris and trade in raw jute, see Birla, *Stages of Capital*, 197, and Dipesh Chakrabarty, *Rethinking Working-Class History: Bengal 1890–1940* (Princeton: Princeton University Press, 1989), 54.

170. It had set aside 25,000 rupees. 'Earthquake Relief; Mayor's Fund over Two Lakhs', *The Statesman*, 30 January 1934.

171. Indian Jute Mills Association was the voice of British jute mill-owners and managing agents. Birla, *Stages of Capital*, 190; Chakrabarty, *Rethinking Working-Class History*, 4–5.

172. Indian Jute Mills Association donated 54,140 rupees. 'Earthquake Relief (...)', *The Statesman*, 31 January 1934. Hanuman Mills and Adamjee Mills gave through the association, although both had been expelled on the grounds of breaking working-hour rules. Omkar Goswami, 'Collaboration and Conflict: European and Indian Capitalists and the Jute Economy of Bengal, 1919–39', *The Indian Economic and Social History Review* 19, no. 2 (1982): 141–79, 153, 163; Chakrabarty, *Rethinking Working-Class History*, 54–55.

173. 'Assistance of Mayor's Fund; Relief Measures', *The Statesman*, 26 January 1934.

174. 'To-day's Charity Performance', 'Wednesday's Charity Show', 'Natya Niketan's Charity', *ABP*, 30 January 1934. 'In Aid of 'Quake Sufferers; Charity Performance by Girls', *ABP*, 23 February 1934.

175. 'Assistance of Mayor's Fund; Relief Measures', *The Statesman*, 26 January 1934.

176. 'Ladies Relief Dentre [*sic* 'Centre']; An Appeal to Ladies', *Behar Herald*, 27 January 1934.

177. 'Mayor's Relief Fund: "Flag Day" Fixed for Saturday', *The Englishman*, 22 January 1934. 13,000 rupees was collected in tin cans. 'Earthquake Relief'; (...), *The Statesman*, 31 January 1934.

178. 'Behar Relief Day; Sunday the 28th January; Pl. Malaviya Urges Country Wide Observance', *Behar Herald*, 27 January 1934.

179. Nripendra Nath Mitra (ed.), *The Indian Annual Register: An Annual Digest of Public Affairs of India* (Calcutta: The Annual Register Office, Vol. II, July–December, 1934), 356.

180. George Schuster (Finance member), 14 February 1934, in GOI, *Legislative Assembly Debates* (Official report), vol. I, 1934 (24 January–16 February 1934), 830–31.

5

Categories of Victims

Introduction: Victimhood

This chapter examines how categories of relief receivers were defined by the government and select relief societies according to the effects of the earthquake, social relations and the political economy of the government. By examining the way categories of relief receivers and damages were defined, the chapter seeks to explore how socio-economic categories and the particular damages of the earthquake intersected and created needs for relief that would come to shape the rehabilitation phase.

After the earthquake, the idea of relief as a compensatory scheme of relative provisions, allocated according to needs based on social and financial class, in many ways bears resemblance to divisions in famine relief. During famines in the nineteenth century, relief societies and the government both allocated and distributed gratuitous relief to categories of relief receivers divided into 'classes' defined by social standing and financial losses. The 'middle classes' became a class apart among relief receivers as charity and philanthropy were increasingly institutionalised in famine relief. Labourers and the so-called able-bodied carried out 'works of public utility', for instance, on the notorious famine works, while the rest were left to charity of the public and private kind.[1] The government's definition of 'able-bodied' was not uniform, as in the case of the 1892 Orissa famine when the local government classified workers according to skills, physical abilities and whether or not they were considered accustomed to hard labour.[2]

Famine relief by the colonial state divided people according to who were 'the deserving and the undeserving', according to Sanjay Sharma: 'By introducing new measures of need, by attempting to distinguish between ordinary beggary and crisis-destitution, and by exacting work in return for relief to prevent indolence, the colonial state set the parameters in which new notions of the deserving and the undeserving crystallized over a period of time.'[3] In the context of the eighteenth-century Madras Presidency, Ravi Ahuja has noted how famine relief classification detailed subsistence and means for survival.[4] The colonial administrators allotted a right of subsistence unevenly to different groups by giving preferential treatment to house-owners, occupational groups of strategic value, 'poor Europeans', so-called Eurasians and sepoys and 'possibly' Brahmins.[5] Later policy documents such as the Bengal Famine Manual from 1941 continued the tradition of needs-based relief with stratification of relief according to class and physical abilities. In order to enable poor villagers to buy a basic diet in the market, the government provided 'test' relief for those prepared to work, gratuitous relief for those incapable of labour and agricultural loans for those with land to cultivate. The so-called able-bodied members of indigent *bhadralok* families, unwilling to undertake manual labour, were provided for from private donations to charitable relief funds administered by district relief committees.[6] While famines and 'natural' disasters undoubtedly have different causes and effects on society, categories of relief after the earthquake shared many definitions with categories drawn up in famine relief, most importantly the classification of middle classes as a privileged category and the ability of labourers, agriculturalists and a category of so-called poor to undertake manual labour. In the colonial period, 'labourers' mainly referred to agricultural wage labourers but also included a general category of people who carried out manual labour,[7] as well as a so-called working class of agriculturalists among the peasantry.[8] While damages to property and loss of income due to the earthquake played a role in defining the needs for compensation for the middle classes, perceptions of social classes also influenced relief provisions and the allotment of financial aid. The middle classes emerged as the primary category of relief receivers both for charitable relief as well as government loans. The urban middle classes were univocally portrayed as in need of aid to rebuild their houses, even though data on ruined houses varied starkly, while rural damages and rural needs for relief varied greatly in official reports and documentation of damages by the Revenue Department. The definitions of relief receivers and of property would come to occupy the relief and reconstruction process, showing the importance of both material losses and social standing in defining needs for relief according to different categories.

The categories of earthquake victims can be understood as based on categories drawn up during previous disasters, primarily famines, each of which had been created to respond to the demands of its corresponding social group (for instance, labourers, middle-class persons). The earthquake's aftermath represented a moment when the needs of these categories would be redefined in relation to damages, while still being constituted on previous understandings of socio-economic relations. By addressing how first of all the middle classes were conceived as a category of relief receivers, the chapter shows how the category was produced in relation to other groups considered less deserving of relief. In a larger perspective, these relief categories may have further entrenched or increased the vulnerability of poorer communities in future disasters. Financial aid to the middle classes enabled them to rebuild better houses, that is, with improved constructions and material, while labourers and the poor reconstructed with smaller budgets and recycled building materials assembled by their own capacity and with limited amounts of charity.

In this sense, the urban middle classes emerged as winners in the relief and reconstruction phase.[9] They were, however, portrayed as the biggest losers in terms of having lost urban property and sources of income according to contemporary spokespersons for these classes in the Legislative Assembly and newspapers. In the aftermath the middle classes received considerable charitable relief and subsidised loans with low interest rates. At the other end of the spectrum, rural and to some extent urban labourers, according to the same logic, received less attention in compensatory relief schemes: labourers had lost the least in the earthquake. Since they owned nothing valuable before the earthquake, they could not have lost anything: they did not own property according to the official definition, had no regular income and, most importantly, their only asset, 'the ability to labour', was intact and in demand. In the rhetoric by the advocates of financial relief to the middle classes, those with the ability to labour emerged as winners.

Surveys of Rural Damages

'Labourers', 'agriculturalists' and the 'poor' were in newspaper accounts, government reports and official debates generally not portrayed as the primary victims and sufferers in the aftermath; rather, they were seen as only marginally affected by the earthquake. In the immediate aftermath, the labouring classes and to a great extent the rural population were, in fact, seen as unaffected by the disaster—so far. Rural relief instead was directed towards preventive measures in view of the negative effects that the earthquake was anticipated to have on soil productivity and the vulnerable flood landscape during the upcoming monsoon. Broken embankments and large tracts of agricultural land under water—observations made by local government officers early on signalled that the earthquake would have a significant impact on waterways.[10] A connection between increased flood vulnerability and earthquakes have been documented in Assam, where both the 1897 earthquake and the 1950 earthquake contributed towards more severe and changed patterns of floods. Geological changes brought on by the earthquakes and man-made engineering solutions meant to 'manage' rivers led to more instances of floods and increased vulnerability.[11] In Bihar, changes in land levels affected, above all, the river beds: like in 1934, the earthquakes of 1833 and 1988 impacted the river Kosi's flow.[12] In the immediate aftermath of the 1934 earthquake, however, government officials undertaking the air and land surveys were divided in their opinions regarding the effects of sand and water on agricultural land.

Two early reports by the Commissioner of Tirhut division were based upon an air survey and a tour by road across parts of the worst-affected rural areas.[13] Another report by the Director of Agriculture and the Director of Industries contained contradictory information.[14] These reports show the difference in appreciation of rural damages in accounts made by high officials in the local administration. In his second report the Commissioner wrote that the 'damage is serious, but not nearly so serious as I feared':

Round Katra and Aurai crops are excellent, fully normal where not swamped by sand, and swamped only to about 5 or 7%. The sub-divisional officer took us out the Sursand road to see 'widespread and irreparable damage'. We consider that even here, not more than from 10 to 15% of the standing crop is affected. It seems certain now that so long as the crop, rather, wheat, oats, barley, even tobacco, has a fair number of leaves above the deposit, it is going to survive, and the deposit brought, and to some extent retains, a good deal of moisture. It is definitely not correct to assume that wherever there is standing water there is damage from deposit. (…) I shall be surprised if by the end of March, when most of this water will have disappeared, the country does not look much more normal and healthy.[15]

Though the Commissioner of Tirhut found the damage 'serious', he dismissed the sub-divisional officer's description of 'wide-spread and irreparable damage' to crops. His second report thereby reconfirmed his initial findings which described damages as 'negligible', and 'no where' [sic] did the damage exceed 10 per cent of the crop, in some areas less than 2 per cent, according to him. Contrary to the previous negative effects feared as a result of the sand deposits and standing water, he believed it could have a positive impact and make it appear 'much more normal and healthy'. As he had noted in the first survey a week after the earthquake, more worrying than the outcome of the yield was the effect of 'very extensive mud deposits' on future crops. However, the damages were patchy: the Commissioner did not estimate 'that outside this area [i.e. the area between Sitamarhi and Muzaffarpur] we shall require to give any assistance to *raiyats* or villagers on the score of damage to houses or fields, nor do I think there is any risk of water supply or any call for medical assistance'.[16] Despite the Commissioner's optimistic take on damages to the land, he thought it difficult to translate the estimates into figures in terms of outcomes on the harvests and thereby revenue. On top of that, floods had affected the area in the previous year and 'a very poor yield' had been expected.[17] His reports thereby recognised the need for assistance in sand clearing in some areas but large-scale relief, economic compensation or medical assistance for the rural population on a broader basis were not regarded as necessary.

The Director of Industries and the Director of Agriculture, instead of agreeing with the Commissioner's perception of rural damages, raised alarm about the sand deposits' impact on the soil's productivity in a report submitted a few days after the Commissioner's first report. Contrary to the Commissioner's report that had found extensive 'mud deposits', also referred to as 'silt' which normally provides nutrition to the fields in annual inundations, their report stressed that a sample sent for analysis showed that it was pure sand. Unless the sand mixed with the soil, the land would become 'infertile and unproductive', or even worse: 'Where the deposit is thick the area will within a short time assume the appearance of a desert.' Assessment of the impact on the crops would only be possible after a detailed survey of the land, but in the areas 'within a radius of 7 to 8 miles round Sitamarhi and Riga, the *rabi* crop may be taken as a total failure'.[18] These two reports carried out in the same area in the weeks following the earthquake, reflect the differences in perceptions of the damages among government officials.

After the initial superficial and contradictory land surveys, the government announced that for relief in rural areas two acts previously applied foremost during rural distress and famines would be used.[19] The Agriculturalist's Loans Act, 1884 (Act XII of 1884), and the Land Improvement Act, 1871, had served to distribute grants and *taccavi*, a system of agrarian loans provided by colonial and Mughal rulers during agrarian distress or famines.[20] The two acts enabled the government to use the Bihar and Orissa Provincial Famine Relief Fund, the government announced in February.[21] The famine fund was normally used for relief after 'natural calamities' such as floods and droughts, and after the province split into Bihar and Orissa, the Bihar Famine Relief Fund Act would relieve agriculturalists and *rayiats* in 'distress' after 'natural calamities' by relying on the Bihar Famine Relief Fund.[22] However, this was a temporary solution since the government at the beginning of March decided to cover the amount from the VERF set aside for small grants to remove sand.[23] The Provincial Famine Relief Fund covered agricultural loans of a little more than one million rupees to those affected by the earthquake and the subsequent floods, and about 450,000 in grants for sand clearance.[24] This was considerably more than its yearly average expenditure on disaster relief of 100,000 to 150,000 rupees.[25] However, as Brett notes in his report, 'two schools of thought' developed as to the sand's possible damage on the soil and waterways: one claimed that the sand would mix with the soil relatively soon with the help of rain and wind, while the other argued that it was necessary to remove the sand. The local government and the Agricultural Department sided with the latter position, which was supported by a set of surveys discussed next. However, the GSI's comprehensive report on the earthquake published in 1939 claimed to have difficulties in finding reliable observers of the phenomenon of sand vents, limiting their accounts of sanding to narratives by mainly Europeans in high positions or those involved in the sugar cane industry. Yet the volume devoted a section to explain and compare the phenomena of sand and water emerging from vents in the land and their occurrence in historical earthquakes. According to the GSI, the extent of sanding was 'popularly much exaggerated' and 'the actual damage due to sanding would be almost negligible'; not unlike the Commissioner of Tirhut's perception of the areas covered by sand and water, the geologists thought the land to have become more fertile.[26]

A report commissioned by the local government, based on a brief survey conducted in the first half of March 1934 by K. S. Caldwell, a professor in Chemistry at Patna Science College, expressed the view that the sand needed to be removed.[27] Regarding the sand's negative effects, the important point was first of all to clear waterways since it had blocked roadside drains and *nullahs* which risked to breach the bunds of small landholders. In moderation, the sand had no harmful effect on the quality of the land, but thick deposits had to be removed or diluted, according to him. Based on the unknown effects of the sand, coupled with the serious risk of floods in the ensuing monsoon, he recommended the government to 'reward' peasants in order to expedite sand clearing, a process which otherwise worms and ants or rain and wind would gradually take care of.[28] Caldwell's report and the GSI's *Preliminary Report** on the North Bihar Earthquake* were used by the Japanese earthquake expert Nobuji Nasu (1899–1983)[29] from the Earthquake Research Institute at Tokyo University who visited the earthquake area for 50 days.[30] Japan's earthquake expertise was by 1934 well established, based on the catastrophic experiences of the Nobi Plain. Japanese seismologists conducted research expeditions to Assam in 1897 and to epicentral zones of major earthquakes such as the 1906 San Francisco and the 1908 Messina earthquakes, sharing advice and using methods based on lessons from the 'earthquake nation'.[31] Nasu agreed with Caldwell that the sand originated from the layer of water-bearing sand from a depth of 20–30 feet, and not 300 to 400 feet as 'frequently reported'.[32] In this context, the Muzaffarpur District Board commissioned the publication of a booklet with guidelines for how to instruct the peasants to remove sand, use scrapers, fertilizers and seeds, with detailed costs for the equipment.[33] The local government arranged 400 ploughs for the peasants to remove or mix the sand with the soil. The ploughs were not for free and since 'very few' were sold, the government lent them to the *chaukidari* unions who were expected to oversee their utilisation.[34]

In view of distributing rural relief and based on the initial reports by the two directors, the Revenue Department by the end of January started preparing for a survey of land damages. The survey from 10 March to May 1934 mapped the earthquake's effects on agricultural land in terms of sanding, standing water and changes in land levels. The findings were presented in *Final Report on the Survey of Lands Damaged by Earthquake in North Bihar in 1934* (short title: *Final Report on the Survey of Lands Damaged*) submitted in July 1934 and published in September the same year.[35] The survey formed the basis for the distribution of grants and *taccavi*.

Taccavi, Grants and Revenue Remission

Since reports on rural conditions in the earthquake area contained little comprehensive information, the local government and the Government of India hesitated to estimate costs of rural relief and reconstruction until the Revenue Department's survey had provided data.[36] The central government, however, assured financial support since it was clear that the local government would be unable to bear the expenditure.[37] The lack of information about damages in rural areas can be explained by the urgency of relief in the often devastating destruction of brick buildings in towns: it was only after the situation in the towns was under control at the beginning of February that the administrations in the worst-affected districts were requested to submit reports on relief work and damages in villages.[38] While waiting for information on the nature of rural relief, the district administrations in the affected districts had gone ahead to deal with the effects on land with only cursory support by the local government in Patna. Contrary to the perception of the Commissioner of Tirhut, the district officer of Muzaffarpur foresaw difficult times for the rural areas. He anticipated the situation to get worse once the effects of the soil and the lack of water had taken its toll on resources. In the Tirhut division, the impending monsoon floods and difficulties in extracting the *rabi*[39] crop from the sand-covered fields were expected to worsen the situation for the agriculturalists. In anticipation of an increasing need for relief among the rural population, he saw large advances as necessary 'for improvement of lands or many cultivators will be almost completely ruined'. Contrary to the almost positive account impact on the landscape by the earthquake according to the Commissioner of Tirhut, he thought 'that the problem of rural areas would become more and more acute as time goes on'.[40] Similar accounts appeared in the reports by other district officers in north Bihar. The district officer in Champaran had eased conditions of debts and payments in the rural areas and, without waiting for instructions, he had granted remission of rent for destroyed standing crop and areas permanently thrown out of cultivation. Rent and arrears, as well as certificate sales and proceedings, had been postponed until March. The relief work in Champaran was facilitated by the fact that the Bettiah Estate made up 1,350 square miles out of 1,700 square miles in the worst-affected area. Since the estate's administration had taken responsibility for *taccavi* loans in by far the largest part of the district, the district officer was in charge of only 350 square miles 'where the Sub-divisional Officer is constantly touring, and the Kanungo is preparing estimates of sand deposits, with a view of granting *taccavi* loans immediately'.[41] The anticipation of a widespread and growing need for rural relief proved to converge well with the previously mentioned report by the Directors of Industries and Agriculture, who had predicted aggravating conditions in Tirhut. Despite the local government's hesitant stance towards announcing assistance to rural areas, the administration in the districts saw it necessary, if not to provide relief, at least to temporarily relieve the rural population with regular payments in order to cope with the apparent effects of the earthquake on agricultural land.

Based on the initial land surveys by the GSI and government officials, ahead of the publication of Caldwell's report, and based on the Revenue Department's survey from 10 March to 28 May 1934, the government announced that it would distribute large sums in *taccavi* and in gratuitous relief to cultivators for clearing sand from their fields. Since the sand deposits were feared to cause waterlogging once the rains started in June, the government was in a hurry to initiate the work. The survey—resulting in the Revenue Department's *Final Report on the Survey of Lands Damaged*—and the distribution of relief proceeded in tandem: officers distributing *taccavi* and grants followed in the footsteps of surveyors from the Revenue Department. In order to ensure that the work of sand clearance was completed, half of the grant or loan was to be paid after the work had been carried out. The Board of Revenue's relief measure included the postponement of land revenue due in March, to be paid instead in June 1934 in the areas with most severe agricultural damages, that is, Champaran Sadr, Muzaffarpur Sadr, Sitamarhi, Darbhanga Sadr and Madhubani.[42]

The distribution of *taccavi*, like the distribution of loans and grants, suffered from a lack of staff. The 120 survey officers expected to cover more than 4,000 acres of land and 6 million plots in three months, before the rains that were expected to start in June (Table 5.1), were from the outset found to be insufficient for the task.[43] Instead of the initial survey method proposed by the Board of Revenue, the new, 'speedier method' referred to as *nazar paimaish* (literally 'eye measurement' or 'eye survey') required less staff since surveyors were only required to 'make a guess of the areas of each plot damaged' and take the average depth of sand in each plot.[44] In practice, survey officers speeded up the progress of the survey further by estimating the damage based on the *nazar paimaish* of the villagers, not even setting eyes on the land themselves. According to the *Final Report on the Survey of Lands Damaged*, the majority of the damaged land was covered by 6 inches to 1 foot of sand, and sand measuring 1–2 feet covered a substantial area (Table 5.2). These estimates meant that the majority of the agriculturalists could ask for a *taccavi* of 20–30 rupees per acre (Table 5.2).

Proof of being a landholder was initially an essential requirement for obtaining a loan or a grant, a rule which in practice had to be bent several times. The district administration instead organised for distribution of grants and *taccavi* according to the districts' own systems and the *Final Survey* mentions local practices for grant distribution.[45] In Champaran, the *khesras* (official village field book)[46] had been destroyed and the *khatian* (land register of the full holding),[47] for some unidentified reason, could not be taken out of the record room, which obstructed the work. Possible cases of attempts to fraud, or perhaps what can be seen as a chance to easily access loans, arose in the cases of *raiyats* claiming loans for land reclamation of plots which, according to the last survey, had been recorded as uncultivated land. The holdings of the *raiyats* were, however, small and, with the time constraint in mind, it was decided 'to roughly survey' the entire area as one plot and record the tenants as 'joint owners', a system which meant that they collectively took a loan. Similarly, 'a few cases' arose where a considerable area, recorded as *zirat*[48] of the landlords, had been settled with tenants as separate

Table 5.1 Damages of area and plots surveyed in 4,152 villages

	Total survey	Acres/number damaged	Percentage of the surveyed area/ plots damaged
Area	2,647,591 acres (4,137 sq. miles)	393,977 acres (616 sq. miles)	15 %
Plots	6,028,210	1,810,958	31 %

Source: Appendix E in *Final Report on the Survey of Lands Damaged*.

Table 5.2 Sanding, *taccavi* allowance payable per acre, and percentage of the damaged lands according to the survey

Classification of damages	Degree of sanding	Maximum *taccavi* payable per acre	Sanded [damaged] area in sq. miles	Percentage
Class I	Less than 6 inches	10 Rs	28,160 acres 44 sq. miles	7 %
Class II	Less than 1 foot	20 Rs	206,080 acres 322 sq. miles	52 %
Class III	More than 1 foot	30 Rs	145,920 acres 228 sq. miles	37 %
Class IV	2 feet and above	35 Rs	13,440 acres 21 sq. miles	4 %

Source: Compiled data from *Final Report on the Survey of Lands Damaged*, cf. 1–20.

holdings since the last settlement.[49] Officially, the question of landownership was crucial to determine eligibility for a loan, and only owners of the fields, zamindars and *raiyats* were recorded in the 'Damage *khesras*', as the new survey document was named. Other types of landholders were defined as 'temporary', such as *zerpeshgidars*[50] or *bataidars* (tenant-at-will paying rent in kind) and excluded from the survey, except for *bataidars* who had held the land for over 12 years on a fixed produce rent.[51] In practice, however, alternative solutions were used since papers regarding landholding rights could rarely be submitted.

In addition to the fact that the sand was only occasionally measured, the surveyors' difficulties in cooperating with tenants make the accuracy of the survey questionable. In the beginning, the surveyors reported how the tenants took no interest and how, despite the efforts made by the surveyors, 'they would not come out of their houses to show their fields'. According to the surveyors, this seemingly odd behaviour could be explained by pressure from moneylenders in the villages who hoped to profit from granting loans with high interest. The government countered by mobilising support from 'non-official agencies', perhaps local associations and relief organisations, and conducted 'counter propaganda' of undisclosed character, resulting in the cooperation of the tenants in the survey.[52]

Sugar cane planters and agriculturalists of more substantial means made up an exclusive and favoured relief category. The Government of India from the outset promised to arrange loans[53] and provide a grant of 500,000 rupees exclusively for the disposal of the sugarcane harvest, relief to the cultivators and the mills.[54] Officially, the government's *RPER* claimed the support and control of the sugar cane market to be necessary, as without it 'unscrupulous contractors' would persuade the *raiyat*s to sell cane at nominal prices. According to the local government's opinion, sugar cane cultivation was the means for the 'average Bihari *raiyat*' to earn money to pay rent and buy what was not reaped in the fields.[55] In terms of financial support, the planters were clearly favoured, although the government viewed the grant as a way 'to show our consideration for the cane-grower'.[56] The stated purpose of the Cane Marketing Board was to serve as the only selling agent of cane in order to explicitly prevent the agents of the two 'unscrupulous' factories that were still functional to take advantage of the situation by buying the cane at low rates.[57] As a result, the board fixed the price of cane paid to the cultivators at 'very little less' than what was received normally, a measure which benefited five out of the eight severely damaged factories which could resume crushing and continued working 'well beyond' the normal season, the local government noted.[58]

Instrumental in securing relief to plantation owners was the Bihar Planters Association and the local government who cooperated in submitting proposals for taking steps in speeding up the grant and loan process. In Champaran, one of the larger cane-growing areas, the government regarded a chief concern the urgent disposal of sugar cane crop valued at above 1 million rupees.[59] When the earthquake struck, 54 estates farming from 500 to 5,000 acres (202 to 2,023 hectares) all over north Bihar produced sugar cane. The case was urgent since the cane was ready to be harvested and the local factories were rendered non-functional by the earthquake. The government grant was motivated by the value of the harvest and spent on the conversion of 6 million *maund*s (almost

224 million kg) of sugar cane into *gur* (jaggery) and to a lesser extent *khandsari* sugar by country mills and pans, and to some extent on freight concession on the railways for transports to undamaged factories.[60] A return to local production methods of *khandsari* sugar and *gur* was a temporary solution financed by grants from the Government of India. The production method was normally confined to the interior areas without access to sugar factories and it was by comparison more labour-intensive and did not require electricity, as it in this case was powered by bullocks.[61] According to the local government's yearly report, 'the cultivators had to be taught the forgotten art of making good *gur'*. In addition to lacking skills and the additional labour required for the method, producing *gur* meant a smaller profit, which was only accepted by the cultivators after exhausting all options of selling to sugar-producing factories.[62]

Property, Losses and Finding 'Genuine Sufferers'

From the views put forward in the press emerged an idea of needs according to the socio-economic layers contained in the broad category of the middle classes as opposed to the labouring classes and the sub-tenants of the agricultural population. According to an opinion in the newspaper, professionals of the middle classes—'pleaders, *mukhtears* (attorneys), doctors, school-teachers, "*gurus*" (teachers) of *pathshalas* (schools teaching in vernacular languages) and petty businessmen'—after the earthquake had to fend for themselves, while coolies, labourers, *ekkawallahs* (cart drivers) and *taxiwallahs* (taxi drivers) could easily find work.[63] Such attempts to emphasise the suffering of the middle classes, forcefully voiced in the Legislative Council as well as in the press, amplified the strong lobbying carried out on their behalf by persons in influential positions such as council members and representatives of relief societies.[64] In particular, in the Legislative Assembly, the middle classes were well represented by lawyers and landholders, who formed a substantial share of the Provincial Councils at the beginning of the twentieth century. With the emergence of political rights according to groups and collectives in the first decades of the twentieth century, political representation included group interest as well as individual representation.[65] Planters formed one such group which was wholeheartedly in support of the view that the middle classes were entitled to relief for reconstructing houses. In addition to a likely self-interest in arguing for the needs of the middle classes, there was the fact that franchise in the province was, like elsewhere in India, based mainly on property.[66] With franchise in the province being dependent on the payment of a certain amount of revenue, rent or cess in rural areas and on the payment of municipal tax in urban areas, people who had the right to vote also had an interest in the reconstruction of property. Although it is beyond the scope of the present discussion to address the possible impact of financial support towards the reconstruction of property on electoral politics, it is interesting to note the relation between disaster reconstruction, property and the possibility of increasing electoral participation in the aftermath. According to the 1931 census, the electorate for the provincial legislature was the lowest in India, at only 1.1 per cent (5 per cent urban; 1 per cent rural). As per recommendations by the report of the Indian Franchise Committee in 1932, franchise to the provincial legislatures was to be increased to 10 per cent of the population.[67] Since this target was to a large extent achieved by extending the existing property qualifications,[68] financial aid towards the reconstruction of property was likely to benefit a group of new voters.

One of the strongest advocates for relief to the middle classes was Speaker Chandreshvar Prashad Narayan Sinha, belonging to the local elite class of landowners in Muzaffarpur. He argued for relief to the broad middle classes and opined that houses of 'permanent nature' should be considered for a loan and the greatest group of potential house-loan takers was the large body of the middle classes inhabiting urban, suburban and rural areas.[69] The abilities of the middle classes to voice their need for relief in public and to the authorities appeared as strong in the rural as in the urban areas. The police in Champaran reported a case of unrest where the insufficient relief to the middle classes from the government and the Bettiah Raj was the cause of complaint by a leader of a local relief society.[70] In such complaints, the middle classes forcefully expressed a critique of the local government and portrayed themselves as a deprived group. Although the middle classes as a group was often argued for based on whether they were house-owners, as a category it was differentiated in terms of quality of property and professional and financial status.

In framing needs for relief, the middle classes were often portrayed as dependent on each other, yet markedly different from each other. As Sanjay Joshi writes, being middle class was a project of 'self-fashioning'.[71] In arguing for relief, the middle classes fashioned themselves as being in between and, foremost, above the 'labouring' classes. The middle classes were demarked as a category by both social and economic criteria which made them different from each other, and yet dependent on each other as well as on other relief-receiving categories in the aftermath. This interdependency of skills and assets was largely articulated from the perspective of the middle classes and financial elites such as planters from the sugar industry. The middle classes of Bihar fit within the standard definition of the group in colonial India, often distinguished by belonging to the upper strata of society, without being at the very top.[72] In colonial India they were, as Partha Chatterjee writes, 'simultaneously placed in a position of subordination in one relation and a position of dominance in another'.[73] Among Bihar's largely rural middle classes in towns and villages, the government, under normal circumstances, relied to a great extent on the well-to-do peasants for the administration of the rural areas. These persons constituted the top layer of the peasantry and employed other lower categories of the rural population, the agricultural labourers and the under-*raiyats*.[74] The colonial government mostly relied on these well-to-do landed *raiyats* as intermediaries in exercising its power in the districts.[75]

There were people who noted the relative silence on the rural situation and a tendency to speak in favour of town residents even as the village population remained 'not vocal like its brethren in the towns'.[76] A speaker from Darbhanga argued for relief to the rural population who remained marginally addressed as a group in need of financial aid:

> The prevailing idea is that the villagers have got merely huts and mud-wall buildings and therefore they have not lost much. In the local committee this sort of view was expressed, but it was perhaps not remembered that these villages, who previous to this calamity were heavily indebted and whose produce was selling very cheap, were even before the quake financially in a very straitened condition and had to purchase their necessities of life such as kerosene oil, salt and cloth at a higher rate than what was prevailing in the towns. (...) They were already in a bad plight and it was on account of their poverty that they had mud-walls and very few brick walls. But all the same they have all suffered and their mud-walls were for them like brick walls. I think their troubles were not fully realised and consequently their claims were brushed aside in giving them immediate relief.[77]

The speaker's statement addressed 'the prevailing idea' that the villagers had not lost much since they did not own much in terms of property, by arguing that though the loss was relatively less compared to sugar-factory owners, it was still a loss which was felt financially. The 'immaterial' value of rural houses was contrasted with the middle classes' houses as 'assets'. In the relief process, a house figured to the middle classes as an investment accumulated over the years. With the destruction of the house, they had lost the invested earnings and inheritance.

As Chandreshvar Prashad Narayan Sinha put it in the Legislative Council, this group of middle class men was positioned between the lowest class, the 'labourers', and a class of people with substantial means, 'the bigger *zamindars* and planters'.[78] The one thing in common among the middle classes according to the argument forwarded: to have lost a house built of bricks, the most common type of building defined as a house in the towns. Houses were further assessed as a means of income: in Monghyr and Jamalpur, the government deemed the reconstruction of houses of 'destitute Anglo-Indians and Europeans' eligible for assistance since these served as a means of income. Similarly, widows of railway subordinates in Jamalpur, who claimed to have invested all their savings in house property, represented 'hard cases' in need of relief, and the same held true for an 'old Anglo-Indian lady' in Monghyr who had lost five houses and thereby her whole income derived from rents.[79]

In his report from 1935, Relief Commissioner Brett wrote that many attempts had been made to estimate the number of houses damaged and to compute the financial loss involved but the attempts 'proved to be of very little value' since the houses varied in their construction and damages.[80] The disparate figures in the appreciation of damaged houses are to a large extent explainable by the fluid definition of a house that resulted from the variety of constructions in terms of building material. Official reports recognised three common types of constructions: *kuccha* buildings, foremost in villages, and *pucca* buildings used for official constructions in towns, and *kuccha-pucca* houses, in both urban and rural areas. The vast majority of the rural village population, who also formed the large majority of Bihar's population, lived in *kuccha* buildings of mud, or mud and wattle, with a roof carried on bamboo poles and walls of bamboo-wattle work covered with a thin layer of mud. The GSI regarded this type of construction 'equally liable to damage' during regular monsoons, noting that they should 'never have heavy roofs' in order to at least reduce mortality in case of collapse in a future earthquake.[81] Such *kuccha* constructions were commonly referred to as 'huts' and generally excluded from the category of buildings which qualified as 'houses'.[82]

A combination of the *kuccha* constructions, mud, bamboo or straw and the *pucca* material bricks became a *kuccha-pucca* construction as long as it was built without a fixating substance such as lime or mortar. A *pucca* house was in general made of bricks or stones, fixed with cement or lime, or if of a better standard, with a structure of concrete. The majority of the damaged houses in north Bihar were of the type *kuccha-pucca* and constructed with 'mud mortar'. With little to bind the bricks together, they had collapsed in the central area of the earthquake.

Similarly, townhouses made of bricks were described as 'merely laid in mud' without being fixated. Adding to their fragile structure, they were often built with numerous additions over a period of time and were of considerable height in the bazaars. These most common brick houses, sometimes fixed with mud and sometimes built with lime or mortar in the towns, and the *kuccha-pucca* houses in the villages were the most severely affected according to Brett and the GSI. Without a uniform standard and a variety of material, they formed the majority of the damaged houses which needed to be reconstructed.[83] An accepted idea of a 'house' therefore ranged from brick buildings made by cement or mortar to constructions made of brick and mixed with a variety of materials such as mud, lime, bamboo and grass.

The loss of property was according to Brett 'the greatest and the most universal of the losses', yet data with approximate numbers to sustain such a claim are missing from his report. The scheme of distribution set up by the VERF according to him 'pre-supposed' that recipients needed money to rebuild houses. Another rather contradictory explanation for the lack of data was that it would have been 'inadvisable' to record statistics on the damages since they would have been of 'no practical value' considering the urgency to reconstruct.[84] Though neither the exact number of damaged private properties nor the nature of damages was known, the destruction was regarded as extensive and the category of reconstruction of houses received a large share of charitable relief and government-sponsored loans.

The official lack of initiative for recording damages to private property in Bihar, except for general references by the GSI to the destruction of buildings while mapping isoseismals of the earthquake,[85] partly explain the confusion in counting the number of damaged houses which varied greatly depending on sources. Towards the end of February, as the budget for reconstruction was being negotiated, the number of houses and financial relief was intensely debated in newspapers and in the Legislative Assembly.[86] Two examples of the 'many attempts' at estimating the scope of ruined houses mentioned by Brett are given in the Marwari Relief Society's (1935) and the BCRC's publications— *Report for the Period Ending 30th June 1934* and *Devastated Bihar*.[87] According to the 1931 Census, the total number of inhabited houses in the five towns of Muzaffarpur district was 16,739, as quoted by the BCRC.[88] Both the BCRC and the Marwari Relief Society appreciated 'considerable' damages to 318,175 'houses' and 'house properties' in Muzaffarpur,[89] that is, the damaged houses were many more than the number of houses according to official records in the main towns of the district.[90] Another sign of the Marwari Relief Society's concern for house-owners, and to some extent involvement in their interests, is evident in a telegram sent two weeks after the earthquake in which its general secretary requested the local government to send engineers for giving advice on 'cracked' houses in Muzaffarpur.[91] As evident from the data, these reports' classification of houses included constructions other than of those of the *pucca* quality. For instance, the BCRC included 'mud houses' as a type of 'house'.[92] The criteria put up by relief societies thereby differed from the official criteria which, according to Relief Commissioner Brett, defined a 'house' as made of bricks and mud or mortar. Though the two relief societies' reports do not describe damages in detail, the fact that dynamite was used to demolish houses still standing but dangerous to inhabit indicate that solid materials such as cement, concrete and/or bricks constituted construction material to some extent.[93]

The much broader definition used by the BCRC and Marwari Relief Society for a house may be seen as attempts at widening the need for relief measures, and this also broadened the classification of the middle classes and thereby expanded the distribution of aid. Arguing for relief to a broader category of houses-owners may at the same time have been a strategy to consolidate the needs of people who would cast their votes in the upcoming elections. In Bihar, the Indian Franchise Committee in 1932 had recommended to increase the franchise from 1.1 per cent to 9 or 10 per cent by lowering qualifications based on municipal tax in urban areas.[94] Data in *Devastated Bihar* estimated that half of the 70,000 houses in urban areas hit by the earthquake had to be rebuilt for a cost of 100 rupees per house, covering construction costs and building materials. In the BCRC's calculation, 3.5 million rupees would cover the cost for reconstruction of urban private property, while rural houses could be rebuilt for 20 rupees per house, indicating perhaps cheaper construction material as well as low-paid or unpaid labour as will be further discussed in this chapter. The number of buildings defined as 'houses' in rural areas was, however, considerably more than in the towns: out of a total of 1.03 million houses, roughly half of them, that is, 506,000 houses needed to be rebuilt or repaired at a total cost of slightly more than 10 million rupees. In the BCRC's calculation, the sum 13.62 million rupees was needed for reconstructing both rural and urban private property.[95] To further complicate the disparate figures, the BCRC's later publication, *Report for the Period Ending 30th June 1934*, mentioned 1,011,967 'damaged and ruined houses' in north Bihar and Monghyr, excluding the districts Patna, Purnea and North Bhagalpur for which data had not been collected.[96] This figure almost doubled the number of 541,000 houses first mentioned in *Devastated Bihar*, that is, 506,000 rural houses and 35,000 urban houses. The considerably higher number may have been the result of revised definitions of damages and appreciation of the need for repairs. Even if providing far from reliable data, these sources reveal the difficulties in appreciating the number of damaged houses and the actual cost of rebuilding as clearly several definitions of a house were in use. With these figures at hand, it is therefore difficult to state even an approximate figure of damaged houses. The rather wide range in the number of damaged or ruined houses—somewhere between 500,000 and 1,000,000— according to the figures from these two relief societies shows the diverging appreciations of damages as well as different definitions of a house.

Reconstruction of Private Property: Middle Class Relief

The Bihar and Orissa Natural Calamities Loans Act was passed in order to support the reconstruction of damaged private houses: 'to grant loans for building to the owners of buildings which have been damaged or distroyed [sic] by earthquakes [sic] or other natural calamities'.[97] An emergency act for lending money to the public on the security of house property, it was a method hitherto untested by the local government.[98] The government referred to the conditions as a clear deviance from practice in order to arrange loans for those who normally were able to borrow money with their house as security. The act was passed in the February 1934 session of the Legislative Council without much ado, the applicable rules were published in the middle of March and loans were issued early in April.[99] The need for an act to specifically aid the reconstruction of private property was argued for based on an unwillingness among the middle classes to accept charity. A speaker in the Legislative Council argued that the fragmented group of the middle classes 'would much rather starve and die before they take help from any charitable society or from any organisation'.[100] Despite this description of the middle classes as being reluctant towards accepting charity, the middle classes as a relief category received large amounts in charitable aid while loans constituted a comparatively small share of the amounts distributed for reconstruction (Table 5.3).

Next to the government's loans scheme, Bettiah Estate and the Darbhanga Raj granted loans towards the reconstruction of private property. Bettiah's management announced substantial amounts for both *taccavi* and house building loans,[101] making a distinction between the two categories of relief receivers similar to the colonial government, while the Darbhanga Raj's scheme did not differentiate between loans for restoring agricultural land and reconstructing houses—one type of loan covered both and at a lower rate than offered in the government act. However, the Darbhanga Raj also conflated loan-takers with the middle classes, as it granted a minor amount of loans to 'Gentlemen of the middle class' who were not tenants of the Raj.[102]

By May 1934 a clause was added to the Bihar and Orissa Natural Calamities Loans Act which further strengthened it as a form of relief to, first of all, propertied urban middle classes: loans could only be issued for urban houses, partly because of unspecified legal issues, but mainly for the reason that the local government after passing the act had realised that there was no free market for rural property. The additional rule for rural house loans, however, restricted loan-takers to a much stronger financial group than what initially was promised. As a result, a large number of people in rural areas instead applied for grants, in most cases of smaller amounts. Another practical reason for the local government to resort to grants in rural areas was that the loans demanded more time and paperwork than grants and thereby increased work pressure on the district administration.[103]

Rural house loans were from May 1934 onwards conditioned on extra security in the form of additional land. In effect, a so-called ordinary *raiyati* house or holding was ineligible for a loan and the majority of rural house loan applications were rejected. Another explanation for the large number of rejected loan applications was, according to Brett, the 'mistaken impression' that loan-takers would in due time be exempted from repaying the loan. The loans came in two categories, with different interest rates according to the financial strengths of the 'classes', a differentiation that became another source of public discontent. The smaller type of loans ('A') of maximum 1,500 rupees were given on 'easy terms' with a rate of interest at 4 ½ per cent and repayable in 6 to 9 years.[104] These loans were a form of government relief, as George Schuster, the Finance Member of the Government of India, underlined by describing them as for the 'poorer class of borrowers' and given 'not strictly on a commercial basis'.[105] The smaller loans were clearly seen as favoured by lenient loan terms while the larger loans, meant for a financially stronger group who because of the earthquake had difficulties in raising money 'at reasonable rates', had to bear the default costs of both types of loans. Initially, these loans were available at an interest of 6 ¼ per cent repayable in 12 to 15 years, but after pressure from the loan-takers, the interest was lowered to 5 per cent within a year.[106] Later, the government refused to lower the interest rate further, with the argument that the 'really deserving cases' had been granted 'heavy remissions' and the loan terms were better than under the Agriculturalist Loans Act.[107] The major objection came from the large loan-takers whose higher rate of interest was meant to cover for loans that could not be recovered in both the categories, even though the smaller loan-takers were the ones expected to default.[108] Although the rate of interest for the larger loans was comparatively low, the scheme's conditions were described as 'onerous' and amounting to 'a denial of relief' in a petition.[109] Despite criticism against the loan scheme and considering its prioritisation of urban applicability, the amounts and number of applications surpassed expectations and the initial sums allotted for larger loans had to be tripled when the revised budget increased the amount of both types of loans.[110] Judging by the popularity of the loans, the local government assumed borrowers used the opportunity to borrow more than needed, perhaps to lend it out at higher interest rates since the market rate for loans, with a house as security and not only a plot, was expected to be about 14 per cent.[111]

Charitable relief in the form of grants to the middle classes served, first of all, to reconstruct private property. The government and the VERF divided the middle classes into three sub-categories according to social, economic and professional status. In addition to relief towards the reconstruction of houses, the VERF gave grants of about 200,000 rupees to 1,900 cases as assistance for loss of income, unemployment, loss of businesses, severe expenses and loss of movable property.[112] According to the VERF's chart of disbursements, 'gratuitous relief' incorporated foremost house reconstruction of various kinds. The largest head was 'House-building grants' of about 2.7 million rupees and grants for house materials and semi-permanent shelters of almost 1 million rupees.[113] Under the heading 'House building grants', 'Middle class' relief as a sub-category increased significantly, from 31,875 rupees by the end of July to 227,088 rupees by the end of October 1934.[114] The middle classes made it into every relief category that pertained to the reconstruction of houses.

The government gave grants of 300 to 1,000 rupees to specifically one group of the middle classes described as those of 'poor circumstances' and 'too poor to rebuild their houses'.[115] This group of the middle classes was defined as having owned property ruined in the earthquake and at the same time unable to take a loan. The grant amount was at first 300 rupees but the VERF committee decided to increase the amount after officers in the field had reported the sum as insufficient. By increasing the amount, the additional grant almost doubled the total allotment to this group (Table 5.3). The officers were encouraged to give the grant in larger amounts to a fewer number of applicants, but the instruction was apparently not being followed as most grants did not exceed 300 rupees. The average grant of this type amounted to 324 rupees, even after the VERF's Committee had again instructed the District Magistrates to give more in each grant. Above the category of the middle classes were persons of 'higher social status' as a separate category and appeared to have been composed of rich rural people whom officers in the field had defined as a group in need based on their social status. These cases pertained to people in rural areas whose only safety to borrow against had been a house and now they stood without a chance of obtaining a house loan since rural plots without extra security did not qualify for a loan. According to Brett, their social status 'required that they should occupy houses of some pretensions' and they were given grants exceeding 1,000 rupees in order to obtain a 'reasonable amount of shelter'.[116]

The local government claimed to initially have had problems in reaching 'the lower middle classes', described as 'deserving' and 'those who really need relief' as opposed to the so-called professional beggars who collected blankets at relief centres.[117] The 'lower' middle class were at the same time the most difficult for the government to differentiate from the labouring classes in terms of property, assets and financial standing since they were perceived as belonging to the middle classes primarily in terms of social standing. According to the government's definition, 'small shopkeepers and poor middle class families' were unable to labour based on social status, and thereby eligible for a grant of a maximum of 300 rupees. Social standing either 'embarrassed', as Brett put it, or hindered them in carrying out manual labour.[118] A combination of socio-economic class and inability to 'labour' thereby became defining features for eligibility of this smallest of the grants. Though the grant was limited to 300 rupees for this diverse group of 'small house-holders' in urban, semi-urban areas, and sometimes in villages, as per official reports as well as instructions to the districts, the amount was usually expected to be considerably less.[119] In the end, the recipients of the grant were those who had been denied house loans or who had applied for less than 100 rupees with 'doubtful' security.[120] This indicated that people of insufficient means, with a property of lesser value or who lacked the required paperwork, attempted to apply for loans.

The railway workers in Jamalpur provide a distinct example of how socio-economic class and profession impacted the ability to 'labour' and was used in order to qualify them for a grant. Their socio-economic class and the inability to undertake labour placed them in a relief category between labour and the middle classes. According to the railway authorities, the 'workers' fitted into the category of relief receivers with insufficient assets to take loans; at the same time, the repairs of their 'huts' had to be carried out by 'labour', in contrast to the agriculturalists 'who usually have to build their own houses every two or three years'.[121] These men were viewed as 'workers', yet their socio-economic class set them apart and made them unfit for 'labour' by which the railway authorities argued that their requirements for grants differed from the labourers.

Relief societies, in general, followed the same criteria as the VERF and the government in creating categories of relief and prioritising the middle classes. As mentioned in Chapter 3, the BCRC had a committee managing middle-class relief and it was the only category of relief receivers given cash in aid, while goods such as clothes, blankets and huts for shelter were distributed across the social spectrum.[122] The Marwari Relief Society prioritised and selected house-owners as recipients of its grants, just like the government equalling private property possessions with the middle classes for its grants. As discussed earlier in the section on definitions of house damages, the relief society's estimate of damaged houses was, like the BCRC's, considerably higher than the government's estimates. This may indicate that they used a much broader definition of a house, thereby including classes officially considered below the lower middle classes. In effect, the broader definition of a house served to expand the middle classes as a relief category.

The Marwari Relief Society from Calcutta became known for providing so-called middle class relief for families 'shy to accept doles in the open', who, instead of visiting the relief society's centre, received help through 'special arrangements'. Similar to the local government, the society described the middle classes as hesitant to accept charity in public. Reading the report against the grain, an idea forms of how poor persons and those without property tried to access financial aid, as 'professional beggars' and 'unreal cases' were suspected of trying to access relief funds meant for 'genuine sufferers'.[123] For the Marwari Relief Society, a 'complete change' of their previous practices had to be implemented in order to avoid being 'made dupe' by people who did not belong to the middle classes. Social networks and local familiarity played a role as it entrusted the society's workers and 'respectable persons from the locality' to make 'exhaustive investigations' in order to identify middle-class people.[124]

Women from the upper strata of society engaged in the distribution of so-called middle-class relief, partly since it was an activity in private spaces, at people's houses, or temporary quarters one may assume, according to the Marwari Relief Society. Women of the upper middle classes or local elites took on the task as organisers of female relief workers. In Motihari, the wife of the town's magistrate presided over the Mahila Samiti which confined its relief work to the middle classes.[125] In Saran, too, three women 'occupying high positions in the society'— of which one was the wife of the Collector, and another the wife of the doctor in charge of coordinating the relief efforts—distributed relief to the middle classes.[126] Presumably, the female relief workers in this manner approached not only the middle classes but specifically women among the middle classes who to a limited extent occupied public spaces.

The middle classes did not only need shelter after their brick houses had been ruined but also food, which the Ramakrishna Mission restricted to the middle classes from May onwards, while people of all classes were given rice in rural areas.[127] The same month the association's work shifted to the construction of semi-permanent houses in urban areas, and arrangements were made at Monghyr, Muzaffarpur, Sitamarhi, Motihari and Laheria Sarai for building such houses for 'those who do not possess land of their own'.[128] This indicated that people who had lived in rented or leased houses faced hurdles in the reconstruction process, perhaps involving a long wait during the reconstruction period or being unable to pay an increased rent that was likely to come with a new building. In all, the Ramakrishna Mission had undertaken to construct 200 such houses and supplied material to repair houses for more than 50 middle-class families. By May 1934, the Ramakrishna Mission had spent 55,000 rupees on various items of relief, including the purchase of housing materials and construction of semi-permanent houses with roofs of corrugated iron or country tiles. The earthquake relief operation by the society received a substantial amount of 60,470 rupees, more than half of the collection, from the Mayor's Earthquake Relief Fund in Calcutta.[129] Out of the total collection of 116,828 rupees[130] for earthquake relief, 50 per cent was allocated for house constructions and repairs, underlining the relatively large share of financial resources given primarily to persons who had lost property or had difficulties to afford the higher rent of a new house. By September, the Ramakrishna Mission closed down relief centres in Bihar, but flood relief in the form of food distribution to 1,500 people in Monghyr continued into October.[131]

Self-Help and 'the Capacity to Labour'

Similar to how the urban middle classes emerged as a relief category based on holding property and social status, the needs of the rural and agricultural population as a relief category were defined by their ability to labour. Both these definitions were, however, chartered by the middle classes who portrayed and positioned themselves in the categories of relief by describing their needs as different from the poor and labouring classes. The two broad, and internally diverse, categories of relief receivers, the middle classes and the labouring population, experienced the disastrous consequences of the earthquake differently in terms of losses and on a time scale. For the urban population, the destruction of houses and deaths had happened in an instance. For the rural population, often equalled to the labouring population in terms of relief categories, damages to agricultural land had a long-term effect on livelihoods. Having lost property was the defining feature of the middle classes as a relief category, while the ability to labour became the defining feature of the rural and agricultural population. In their capacity as labourers, sources refer to how they could resort to 'own labour' as a form of relief, not only to earn, but also to repair their own dwellings or rebuild better, that is, a house. Hence, 'labour' was portrayed as an asset in self-help for the poorer strata and a domain off-limits for the middle classes. The large 'divider' in allocating relief was not only property, but also the ability to labour.

The division between the middle classes and the labouring classes, between houses and 'huts' and between rural and urban settings emerges in the novel *Dhoday Charitmanas* (1949–51) by the Bengali writer Satinath Bhaduri (1906–65).[132] The social realist novel borrows freely from historical events in describing the politics of reconstruction in a rural area through the eyes of the protagonist Dhorai, a tribal Tatma from a village in the district Purnea. In the earthquake aftermath, Dhorai settles in a village among the Koeri, a low caste of sharecroppers and labourers, who are promised 'relief' that never arrives. After the village has been surveyed by government officials and INC volunteers, they hear for more than a year that relief is coming. In the end, they are told that the survey had found that the Koeri huts of mud walls and thatched roofs could be repaired easily by the Koeris themselves, while the brick houses of the high castes, the landlords, had suffered severely and would get most of the relief.[133]

The fictional account by Bhaduri appears to have captured the experience of the rural poor with not only the government's relief programme but also the local elite's influence over the relief programme of the BCRC. A weekly communiqué by the local government announced to the public at the end of March 1934 that '[a]ctual experience has shown that in the humbler type of dwelling, when the materials have not been destroyed, the house can be repaired, usually be [*sic*] the man's own labour, for a comparatively small sum'.[134] The conclusion was reached after the district administration had made enquiries into the situation of the rural population and started rural relief by the end of February.[135] 'Dwellings' made by mud, bamboo and straw could be rebuilt by 'own labour' without financial aid. Two village accounts from Sursand and Jhapaha were described as typical of the situation in the affected areas by district officials in Muzaffarpur:

> The poorer *raiyats* have not suffered much in respect of their houses or clothing, as they lived in mud wall houses or grass huts which are usually repairable. It is only the bigger cultivators who have suffered much damage in loss of houses and property.[136]

Rather than providing financial aid, district officers were asked to encourage villagers to 'clean up' their villages and to 'dig out their wells' since 'the earthquake had left unaffected their capacity for labour'.[137] Explicit in such correspondence at district level was the message that villagers and agriculturalists were not supposed to expect compensation, whether as relief or by remuneration, for carrying out the task. The local government was steadfast in its position that no general help was to be expected since it was the 'duty' of villagers to carry out labour tasks: 'the *raiyats* are taking the attitude that it is not their duty to clear their wells or to clean up their lands and are waiting for Government to do this'.[138] In terms of building material, the rural population was expected to rebuild by using the old materials. The local government meant that a rural peasant house had suffered 'no more damage than it often suffers in the rains' and had 'his own labour and will not require any grant'. The argument that the cultivators could use 'own labour' and old construction material for rebuilding, implied that there was a need for financial aid to cover labour or building materials: only in some cases smaller sums were granted for buying materials, or for hiring labour, if the peasant suffered from physical impairments.[139]

In contrast to the self-help suggested to the rural population, the middle classes in towns benefited from the government-imposed price control and subsidised rates. When the demand for bricks increased in the summer of 1934, the government stepped in to control prices and supplies of building materials. Noteworthy is the stark revaluation of subsidies for bricks that may be indicative of the demand for it, or the government's willingness to support house constructions: from the initial 1,000 rupees, it increased to 98,000 rupees.[140] In Bhagalpur, the district administration arranged building materials such as timber and corrugated iron sheets also for rural middle classes, while many were supposed to manage with re-using the material from wrecked houses.[141] A common argument by house owners, as claimed by W. H. Meyrick, an estate manager and planter from Motihari,[142] who advocated the interest of planters and zamindars, was that 'the man in the *tatti* [in this context meant a house made of bamboo paring reeds or grass] house has not been hit so much as the man who lived in a *pukka* [*pucca*] house'.[143] Not surprisingly, initial reports of destruction and financial relief for houses in Jhapaha was found to be necessary in the case of 'middle class people living in *pucca* houses' and stretched to cover 'well-to-do' *raiyats* living in mud houses.[144]

Compared to the financial aid provided for the middle classes, advocates of middle class relief claimed that 'labourers' had benefitted from job opportunities in the wake of the earthquake. According to a speaker from Saran in the

Legislative Assembly, labour wages had increased from 3 to 8 *annas* per day, and it was difficult to find a coolie or labourer for that amount. In effect, the speaker argued that the earthquake had turned out to be 'a rich harvest' for the 'labour class' while the middle classes, 'the dumb-mute people ... who got some pride in them', were left in a 'pitiable' condition, since they could neither labour nor accept charitable relief according to his line of argument.[145] When Chandreshvar Prashad Narayan Sinha argued for relief to the middle classes in the Legislative Council, he compared their situation to that of the labourers, whom he considered 'better off than what they were before' as the earthquake had given rise to an increased demand for labour.[146] After the Assam earthquake in 1897, almost identical perceptions of the labourer as profiting on the disaster surfaced. Coolie wages and prices rose after the earthquake and the labourer, who was 'about to amass a small fortune at the expense of those who can ill afford it, has himself lost practically nothing, for the excellent reason that he has nothing to lose...'[147]

The earthquake being considered an opportunity for labourers to earn, as an effect of their increased demand, became linked with financial aid to the middle classes. Those who had not lost what was defined as a house were perceived as benefitting from the increased demand for labour by those who had lost property and would be able to pay for reconstruction with a grant or a loan.[148] Similar logics were deployed by the European planters and sugar cane estate owners to argue for grants and loans in order to rebuild their factories: as long as the mills did not run, they could not employ labour, and the workers would also suffer from loss of income and lack of jobs, argued one speaker representing their interest in the central Legislative Assembly.[149] Another argument claimed that loans to bigger zamindars and planters automatically solved the question of charitable relief since the money was needed to keep staff employed and at the same time hire labour for the reconstruction.[150] Relief was argued for based on labour relations existent before the earthquake and reflected labourers' dependency on wealthier socio-economic groups.

While labourers may have been in demand as the increased salaries for labourers in Saran indicated, the loss of cultivation due to flooding and sand deposits released many labourers in the countryside. The hurry to initiate unemployment relief was partly motivated by the loss of work among the rural population since large tracts of agricultural land had been ruined, but with the *rabi* harvest in April the labourers could again take up work in the fields.[151] Coupled with the low wages offered by the BCRC for clearing sand deposits and retrieving wells,[152] as well as the large number of unskilled and skilled labour hired on the Darbhanga Raj's major reconstruction projects,[153] the overall profit for labourers as an outcome of the increased demand appear unsubstantiated. The perception that the large and diffuse group referred to as the labouring classes had benefited from the earthquake in terms of raises in salary appears doubtful, except for possibly in the emergency phase, since it is questionable how often labour was rewarded by compensation in cash or kind, if rewarded at all.

Relief works as a form of aid also confirms an official view of labour as an asset of the rural population, while at the same time it contradicts the perception of financial profits made by the labourers. The government mainly employed women and children as workers whose wages were kept to a bare minimum according to its own policy,[154] perhaps an indication that men could get better-paid labour opportunities elsewhere. The same approach towards labour was voiced by the BCRC which had opened 'a sort of test work' in order to counter the scarcity of food in villages in Muzaffarpur and Champaran. The argument for employing people on the low wages of 4 to 6 pice (1–1 ½ anna) a day, depending on the age and capacity of the worker for cutting earth, repairing village roads and excavating water-channels and tanks, was the ability to labour according to the report. Doles were considered demoralising:[155] 'We made it one of our principles not to pauperise the people by giving doles of grain without getting some sort of work from the recipients except when they were old or infirm and incapable of work.'[156] Up to 15,000 day-labourers and peasants per day were engaged in the BCRC's employment relief on restoring roads and agricultural land, filling up sunken villages, removing debris and, in some cases, re-excavating silted tanks in Champaran. As many as 400,000 persons in Champaran undertook such work and shared about 17,000 rupees in reward for constructing roads, embankments and other labour-intensive tasks for an undisclosed number of days in the first six months of the aftermath.[157] The number of labourers may seem exaggerated, but the local government and the Bettiah Raj also employed large numbers on relief works and as coolies in Champaran and Muzaffarpur.[158]

The relative loss of those who had only labour as an asset was, however, questioned by European volunteers from the SCI, an international volunteer pacifist organisation that in cooperation with the local government and the BCRC had formed the Joint Flood Committee (JFC) in November 1934.[159] Manual labour in international teams with local workers was an essential component in building solidarity and thereby promoting peace according to the philosophy of SCI and its founder, Pierre Cérésole (1879–1945).[160] Cérésole's idea was to use the method, until then only tried in Europe, to improve relations between the colonial government and Indians, specifically the INC.[161] The cooperation focused on building three villages in the Muzaffarpur district for the resettlement

Image 5.1 Newly built thatched houses in rural Muzaffarpur.

Source: SCI International Archives, SCI India Photos: 'Zivildienst in Indien. 2. Teil' (Civil Service in India, Part 2'), 60501.2, January–June 1935.

of about one thousand families of peasants threatened by the floods of the river Bagmati after the earthquake.[162] Compared to Europe, however, the low wages and poor living conditions of manual labourers in Bihar served as an eye-opener that resulted in a revision of the organisation's programme. A small group of Europeans participated as international volunteers and worked as 'leaders' and partly side by side with the Indian workers in digging and carrying soil.[163] Just like in Europe, where the SCI had previously organised similar work-based reconstruction camps in places struck by natural disasters or the First World War, Cérésole's idea was to pay local people for labour in order to not take away work opportunities. According to the scheme in Bihar, the villagers worked in exchange for land and house material granted by the local government and the BCRC under the relief programme run by the JFC. The workers' contribution consisted 'exclusively in supplying labour at somewhat reduced rates',[164] while land and material were given based on the condition that the settlers built 'decent

Image 5.2 New mud house in rural Muzaffarpur.

Source: SCI International Archives, SCI India Photos: 'Zivildienst in Indien. 2. Teil' (Civil Service in India, Part 2'), 60501.2, January–June 1935.

and durable' houses with mud or bricks walls as opposed to the thatched huts they had lived in before: such *kuccha* constructions were prohibited since the settlements were framed as model villages (Images 5.1 and 5.2).[165]

The method of rebuilding villages by engaging landless villagers as labourers in exchange for building materials and land, however, could not be realised.[166] The villagers depended on their labour for making a living, hence labour in exchange for construction materials was planned to provide the villagers with 'houses' or better huts, but the plan proved unsustainable since it did not enable them to feed themselves and their families.[167] As a solution to the untenable situation the JFC agreed to employ full-time workers on standard wages to keep their 'soul and body together'. According to the camp leader of the JFC, extreme poverty did not allow villagers to work on reduced wages as they had 'their daily work and earnings to keep alive'.[168] This was perhaps not surprising, since unskilled labour wages, in general, fell well below the nutritional norms in colonial India.[169]

The committee's perception of the value of labour, voiced foremost by the SCI members, contradicted the general official categorisation of labourers as endowed with the asset to labour without much regard for its income-generating purpose. According to the SCI's impression of the labour conditions, the labourers suffered a loss of income when they supplied labour in exchange for building material. It should also be noted that the JFC intended to improve the housing conditions of the villagers by upgrading building materials from *kuccha* to *pucca*, an aspiration that undoubtedly required a labour effort that extended beyond using or reusing *kuccha* materials from destroyed houses.

The poor living condition of the labourers was also noted by the European volunteers of the SCI. That the Europeans in the camp ate more per person than an Indian peasant family survived on made them question their own presence and their role as volunteers.[170] Based on one of the volunteer's diaries—that of the schoolmaster Frazer Hoyland from Dorset, sent home in January 1935—the Quaker journal *The Friend* published a series. Altogether four European and seven Indians volunteers lived in the camp and employed about 30 to 40 men to dig and transport earth.[171] According to Hoyland, the local zamindars would pay three glasses of rice a day to a worker which was supposed to feed a family of father, mother and three or four children. To the foreign volunteers, the salaries paid to the rural labourers appeared grossly inadequate, to the extent that they opposed the local labour rates and increased the salary to 5 glasses of rice, despite protests from the zamindars.[172] They were not only appalled by the labour conditions under the zamindars, but also seemed more surprised to note that 'even the local English planter' paid boys 1 *anna* per day for walking on their knees 8 to 9 hours per day in the fields, the same rate for unskilled female labour, when the official minimum wage was supposedly 3 *annas* per day.[173] According to these European eye-witness accounts and the administrative documents of the JFC, labourers and peasants did not earn enough to eat properly, with their earnings being below the minimum wage rather than reflecting an increase in salaries that the increased demand for labour supposedly had triggered. Regardless of their earnings, their employment in large numbers in reconstruction projects by the JFC, on BCRC's 'test works' and by the local government facilitated recovery at a regional level.

Administering Loans and Grants: Chaos and Collapse

The local government's distribution of grants and loans was marked by a gross miscalculation of the burden it would impose on its administration. The confusion was a fact as the distribution of charitable aid from the VERF in the form of 'house building grants' started before the government announced the loan conditions under the Natural Calamities Loans Act by the middle of March.[174] The local government administration handled both types of monetary aid simultaneously, a factor that directly contributed to misunderstandings and complicated applications, as will be discussed in this section.

The distribution of *taccavi* and charitable relief in the form of grants to agriculturalists suffered the same confusion. The local government administration distributed charitable grants from the VERF to private persons: in rural areas, this was done by government officials under the Director of Agriculture and additional staff who partly were paid by funds from the VERF.[175] The fine line between the administration of local government funds for gratuitous relief and those of the VERF's collection existed on paper but was hard to discern in practice.[176] That the local government had underestimated the dimension of work involved in processing applications and to distribute relief became evident when the relief programme collapsed after the summer as a result of staff shortages and administrative chaos.

The *Final Report on the Survey of Lands Damaged* described a relatively unproblematic distribution of *taccavi* and grants, contradicting the experience of the administration and applicants who struggled with muddled guidelines and insufficient numbers of staff. By April reports from survey teams in the area questioned the low number of grant applications compared to the number of loan applications. Large landholders had been the first and most efficient to apply for loans. According to field reports, one reason for the fewer-than-expected number of applications may have been the definition of 'severe spoilation' being set too high; another reason could have been that the small landholders of less than an acre of land had not come forward since they had not understood the rules.[177] The time-consuming land survey was the primary reason for delays in the distribution of all types of grants and loans according to the Commissioner of Tirhut: 'The present difficulty is lack of staff. Almost every available officer is employed on sand *taccavi* either as enquiring officer or disbursing in order to get the work completed by the end of May.' In the subdivision of Madhubani, with 8,000 villages, the envisioned inspection of damaged fields in person was regarded as impossible by the Commissioner of Tirhut, even if only half of them had to be visited, at least four to five officers were needed.[178] Similarly in Darbhanga, the district officer claimed to need at least 40 officers for what he perceived to be a colossal task of distributing house-building grants in 3,000 villages, in addition to agricultural loans, and carrying out other regular tasks.[179] Surveying agricultural land before the rains arrived was given priority because of the impact sand was feared to have on waterlogging and in aggravating floods if not removed in time. But the number of staff was insufficient for the task, and few members of staff remained to process house loans and house grants.

Contrary to the district administration, the provincial administration in Patna did not find fault with the administrative set-up, but thought the delays depended on *raiyats* being 'chary' of taking loans and appearing 'suspicious'.[180] The raiyats' attitude, according to Brett, was to rather 'sit and wait' for the monsoon to carry away the sand than accepting loans and grants in order to start the work.[181] Towards the end of April, the district officers had not yet submitted distribution reports for agricultural relief, and progress reports supplied by the Commissioner of Tirhut showed insignificant results compared to the expectations.[182] When the Commissioner of Tirhut plainly listed the reasons for the delayed distribution by the end of April, the provincial administration in Patna appeared taken aback by the district administration's workload. In spite of repeated warnings from the Tirhut Division about the failures in distribution, the governor considered it 'absurd for the Muzaffarpur officials to leave us entirely in the dark about the problems in the distribution of *takavi* and grants',[183] thereby finding the problem partly rooted in a lack of communication by the division and district administration. The slow process of administrative communication was in fact ignored by the Additional Commissioner in Tirhut, appointed to deal with the extra work after the earthquake, who went ahead distributing grants and agricultural loans without the government's approval. He had authorised eight officers with the powers of Collector in order to 'enable loans to be distributed in reasonable time'.[184] The apparent understaffed administration had resorted to breaking protocol in order to distribute relief. The local government had to 'make legal' the distribution of grants and loans by extending the power of the Collector to the loan-distributing officers as an ad hoc measure.[185] According to the rules, the police was trusted to distribute grants up to 25 rupees, while sub-inspectors, sub-deputy collectors were trusted to distribute grants up to 40 rupees; and finally, sub-divisional officers or collectors distributed any larger amounts, up to a maximum of 300 rupees.[186] The power of the Collector had thereby been necessary to distribute grants of larger amounts. In this way most of the grants from the VERF had by May 1934 been distributed or allocated to people who had lost houses or needed temporary quarters. Rural relief to the poor from the VERF amounted to 166,350 rupees of 'petty' grants for repairs of houses and wells. At the end of 1934 so-called general grants of 'max 300 rupees' for almost 2.8 million rupees had been distributed, and urban and rural middle-class persons had received middle-class grants of 300 to 1,000 rupees for the amount of almost 1.5 million rupees (see Table 5.3).

In June, after the rains commenced, the Commissioner in Tirhut had tried to stop further distributions since the administrators thought only 2 to 10 per cent of the *taccavi* had been used for clearing sand: the *raiyats* had used the rest on 'domestic expenses, often marriages and social ceremonies, and trusted nature to dissipate the deposits'.[187] Yet, Brett had by May when the land survey was in progress, estimated to spend 1.2 million rupees on sand-clearance grants, and half of it in Muzaffarpur district.[188] It turned out, according to the Commissioner of Tirhut, that the sand's negative effects had been exaggerated by everyone, including himself: only in a small area sand deposits of 2 feet were considered a grave problem. The other argument against distributing a second instalment was the workload it imposed on the administration by 'duplicating the laborious and complicated work of the past four months'.[189] The problem entailed with the distribution of *taccavi* was solved by the cancellation of a second installation in September 1934. The relief programme had misjudged the need for relief and lacked adequate administrative capacities to follow it through. Even if the need for financial assistance to remove sand was, according to the government's appreciation, less than expected, it found that the rural population had made good use of the aid. In retrospect, Brett, like the Commissioner of Tirhut, saw the positive side of loans and grants. Even if the major parts of the grants for clearing sand had been used for another purpose, he thought the money of incalculable value as it enabled the receivers to 'repair their houses, pay their rent and resume the normal course of their lives'. According to the local government, the grant had helped people out of a sense of despair, reversing 'a general state of despondency which induced the peasants to sit idle and refuse to pay rent and taxes'.[190] By extension, however, the loans and grants had not only benefited the relief receivers in the reconstruction of houses and reclamation of land, but the financial aid had also served the needs of the local government and the landlords who could continue to collect rents and taxes. The outcome of the disaster was in this way highly unequal for those who wielded power and, in addition shared interests of rent and revenue collections, the government and the landlords, compared to the peasants.

The loan scheme for rebuilding private property in towns under the Natural Calamities Loans Act went wrong in the same way it had done for the *taccavi* and grants for rural areas. In writing the report at the end of 1934, Brett recognised that the loan application process had failed in particular in Darbhanga and Muzaffarpur, while the scheme was deemed successful in Patna with 761 loans distributed in six months. As Brett concluded, by the end of 1934, people liberally applied for grants of maximum 300 rupees in both rural and urban areas. Also in towns, 'for which the Act was originally intended' according to Brett, the number of applications requested more than the requirements in the government's estimates, as a result 'only' 15 per cent of the applications were granted.[191] Although Brett's final report posthumously notes the failure of the relief programme to follow through, the administrative issues were discovered early in the process.

In comparison to the success of the scheme in Patna, 17,787 out of 31,602 loan applications in Darbhanga had been rejected by September 1934. At that point, the administration confessed to being overburdened by the number of applications as 'nothing was being done except to weed out cases capable of rejection'.[192] The great number of applications for grants and house loans in both rural and urban areas in the whole earthquake area required substantial efforts by the district administration. According to Brett, many of the 24,226 applications for a house grant in urban areas, and of the 202,539 applications for house grants in rural areas were invalid and only served to burden the administration. Similar to rural aid, people appeared to have been misinformed about the rules or lacked the required paperwork.[193] The district administration in Muzaffarpur made 'painfully slow' progress under the sheer volume of loan and grant applications: half of the more than 800 urban middle-class building grants had been approved, half of them had been rejected and more than 10,000 loan and grant applications were still pending in September. By the end of September, 8,148 loan applications from rural areas and 853 cases in urban areas in Muzaffarpur were dealt with at a snail's pace of two cases a week. In the rural areas merely two out of the 8,148 loan applications had been sanctioned. Only districts such as Saran with a low number of applications for rural house loans managed to dispose of a fair number of the applications.[194] Up to 31 August 1934, house loans ranging from 100 rupees to 12,000 rupees had been distributed up to a total of 856,000 rupees in Patna, Saran, Monghyr and Bhagalpur, and 500,000 rupees in other affected districts.[195]

Darbhanga repeatedly revealed the weaknesses of the scheme. The erratic administration of loans and grants was to a large extent caused by a misinformed, overburdened or defective district administration. For instance, the Darbhanga District Officer's estimates of 200,000 rupees for house-building grants at the end of February never reached Brett[196] and, as a result, the district's funds were exhausted before the mistake was discovered.[197] Early on, Brett foresaw a 'defective' administration of grants in Darbhanga which he thought would cause a 'serious delay' in distribution but such warning signals were not taken seriously.[198] Officers in charge in Muzaffarpur and Darbhanga wrongly rejected loan applications from towns, based on a misconception that it was necessary to demand security other than the house itself, even though this rule clearly only applied for granting house loans in rural areas. The district officials appeared badly informed about regulations, and partly created some of the chaos by delaying reports, underestimating sums required and accepting invalid applications. In retrospect, Brett complained that the officer in charge of Muzaffarpur district had neither acquainted himself with the specific regulations nor instructed the subordinates on the subject.[199]

Applications for middle class grants in rural areas in Darbhanga increased significantly after the rule of extra security for a house loan was announced. The increase in applications for grants was interpreted as a sign of a distribution that was too wide and spurred Brett to immediately visit Darbhanga to review the situation. According to him, the grants appeared to have been distributed to 'classes' below the middle classes, and in the villages 'irrespective of whether the owner of the house can repair it with his own labour'.[200] The initial estimate of 200,000 rupees for house-building grants in Darbhanga doubled to more than 400,000 rupees remitted by the end of April, and the estimate for grants was revised to the substantially higher figure of 650,000 rupees.[201] The total sum requested for rural house-building grants in Darbhanga by June amounted to 750,000 rupees, more than any other area at that point in time.[202] The increase in grants also reflected the district administration's idea of a larger need for relief in rural areas than what the administration in Patna claimed. For instance, the Commissioner of Tirhut and Brett both disagreed with the high estimates provided by a sub-district officer for rural house grants in Darbhanga, but the persistence and support of the District Officer resulted in a grant of an unusually high figure. Even though the Commissioner remained defiant that the figures were 'too high', he considered it 'better to err on the side of generosity', cautioning the Sub-district Officer against what was considered a too wide distribution in rural areas.[203] Brett had asked district officers to revise the amounts for distribution already in March since the officers had 'far too liberal ideas' in distributing grants; they had included schools and other types of community buildings and were consequently reprimanded to apply the grants only to private houses. In order to limit disbursements, sub-inspectors were entrusted to give out grants of maximum 5 rupees per case in order to speed up the distribution of small grants in Darbhanga.[204] The amounts distributed differed greatly between Darbhanga and the other districts: for instance, 7 rupees was the average rural grant distributed to 66,000 people in Champaran, and 32 rupees the average urban grant handed out to 3,000 urban households in the same district, while in Muzaffarpur district, rural grants were on an average 32 rupees and limited to 100 rupees per grant in urban settings, totalling 400,000 rupees.[205]

There were, however, shortcuts to obtain grants. According to the newspaper *Ittihad*, the persons who had derived the largest benefit from the grants were those who could approach the officials in charge and those with access to distributors of the fund. Among the *amlas* (police officers) of the lower rungs, bribes were reportedly rampant and grants distributed according to communal belonging. Issues in distribution and corruption, the newspaper explained with mismanagement caused by the relief committees and a collector who did not personally look into cases.[206] The Relief Commissioner himself recognised that the distribution of aid by government officials, police staff and relief committees was fraught with corruption and mismanagement, as he repeatedly reprimanded and investigated senior officers in the districts. For instance, in Darbhanga, the District Officer let unauthorised persons hand out house building grants in urban areas in order to speed up distribution, which Brett put a stop to.[207] Despite the administration's diverging perceptions of rural and urban needs for house-building grants, the distribution of grants in rural areas, in the end, was more than the amounts given to urban areas, partly a result of the change of rules which restricted loans to primarily urban houses. When Brett was asked to present the figures of urban and rural relief, respectively, by the end of July 1934, he grudgingly informed his superior that 'Tirhut "returns" are sui generis'.[208] In particular, the Darbhanga district administration remained a problem to Brett by ignoring his repeated requests for reports of disbursements.[209] The distribution of grants seemed to have gone out of control for the reason of the time- and staff-consuming land surveys and the massive amount of house-loan applications that the grants were in theory expected to help to bring down. The district administration proved insufficient for the task and distributed more grants in rural areas rather than in urban settings, contrary to what the Relief Commissioner had instructed.

The house-building loans under the Natural Calamities Loans Act were seen as necessary in order to enable rebuilding, but considering the huge round of applications, garbled application guidelines and the insufficient administrative workforce, house loans seem to have caused considerable damage in terms of taxing the administration to its utmost and incurring additional expenses for the local government in terms of extra staff and travelling. As on 31 January 1936, the local government had distributed loans in accordance with Bihar and Orissa

Table 5.3 Grants and loans distributed until 31 December 1934

	House Loans (Bihar & Orissa Natural Calamities Loans Act)			General Grant of 'Max 300 Rupees'			Grant to Middle-Class Families (300–1,000 Rs)	Additional Grant to Middle-Class Families (300–1,000 Rs)
	At 4½ per cent 2,205 loans, most of them 300–500 Rs	At 6½ per cent 821 loans	Total	Urban	Rural	Total		
Patna	316,000	335,000	651,000	237,000	87,000	324,000	75,000	–
Monghyr	163,000	120,000	283,000	210,000	22,000	232,000	100,000	200,000
Saran	99,000	98,000	197,000	55,000	130,000	185,000	50,000	40,000
Bhagalpur	70,000	78,000	148,000	72,000	138,000	210,000	50,000	–
Champaran	79,000	127,000	206,000	99,000	469,000	568,000	50,000	75,000
Purnea	16,000	42,000	58,000	7,000	1,000	8,000	5,000	–
Gaya	26,000	35,000	61,000	11,000	11,000	22,000	–	–
Muzaffarpur	66,000	34,000	100,000	251,000	237,000	488,000	300,000	200,000
Darbhanga	91,000	46,000	137,000	138,000	578,000	716,000	100,000	185,000
Shahabad	11,000	17,000	28,000	8,000	12,000	20,000	10,000	–
Total	937,000	932,000	1,869,000	1,088,000	1,685,000	2,773,000	790,000	700,000

Source: Compiled with figures provided in Brett, *A Report on the Bihar Earthquake:* 61, 63, 64.

Note: Units in rupees. Empty box means that data on the amount is missing. As per 31 January 1936, the local government had distributed loans according to the Bihar and Orissa Natural Calamities Loans Act ('House Loans') for 2,700 976 rupees. 'Grant of Loans on Account of Earthquake' (Question no. 223), 28 March 1936, *BOLCP* 34 (22):1419.

Natural Natural Calamities Loans Act amounting to about 2.7 million rupees, a petty sum next to the amount extended in grants by the end of 1934 (Table 5.3).[210] When members of the Legislative Assembly of Bihar and Orissa argued for a loan scheme a month after the earthquake, they claimed that out of the 60 per cent of the middle and upper classes living in *pucca* houses and bungalows who had lost their houses, 25 per cent needed grants for rebuilding, while 75 per cent were able to take loans.[211] In the end, grants made up a larger share than loans as a form of relief. Against the backdrop of the complications surrounding the house loans, the government's recourse to gradually turn to charity and grants also for rebuilding houses seem to reflect a loan scheme insufficiently planned, with little grasp of administrative capacities at hand.

Conclusion: The Social Construction of Needs

This chapter has examined the foundations for how categories of relief emerged in the earthquake's aftermath. Socio-economic status, rural or urban spaces and damages to property were variables used to define categories of relief. While earthquake relief relied on previous experiences from famine relief in both urban and rural areas among the middle classes, labourers and agriculturalists, urban material damages to houses cast categories in a new light.

Middle class relief after the earthquake catered to victims of the earthquake whose property was damaged or ruined, or/and whose social status inhibited them from accepting relief in public spaces or, to a lesser extent, to those who regardless of social status were physically unable to labour. In this way, both social and financial class influenced middle class relief. The middle classes as a category of relief receivers was a diverse group which benefitted from fundraising and government schemes launched in the aftermath, as well as from house-building initiatives and charitable relief. The two main sources of relief to compensate for the loss of property were the loan scheme under the Bihar and Orissa Natural Disasters Loans Act and grants. Middle class grants and house-building grants distributed by government officials were sourced from the VERF. A large portion of funds went towards grants for the relief category of the middle classes, and the same category was the target of house reconstruction grants from relief associations. Similar to how middle classes had been treated as a separate category in famine relief, they were in the earthquake's aftermath distinguished from the so-called labouring classes based on needs. Their needs were portrayed as more than the labourers' and agriculturalists' needs, based on the loss of property which made them eligible for higher grants and the subsidised government loan scheme.

The relief scheme for the rural population below the middle classes in the hierarchical categorization of relief was foremost based on measures implemented in times of so-called agricultural distress, which meant unemployment relief, *taccavi* or agricultural loans, charitable grants and remission of revenue to agriculturalists. A significant difference which separated the rural population from the middle classes in the scheme for relief was its ability to labour and status as inhabitants of huts rather than houses. Compared to the relief category of the middle classes, they supplied labour to rebuild their huts of immaterial value. According to this form of relief policy, labourers were considered to be helped by both an increased demand for labour and by so-called unemployment relief in the form of minimum salaried wage labour in removing sand and rebuilding infrastructure. The category of middle-class persons was instead given unemployment grants in compensation for the disruption of income that the earthquake meant.

The afore-described logic in relief measures for the labouring rural population suggests a perception of their needs as constant regardless of the type of 'natural' disaster inflicted upon them, that is, agricultural distress, famine, flood or earthquake had the same effects and prompted the same needs in rural settings. To some extent, rural relief measures expressed an idea of the disaster not yet having reached the rural population. As such, they had not lost property and could benefit from increased labour demand. The measures taken to extend agricultural grants and loans were described as preventive, bearing in mind future decreased soil productivity and the sand's potential aggravating effect on floods. In this respect, rather than the needs of the rural population, the financial implications of the environmental effects of the earthquake were taken into consideration. Relief was not mean to ameliorate the situation of a peasant but the restoration of business as usual—that is, ensuring the collection of revenue. A foreseeable revenue loss motivated *taccavi* according to the survey of the Revenue Department.

If previous disasters such as famines and floods had first hit the rural population, and subsequently the urban population, the earthquake was treated primarily as an urban disaster during the first two weeks of the aftermath. Yet the earthquake had an instant and prolonged impact on both rural and urban settlements. This was a major difference from earlier disaster experiences. For the district administration, the ambition to manage two different types of loan and grants schemes for houses and for agricultural damages meant an organisational disaster. The work of simultaneously assessing damages and needs for relief and organising the distribution of funds was further complicated by the involvement of both the new Reconstruction Department and the Revenue Department. Adding to the administrative chaos, these two departments struggled to extract information from the districts in order to have funds released from the VERF. The administration's dependence upon the relief fund slowed down the processing of grants. Though the *taccavi* loans were far from a novelty to the administration, the land survey on damages and shortage of staff complicated the task, partly due to the need to process house loans and grants according to another set of rules, which was new to the administration. The distribution of relief burdened the administration until it was on the brink of collapse and, as a result, relief was delayed and rules were amended to hasten the process. Apart from the problems that the failures in distributing grants and loans created for those in need, perhaps the relief programme's most significant weakness was the stress categorisation of victims and relief put on the administration. In the end, the management of relief added another layer of disaster to the aftermath.

Notes

1. Sharma, *Famine, Philanthropy and the Colonial State*, 182, 190–91.
2. Bhatta, *Natural Calamities in Orissa*, 214.
3. Sharma, *Famine, Philanthropy and the Colonial State*, 181.
4. Ahuja, 'State Formation and "Famine Policy" in Early Colonial South India', 379.
5. Ibid., 354.
6. Brennan, 'Government Famine Relief in Bengal, 1943', 542.
7. Within the labour hierarchy, the cotton-mill worker and the field labourer are at two ends. The daily wage rate of agricultural labour was in general 70–80 per cent of the nearest comparable labour markets in industries and mines. Roy, *Rethinking Economic Change in India*, 86–87.
8. The 'peasantry' is problematic to differentiate or to position in relation to an internal hierarchy, ranging from working classes to large capitalist landholders. The agriculturalists referred to as 'labourers' appear to have belonged among the poorest, landless peasants and, to a limited degree, among groups who resided on leased land. Rothermund, *India in the Great Depression: 1929–1939*, 110.
9. For an example of 'winners' and 'losers' in terms of benefitting from the reconstruction phase, see Sanderson and Sharma, 'Winners and Losers from the 2001 Gujarat Earthquake'.
10. 'Extract from D.O. letter no 690 dated 1st February 1934', The Commissioner, Bhagalpur Division, to the Chief Sec. to Government, B&O, File: 'Opinion of the

Director of Geological Survey of India regarding possibility of severe shock in Bihar', BSA RE 495/1934.

11. Arupjyoti Saikia, 'Jute in the Brahmaputra Valley: the Making of Flood Control in the Twentieth-Century Assam', *Modern Asian Studies* 49, no. 5 (2015): 1405–41.

12. R. P. Agarwal and R. Bhoj 'Evolution of Kosi River Fan, India: Structural Implications and Geomorphic Significance', *International Journal of Remote Sensing* 13, no. 10 (1992): 1891–901. On earthquakes in relation to historical flood management, see Singh, 'The Colonial State, Zamindars and the Politics of Flood Control', 248.

13. The Commissioner's first report contained observations from an aeroplane survey made from 8:40 a.m. to 1:45 p.m. on 21 or 22 January 1934: D.O. J-297, 'Notes of reconnaissance by aeroplane from Muzaffarpur to Bettiah and back via Raxaul and Sitamarhi' (6 pp.), J. E. Scott to P. C. Tallents, Muzaffarpur, 21–22 January 1934. The second report was compiled after a survey 'by car and on foot' about two weeks later: D.O. J-822, 'By car along main Darbhanga road to Keotra (22 miles); then through Katra and Runisyedpur to Sitamarhi; 5 miles along the Sursand road and back; returned by car and on foot by direct road Sitamarhi–Muzaffarpur', J. E. Scott to J. T. Whitty, 7 February 1934, BSA RE 23/1934.

14. Unpublished government report by the Director of Industries, S. Lal [alt. Lall] and Director of Agriculture, D. R. Sethi, submitted 26 January 1934 (21 pp.), in D.O. 223, P. C. Tallents to J. E. Scott, Patna, 9 February 1934. BSA File: 'Staff-allotments of grants required for Relief Engineers of Town Engineers', BSA RE 76/1934.

15. D.O. J-822, J. E. Scott to J. T. Whitty, 7 February 1934, BSA RE 23/1934.

16. D.O. J-297, 'Notes of reconnaissance by aeroplane...', J. E. Scott to P. C. Tallents, Muzaffarpur, 21–22 January 1934, BSA RE 23/1934.

17. D.O. J-822, J. E. Scott to J. T. Whitty, 7 February 1934, BSA RE 23/1934.

18. Report by the Director of Industries S. Lal [or Lall] and Director of Agriculture, D. R. Sethi, 26 January 1934, in D.O. 223, P. C. Tallents to J. E. Scott, Patna, 9 February 1934, BSA RE 76/1934.

19. Notes by J. W. Houlton, 29 January 1934, File: 'Loans under Agriculturalist's Loan Act and Land Improvement Loans Act to Persons Affected by the Earthquake', Revenue Dept, L. R. Branch, December 1934, BSA R-LR IIIA/19/1934.

20. The 1871 Land Improvement Act was a colonial law specifically intended to grant and recover *taccavi* loans from peasants. Hall-Matthews, *Peasants, Famine and the State in Colonial Western India*, 114–15. *Taccavi* loans at 6 per cent interest were, until the end of the nineteenth century, the only direct government assistance to agricultural development. It already existed in Mughal times and was continued

by the British from the end of the eighteenth century. The object of the loans was to enable the peasants to improve their holdings or to restart cultivation after a calamity. They were, however, unpopular as the ordinary cultivator often preferred to deal with a local known moneylender rather than with the physically distant, unfamiliar and known to be inflexible administration of the government. The total amounts of these loans were generally small (in the example of Champaran by Pouchepadass) and they mostly went to the more influential and well-to-do agriculturalists. Pouchepadass, *Land, Power and Market*, 542–43.

21. Appendix 1, in Brett, *A Report on the Bihar Earthquake*, 93.

22. The funds was meant for 'utilization on occasions of distress caused by drought, flood or other natural calamities in the said province'. 'The Bihar Famine Relief Fund Act, 1936 (Bihar Act V of 1936), in *Manual of Bihar Local Laws: 1790–1991* [Civil, Criminal, Revenue, Labour & Taxation Laws], ed. S. K. Pandey, vol. 3 [C-E], Containing: Bihar Acts, Rules, Orders & Notifications issued by State Government with Up-to-date Amendments with Latest Case-laws (Allahabad: National Law Agency, 1985).

23. D.O. 533, 'Weekly Bulletin, 9 March 1934 RD', W. B. Brett to M.G. Hallett (Home Dept.), Patna 9 March 1934, NAI H. Pol. 34/1B/1934.

24. 'Presentation of the Budget for 1935–36', 13 February 1935, BOLCP 32, no. 4, 271.

25. 'The Bihar Famine Relief Fund Bill, 1936 (no. 17 of 1936)', 18 November 1936, 37–38 in *Bihar Legislative Council Proceedings (BLCP)* 36, no. 1, Official Report. (Patna: Superintendent, Government Printing, 1937).

26. Dunn et al., 'The Bihar–Nepal Earthquake of 1934', 33, cf. 33–37.

27. Caldwell noted that he 'had no measuring instrument and very limited time', making the reservation that his observations 'must be taken as merely very general impressions'. Though such shortcomings obviously hampered the survey, his observations and details are unparalleled. Other surveys and observations were either done in a greater haste and are thus more superficial and less methodological, or at a later stage after human beings and the weather had impacted the land. K. S. Caldwell, *Note on Sand Deposit*, 17 March 1934, 5 pp., printed at the B&O Government Press, 28 March 1934, submitted to the Govt of B&O and GOI, Home Dept., New Delhi; NAI HP 34/1B/1934. Caldwell's note is also mentioned in 20th Communiqué: Bulletin for the week ending the 21st March 1934 (same file as above).

28. Caldwell, *Note on Sand Deposit*, 3, 5.

29. William H. K. Lee, Hiroo Kanamori, Paul Jennings and Carl Kisslinger, *International Handbook of Earthquake and Engineering Seismology*, Vol. 81B in the International Geophysics Series (Amsterdam: Academic Press, 2003), 1379.

234 • Acts of Aid

30. Nasu commented on seismic damages and possibilities of giving recommendations on earthquake-safe buildings. Nasu, 'No. 30, The Great Indian Earthquake of January 15, 1934', 417, 418n2. Nasu wrote an article in Japanese on 'seismic damages' which has not been consulted due to linguistic limitations. Shinji [an alternative reading of the Japanese characters for 'Nobuji'] Nasu, 'Seismic Damages caused by the Great Indian Earthquake of Jan. 15, 1934' (in Japanese), *Journal of Architecture and Building Science* 48, no. 591 (11 May 1934): 1182–293. My initial confusion regarding the name of the author could be cleared thanks to Amelia Bonea's knowledge of Japanese.

31. Gergory Clancey, 'The Meiji Earthquake: Nature, Nation, and the Ambiguities of Catastrophe', *Modern Asian Studies* 40, no. 4 (2006): 909–51, 931.

32. Nasu, 'No. 30, The Great Indian Earthquake of January 15, 1934', 418n2, 419–20.

33. A. M. P. Cliff, *Bālū kaise hategī? Bhūkamp ke kāraṇ khetoṃ meṃ jo bālū jamā ho gayā hai uske miṭne ke kucch upāy* (How to Remove the Sand? Some Remedies for Removing the Sand in the Fields Caused by the Earthquake), published on behalf of Muzaffarpur District Board, by R. P. Roy Sharma, 70 Dharmatala Street [Calcutta]: Rashtrabandhu Press, [1934], 8 pp.

34. Brett, *A Report on the Bihar Earthquake*, 37–38, 40.

35. The survey was carried out from 10 March to 28 May 1934 by the Revenue Department, *Final Report on the Survey of Lands Damaged by Earthquake in North Bihar in 1934* (Bihar and Orissa, Patna: Department of Land Records and Surveys. Superintendent, Government Printing, 1934).

36. Telegram from GOI to Sec. of State for India, New Delhi, 11 February 1934. In 'Earthquakes. Earthquake in Bihar, Bengal etc. 1934. Financial Assistance to Provinces', Collection 109: Earthquakes Collection, IOR/L/F/7/913.

37. Telegram from India Office to the GOI, London, 14 February 1934, 'Earthquakes. Earthquake in Bihar, Bengal etc. 1934. Financial Assistance to Provinces', Collection 109: Earthquakes Collection, IOR/L/F/7/913. However, it should be noted that the financial responsibilities of the GOI or the Govt of B&O changed over time as funding and economic policies changed with budget proposals. 'Table of Expenditure' in Wasi, *Bihar and Orissa in 1936–37*, 20–24.

38. Memo, J. T. Whitty to P. C. Tallents, 3 February 1934, forwarded from P. C. Tallents to all District Officers of Patna, Tirhut and Bhagalpur Divisions', 4 February 1934, BSA RE 501/1934.

39. *Rabi*, winter crop. In Bihar, the *rabi* crops were mostly rice but also included wheat, barley and pulses. David Ludden, *An Agrarian History of South Asia* (Cambridge: Cambridge University Press, 1999), 23.

40. D.O. 123-A, Muzaffarpur District Office to P. C. Tallents, Muzaffarpur, 8 February 1934, BSA RE 501/1934.

41. D.O. 1539, S. L. Marwood (Champaran District office, Motihari), to P. C. Tallents, 8 February 1934, BSA RE 501/1934.

42. D.O. 533 R.D., 'Weekly Bulletin, 9 March 1934', W. B. Brett to M. G. Hallett (Home Dept.), Patna, 9 March 1934 (received 12 March 1934), NAI H. Pol. 34/1B/1934.

43. The survey was supervised by the 'Special officer, Land Damage Survey', Babu Nila Lohita Bhattacharya, Sub-Deputy Collector, who joined at Muzaffarpur on 10 February 1934. With two Head Inspectors from Chota Nagpur Settlement, he began an experimental survey of five villages around Musari, five miles from Muzaffarpur. *Final Report on the Survey of Lands Damaged*, 1–2.

44. The Board of Revenue suggested that the survey should mark the extent of sanding in the fields based on maps prepared 40 years earlier (around 1894), which the officer in charge found to be still fairly accurate, as well as on information obtained locally from tenants, *khesras* and maps from the last settlement. By night, the surveyor would use chalk and mark with red on a map the areas (*a*) with 'some sand, but less than 6 inches', (*b*) 'more than 6 inches' and (*c*) 'more than one foot'. The officer in charge concluded, from the experimental survey, that a surveyor could not cover more than 150 acres a day, and as the area to survey was more than 4,000 square miles and the number of surveyors were set to about 120, meant that it would have been impossible to complete the survey before the rains started in 1934. Therefore a 'speedier method' was approved by the Board of Revenue on 26 February 1934. *Final Report on the Survey of Lands Damaged*, 2.

45. D.O. 674 R. D., W. B. Brett to J. E. Scott, Commissioner, Tirhut Division, Patna 17 March 1934, BSA RE 43 IV/1934. *Final Report on the Survey of Lands Damaged*, 3.

46. *Khesra/khasra*: Official village field book containing the list of plots and showing their areas, crops and details of occupancy.

47. *Khatiyan*: Land register containing the full description of each holding (plots, areas, boundaries, details of ownership and tenancy, rents and dues). Pouchepadass, *Land, Power and Market*, 22.

48. *Zirat*: private land of a zamindar.

49. *Final Report on the Survey of Lands Damaged*, 3.

50. *Zarpeshgidar*: Holder of a zarpeshgi lease, that is, holder of a mortgage with possession.

51. According to the report. *Final Report on the Survey of Lands Damaged*, 3.

52. Ibid.

53. Appendix I, in Brett, *A Report on the Bihar Earthquake*, 93–94.

54. Ibid. See telegrams from GOI to Sec. of State for India, New Delhi, 11 February 1934; from India Office to the GOI, London, 14 February 1934, 'Earthquakes. Earthquake in Bihar, Bengal etc. 1934. Financial Assistance to Provinces', Collection 109: Earthquakes Collection, IOR/L/F/7/913.

55. Brett, *A Report on the Bihar Earthquake*, 15.

56. Telegram from GOI to Sec. of State for India, New Delhi 11 February 1934. 'Earthquakes. Earthquake in Bihar, Bengal etc. 1934. Financial Assistance to Provinces', Collection 109: Earthquakes Collection, IOR/L/F/7/913.

57. Wilcock, *Bihar and Orissa in 1933–34*, 22.

58. Ibid.

59. D.O. 1539, S. L. Marwood to P. C. Tallents, Champaran District office, 8 February 1934, Motihari, BSA RE 501/1934.

60. Wilcock, *Bihar and Orissa in 1933–34*, 17, 22. 'Relief Measures—Official Account', *The Nation*, 25 April 1934.

61. 'Sugar–Cane Bill' in the Council of State Debates 1, 26 April 1934, 919–20. Both *gur* and *khandsari* sugar belongs to so-called non-centrifugal sugar produced in India. J. H. Galloway, 'Sugar', in *The Cambridge World History of Food*, vol. I, ed. Kenneth F. Kiple, Kriemhild Coneé Ornelas, 437–49 (Cambridge: Cambridge University Press, 2000).

62. The cost of the mills and pans was 200,000 rupees. Wilcock, *Bihar and Orissa in 1933–34*, 22.

63. 'Relief for Middle Class People', *ABP*, 23 March 1934.

64. 'Relief by Calcutta Marwari Relief Society', *ABP*, 25 March 1934; 'Poor Middle Class Men! Need for Relief', *ABP*, 23 February 1934. 'Effect of Earthquake on Society: Labourers Finds Work', *ABP*, 29 March 1934.

65. Niraja Gopal Jayal, *Citizenship and Its Discontents: An Indian History* (Cambridge, MA: Harvard University Press, 2013), 46.

66. Ibid., 44–45.

67. Indian Franchise Committee, *Volume I: Report of the Indian Franchise Committee*, 2nd ed. (Calcutta: GOI Central Publication Branch, 1932), 66–67.

68. For the case of Bihar, see ibid. The expansion of franchise in this period is discussed in Tomlinson, *The Indian National Congress and the Raj, 1929–1942*, 70–73.

69. Speaker Chandreshvar Prashad Narayan Sinha, Muzaffarpur District, 15 February 1934, *BOLCP* 30, no. 2, 138–39.

70. Memo 2623-26/S.B, 'Extract from D.I.G.'s report, II-Agitation, Kisan Sabha and Agrarian Agitation', 21 March 1934, BSA PS 33 VI/1934.

71. Sanjay Joshi, 'Introduction', in *The Middle Class in Colonial India*, ed. Sanjay Joshi, xv–lvi (New Delhi: Oxford University Press, 2010), xix.

72. Sanjay Joshi, 'The Spectre of Comparisons: Studying the Middle Class of Colonial India', in *Elite and Everyman: The Cultural Politics of the Indian Middle Classes*, ed. Amita Baviskar and Raka Ray, 83–107 (New Delhi: Routledge, 2011), 91.

73. Partha Chatterjee, 'The Subalternity of a Nationalist Elite', in *The Middle Class in Colonial India*, ed. Sanjay Joshi, 94–117 (New Delhi: Oxford University Press, 2010), 95.

74. Pouchepadass, *Land, Power and Market*, 332–34.

75. Anand A. Yang, *The Limited Raj: Agrarian Relations in Colonial India, Saran District, 1793–1920* (Berkeley, California: University of California Press, 1989), ch. 5, 90ff.

76. Saghirul Haq, Saran District, 15 February 1934, *BOLCP* 30, no. 2, 157.

77. Maulavi Shaikh Muhammad Shafi, Darbhanga District, 15 February 1934, *BOLCP* 30, no. 2, 162.

78. Speaker Chandreshvar Prashad Narayan Sinha, Muzaffarpur District, 15 February 1934, *BOLCP* 30, no. 2, 133–34.

79. A Mrs Hogan obtained her livelihood by letting out her bungalow to boarders. It had been completely destroyed and she had asked for 12,000 rupees to build a new house. Miss Curtiss valued the loss to 47,000 rupees, including the cost of the destroyed furniture. 'Some Political and Other Aspects of Earthquake Relief in Bihar', M. G. Hallett, 31 March 1934 (Unofficial report of a 'short visit' to Bihar of two days in Patna, two days in Monghyr and two days in Muzaffarpur, 18 unnumbered pages out of which one appear to be missing), NAI HP 34/1/1934.

80. Brett, *A Report on the Bihar Earthquake*, 57.

81. Dunn et al., 'The Bihar–Nepal Earthquake of 1934', 167–71.

82. Brett, *A Report on the Bihar Earthquake*, 56.

83. Dunn et al., 'The Bihar–Nepal Earthquake of 1934', 30, 167.

84. Brett, *A Report on the Bihar Earthquake*, 56–57, 65.

85. See the chapter on isoseismals, in Dunn et al., 'The Bihar–Nepal Earthquake of 1934', 201–73.

86. 'The Reconstruction Problem; Mr. Mookerjea's Suggestions in Bihar Council', *ABP* 23 February 1934.

87. Marwari Relief Society, *Report of the Behar Earthquake Relief Work*, 9. BCRC, *Report for the Period Ending 30th June 1934*, 22.

88. Table I, BCRC, *Devastated Bihar*, 65.

89. Marwari Relief Society, *Report of the Behar Earthquake Relief Work*, 9. BCRC, *Report for the Period Ending 30th June 1934*, Proceedings, 22.

90. Census data (1931) recorded: Muzaffarpur: urban population 82,241, number of occupied houses 16,739; Darbhanga: urban population 104,823, number of

occupied houses 21,184; Monghyr: urban population 126,008, number of occupied houses 24,674. From Appendix E: 'Census Report of India 1931', in BCRC, *Devastated Bihar*, 65.

91. Honorary Sec. Kanoria, Marwari Relief Society, to Sec. Behar Govt, Calcutta 29 January 1934, RE 65/1934.

92. BCRC, *Report for the Period Ending 30th June 1934*, 22.

93. Marwari Relief Society, *Report of the Behar Earthquake Relief Work*, 9.

94. Indian Franchise Committee, *Volume I: Report of the Indian Franchise Committee*, 69.

95. BCRC, *Devastated Bihar*, 51.

96. Table 'Approximate Figures of Damage Done by the Earthquake on 15th January, 1934, in the Districts of North Bihar and Monghyr', in BCRC, *Report for the Period Ending 30th June 1934*, 93.

97. Gaya Prasad Singh, elected member of the Central Legislative Assembly from Muzaffarpur-cum-Champaran, and Syed Abdul Aziz, Minister of Education in Bihar, were key persons in the proposal. 15 February 1934, BOLCP 30, no. 2, 154. 'The Bihar and Orissa Natural Calamities Loans Rules, 1934', *Manual of Bihar Local Laws: 1790–1991* [Civil, Criminal, Revenue, Labour & Taxation Laws], vol. 12, ed. S. K. Pandey (Allahabad: S. B. Malik for, National Law Agency, 1991): 91–108, 91. Reproduced from The Bihar and Orissa Natural Calamities Loans Act, 1934. *Bihar and Orissa Act I of 1934* (Patna: Superintendent, Government Printing, Bihar and Orissa, 1934).

98. Brett, *A Report on the Bihar Earthquake*, 58.

99. *RPER*, 8.

100. Speaker Birendra Nath Chakravartti, 15 February 1934, BOLCP 30, no. 2, 172.

101. Bettiah estate promised 500,000 rupees in 'house-building loan' to private persons in Motihari, Bettiah and bazaar areas in rural towns, which was about 80 per cent of the damaged area according to the district administration in Champaran. For rural areas, the estate had allocated 200,000 in *taccavi* loans. As a result of the relief extended by the Bettiah estate, the district administration in Champaran estimated that the local government would only need to distribute *taccavi* of 300,000 rupees in the Sadar subdivision which was the hardest hit. D.O. 1943/E-31, Marwood to P. C. Tallents, Motihari, 15 February 1934, RE KW 20/1934.

102. 'Long term loans' at 2 per cent per year of the total sum of 313,145 rupees were distributed to tenants of the Raj. The Darbhanga Raj sanctioned loans in 10 circles (an administrative unit) and the amount granted in one circle varied from 833 rupees to 73,365 rupees. Appendix 3, in Sinha, *The Bihar Earthquake*, 107. Forty thousand rupees was distributed to tenants outside the estate. Ibid., 25.

103. Comments to the weekly reports from Tirhut Division, Brett to H.E., Patna/ Ranchi 30 April 1934, BSA RE 13/1934.

104. The loan amount was unlimited per se; however, there were certain clauses in place with regard to the claims. Most significantly, the loan could not exceed the value of the original house, nor could it exceed the cost of repairing the house. If a loan exceeded 1,000 rupees, the limit was 50 per cent of the value of the house, and for lesser amounts loans were given for up to 75 per cent of the value of the reconstructed house. The smaller class of loans ('A') were free of interest for the first year, which in practice lowered the total rate of interest to less than 4 per cent. Brett, *A Report on the Bihar Earthquake*, 9, 59–60.

105. 'Loans to 'Quake Sufferers, Bihar Government Demanding High Rates of Interest, Interpellations in the Assembly' (New Delhi, 17 March 1934), *ABP*, 22 March 1934.

106. Resolution: 'Reduction of Rates of Interest on 'A' and 'B' Class Loans Advanced under the Natural Calamities Loans Act, 1934', 7 February 1939, in Bihar Legislative Council Debates (*BLCD*) 4, no. 4. Official Report. (Patna: Superintendent, Government Printing, 1940), 173.

107. Cf. 'Question no. 149', 9 August 1938, *BLCD* 3, no. 41. Official Report. (Patna: Superintendent, Government Printing, 1939); 7 February 1939, *BLCD* 4, no. 4, 173.

108. 'Short Notice Question', Reg. no. 741 (7 March 1934), NAI H. Pol. 3/2/1934. Also in 'Loans to 'Quake Sufferers, Bihar Government Demanding High Rates of Interest, Interpellations in the Assembly' (New Delhi, 17 March 1934), *ABP*, 22 March 1934.

109. 'Week ending 31 March' (Monghyr) DIG to McDowell, Inspector General, CID, BSA PS 33 III/1934.

110. App. No. 37, 'Supplementary Demand under the Head "Loans and Advances by the Provincial Government"', 28 March 1936, *BOLCP* 34, no. 22, lvi.

111. D.O. 3656, W. B. Brett to Rajendra Prasad, 17 September 1934, NAI H. Pol. 22/21/1936. Brett, *A Report on the Bihar Earthquake*, 59.

112. Ibid., 66. In the category 'Professional grants', yet again vaguely defined, Brett mentioned specifically 'legal practitioners and their employees', the maximum grant was set to 300 rupees, in distribution the average was approximately 100–120 rupees. 'Progress of Work: Statements by Districts', summary by W. B. Brett to J. T. Whitty, Patna/Ranchi 28 September 1934, BSA RE 13/1934.

113. The exact amount was 930,255 rupees. House-building grants of 2,720,635 rupees were divided into 'Urban' 1,072,737 rupees; 'Rural' 1,420,859; 'Middle-class' 227,088 rupees. Appendix 3, in Brett, *A Report on the Bihar Earthquake*.

114. 'His Excellency the Viceroy's Earthquake Relief Fund, Bihar and Orissa Branch, Balance Sheet, 31 July 1934', NAI HP 1/41/34; Appendix 3, in Brett, *A Report on the Bihar Earthquake*.

115. *RPER*, 9–10.

116. Brett, *A Report on the Bihar Earthquake*, 63–65.

117. Second-half of January, P&J (S) Dept., 'Fortnightly Report' in B&O Local Government's Reports, Patna 1934. IOR/L/P.J/12/743.

118. 'Grant of free grants from the V.E.R.F. for house-building', No. 540/49 R.D., W. B. Brett to the District Magistrates of Monghyr, Purnea, Muzaffarpur, Saran, Champaran, Darbhanga, Patna, Gaya, Bhagalpur, Arrah, 9 March 1934, File: 'Grants sanctioned from the VER fund (Darbhanga district)', BSA RE 43 V/1934.

119. Ibid.; *RPER*, 8; Brett, *A Report on the Bihar Earthquake*, 61–63. 'No. 348-V.R. Viceroy's Earthquake Relief Fund, Bihar and Orissa Branch', H. C. Prior, Honorary Sec. VERF, to the District Officer Bhagalpur, Patna, 2 March 1934, BSA RE 43 V/1934.

120. 'Tirhut Weekly Report', W. B. Brett to J. T. Whitty, 2 August 1934, BSA RE 13/1934.

121. Confidential D.O. A.C. 56/R, A. V. Venables (Agent, East Indian Railway, Calcutta) to R.E. Russell, Sec. Revenue and Commerce Dept, Govt of B&O, 18 May 1935; Confidential D.O. 2136-C, Russell, to A. V. Venables, Ranchi, 4 June 1935, BSA PS 11 IV/1935.

122. BCRC, *Report for the Period Ending 30th June 1934*, vi.

123. Marwari Relief Society, *Report*, 10.

124. Ibid., 10–11.

125. 'Flying Visit to Motihari Town; Ladies Astir' (26 March 1934), *ABP*, 28 March 1934.

126. Speaker Birendra Nath Chakravartti, 15 February 1934, *BOLCP* 30, no. 2, 172.

127. Fifty tons of rice was distributed in Champaran. *Prabuddha Bharata*, no. 5 (May, 1934): 260.

128. Ibid.

129. The Ramakrishna Mission, *The Eighth General Report of the Ramakrishna Mission (1934–35)* (Kolkata: Ramakrishna Mission, Belur Math, reprint [no date; photocopy March 2010]). The lesser amount of 50,000 rupees is provided in *Prabuddha Bharata*, no. 5 (May, 1934), 260.

130. A total amount of 116,828 rupees had been collected by September, including a contribution by the Mayor of Calcutta's fund, out of which 114,028 rupees had been disbursed. *Prabuddha Bharata*, no. 9 (September 1934), 260, 430.

131. *Prabuddha Bharata*, no. 10 (October, 1934), 520. 'Quake Relief', in The Ramakrishna Mission, *The Eighth General Report of the Ramakrishna Mission (1934–35)*.

132. Satinath Bhaduri, *Dhoday Charitmanas*, original in Bengali, Hindi translation by Madhukar Gangadhar (2nd ed., the original novel was published as part one and two in 1949 and 1951; Allahabad: Lokbharati Prakashan, 1981). Satinath Bhaduri was a leading functionary in the Congress organisation in Purnea district. The novel depicts several political events through the eyes of a number of community members in rural parts of north Bihar. Partha Chatterjee, 'The Nation in Heterogenous Time', *Indian Economic and Social History Review* 38, no. 4 (December, 2001): 406–40, 406–407. Shirshendu Chakrabarti, 'The Matrix of History: A Study of Satinath Bhaduri's Dhorai Charit Manas (1949–51)', *Journal of Arts and Ideas* 9 (October–December 1984): 49–56, 49–51.

133. Chatterjee, 'The Nation in Heterogenous Time', 412.

134. '20th Communiqué: Bulletin for the Week Ending the 21st March 1934', NAI HP 34/1B/1934.

135. No. 1755-60. P. C. Tallents to District Officer of Saran, Chamapran, Muzaffarpur, Darbhanga, Monghyr and Bhagalpur Patna, 21 February 1934, File: 'Grants from the Viceroy's Earthquake Relief Fund for House Building Purposes', BSA RE 43/1934.

136. D.O. 123-A, Muzaffarpur District Office to P. C. Tallents, Muzaffarpur, 8 February 1934, BSA RE 501/1934.

137. D.C. 38/41, J. E. Scott, Muzaffarpur, to all District Officers, 19 February 1934, BSA PS 33 IV/1934.

138. D.O. 323 P.C., P. C. Tallents to District Commissioner J. E. Scott, 18 February 1934, BSA PS 33 VI/1934.

139. No. 540/49 R.D., 'Grant of Free Grants from the V.E.R.F. for House-building', W. B. Brett to the District Magistrates of Monghyr, Purnea, Muzaffarpur, Saran, Champaran, Darbhanga, Patna, Gaya, Bhagalpur, Arrah, 9 March 1934, BSA RE 43 V/1934.

140. Appendix 30, 'Supplementary Demand under the Head "Miscellaneous"', 28 March 1936, *BOLCP* 34, no. 22, xliv.

141. D.O. 1192, District Officer, Magistrate's Office, Bhagalpur to P. C. Tallents, 5 February 1934, BSA RE 501/1934.

142. W. H. Meyrick (or Meyerick), planter and resident of Motihari, was Secretary of Bihar Planters Association and in 'close touch' with the local administration regarding the distribution of sugar cane after the earthquake. 'Progress Report for the Week Ending 1 March 1934', District Officer S. L. Marwood to J. E. Scott, Commissioner of Tirhut, Motihari 2 March 1934, BSA RE 13/1934. According

to Meyrick himself, he managed an estate of 70 square miles covering four *thanas* in south Champaran. W. H. Meyrick, 15 February 1934, *BOLCP* 30, no. 2 (Superintendent, Government Printing: Patna, 1934), 149.

143. W. H. Meyrick, Champaran District, 15 February 1934, *BOLCP* 30, no. 2, 149.

144. 'Extract from a Report from Mr Gill of Jhapaha Factory', spokesman for the local Relief Committee of Jhapaha (5 February 1934), in D.O. 123-A, Muzaffarpur District Office to P. C. Tallents, Muzaffarpur, 8 February 1934, BSA RE 501/1934.

145. Speaker Birendra Nath Chakravartti, 15 February 1934, *BOLCP* 30, no. 2, 172.

146. Speaker Chandreshvar Prashad Narayan Sinha, of Muzaffarpur District, 15 February 1934, *BOLCP* 30, no. 2, 138.

147. 'The Earthquake in Bengal and Assam', a letter reprinted in *The Englishman*, in Roy, 'State, Society and the Market', n49 and cf. 276–77.

148. D.O. 123-A, Muzaffarpur District Office to P. C. Tallents, Muzaffarpur, 8 February 1934, File: 'Earthquake Relief in Affected/Rural Areas', BSA RE 501/1934.

149. Mr E. Studd (Bengal: European), GOI, *Legislative Assembly Debates* I, 1934, 819.

150. Speaker Chandreshvar Prashad Narayan Sinha, Muzaffarpur District, 15 February 1934, *BOLCP* 30, no. 2, 138.

151. See 'Proceedings from the Second General Meeting' in BCRC, *Report for the Period Ending 30th June 1934*, iii.

152. Andrews, *The Indian Earthquake*, 85.

153. In Darbhanga, 20,000–25,000 men of the 'skilled and unskilled labour class' were employed by the Raj in the peak reconstruction period. 'Notes on Reconstruction of Raj Buildings', in Sinha, *The Bihar Earthquake and the Darbhanga Raj*, 106.

154. 'Tirhut Weekly Report', Brett to J. T. Whitty, Patna 2 August 1934, BSA RE 13/1934.

155. Appendix 'Proceedings of the Second General Meeting of the Bihar Central Relief Committee' (3 August 1934), in BCRC, *Report for the Period Ending 30th June 1934*, iii.

156. BCRC, *Report for the Period Ending 30th June 1934*, 13.

157. In Muzaffarpur, relief to the unemployed amounted to 19,000 rupees for the same period, and in Darbhanga 2,430 rupees; unfortunately, data is missing for the other towns and districts. Ibid., 52–53, and 'Proceedings from the Second General Meeting', iii.

158. 'Tirhut Weekly Report', W. B. Brett to J. T. Whitty, Patna, 2 August 1934, BSA RE 13/1934.

159. 'Bihar Central Relief Committee: Proceedings of the Managing Committee' (2 pp.), meeting held on the 11 January 1935, 2 p.m., at Sadaqat Ashram, Patna,

BCUL PC 1006: 1. Brett's report ignored the SCI's central role and referred to the scheme as jointly financed by VERF and BCRC. Brett, *A Report on the Bihar Earthquake*, 35.

160. The life of Cérésole and the initial years of the SCI are outlined in Hélène Monastier, *Pierre Ceresole: Ein Kämpfer für den Frieden* (Vienna: Sensen-Verlag, 1950).

161. Eleonor Marcussen, 'Cooperation and Pacifism in a Colonial Context: Service Civil International and Work Camps in Bihar, 1934–1937', in *HerStory: Historical Scholarship between South Asia and Europe: Festschrift in Honour of Gita Dharampal-Frick*, ed. Rafael Klöber and Manju Ludwig, 83–101 (Heidelberg; Berlin: CrossAsia-eBooks, 2018).

162. Villages in Sonathi and Minapur *thana* in the Muzaffarpur district were transferred. 'Memorandum of Discussion held on 26th November 1934', BCUL PC 998: 2. 'Memo No. R 5554-55', J. E. Scott, Commissioner, Tirhut Division, 8 December 1934 (Discussion held on 7 December 1934) Commissioner's Office, Muzaffarpur, copy sent to P. Cérésole, Muzaffarpur, Central Relief Camp, for information. BCUL PC 999. In 1936, 1870 families intended to move, almost double the number of the initial 1,000 families. 'Report on the Work of the Committee for the Removal on New Sites of the Flooded Villages in Muzaffarpur District', by P. Cérésole (12 pp.), 30 January 1936, BVCF SCI 20342.

163. 'Report on activities of the Joint Committee upto October, 1935 for Sonathi Scheme' (19 pp.), by Phanindra Mohan Dutta, camp leader of Sonathi, 10, 18, BCUL PC 1007. Similar description in 'Notes on Indian Film' (5 pp.), explanatory notes and background to 'Indian Film 1934–37', 2, enclosed with 'Introduction to Indian Film 1934–37' (5 pp.). Recorded by the SCI 14 months after the earthquake, BVCF SCI 30401.

164. Cérésole, 'Report on the Work of the Committee', 12. BVCF SCI 20342.

165. The roofs were thatched or covered by tiles bought from Dam Chuak colony, which was standing empty in Muzaffarpur in the aftermath of the earthquake. The tiles were sufficient to cover the roofs of 150 houses. The thatched roofs were made of straw and bamboo. 'Report on Activities of the Joint Committee upto October, 1935 for Sonathi Scheme' (19 pp.), by [Phanindra Mohan Dutta, camp leader of Sonathi], 10, 18, BCUL PC 1007.

166. The labour cost supplied by the villagers corresponded to 4–5 rupees, or 25 per cent of the cost of the walls (material, including transport by cart and boat), which was approximately 18 rupees. In Shantipur 60 per cent of the houses were built with walls of mud (14 rupees) and 40 per cent of bricks (18 rupees). 'Detailed Estimate for the Construction of Shantipur, Jamalabad, Minapur, Turki Kharao, Karanpur, Kalahia' (s.l., n.d.), BCUL PC 1050.

167. 'Memorandum of meeting held at Commissioner's Residence 28 March 1935' (2 pp.), by J. E. Scott, Muzaffarpur, 29 March 1935. BVCF, SCI 20342. 'Return of Expenditure of Joint Committee Scheme from March 1935 to February 1936', Muzaffarpur, BCUL, PC 1049.

168. 'Report on activities of the Joint Committee upto October, 1935 for Sonathi Scheme' (19 pp.), BCUL, PC 1007.

169. Roy, Rethinking Economic Change, 87.

170. 'Earthquake Relief Service in India: Frazer Hoyland on His Work and Experiences', The Friend, 8 February 1935: 115–16. Recounted in a publication by his brother: John S. Hoyland, Digging for a New England: The Co-operative Farm for Unemployed Men (London: Alden Press, 1936), 105–6. Frazer Hoyland, 'From an Indian Diary', The Friend, 15 March 1935: 230–31.

171. The Indian volunteers mentioned by name were 'Biren' and 'Bannergee' [Bannerjee], the latter described as an ex-army officer who served in Salonica during the war. 'Notes on Indian Film', 5. BVCF SCI 30401.

172. In addition to Ceresole, Joe Wilkinson, 25 years old, from the British branch of the SCI, the International Voluntary Society for Peace (I.V.S.P.), Paul H. Schenker, a Swiss SCI camp leader, and Hoyland (see previous footnote). The Friend, 30 November 1934. Hoyland, in The Friend, 8 February 1935.

173. 'Introduction to Indian Film 1934–37' (5 pp.), 2, BVCF SCI 30401.

174. No. 540/49 R.D., 'Grant of Free Grants from the V.E.R.F. for House-building', W. B. Brett to the District Magistrates of Monghyr, Purnea, Muzaffarpur, Saran, Champaran, Darbhanga, Patna, Gaya, Bhagalpur, Arrah, 9 March 1934, BSA RE 43 V/1934.

175. D.O. 223, P.C. Tallents to the Commissioner, Tirhut Division, Political Dept, Patna, 9 February 1934, BSA RE 76/1934.

176. 'Progress Report for the Week Ending 1 March 1934. District officer S. L. Marwood to J. E. Scott, Commissioner of Tirhut, Motihari, 2 March 1934, BSA RE 13/1934.

177. D.O. No. R 1523, J. E. Scott, to all District Officers (Tirhut, except Saran), Laheria Sarai (Camp) 23/25 April 1934. File: 'Progress Report on the Distribution of Takavi Loans and Free Grants in North Bihar due to Earthquake', BSA R-LR IIIA/32/1934.

178. One village in Tirhut was on average 1 square mile according to the Census. Margin notes by J. W. Houlton, added to, 'House Building Grants', (memo) by J. E. Scott, received by Revenue Dept, 23 April 1934, BSA R-LR IIIA/32/1934.

179. D.O. 4438 RF, T. A. Freston to W. B. Brett, Laherisarai 9 April 1934, BSA RE 43 V/1934.

180. Notes by J. D. S[ifton]., 27 April 1934, in Memo by W. B. Brett to Revenue Sec., Ranchi 24 April 1934; Notes by J. D. S[ifton], 5 May 1934, to 'House Building Grants' (memo) by J. E. Scott, 23 April 1934, to Revenue Dept, BSA R-LR IIIA/32/1934.
181. Memo by W. B. Brett to Revenue Sec., Ranchi, 24 April 1934, BSA R-LR IIIA/32/1934.
182. Only 1,689 rupees had been given as free grants, and loans of 139,000 rupees had been approved but not distributed. Memo by W. B. Brett to Revenue Sec., Ranchi, 24 April 1934, ibid.
183. Notes and orders by J. D. S. [Sifton], 26 April 1934, ibid.
184. R1685, Rai Bahadur C.C. Mukherji O.B.E., Additional Commissioner of the Tirhut Division, to W. B. Brett, Muzaffarpur, 10 May 1934, File: 'Investment of Certain Officers Engaged in Distributing Sand Clearance Loans in North Bihar with Powers of a Collector under the Agriculturalist's Loans Act, 1884', BSA R-LR IIIA/35/1934.
185. 'Powers of Officers for Disbursement of Loans', J. E. Scott to the Sec. to Govt of B&O, Revenue Dept., Muzaffarpur, 22 May 1934; 'Vesting Officers Engaged in Sand Clearance Loans Work with Powers of a Collector', J. E. Scott to Sec. to Govt of B&O, Revenue Dept., Muzaffarpur, 5 August 1934, BSA R-LR IIIA/35/1934.
186. D.O. 674 R.D., W. B. Brett to J. E. Scott, Patna, 17 March 1934, BSA RE 43 IV/1934.
187. J. E. Scott to Revenue Dept, Govt of B&O, Ranchi, Muzaffarpur, 21 June 1934, File: 'Loans under Agriculturalist Loan Act and Land Improvement Loans Act to Persons Affected by the Earthquake', BSA R-LR IIIA/19/1934.
188. Notes by W. B. Brett to J. D. Sifton, 6 May 1934, BSA R-L II 7/13/1935.
189. Only 4 per cent was covered by more than 2 feet of sand. J. E. Scott to Revenue Dept, Govt of B&O, Ranchi, Muzaffarpur, 21 June 1934, BSA R-LR IIIA/19/1934.
190. Brett, A Report on the Bihar Earthquake, 39–40.
191. Ibid., 60, 62.
192. 'Progress of Work: Statements by Districts', summary sent by W. B. Brett to H. E. (J. T. Whitty), Patna/Ranchi, 28 September 1934, BSA RE 13/1934.
193. The grant application forms contained information about occupation, income, house tax receipt from December 1933 in case of urban houses, and chaukidari tax in rural areas, and the amount applied for (in Hindi; blank and undated): 'Muzaffarpur zile ke dehāto mem makān marammat karne yā banvāne ke liye khairāt madad kī darkhāst kā fārm' (Application Form for a Grant Towards

the Repair or Construction of a House in Rural Muzaffarpur District) and 'Muzaffarpur meṃ makān marammat karne yā banvāne ke liye khairāt madad kī darkhāst kā fārm' (Application Form for a Grant Towards the Repair or Construction of a House in Muzaffarpur [Town]), BSA RE 43 IV/1934.

194. 'Progress of Work: Statements by Districts', summary sent by W. B. Brett to H. E. (J. T. Whitty), Patna/Ranchi, 28 September 1934, BSA RE 13/1934.

195. 'Q. 94', 10 September 1934, *BOLCP* 31, no. 10, 421.

196. D.O. 851 R.D., W. B. Brett to T. A. Freston, 27 March 1934, BSA RE 43 V/1934.

197. T. A. Freston to W. B. Brett, Laherisarai, 9 April 1934. The same issue mentioned in 540/49 R.D., 'Grant of Free Grants from the V.E.R.F. for House-building', W. B. Brett to the District Magistrates of Monghyr, Purnea, Muzaffarpur, Saran, Champaran, Darbhanga, Patna, Gaya, Bhagalpur, Arrah, 9 March 1934; and '1290-99 R.D.', Brett to the District Magistrates of the before-mentioned districts, Patna, 25 April 1934, BSA RE 43 V/1934.

198. 'Memo to His Excellency', W. B. Brett, Patna, 16 March 1934, BSA RE KW 20/1934. Also in 'Extract from file E.-20 of 1934' [to H. C. Prior], BSA RE 43 V/1934.

199. R.D.O. 5472, Comments by W. B. Brett, in notes attached to Tirhut fortnightly report, W. B. Brett to J. T. Whitty, 14 December 1934, BSA RE 13/1934.

200. W. B. Brett to H. C. Prior, 23 June 1934, BSA RE 43 V/1934.

201. D.O. 4438 RF, T. A. Freston to W. B. Brett, Laherisarai, 9 April 1934, BSA RE 43 V/1934.

202. W. B. Brett to H. C. Prior, 21 June 1934, BSA RE 43 V/1934.

203. Sub-district Officer W. G. Archer, see W. G. Archer, 'The Bihar Earthquake', [s.l.] February 1934, Mss Eur F236/1, Papers of William G. Archer and Mildred Archer. Scott approved of 300,000 rupees for house building grants in rural areas, and 100,000 in urban areas, as compared to 16,000 to max 50,000 in the other districts. D.O. 1519R, Scott to Brett, (Camp) Laheria Sarai, 23/25 April 1934, RE 43 V/1934.

204. D.O. R 988, J. E. Scott to W. B. Brett, Muzaffarpur, 27 March 1934, BSA RE 43 V/1934.

205. 'Progress of Work: Statements by Districts', summary sent by W. B. Brett to H. E. [J. T. Whitty], Patna/Ranchi, 28 September 1934, BSA RE 13/1934.

206. Similar complaints were also raised in the same newspaper on 12 August and 19 August 1934. Extract from *Ittihad* (Patna), 16 August 1934, 'Report on Newspapers in Bihar and Orissa', No. 9, September 1934, NAI HP 1/41/1934.

207. Notes by Brett to Whitty, 13 July 1934, 'Tirhut Weekly Report', Brett to Whitty, 10 August 1934, BSA RE 13/1934.

208. W. B. Brett to H. C. Prior, 22 July 1934, BSA RE 43/1934.

209. W. B. Brett to T. A. Freston, 10 August 1934, and again 12 September 1934, BSA RE 43 V/1934.
210. The amount was 2,700,976 rupees (1,948,000 rupees in 1934–35, and 752,976 rupees in 1935–36). Appendix No. 37, 'Supplementary Demand under the Head "Loans and Advances by the Provincial Government"', 28 March 1936, BOLCP 34, no. 22, lvi.
211. 15 February 1934, BOLCP 30, no. 2, 154.

6

Congested and Contested Spaces

Introduction: Urban Renewal

The earthquake was, according to the local colonial government, administrators, engineers and segments of the population, an ideal scenario for rebuilding with better standards and for better socio-economic conditions. The devastation was effectively used to implement new town plans by arguing that reduced risk in future earthquakes could be achieved by changes in the plans of the bazaars. Conveniently, planning for earthquake-safe bazaars conflated with improvements of sanitary provisions and roads. In reply to an initial proposal for town planning in the larger towns of Muzaffarpur and Darbhanga, the Commissioner of Tirhut expressed his views regarding suggestions for town planning in Tirhut. The earthquake was an opportunity to transform Darbhanga into 'the model town': 'Theoretically the clean-sweep made by the earthquake is the Godsent [sic] opportunity to replace dirt, discomfort, and irregularity, by the model town'.[1] In Monghyr and Muzaffarpur, too, the rebuilding phase from 1934 to 1937 was viewed by the government and engineers as an opportunity for making changes in the social and material fabric of society, underlining the positive outcome of the earthquake as a form of creative destruction. The transformative aspect of disasters is a recurrent theme in urban history.[2] As suggested in the case of North American disasters, to rebuild better after disasters is an integral part of a capitalist system which feeds on disasters and upheavals.[3] In its most extreme form, disaster research has compared the phenomenon of reconstruction after disasters to a phoenix rising from the ashes.[4] The Great Fire of London in 1666 is often taken as an example of changes in architecture and construction types as a result of large-scale destruction.[5] In a long-term perspective, particularly important since seismic events may have long intervals in between, the question is to what extent the disaster provides lessons learnt with future events in consideration.[6] Japan is one such example where construction materials and methods for building earthquake-resistant buildings evolved through experiences with major catastrophes.[7] But also when there is learning from a disaster, several other variables such as public facilities, transport routes and access to water play a major role in urban reconstruction.

This chapter addresses how the rebuilding phase became a site for transformations that reflected contemporary notions of town planning, guided by sanitation engineering and interests in improving trade conditions.[8] Even though official rhetoric made a point out of 'learning' from the disastrous consequences of unrestricted constructions and congested areas, planning was generally undertaken with contemporary conceptions of improvements in sanitation and trade in mind, rather than minimising risk in future earthquakes. In this sense, reconstruction plans after the earthquake treated it as a singular event overshadowed by an agenda of improvements of living conditions and commercial infrastructure, as defined by the local colonial government and sections of the urban population. While these improvements guided the reconstruction phase, the government used earthquake safety as an argument for widening roads and lowering population density with the help of the financial aid that followed in the wake of the earthquake.

The principles of 'improvements' underpinning town planning followed a strategy that had been used to implement sanitation and transport facilities in urban South Asia in the late nineteenth and early twentieth centuries. While urban planning in smaller towns like in Bihar was a relatively unchartered territory, town planning in metropoles under colonial rule was carried out under the banner to improve hygiene and trade conditions, and to secure military and disciplinary control from the state's point of view.[9] As will be further discussed in this chapter, the outcomes of town planning in Bihar displayed a scenario similar to what Nandini Gooptu has argued in the case of urban planning:[10] it had a marginalising effect on settlements of the urban poor by removing them from the centres in order to carry out modernisation and hygienic 'improvements'. Sanitation engineering included rebuilding more spaced and simpler structures, and the widening of roads would facilitate movement: in effect, these changes meant buildings would be less likely to kill people in future earthquakes. In order to achieve these improvements—interchangeably argued to be for the betterment of transport access, sanitary provisions and earthquake safety—population density in the bazaars had to decrease, buildings techniques had to be reviewed, roads had to be widened and drains constructed. Implementing these changes necessitated a restructuring of space with the result of temporary and in some cases permanent dislocation of residents in a struggle over commercial plots.

Before the earthquake larger towns in Bihar had had their share of town planning in attempts to address public health issues, transport and governance. In Patna, by the end of the nineteenth century, the spread of diseases from the so-called native town to the European settlements motivated municipal committees under the direction of local British administrators to initiate what turned out to be failed attempts at constructing sanitation and water provisions.[11] In the railway hub Jamalpur, Nitin Sinha notes several parallel developments in how planning addressed sanitation and security in the town as compared to in larger urban settings. Providing 'civic' amenities was reserved for European settlements, for the sake of their health, comfort and security.[12] A shift can be discerned after 1857 when structuring communications and defence became prominent features of town planning as a means to enhance control over the cities and residents, according to Veena Talwar Oldenburg's research on Lucknow and north Indian cities.[13] Road widening undertaken for the improvement of Bombay was, according to Prashant Kidambi, motivated by cleaning up a sanitary disorder and to enhance the city's image as a centre of imperial and commercial power where unimpeded circulation and free movement of people and commodities characterised an 'orderly city'.[14] Similar to what secondary sources argue, the district gazetteer for Monghyr from 1960 describes how town planning in select areas of Monghyr after 1857 became an improvement of communications, sanitation and control of the town from the local government's perspective. Reconstruction after the 1934 earthquake featured as an opportunity for the local government to continue what was set in motion during the nineteenth century, a transformation of the town layout in terms of sanitary provisions, transport and security. In 1859 and 1867, private individuals petitioned the government with proposals to 'improve' the fort area and surrounding settlements. Consequently, in the 1860s and 1870s the area, 'densely crowded with native huts and kutcha houses surrounded by low jungle and in the most filthy state', transformed as the occupants of the huts were bought out and instead 'good bungalows' were erected, many still in existence in the 1950s.[15] Earthquake reconstruction to a large extent continued these nineteenth-century initiatives in altering transport and hygiene provisions by stressing a need for improved sanitation and better living standards. According to the district gazetteer, the construction of drainages and roads in the town's bazaar after the earthquake were the major improvements undertaken from the

1930s to the 1950s.[16] The earthquake interrupted and ruined a substantial part of the reorganisation of water infrastructure, leaving the town with only 50 per cent of the original water supply for two years after the earthquake. Water supply to the town was, however, an issue since the beginning of the twentieth century as the municipality had bought unfiltered water from the East Indian Railway Company's pumping station at Jamalpur, before organising its own facility, which soon broke down and it again reverted to its old provider. The water scheme was further expanded after the earthquake and again subject to rounds of planning during the next five years.[17] The earthquake had ruined infrastructure across the town, yet it was in retrospect perceived to have facilitated the reconstruction of the Chowk area in particular, which after the earthquake got broader roads, lanes and *pucca* drains.[18] Apart from town planning and water infrastructure, the reconstruction of Monghyr after the earthquake helped the local government become the largest builder in the town. The gazetteer does not mention who was the largest builder before but, as discussed in this chapter, the reconstruction of the Chowk bazaar necessitated reclamation of land in Bekapur, which later would be known as the shopping area of Raja Bazaar (also referred to as the Raja bazaar), where the management of land and semi-permanent buildings was later transferred from the municipality to the local government. The new plan for the bazaar meant a number of new plots in the town, and it may also have been part of the town's lateral growth noted in the district gazetteer. Next to the government, house-owners, described as people of a 'higher income group', benefitted by rebuilding 'better type' *pucca* houses,[19] a process set in motion by the earthquake as will be discussed in this chapter.

The following sections address how the idea of town planning was conceptualised by government officials in the earthquake's aftermath as a project of improvements (An Opportunity for Improvements) and how practical concerns were dealt with by restricting attempts at repairs or reconstruction of houses along roads (Paving the Way for Town Planning). In order to oversee reconstruction, a superintending engineer assisted by a number of engineers was hired to manage practical and technical questions (Engineers: Rebuilding Better). The town planning of bazaars shows how reconstruction 'improved' towns according to 'hygienic' standards and consolidated the interests of large leaseholders and shopkeepers ('Improving Slums': Planning Bazaars). The plan for how to undertake such planning in several ways underestimated the human side of urban renewal as the relocated residents, their financial compensation and tenancy rights appeared more complicated to address than rebuilding houses and restructuring space (Protected Interests, Protected Spaces).

An Opportunity for Improvements

The destruction and death in Monghyr's bazaars figured as an example par excellence of the need for town planning. The bazaar's layout, its crowds, narrow lanes and uncontrolled constructions posed as the cause of death to which the remedy was control through a plan that widened roads and lowered population density. The earthquake turned Monghyr's Chowk bazaar into 'a heap of bricks presenting the appearance of a huge brick Kiln [sic] with its bricks scattered all around without any order'.[20] The bazaar was a 'gigantic rubble heap, piled 15 feet high' and it was impossible to tell where the roads and lanes had been, as amply illustrated by photographs.[21] Other bazaars of the town had also toppled down and most of the injuries and deaths had occurred in Topekhana bazaar, Bari bazaar and the Chowk bazaar.[22] Congestion and narrow lanes became death traps, while in less congested *mohallas* the number of deaths was much smaller (Images 6.1 and 6.2).[23] In a spacious residential area of the Chowk bazaar, 80 persons had been dug out within one and a half hours, leaving the number of

This picture, taken three days after the earthquake, when bodies were still being extricated from the ruins, depicts the hopeless confusion that existed in the demolished bazaar area of Monghyr.

Image 6.1 One of many photos of the vast destruction in Monghyr bazaar published by the newspapers. This one was taken three days after the earthquake, hence before partially ruined constructions were demolished and the rubble cleared.

Source: Moore (ed.), *Record of the Great Indian Earthquake*, 21.

The gateway of the old Fort at Monghyr—once occupied by a Regiment of " John Company " troops. The European residents of the city of Monghyr live inside the Fort.

Image 6.2 The remains of the clock tower-cum-gateway to the fort in Monghyr were like the destroyed bazaars widely published in the newspapers.

Source: Moore (ed.), *Record of the Great Indian Earthquake*, 35.

people buried under the debris to be 'well imagined' in the narrow and congested roads and lanes.[24] Those who escaped through the dust and darkness as the houses fell, ran for open space such as the maidan of the fort in Monghyr where eye-witness accounts described thousands to have sought refuge.[25]

Government officials too told of the dangers of the bazaar. In the announcement of a new town plan for Monghyr, the Chowk bazaar was described as congested: its narrow lanes and high buildings had formed a 'death trap' which the government set out to amend by widening the roads.[26] Reconstruction in towns was viewed as an opportunity by the local government 'to take advantage' and make desired changes in terms of facilitating transport and widening 'the principal thoroughfares of these towns'.[27] In Bihar, communication was a fundamental part of colonial expansion and access to trade within the province as well as by linking up with larger transport arteries to the city of Calcutta.[28] Communication and modes of transport in the region not only affected trade and the physical presence of the colonial powers, but would also come to shape ideas and practices of rule in the earlier colonial period.[29] Communication and infrastructure between settlements—towns, trade centres, production centres, districts and nearby cities—were essential features of the state's presence in the province.[30]

As Relief Commissioner Brett, in charge of coordinating town planning, argued in the Legislative Council when the town plan for Monghyr was finally approved in September 1934: deaths could easily be avoided in future earthquakes by thorough town planning with open spaces and wider roads.[31] While the plan was being drafted, the government announced that '[t]he new scheme will remove congestion, provide better sanitation, and is likely to be conducive to economic improvement and minimise the risk to life'.[32] In particular in bazaar areas, the GSI's recommendation on reconstruction supported the implementation of a minimum standard width for roads and park areas, as larger open areas were 'as desirable for health reasons as for earthquake-escape routes'.[33] As mentioned in Chapter 1, town planning in Motihari and Jamalpur had arguably saved people's lives by making it less densely populated. In Jamalpur, though the material destruction was extensive, the reason for the relatively low number of deaths was thanks to the town being 'not so congested and not so populous as Monghyr is'.[34] As the planning process progressed, statements in the press hailed the 'scientific town plan' projected for Monghyr's bazaar in which new wide roads ran through the 'most densely populated quarter'.[35] The same arguments applied to Darbhanga's town plan: 'designed to improve and replan the congested areas in Darbhanga town so as to render them safer in terms of another earthquake, and to provide better sites for the population'.[36] Reconstruction was perhaps nowhere as frankly framed as an opportunity for improvements as in the Commissioner of Tirhut's vision of a Darbhanga relieved of 'dirt, discomfort and irregularity'.[37] The position reflected a general negative perception of life in the bazaar as unhygienic and disorganised among government officials, not unlike that of his predecessors in the town administration.[38] Congestion and overpopulation explained the many deaths in the bazaars and the same factors posed as the major cause of 'unsanitary' conditions, which the chief engineer in charge of Monghyr's town plan would address in his attempts at 'improving' sanitation as discussed in a sub-section of this chapter. Wider roads and lanes, and more sparsely populated areas and lower houses were measures likely to prevent deaths on the same scale in future earthquakes.

As noted in the secondary literature on earthquake engineering in India, 'serious and systematic efforts' at building earthquake-resistant constructions and for developing earthquake codes were made in India after the 1935 Quetta earthquake.[39] In 1934, such ideas were discussed and the wholesale reconstruction after the 1923 Kanto earthquake was mentioned as a suitable model but played a marginal role in the actual reconstruction process.[40] The 1935 Quetta earthquake posed an altogether different set of circumstances that resulted in a more systematic and controlled reconstruction process. The success in developing earthquake-resistant features in Quetta was partly explained by the town's status as a military area, which made it easier to rebuild railways, military and the civil administration.[41] The military's control of Quetta and the ban on residents to return in both the immediate aftermath and during the reconstruction phase solved the problem of having to erect temporary housing and facilitated rebuilding permanent structures—a measure which would have been difficult to justify in Bihar where town inhabitants mostly remained displaced within or on the fringes of the towns.

More importantly, however, the development of new engineering techniques in Quetta emerged from the opportunity to review learning from a recent earthquake nearby. After the 1931 Mach earthquake in Baluchistan, an engineer undertook the rebuilding of railway buildings according to an earthquake-resistant technique developed specifically for the seismic area affected by both earthquakes.[42] As the 1935 earthquake struck, the earthquake-resistant railway quarters located in the area of maximum intensity were the only houses that escaped undamaged. The experience served as evidence of not only the successful building technique, but also the importance of investing in research and buildings to prevent damages and deaths.[43] The earthquake-resistant buildings proved what secondary sources are soon to point out in the often-tragic aftermaths of earthquakes: buildings kill people, earthquakes do not.[44]

Even though the 1935 Quetta earthquake happened more than a year after the Bihar earthquake, Quetta's rebuilding plan was soon ahead of Bihar's. It was praised as a model example of a building code with rigidly enforced reconstruction. However, an encompassing 'Indian' building code for earthquake-safe constructions was yet to be conceived in 1934, the reason being, according to the GSI, the 'unique' structures of mixed materials, *kuccha-pucca* and *kuccha*. At the same time the destruction in Bihar proved to the GSI the necessity of a code for Indian building standards, in particular in larger towns and villages.[45] A Punjab government publication on 'earthquake-resisting design' from 1934 gave another explanation for the lack of a general building code, namely financial constraints of private individuals: 'forms of construction within the means of the people are often so restricted that no general Code is practicable'.[46] Simultaneously, the publication provided several local examples of earthquake-resistant designs from major earthquakes such as the 1905 Kangra earthquake. The GSI, on the contrary, expressed the contradictory view that earthquake-safe houses could be built with the same costs as ordinary buildings, as long as simplicity was maintained.[47] According to the initial GSI report mainly concerned with reconstruction, the average Indian householder could not afford the necessary high-grade materials, thereby echoing the view of the Punjab government publication mentioned before. The loss of life in Bihar was seen as a combination of faulty constructions and financial constraints: many could only afford to build houses of *kuccha-pucca* material, which had been the most severely damaged type of house.[48]

In addition to the lessons learnt from recent earthquakes, the GSI had recorded several earthquake-resistant building techniques since the 1897 Assam earthquake. An indigenous construction of very old *kuccha-pucca* timber houses had survived the 1934 earthquake remarkably well, and so had earthquake-resistant constructions with a framework of split bamboo on a masonry plinth in the 1930 Dhubri earthquake.[49] The latter was a technique that let the house structure move as a whole while other buildings of same material with the frames attached to the plinth were 'considerably damaged'.[50] Similarly in Chapra and Muzaffarpur, brick or mud houses raised on timber frames had collapsed with less frequency compared to the ordinary brick houses, and those which were damaged could be repaired rather than rebuilt,[51] making them both life-saving and cost-efficient constructions. These constructions appeared to have formed the basis for the GSI's recommendation for the government to 'encourage' reconstruction with timber pillars and frames in both kuccha and *kuccha-pucca* buildings.[52]

Apart from examples of these local construction methods and materials, the GSI thought 'good quality mortar and brick-work' to be the 'best insurance against earthquake damage'.[53] While the quality of materials and control over constructions explained the wholesale damages to bazaars and private properties, even official buildings with a controlled construction plan had suffered badly. According to the GSI, the scope for 'the greatest improvements' were in the construction of larger *pucca* houses and government buildings.[54] Eye-witness accounts and the press confirmed the perception of how 'modern' buildings, such as the Patna Hospital, the English Church at Patna and the buildings of the Imperial Agricultural Research Institute at Pusa could not withstand the earthquake, as compared to Patna's landmark building the Golghar, built in 1786, which was left with 'barely a scratch'.[55] Although the GSI acknowledged the need to upgrade especially the quality of mortar and bricks, the use of 'high quality materials' had not helped to prevent slumping and cracks in heavier buildings such as the sugar mills in north Bihar. In order to reduce the risks of damages and high mortality, the GSI recommended improving designs by ensuring strong foundations in heavy buildings.[56] Advertisements for 'cheap earthquake proof pucca houses' by contractors in the local newspapers[57] might have struck a chord with the public since the cost of bricks was prohibitive to many. The concrete and cement companies' attempts at selling their products in the reconstruction phase have been described as a sign of the industry's early interest in 'earthquake engineering'.[58] A later government publication claimed reinforced concrete, reinforced brick work and Portland cement to have replaced the use of 'mud, mortar and lime'.[59] Although the Cement Marketing Company of India offered reduced prices of up to 12.5 per cent in Muzaffarpur and 20 per cent in Monghyr,[60] it targeted factories and houses of the wealthier sections rather than a general town population, judging by the types of large constructions advertised in, for instance, *The Indian Concrete Journal*'s special issue, *The Great Indian Earthquake*.[61] Likewise, advertisements by the Concrete Association of India aimed at a select number of people with its examples of 'earthquake proof buildings', illustrated with photographs of sizeable and undamaged concrete houses in Darjeeling.[62] As a part of the recommendation to rebuild simpler structures, the GSI discouraged buildings of more than one storey in the earthquake area north of the Ganges and, in order to make structures lighter, it recommended the material of the roof to be kept as light as possible and all ornamental work such as cornices and balustrades were to be avoided.[63] Interestingly, Katharina Weiler notes the opposite development in the use of ornamental works in Kathmandu where they became distinctive features of 'New Road' (Juddha Sadak, that is, Juddha Road), which after the earthquake was rebuilt as an elegant boulevard with eclectic neoclassical architecture of plastered façades and aspiring columns.[64] Though the use of ornamentation may have negatively affected earthquake safety, according to the GSI officers, it is noteworthy that the renewal in Nepal was mostly restricted to the façade while local forms were preserved in building design.[65]

In addition to passing recommendations on materials and construction models, the GSI advised—in the absence of an earthquake code—that 'much could also be done by legislation in controlling the height of buildings and the width of streets'. Rather contradictory—considering the serious damages and number of lives lost—opposition against legislation to control reconstruction had been voiced with the argument that earthquakes were relatively infrequent. The lapse of one hundred years since the 1833 earthquake had given rise to speculations regarding a cyclical pattern, but the GSI refuted the possibility to say anything with regard to 'periodicity' and frequency. Regardless of when and how frequently earthquakes visited the region, the GSI stood by the opinion that controlled reconstruction would benefit earthquake-safety: according to their suggestion reconstruction in villages needed to be supervised by the *thana* staff and in urban areas by the municipalities, while engineers and architects of public buildings and heavier construction should ideally be guided by a building code.[66] Improved building materials and technical solutions thereby represented but one side of earthquake safety. The GSI's recommendation about taking control over how and where people reconstructed their houses with the help of municipal laws was seen as a way to prevent large-scale urban death and destruction in future earthquakes. Within the town planning schemes drawn up by the provincial government, engineers, municipalities and, to some extent, local representatives, earthquake-safety legitimised a control over reconstruction and urban spaces by legislation. At first sight, town planning may appear to have been a relatively low-cost and easy-to-implement solution compared to a building code, but it entailed a contested period of altering property relations and relocating segments of the urban population.

Paving the Way for Town Planning

The prolonged process of town planning of the important market towns of Darbhanga and Muzaffarpur in Tirhut and of Monghyr south of the Ganges started in the last week of January 1934 and soon involved the public, engineers, district officers, the municipalities and the local government. Rebuilding the bazaars in the towns offered the government a 'chance' to restructure urban spaces since the earthquake had in a cruel way facilitated town planning by demolishing houses and the dislocated residents had migrated to streets, parks and open spaces within or on the fringes of the towns. It presented a scenario different from town planning in Bombay in 1898, when the acquisition of land and properties as well as arrangements for temporary accommodation had caused delays.[67] Already by the end of January 1934, the government realised the need to stall individual plans for rebuilding houses in order to implement a reconstruction plan. The decision to impede reconstruction in towns subject to town planning was partly justified by technical concerns raised by officers from the GSI who cautioned against rebuilding based on a fear of aftershocks lasting 'for some months'.[68] Until after the monsoon, a far bigger issue was the earthquake's impact on land levels and river courses. A measuring of land levels in Tirhut showed a depression of 2 feet and was further investigated by drainage engineers.[69] These concerns were from the outset voiced at the district level, since according to the local appreciation 'very little' could bring about 'very great changes in these rivers' and consequently affect the drainage system.[70] The local government was, however, keen to put in print in a communiqué that initially was a verbal advice by the GSI. The recommendation to wait with reconstruction until after the rains when the land had settled gave the local government more time for realigning roads before private individuals started rebuilding.[71] Consequently, the geologists' first appreciation of the situation was published in a government communiqué as an 'expert advice' against reconstruction of *pucca* buildings in north Bihar until after the monsoon.[72] Later, the first report by the GSI submitted to the local government in May 1934 contained recommendations for reconstruction, which would again be reiterated in the final GSI volume on the earthquake.[73] With the reconstruction process in mind, the local government decided, with the consent of the GSI, to publish the report as a 'preliminary report' for public consumption, and later the same year, the GSI published its official version of the report as an 'account'.[74] For towns subject to planning, the Judicial Department found two paragraphs in the Municipal Act for taking over plots for road widening and planning public lights and drainage. With the act, the government could define new or wider roads and claim more space. According to two other sections of the act, any alteration or re-erection of property had to be on notice with the Commissioner for one month, thereby giving the government time to discuss the outline of the new town plans.[75] The local government's plans of widening roads and, in particular, acquisition of roadside space was central to the envisioned town plans. With the support of the acts, the local government efficiently put a temporary halt on all attempts at reconstruction in the town areas under investigation.

However, in towns where large-scale reconstruction was still necessary, but *not* town planning, building regulations were on the contrary relaxed immediately in order to speed up the erection of temporary shelters and urgent repairs.[76] In this way, the local government controlled reconstruction in areas where it had decided not to undertake town planning: rather than to halt repairs and rebuilding of houses, the government was keen on speeding up the process. An Additional District Magistrate in charge of the Patna City Municipality had already, by end of January, issued an order dispensing with the ordinary notice required for the reconstruction of houses damaged by the earthquake.[77] The permission to rebuild served its purpose: to hasten reconstruction. Already at the beginning of February 1934, four temporary assistant surveyors were appointed to deal with inspections of damaged private property in Patna.[78] Their conclusions reflected what eye-witnesses described: while the three-storeyed mud and brick houses in Bankipore bazaar collapsed, similar to in the bazaars of Monghyr, Muzaffarpur and Darbhanga, many residential 'modern' bungalows and brick houses in Patna experienced relatively minor damages, such as cracks and damages to arches.[79] The local government's approach and the type of damages explain the initial rapid reconstruction in Patna. Contrary to towns subject to planning, little concern was voiced regarding public health, sanitary provisions or undertaking 'improvements'. The District Magistrate noted, after having crossed the town on an initial inspection of damages, that in the case of roadside shops it was 'difficult to improve the sanitation' since they were situated by the side of the road. The decision to hurry reconstruction and repair of damaged houses was reconsidered at the end of May 1934 when the government informed the municipalities to again apply regulations restricting rebuilding. The change of rules was motivated by the need to prevent the erection of dangerous houses, particularly in the case of masonry buildings since only a few towns had qualified engineering staff to oversee the process.[80]

While the local government officials dealt with the paperwork necessary to realise the envisioned plans, the municipalities faced financial and practical problems with housing people rendered homeless by the earthquake and further displaced by town planning. The decision to postpone repairs and reconstruction affected the municipal house tax. In April 1934 an Emergency Act was passed by which the municipalities had the right to reduce or remit house tax of plots with destroyed or damaged houses.[81] The act was applied with retrospective effect from 1 January 1934 when taxes for the first quarter had been paid. The act was meant to facilitate decisions by the municipalities where the shortage of staff made the inspection of houses for claiming remission impossible.[82] The tension between the interests of the municipalities on the one hand and the local government on the other was apparent in the towns subject to town planning as the municipalities lost the decision power over urban improvements to the town planners. The schemes for town planning, or in the case of Darbhanga, a trust in the form of a legal act, transferred the power over key urban developments from the municipalities to appointed officials, a common administrative hurdle in the planning of larger cities during the colonial period.[83] With regard to Darbhanga's Improvement Bill, Relief Commissioner Brett was concerned about how the scheme, once it became law, would serve to centralise decisions to Patna at a distance from people affected by the planning.[84] Town planning was, as the period between January and September proved, a lengthy process, which brought uncertainty in terms of municipal finances and decision power in the administration, as well as complicated living conditions for the displaced residents. People were waiting to know both when and where they could rebuild their houses, and on top of it, if they could afford it, while living in provisional or semi-permanent houses. Following the advice by the officers of the GSI, as mentioned earlier, permanent rebuilding was not planned to start until after the monsoon, in September 1934. Meanwhile, in order to set up semi-permanent buildings for the homeless, to control rebuilding and acquire new spaces for expanding bazaar areas, many practical questions such as ensuring at least temporary reconstruction of infrastructure, supply of building materials, finances and new plots needed to be addressed. In order to supervise these steps involved in rebuilding private and government property, as well as roads and bridges, a body of engineers was hired.

Engineers: Rebuilding Better

After the local government urged other provinces to send 'really experienced' Executive Engineers for a year of service,[85] three engineers arrived for the towns of Darbhanga, Muzaffarpur and Monghyr.[86] While the recruitment of engineers was in process, the appointment of the chief technical adviser, Relief Engineer and Supply Officer Colonel F. C. Temple[87] was carefully considered. He joined on 5 March 1934,[88] almost a month after some of the first engineers had arrived. The extensive damages and the envisioned improvement scheme in Monghyr's Chowk bazaar motivated the government to prioritise the town, therefore Executive Engineer A. H. Nunn was deputed to Monghyr and H. V. Williams was appointed Town Engineer for Bhagalpur, sent by the government of Bengal.[89] At least two engineers came from the neighbouring United Provinces: Assistant Engineer Rai Sahib Pandit Ram Chandra and, one of the last and most experienced to be hired, Devi Dayal was appointed District Engineer and worked outside the towns mentioned.[90] Like in the cases of the engineers Nunn and Williams, Ram Chandra from Lucknow joined on deputation. After a week in Chapra, he arrived in Muzaffarpur where he was supposed to be based under the supervision of the Superintending Engineer and the Commissioner of Tirhut J. E. Scott,[91] who had prepared a detailed programme for a month, including visits to the district headquarters and subdivisions seriously affected. Scott was more than pleased with him, 'quick and definite' at work and 'much appreciated by the public'.[92] To start with, Ram Chandra advised on public buildings, potentially dangerous houses and a few of the private residences, and in a second round he continued with the row of private houses listed by Scott.[93] By the end of March, there was still no news about an engineer for Darbhanga, and Scott deputed Ram Chandra as its Town Engineer until a permanent engineer joined in the middle of April.[94]

Though partly successful, the recruitment of engineers appeared as marked by chance in terms of availability and the willingness of experienced engineers to relocate for the job at short notice or of the respective local government to do without the staff. For instance, the Government of Bengal offered to send three engineers soon to be unemployed. A travelling allowance and other types of compensation were offered in addition to salary. Harold Easton Bruce (1897–s.d.), in his reminiscences from his time with Tirhut's police force in the earthquake aftermath, described the 'miracle' of restoring railways and bridges as achieved by 'blasphemous Scottish engineers, provided with free whiskey for a month by the Company [East Indian Railways]—after the job was done'.[95] Though no special rewards were mentioned in connection with the engineers hired by the local government, the positions appeared as reluctantly accepted. The tasks were described as unfamiliar even for experienced engineers, and because of damages and the nature of work, they had to bring their own tents.[96]

The engineers reported to Relief Engineer and Supply Officer Colonel F. C. Temple who, according to Brett, was 'anxious for a title which would assist him when he returns to his ordinary work' and therefore was granted the title 'Relief Engineer' in addition to 'Supply Officer'.[97] He received the maximum pay for a Superintending Engineer and had a good number of staff attached to him.[98] Although Temple was privately employed at the time, his background as a sanitation engineer to the Government of Bihar and Orissa and extensive experience from designing the new town plan for Jamshedpur, also known as Tatanagar or 'the town of Tata' in 1919 made him a choice well fitted with the local government's ambition to improve sanitation and roads in the reconstruction process.[99] The 'Temple Plan' for Jamshedpur had been innovative, influenced by garden-city planning and perhaps by Patrick Geddes' work in India on civic improvement.[100] As a widely acclaimed town planner, Geddes' engagement with 'civics', or 'the good life', gained currency for its sensibilities in designing town and city plans in accordance with ecological local conditions and human well-being in mind.[101] The modern industrial cities with slums as a defining feature he called 'Paleotechnic', while the so-called Neotechnic town of the future was achieved by town planning that removed the slums by promoting health, hygiene and order. For Geddes, town planning was a way of transforming life, a 'civilisational transition' where the removal of slums was essential to achieve health, hygiene and order.[102] In the fast-growing industrial town of Jamshedpur, Temple had concentrated on accommodating the increasing number of workers in a town plan with open spaces and an improved water and sanitation system for the upkeep of hygienic facilities, despite overcrowding.[103] Temple's senior expertise in sanitation engineering carried considerable weight in qualifying him for the appointment in 1934, but at least equally important was his regional contacts with contractors and the local government administration.[104] This was particularly valuable since supply and delivery of construction materials, such as bamboo from Chota Nagpur and steelwork and steel sheets from the Tata Iron and Steel Company in Jamshedpur and Calcutta, were key to rebuilding towns and infrastructure.[105]

In addition to his central role in town planning, Temple took part in committees for planning infrastructure and designs of culverts, bridges and embankments. Reconstruction of infrastructure after the earthquake was affected by the changes in the flood landscape for which an engineer was deputed to advise on repairs to embankments and requests for permission to excavate drainage channels.[106] Temple spent considerable time and effort on preparing and planning the reconstruction of infrastructure together with the Embankment Engineer and the Inspector of Local Works. This work had to take into consideration past flood levels, a variety of embankment constructions and roads, settlement patterns and water needs, as well as the unknown future changes of the water bodies which the earthquake was assumed to have set in motion.[107]

In the towns, Temple's supervision and expert advice on town planning followed in conjunction with the work of the newly employed engineers. His tasks were numerous: overseeing the demolition of dangerous buildings, securing bricks and building materials, price control, construction of municipal buildings such as hospitals and other public institutions, pass municipal building plans and control ground conditions, grant loans to contractors for supply of building materials and supervise drain and road construction as well as the erection of temporary quarters while reconstruction was undertaken. Although the tasks to a great extent were executed by the town engineers under his supervision, they prioritised to arrange temporary housing and evaluate the safety and prospects for renovating private properties.[108] The condition of standing buildings would also give a clue to the number of temporary houses needed, the amount for house-building loans or grants, materials to order, while the work on repairable buildings could start before the rains that were expected to arrive in June. The multifarious tasks that came with Temple's position entailed extensive touring and coordination, every step carried out in close cooperation with the headquarters in Patna and with the engineers, magistrates and commissioners in the districts and, according to Brett, 'a constant hammering' at the railways and suppliers to send goods.[109] Temple's description of the very busy schedule served to make Brett apply for further staff on his behalf, though several staff were already attached to him. A qualified engineer as 'Technical Assistant' and a second steno-typist based in the office were intended to speed up the paperwork, a major bottleneck in the workflow according to the application.[110] The Finance Department declined the request, motivated by the increase in travel expenses it would incur and that the Chief Secretary was the only person with two steno-typists, implying that it was only required by the top administrators of the local government.[111] Overall, the case was characteristic of the hectic period of initial reconstruction and the slow process of hiring staff, an outcome of administrators being at loggerheads regarding budget and staff requirements in the aftermath. The local administration's and the Reconstruction Department's protests regarding the amount of work and lack of staff were similar to the problems in the distribution of relief, as discussed in the previous chapter. The problems experienced reflected a barely functional administrative flow, and the calls for resources were louder than the ordinary administrative quibbles over insufficient budget allocations and shortage of staff. The extra expertise and staff called on for the relief and reconstruction work were repeatedly pointed out as inadequate for the tasks prescribed. Though the Reconstruction Department was meant to facilitate the government administration, the new department often found itself entangled in correspondence between departments. The PWD advised on its office and staff requirements such as salaries for the Town Engineers, but it was Brett who controlled the budget even if expenditure was normally under the PWD. In effect, it meant that Brett had to consult both the Finance Department and the PWD for hiring staff.[112] Moreover, Brett had to request sanctioning of staff required by the relief engineers who first applied through Temple. In general, staff and professional positions in the reconstruction process were created in order to complete work as the tasks arose, preferably with minimum qualifications in order to keep the salary on a lower scale, a process which caused delays and left tasks pending.[113]

However, as the work progressed, Brett and Temple successfully joined forces to hire more staff and again requested a sanction for the post of a Technical Assistant. In the middle of April 1934, the work of investigating house plans, securing building materials and, in addition, cooperation with the local administration in evaluation of house loans was well under way. Temple's office in Patna was a hectic hub where the PWD, District Boards and the Town Engineers obtained supplies. The rains were approaching and the repair of bridges was still under way, material and equipment had in some cases not arrived either because several contractors were involved or ruined infrastructure had blocked the roads. The lack of planning for the reconstruction of several bridges, essential for transport of goods and building material, blocked supplies.[114] The District Boards had placed orders for bridge material without any thought of how to approach the reconstruction bridge by bridge. As a result, goods carriers with material were left stranded between rivers, causing a shortage of wagons for transports that further delayed the arrival of other necessary material. Repairs to railways were impeded by engines buried under debris at stations; workshops and blacksmith's shops were damaged; both water and electricity supplies were short after the earthquake; and some of the back-ups such as kerosene, castor and linseed oils in the railway store buildings had been lost in the earthquake.[115] Temple wanted to hire a technical assistant for dealing with the increasingly complicated and slow-moving work shared between the PWD, the District Boards and the Town Engineers. Brett supported Temple's renewed attempt at expanding his staff with an assistant, and this time he managed to communicate the anticipated increasing workload to the Finance Department. Temple had requested a person with 'sufficient technical knowledge' and 'sufficient authority', perhaps hinting that the current staff had neither sufficient education, experience nor the seniority required for the tasks. By using a cost-efficiency argument, which sounded almost like a threat, Brett stressed that 'without this [a person to help in the flow of transport and supplies] rebuilding is quite certain to be delayed for months, a delay which will cost large sums of money'. Reluctantly, the Finance Department granted a post of assistant engineer of junior rank on a temporary basis, several weeks after the initial request in March.[116]

Logistic problems and the slow repair of infrastructure became a vicious circle. Temple had partly addressed the issue in his complaints to Brett regarding the PWD's inefficiency. In addition, earthquake damages to the landscape had changed natural river courses and broken embankments caused waterlogging that hampered the reconstruction of infrastructure. The problem of waterlogging and high water levels were further aggravated by rain and hindered the Local Works Departments and District Boards in planning and executing the rebuilding of roads and bridges. In June 1934, the Local Works Departments in Muzaffarpur, Darbhanga and Champaran districts reported the monsoon to have further complicated the reconstruction of temporary as well as permanent solutions to bridges and roads. The Madhubani–Rampatti Road No. 56 and Barwara–Serai Road No. 74 in Darbhanga were temporarily closed for motor traffic due to the Kamla flood. A masonry bridge in the Darbhanga–Gangwara Road No. 2 had collapsed due to an 'earth tremor' recorded on 2 June 1934 and the road remained closed until the rains were over. Ferry arrangements in Darbhanga were disturbed by the floods in June 1934. The bridge at Bariarpur after the third mile on the Motihari–Mehsi Road No. 19 in Champaran district would be ready by July if the rain decreased.

In addition to seasonal conditions and geological changes, as well as badly coordinated planning in the rebuilding of infrastructure, the human factor played a role in the delay of supplies. Many suppliers had failed in delivering materials required for rebuilding bridges and culverts, perhaps due to difficulties in communication or because of insufficiently available supplies in response to the sudden demand. The Lakhandaya bridge in Sitamarhi, Muzaffarpur district, had not been supplied with material for draining. When the water started rising, the Local Works Department constructed a temporary solution with bamboo. The same applied to several masonry bridges and culverts along the Sitamarhi road which were rendered unsafe but temporarily fixed with a decking of bamboo while waiting for the supply of iron joists to arrive. For the bridges in Darbhanga, too, temporary arrangements had been made to keep the Madhubani–Benipati Road No. 62 open until girders ordered from Calcutta arrived. In Champaran, contractors had not delivered material to the Local Works Department for the construction of a bridge, and in the same district the construction of a temporary wooden bridge was held up since planks had not arrived from Bettiah as had been promised.[117]

Altogether, environmental circumstances such as waterlogging as a result of the rain, broken embankments and shifting land levels after the earthquake, in combination with the government's slow organisation of supplies coupled with difficulties in accessing the areas to deliver materials resulted in a slow reconstruction of infrastructure. Temporary bamboo constructions had to be resorted to for repairs of roads, bridges, buildings and temporary housing and relief shelters from the very beginning until after the monsoon was over.[118] Just like the planning of repairs and ordering of building materials, a lack of planning and damaged infrastructure hampered the provision of temporary material. Initially, the government planned to order the bulk of bamboo from the Forest Department in Palamau in southern Bihar, but an estimate of the cost and quality of the material as well as difficulties in arranging transport, resulted in the choice of bamboo from Sitamarhi and sal[119] poles from the United Provinces, since it turned out more economical and practical to supply to the districts of Muzaffarpur, Darbhanga and Champaran.[120] Besides, both the price and quality of 'Palamau bamboo' were 'repugnant to the public' according to the District Officer in Chapra.[121] The Forest Department in Palamau in southern Bihar could only with difficulties and after help by the local government find railway carriages available to transport bamboo to the northern parts, as well as to Monghyr south of the Ganges.[122] Even if all transport for relief purpose was charged half of the normal rate on the East Indian Railways, prices and costs borne by the local government took time to settle and delayed the distribution of bamboo. Compounded, the damage done by the earthquake and the inability of the local government to plan the reconstruction phase complicated and impeded the tasks of the engineers. Although these practical difficulties affected town planning, the displaced inhabitants and redistribution of tenancy rights posed the major difficulties for the administration and the municipalities.

'Improving Slums': Planning Bazaars

When all the civilized world is actively working for slum removal, it is unthinkable that the Chawk [Chowk] should be rebuilt as a slum, especially with Government as its landlord.[123]

Temple's ideas about town planning to 'improve' urban living conditions and remove what was perceived as insanitary slums would become central to the reconstruction plans. In words and layout he contributed to argue for designs that put sanitation at the core of the new town plans, yet it should not be overlooked that similar visions of 'improvements' were already expressed by administrators in the initial weeks following the earthquake and had partly motivated the recruitment of Temple. His reference to the government as the landlord in the quote earlier was to the *khas mahal* land that the bazaar was built on in Monghyr. In the town-planning documents, Temple and administrators described 'slums' as characterised by congestion, lack of sanitary facilities and population density. These conditions could be built and planned away by decreasing the population density, to relieve the area of 'bad overcrowding' and turn 'a bad slum into a not unreasonable over populated [*sic*] quarter'. The widening of roads was also motivated by the incentive it would have on trade, the essential function of the bazaar. Control over road constructions, width and layout, would facilitate traffic 'in a way that will tend to greater prosperity in the town'.[124] Town planning aimed to provide more uninhabited space. It would be used for making wider roads and improved transport facilities to benefit trade, increase airflow between housing plots to benefit health, and lower population density to improve sanitary facilities and hygiene. The key to this process was the building of roads, which in effect meant fewer residential and commercial plots on lease.

While Temple was foremost concerned with sanitation and road plans in line with contemporary ideals for urban improvements, the Monghyr's town-planning scheme took shape in collaboration with Brett and the District Magistrate and Collector of Bhagalpur district, the Town Engineer, and the Special Officer in charge of the municipality.[125] Among these, the municipal officer was the person most involved in day-to-day communication with the residents as he was responsible for temporary accommodation. In particular, from Brett's comments on the planning process, the diverse and often conflicting interests of planners, administrators and town residents transpired. His approach to town planning reflected the local government's relationship with the town residents in the contemporary sociopolitical context and a growing awareness of the bazaar politics surrounding commerce and leases. According to rough estimates of the number of residents in the bazaar, officially approximately 3,000–4,000 persons had resided in 700 holdings in the Chowk bazaar and adjacent Madhupur bazaar.[126] The municipality estimated that two families had lived in half of its 500 municipal holdings in the Chowk bazaar, giving an approximate number of 750 families.[127] In Brett's calculations, the population in the Chowk had to decrease from 750 families to 450 families, therefore 300 families had to resettle elsewhere. Since Brett suspected that the total number of 750 families was a low estimate, he preferred to count 350 families for which new plots had to be arranged, a number agreed on by Temple.[128] Hence, approximately half of the 3,000 residents of Monghyr's bazaar had to be permanently relocated according to the planners.[129]

In Temple's plan, the optimum population density was fundamental for improving sanitary conditions in the bazaar. In the town plan proposal for Jamshedpur, he followed the same guidelines in accordance with the prevalent garden city ideals of low density which he would argue for in the planning of Monghyr.[130] An increased area helped to create 'hygienic conditions' by lowering population density and he, therefore, recommended acquiring as much land as possible in Bekapur. In his estimate, 47.4 families per acre lived in the 'very badly overcrowded slum area' of the Chowk bazaar before the earthquake. It was regarded as far too many since, according to the standards followed by him, 12 families per acre were 'generally accepted throughout the world as best for practical urban conditions'. Temple's initial plan for Monghyr envisioned playgrounds for children and open spaces in order to improve living conditions, though these features appeared marginal in comparison to the importance of roads and controlled construction of houses in providing space. In the new areas for settlements and with the improvements in the Chowk bazaar, Temple calculated a ratio of 17.5 families per acre. It was a figure he reluctantly conceded to, as it was 'rather too thickly populated judged by ideal standards', but even so 'an immense improvement'. Temple presumed some plots in Bekapur would partly house fewer families per acre, since they would rebuild 'larger and better houses' while he expected higher population density in the Chowk bazaar, perhaps as the result of high rents. The maximum number of families per acre would under the circumstances ideally be limited to 25 per acre, and that too only in a smallholding and on the fringes of an area according to Temple. By placing the most densely populated holdings away from the centre of the bazaar, circulation of both transport and air would benefit, and in case of another earthquake the congestion would be less.[131] His estimate, Brett claimed, was incorrect since many plots were meant for shops; therefore, the population density in residential areas was actually higher than the estimate. Although the conditions had improved, the planning had not had the desired effect as 'congestion in the Chauk bazar [Chowk bazaar] will still be at a fairly high figure'.[132]

A noticeable 'improvement' of the bazaars in town planning, according to the retrospective report of the local government, was the construction of roads. Before the earthquake, the two main roads in the Chowk bazaar, described as 'a tangled labyrinth', were between 20 and 25 feet wide, the side roads 10 to 12 feet wide, and lanes of an average of 7 feet in some places. In the new plan for Monghyr, the roads of the bazaars had become 40 feet wide.[133] Road improvements, such as the new design of Purabsarai, demanded more space at the cost of the plot sizes.[134] In this main artery of the bazaar, the electric poles were moved from the road to the pavement to free up more space for traffic, a measure that further facilitated access to the bazaar area (Image 6.3).[135] Similar to in the Chowk bazaar in Monghyr, the Darbhanga Improvement Trust widened main roads to 60 feet and important roads to 40 feet and interspersed them with open spaces in the three bazaars in order make away with 'the old narrow and filthy service gullies'.[136] The roads were narrow since before the arrival of the railways most goods had been transported on the river and carried by men, pack animals or pulled carts from or to the river bank. When considering the new plan, building away congestion was a priority in the name of, first of all, safety since according to official numbers 311 people had died from falling debris in the streets and alleys. Yet, bringing down the size of the population and widening roads held importance in two other areas: to improve health and hygiene as well as the convenience of commerce and trade. Another two considerations of the planners were aesthetics, or 'beauty', of the bazaar, and the preservation of sound property, which in effect meant houses of wealthy residents and temples, as these were the buildings still standing. One particular contribution towards the beauty of the bazaar was the design of the Oval Market, an oval-shaped bazaar area, on which Temple gave advice.[137] In order to expand the roads

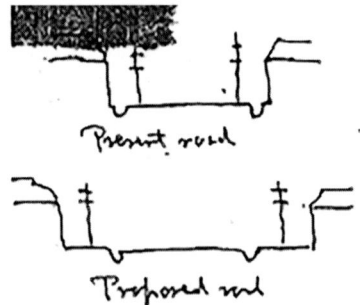

Image 6.3 Drawing of existing and proposed road design for Purabsarai road in Monghyr. The electric poles were moved from the road to the pavement in the proposal. For the Purabsarai road, 0.682 acres had been set aside.

Source: Memo: 'Monghyr Town Planning Scheme', W. B. Brett, 15 April 1934, BSA RE 45/1934.

and decrease congestion, the Oval Market was built on land next to the old bazaar areas that contained mostly houses of mud and thatch, a few gardens, wasteland, patches of palm trees, a lowland where people would excavate earth for construction purposes. This area would become the new 'civic centre', 'a new modern market' for 'better class' shops.[138] The traders and shopkeepers, who in the new plans for the two old bazaar areas, Katki bazaar and Bara bazaar, would lose their plots or get smaller holdings, could lease holdings here, under the Lalbagh New Area Scheme that housed the Oval Market. The fourth scheme in the town plan for Darbhanga concerned resettling people who had lived in the area that was transformed into the new civic centre, a process set in motion by town planning also in Monghyr.

In the new plan for Monghyr, the 12–15 acres of plots in the Chowk bazaar was cut down to 10 acres of plots because of expanded roads and drains. At the same time, each plot contained fewer residents and therefore the town plan extended the bazaar area with 27 acres of arable and wasteland to the south and southeast of the Chowk bazaar.[139] In the two new areas Bekapur and Guhiapokhar, adjacent to the Chowk,[140] 7 acres were set aside for roads and infrastructure and 20 acres were developed as holdings, and later sold to, before everyone else, Chowk bazaar tenants at 200 rupees per acre. Bekapur was mainly laid out on agricultural land, except for a few acres of wasteland, and partly waterlogged and low. This perhaps did not sound like the best preconditions but with three feet of debris as landfill the area stood the test during the first monsoon.[141] The solution of dumping debris in a wetland may, however, have repercussions in a long-term perspective. Land expansion by using debris in the bay area after the 1906 San Francisco earthquake created an unstable soil that resulted in severe ground-shaking and damages to houses in the 1989 Loma Prieta earthquake. Like Yokohama, which to a large extent was rebuilt on debris from the 1923 Kanto earthquake,[142] the new development in Monghyr may be expected to suffer more severely in the next major earthquake. Sanitation engineering and town planning, rather than vulnerability in future earthquakes, was, however, the main concern of the planners in 1934. According to Temple's proposal, Bekapur 'tended to become insanitary rubbish dumps' but the new settlement of 'a well laid out shopping area' would help to 'improve the health and amenities of the town'. In effect, the extended and planned bazaar area became a means to relieve the town from two insanitary areas created by 'rubbish dumps' and cramped infrastructure in terms of drains and roads as well as a site for dumping the debris from the Chowk bazaar.[143] By early April, 150 bullock carts, 15 motor trucks and more than a thousand coolies were emptying the Chowk of debris.[144] Compared to, for instance, the town planning in Darbhanga, available wasteland and debris as landfill levelling and road constructions were circumstances that made the realisation of the plan for Monghyr's bazaars relatively cheap.[145]

Earthquake reconstruction also posed as an opportunity for the local government to access large funds which otherwise sorely lacked for providing public goods such as drains and roads. Monghyr and Muzaffarpur were considered important towns because of their administrative role, population size and positioned as communication and trade hubs. In Darbhanga, the local government had an advisory role in the Darbhanga Improvement Trust, financed with a donation of 500,000 rupees by the Maharajadhiraja, who also lent the remaining amount of 900,000 rupees needed for the scheme.[146] The trust, described by the Governor of Bihar as 'a programme of progressive improvement',[147] was first discussed in February 1934 and passed as an act in the September session of the Legislative Assembly. The mix of two-storeyed *kuccha-pucca* and *pucca* buildings in Darbhanga's Katki bazaar and Bari bazaar suffered severely (Image 6.4), and the areas were rebuilt and expanded as part of the new town plan, as were larger structures such as educational institutions, the hospital and official buildings of the Raj.[148] Earthquake reconstruction of private property, as well as property of the Raj, indeed contributed to the increased and heavy workload of the Darbhanga Raj administration until at least 1936.[149] In the end, however, only a few of the large number of schemes drawn up were realised when the trust came to an end in 1948 due to a lack of finances. In fact, the local government's district gazetteer from 1964 claimed that apart from the Oval Market, none of the bazaar schemes was realised as planned, while more than half of the initial donation made by the Maharadhiraja was spent on acquisition of land, houses and administration.[150]

In Monghyr, the initial budget for town planning of the Chowk bazaar and Bekapur, the area developed as an extension of the bazaar, was considerably less and to a large extent financed by the VERF. The fund made the initiation of the scheme possible with a grant of 50,000 rupees, while the local government's cost was about 11,000 rupees and the municipality was expected to profit from increased revenue from house tax.[151] According to a district gazetteer, however, government grants paid the total cost of 328,564 rupees for constructing roads, drains and buildings in Monghyr's Chowk bazaar.[152] The first budget for Monghyr's town planning stated 65,000 rupees for roads, lighting, water supply and latrines, including the cost of cancelling the *khas mahal* tenancies.[153] In the final moderately expanded budget presented by the Bihar Legislative Council, the municipality started the work with the help of a loan of 25,000 rupees from the government, and a grant of 50,000 rupees from the VERF.[154]

Image 6.4 Katki bazaar in Darbhanga town after the earthquake.

Source: Album reg no 6, titled '1934 Earthquake'. Photographs by Bourne and Shepherd studio, Calcutta, Maharajadhiraj Kameshwar Singh Kalyani Foundation, Darbhanga, Bihar.

Almost two years after the earthquake, the government decided to buy the new settlement Bekapur from the municipality.[155] The acquisition of the land by the municipality was called 'a mistake': the ownership should have rested with the local government since it was responsible for the *khas mahal* tenancies. Second, the municipality had failed in 'obtaining considerable sums by settlement of the acquired land', and therefore the government's decision to 're-purchase' the area was 'help towards the scheme'. The government offered the municipality 150,000 rupees for the land, including certain rights in connection with the temporary huts. The 'generous' price was according to the council's decision fixed after having taken into consideration the purchase price of the land, the development of the area, and the loss of profit that the municipality might have expected from the settlement of the land.[156] With the provision of the VERF and exceptional government measures for earthquake reconstruction, 'improvements' in the form of town planning could be realised in Monghyr.

Protected Interests, Protected Spaces

In *A Great Estate and Its Landlords in Colonial India*, Stephen Henningham addresses the opposition to the Darbhanga Improvement Trust. Although divided along communal lines in voicing concerns against the trust, the poorer Muslims, who comprised almost a third of the population in the bazaar areas, and the Marwaris and other well-to-do Hindu segments were all critical of foremost the scheme's financial burden on the rent-payers. According to Henningham, the Muslims' and Marwaris' open critique of the new plan signalled other sources of support that were relatively independent of the Maharajadhiraja, while his influence was perhaps the greatest among Hindus in the countryside where he could wield his power as the owner of vast lands and in his position as the head of the Maithil community.[157] Although Marwaris, lawyers, businessmen and other professionals often benefitted from interactions and deals with the Darbhanga estate, they had other sources of incomes and were part of networks that linked them with urban centres.[158]

Despite the planning of the new bazaar areas in Darbhanga receiving criticism in public for giving preference along communal lines, and thereby creating tensions foremost between Hindus and Muslims,[159] economic disparities, and thereby wide gaps in building qualities, motivated the dislocation of a 'mostly poorer class [of] Mohammedans', according to the town planners.[160] Town planning was in this sense, like Nandini Gooptu writes, mainly concerned with reclaiming the town for the middle classes and if the urban poor were left without housing and if financial constraints prevented the provision of alternatives, then that outcome had to be endured.[161] In a 'manifesto' published in *The Searchlight* before the bill of Darbhanga Improvement Trust was about to be discussed in the Legislative Council, the plan was described as an attempt to push the poor, and especially Muslims, out of the bazaar since the improvements meant additional taxation. Seventy-four individuals, representatives of associations and proprietors of businesses, many of them pleaders, supported the manifesto, among them were a number of Muslims and mostly Hindus.[162] Arguably, according to the planners, the poor Muslims' old houses of bricks, mud and timber beams had been razed to the ground, while the large and well-built or big modern houses of wealthy Marwaris along the main road of the bazaar had withstood the shaking. The despatchers of the manifesto questioned the priorities made by planners; why make wider lanes and roads when the town was in need of waterworks? The manifesto repeatedly stated the scheme to be contrary to public opinion and against the general wishes of the town citizens.[163] The same opposition was raised in the Legislative Council where the 'improvements' were accused of effectively forcing the poorer segments to relocate, for there were, as one member of the Council[164] dryly noted in a sarcastic comment, 'not many Maharajas of Darbhanga to contribute towards such an improvement scheme'. If town planning was such a 'vast problem', why was it privately financed rather than drawn from the general revenue of the province? Brett answered that if the people of Darbhanga would turn down such a 'generous and public spirited offer' by the Maharajadhiraja, 'they would lose the sympathy of India for large financial aid for which they might apply'.[165] Brett's position echoed the view of the Commissioner of Tirhut, who early suggested that the reconstruction of private property was costly and town planning was a way of providing financial assistance to individuals.[166] At the same time, Brett argued that Darbhanga's town planning was far from catering to the 'rich men' as it was foremost a scheme to resettle people who had to leave the congested area of the bazaar.[167] The Darbhanga Improvement Act did address the apparent power relations and economic interests by having 'a representative of the poorer classes inhabiting the area likely to be effected', as a member of the trust, and the municipality, the state government and the Maharajadhiraja were also ensured representatives.[168] While objections against the planning of a cinema in the proximity of the Katki Bazaar Mosque resulted in moving it to a site at a distance from the mosque, the complaint against the Oval Market for dislocating 'a large number of poorer class Muhammadans' was disallowed since it could not come up with an alternative solution. The conflict of interests in Darbhanga reflected, unlike in Monghyr, the position of people living on land 'developed' into commercial plots for an extended bazaar area. Persons who had lived in the old bazaar areas, benefitted from the expansion of land as they were promised the old rate per acre in the newly developed areas, and if required to relocate they were granted a price reduction of 25 per cent on plots.[169] The persons displaced by town planning in Darbhanga were resettled on a 'very untidily area with a high proportion of waste land' to be developed with roads and plots. The land they had resided on was valuable for extending the bazaar area. In addition, the reconstruction of private property depended on loans and grants and, as discussed in the previous chapter, the latter was a provision that first of all catered to the 'middle classes'. The resettled Muslim community, described as being predominantly of a poorer class, did not fall into this category and were expected to rebuild houses of 'mostly mud' or 'brick[s] in mud' with tiled roof.[170]

Since the whole population of about 3,000 residents of almost the entire Chowk bazaar in Monghyr had to be relocated while the area was cleared of debris and re-planned, the construction of safe and sufficient temporary houses posed a major issue. Many residents were still in need of temporary housing after several relief societies and the local government had erected structures and sold building materials at reduced prices. The VERF funded the material and labour costs for constructing temporary colonies in towns, in most cases 200,000–300,000 rupees, and in return 'small sums' in the form of rents from the huts could be collected.[171] In comparison with the towns of Muzaffarpur and Darbhanga, Monghyr received only a fraction, that is, 10,000 rupees, from the VERF for semi-permanent houses and building material: Darbhanga received more than 200,000 for the purpose. On the other hand, a substantially larger sum of 250,000 rupees in house-building grants was generously allocated in Monghyr in the month of May since rebuilding south of the Ganges could begin before the monsoon was expected to set in and new constructions in, for instance, Bekapur would partly take care of displaced residents.[172]

Many of the temporary accommodations were meant for the middle classes and were made of bricks and asbestos or iron sheets, and sometimes partially grass and thatch. The colony of huts built by the Mayor of Calcutta at Purabsarai in Monghyr was regarded to be of better standards and were partly built with corrugated iron sheets. The 98 huts housed 1,500 people under the supervision of the local housing committee and the local board.[173] The BCRC set up a small group of semi-permanent structures for the middle classes and the Municipality had constructed 50 temporary houses, while 75 more were under way. Like temporary colonies in other towns, fires had been a problem, but water buckets at most of the larger colonies and a water lorry used as a fire engine were provided in order to prevent further dangers.[174] Towards the end of March the huts on the Purabsarai site were nearly all occupied and steps were being taken to fireguard them and render them cooler in preparation for the hot weather.[175]

In many villages in north Bihar, a sub-district officer noticed how houses of bamboos thatch and reeds 'naturally rode out the earthquake without any damage as their materials were both light and resilient'.[176] However suitable these materials were in villages with space between the houses, the experience of huge fires had shown how such constructions posed major hazards in the often congested temporary urban colonies. Mud walls, bricks, tiles and corrugated iron in townhouses controlled the spread of fire, while bamboo and thatched constructions aggravated the problem of fire according to the account by the sub-divisional officer.[177] Even though the dangers of fires in the temporary huts made of grass was commonly known, they still remained the most common type of construction. The frequency of fires in the temporary grass huts was one probable reason for people's reluctance to move into the organised colonies. Notably, when the thatched roofs had been substituted with corrugated iron sheets, applications were in abundance according to the government officials in charge in Tirhut.[178] In the towns, large numbers of grass huts had been constructed as temporary housing[179] and these congested settlements suffered from recurrent fires. Although the corrugated iron sheets may have increased fire safety, they were highly unsuitable in the hot weather. The Marwari Relief Society reported the prevalence of fires among the re-erected huts made of straw and bamboo in villages as well, indicating that the ruined huts had been made of less fire-prone materials such as mud and bricks or with more space in between.[180] While straw and bamboo were to some extent used by the society in erecting huts, corrugated iron sheets became the solution to the frequent fires in the temporary colonies. The Marwari Relief Society remedied several fires in temporary sheds made out of straw and tarpaulin in Muzaffarpur by supplying fire extinguishers and water supplies,[181] and temporary houses had corrugated iron sheets rather than the fire-prone thatched roofs (Images 6.5, 6.6, 6.7 and 6.8).[182]

In Monghyr, the local government soon had to answer to growing discontent among the shop-owners from the Chowk bazaar over the lack of temporary solutions. The organised colonies with temporary huts had been filled up by end of March and a large number of people—most of them came from the Chowk bazaar but also 'all sorts of people' from other parts of the town—had built temporary houses or huts in the Ramlila maidan.[183] By the end of March some moved from the maidan to the colony built by the Mayor of Calcutta, but a survey of the Ramlila maidan's remaining occupants recorded 384 huts yet to be vacated.[184] Subsequently, in June 1934, the Monghyr municipality decided to evacuate and close down the area, as the municipality found it insanitary and cholera had broken out in June. By the end of the month, most of the residents were transferred to Bekapur, and by the end of the first week of July, 250 huts had been vacated and the residents settled in organised temporary huts in Bekapur, Belan bazaar and Purabsarai.[185] In a week's time only 100 temporary huts remained to be evacuated but without alternative accommodation for the residents.[186] According to an intercepted telegram signed by a Sita Ram Khemka, 'the self-styled "Assistant Secretary Town Reconstruction Committee"', addressed to the Viceroy, the Governor of Bihar and Orissa, M. K. Gandhi and the press, the residents were forced away from the Ramlila maidan.[187] The telegram outlined how the property of the temporary settlers had been 'thrown in the dust', and the following day a second telegram expanded on the maltreatment of the 'earthquake strikers'. The event described in the first telegram was also reiterated from the perspective

Image 6.5 Inside temporary quarters in Monghyr.

Source: Turnbull and Ormerod, *The Great Indian Earthquake*, 284. The photographer was most likely Ormerod, who visited the area in February–March 1934.

of the municipal officer, who with the District Magistrate, the Special Officer, the Town Engineer and the *khas mahal* officer accompanied by the police, had paid a visit to shopkeepers and given notice to move to shops allotted in Bekapur. The personal visit by the government officers was motivated by the shopkeepers showing 'great reluctance to move' though they had in the end left 'peaceably and of their own accord'.[188] The alarm expressed in the telegrams and the visit paid by the local government officials indicated that far from everyone was happy with the arrangements. A few days later, when 500 people met to discuss relief to the earthquake 'sufferers', the police reported the local government to be the recipient of the harshest criticism.[189] The public meeting was the result of the 'agitation' in the Ramlila maidan, with the aim quoted as 'to ventilate the "grievances of the people" against the Municipality' and presumably organised by the dispatchers of

Image 6.6 Temporary quarters made of grass and metal or asbestos sheets in Monghyr.

Source: Turnbull and Ormerod, *The Great Indian Earthquake*, 284. The photographer was most likely Ormerod, who visited the area in February–March 1934.

Image 6.7 A demonstration building made of asbestos cement sheets erected by Asbestos Cement Ltd in Monghyr.

Source: Turnbull and Ormerod, *The Great Indian Earthquake*, 284. The photographer was most likely Ormerod, who visited the area in February–March 1934.

Darbhanga—destruction of bazaar area by the earthquake (top left) and congested bazaar area before the earthquake (top right and bottom).
(See page 28).

Image 6.8 Collage of images depicting earthquake destruction and 'congested' bazaar area in Darbhanga before and after the earthquake.

Source: Sinha, *The Bihar Earthquake and the Darbhanga Raj*, 66.

the telegrams and local politicians.[190] At the heart of discontent was the eviction of shopkeepers from the Ramlila maidan where they allegedly were doing 'good business' from temporary shops along the roads.[191] Nripado Mukherjee, the president of the BCRC's Monghyr branch who already by April had pleaded for 200 temporary sheds to accommodate specifically 'middle class' people, was one of the many displeased by the way the government had handled the case.[192] Two articles in *The Searchlight* and the *Indian Nation* dwelt on the discussion in the meeting and accused the municipality and the local administration for 'High-handedness in Excelsis', 'Victimization and discrimination' and 'nepotism' in allocating shops.[193] The District Magistrate admitted a shortage of shops to the government administration in Patna[194] but denied that people were being forcefully evicted.[195] The municipality identified the shop-owners as the source of disgruntlement,[196] and the government singled out in particular 'a small group of well-to-do Marwaris' as opposed to the scheme and described them as 'squealing because they cannot obtain more than their fair share of temporary accommodation at Bekapur'.[197] According to the municipality, it had become the main shopping area, so 'immensely popular that about the entire business town including the new comers [sic] want to get into it', making the Special Officer in charge fear breakouts of 'riot and bloodshed' if the allocation of shops was not strictly controlled. The complaints by the remaining shopkeepers in Ramlila maidan were heard and responded to by the government with an additional arrangement of 100 extra sheds for shops in Bekapur, an insufficient number according to the Special Officer in charge of the municipality who suggested the double amount in order to cover the demand for both commercial and residential plots.[198]

The numerous and multifarious claims on new plots, as outlined by the municipality, reflected the business communities' interest in the expanded bazaar area which would be the temporary main shopping area until the Chowk was rebuilt. The shop-owners lacked neither resources nor voice. According to the Special Officer, some still had houses but had lost their shops and even if their houses were in a part of the Chowk bazaar still standing, these people keenly requested allotments in Bekapur since that was where the bazaar had moved. In one such case, a merchant who held a *khas mahal* lease and occupied two restored houses in the bazaar had been allocated 'a good shop at the crossing at Bekapur so that he might not be a loser' even though his need was not regarded as great as that of those who were homeless. Apparently, his ability to loudly make such claims had paid off, being 'an agitator of the worst type [had] not stood in his way in the least'. The municipality listened to the complaints and calls for an expansion of business opportunities by the commercial and propertied residents of plots in the Chowk bazaar. Only a few shopkeepers presumably lost business opportunities, as in the case of the kerosene depot owner whose shop in Bekapur was denied permit considering safety measures, though he was allotted a plot at a 'safe place' elsewhere. Others were given favoured treatment: all the cloth shops were settled on the main roads, the reason perhaps being to keep guilds together or to grant them preference since cloth was an important trade commodity in the area. The Special Officer and the local administration claimed to have distributed shops according to 'general convenience of the shop keepers' and encouraged 'harmonious arrangements', but they had made exceptions for businesses of higher standards and with a prominent location in the Chowk bazaar. One shop-owner of substantial means, with two shops and a residential house in the Chowk bazaar, had lost 11 family members out of 15 and was described as 'the worst victim' of the earthquake. He was allotted a shop of the same size as others, indicating the inadequacy of compensation as well as the decimated population not merely being an outcome of the reduced number of plots. Only one person from outside the Chowk bazaar, 'also an earthquake-sufferer', had been granted a space in Bekapur based on having obtained an agency from the Bata Shoe Co. Pvt Ltd,[199] hence opening a shop that was considered of a better standard and would add reputation to the new area.[200]

A number of applications for shops in Bekapur had been declined based on either false claims or exaggerated property claims in the Chowk bazaar. In view of the popularity of plots, the 'need' for new shops in the temporary settlement was based on a demand by the established or aspiring business communities. This demand could have been motivated by the pending 'earthquake-boom' in which the demand for goods was likely to increase as the reconstruction progressed. The newly planned areas were seen as an opportunity for expanding business, like for instance in the case of the owner of a 'prominent' *halwai* shop (sweet shop), who requested an extra shop space by arguing that supplies did not satisfy the demand for sweets. The keen interest shown in the new plots was apparent from attempts at applying for shops in the name of family members or a business partner in order to get additional space.[201] If the post-disaster scenario was seen as an opportunity for improving the urban environment according to the government and business interests, financial assistance and restructuring of space indirectly caused conflicts over new land and old rights. In the struggle over claims on old and new spaces, the propertied classes benefitted from the local government's willingness to consider their interests of commercial nature.

At the initial stage of town planning, Brett took notice of the rental conditions for sub-tenants from whom the *khas mahal* holders derived 'a very large income from subletting shops and houses in what was essentially a slum area'. Three of the 'principal' *khas mahal* tenants used to get about 380 rupees per month in rental income for holdings of 'about a third of an acre'.[202] Later in the year, Brett emphasised the eschewed property market by pointing to the fact that 5 persons held 75 *khas mahal* holdings in the resumed areas of 460 *khas mahal* holdings. For 2 acres, these persons had paid about 400–500 rupees per year to the local government while rental incomes had been as much as 1,500 rupees per month or 18,000 rupees per year in total.[203] From the outset, these large rental profits of the *khas mahal* holders were a primary concern of the government in the resettlement of land and residents from the Chowk bazaar. Former *khas mahal* holders were, as Temple had predicted, upset for not only being temporarily displaced by the town planning, but also losing rental income from sub-tenants. According to Brett, the group of former *khas mahal* holders whose land had been resumed 'now suffer in two ways'. First, they were not allowed to rebuild in order to house as many subtenants as previously. Second, the government extended 'the opportunity' to former subtenants to obtain land in the new settlements and as the demand on sub-lets in the Chowk bazaar declined, the rents were expected to follow suit. Hence, the profit that the *khas mahal* holders had managed to extract from sub-tenants was expected to decrease too. In this market transaction, the government intended to intervene by compensating the *khas mahal* holders who lost their leases in the Chowk bazaar by offering additional land in Bekapur in order to sustain their rental profits, that is '50 per cent more land, so that they can accommodate the same number of sub-tenants as they did formerly'. In Brett's calculation, the ejected *khas mahal* tenants would receive in all 3 acres to compensate for the 2 acres which they lost in the old area.[204]

Although *khas mahal* leases in the hands of a few had resulted in high rents and indirectly to overcrowding which had made the bazaars the most vulnerable areas in the earthquake, the planners initially supported the privileged group of *khas mahal* leaseholders by expanding their hold over property. Planning had undoubtedly changed living conditions and safety in the bazaar for the better, but the planners showed less concern for the relocation of sub-tenants, as Brett's support in favour of a few *khas mahal* holders illustrated. Brett advised against letting 'families who were merely sub-tenants' in the Chowk bazaar and people from other parts of town settle in Bekapur, in defence of the old *khas mahal* holders' interests: 'to do so might be harmful to the interests of our old tenants, because it will reduce the pitch of the rents which they can obtain in the future'. The new areas under acquisition were thereby primarily meant as compensation to former *khas mahal* holders, 'whose interests Government is bound to consider'.[205] In addition to showing consideration for the relocated population, the *khas mahal* holders who could stay on in the bazaar were offered to rent the re-drawn and improved plots at the same rate per areal as before the earthquake.[206] According to Brett, the government would have to face a loss in *khas mahal* income as a corollary of the widened roads. The government had, according to Brett, nothing to win by increasing the lease amount in order to cover for the land lost to roads. Brett cautioned against upsetting the leaseholders further: 'the government would not be in a strong position if they insisted on avoiding a loss by taking the same amount of rent for reduced areas', which the widening of roads and construction of drainages would entail.[207]

By the end of the year, in *A Report on the Bihar Earthquake*, Brett claimed that 'the scheme was backed by the more responsible inhabitants of the town, including the majority of the house-owners who stood to lose heavily by the abolition of the old congested conditions and of the high rates which they involved', thereby referring to *khas mahal* holders.[208] Their support was, however, only achieved partially, and by generous compensation in the form of land that guaranteed their profit from the new plan of the bazaar. From the planning process in April to June, until in September 1934, Brett's position regarding the *khas mahal* holders changed. In September 1934, Brett in the Legislative Council described them as the main opponents to the town-planning scheme— since among them were 'certain persons who in the past have derived a large income from subletting shops in the Chauk Bazar [Chowk bazaar]'. As Brett spoke of the benefits of the scheme for shopkeepers and sub-tenants, he showed no consideration for the *khas mahal* holders whose interests he had advocated at the very outset of the planning process. On the contrary, he referred to the persons making money from sub-letting as 'a few malcontents' who were unwilling to give up their incomes for the safe surroundings that the planning entailed for the shopkeepers.[209] In the new expanded bazaar area, double the size of the Chowk bazaar, the government had changed their position and now offered former sub-tenants their own shops. Already in April, the high rents of sub-tenants in the Chowk bazaar indicated that there was an interest in paying a higher rate than the 200 rupees per acre which the new plots in Bekapur would be sold for. Brett saw the opportunity for the government to get higher rates on the *khas mahal* land from subtenants and residents from other parts of Monghyr, who were in April described as a 'non entitled class'.[210] From initially having focused on the *khas mahal* holders' interests in the commercial land, the scheme was now described as benefiting shopkeepers and former sub-tenants, and thereby also beneficial for the local government which could secure a higher price for the plots.

Even so, a consolidation of the financial interests of the *khas mahal* holders remained a priority in the reconstruction phase and the promise of 50 per cent more land to them, as a form of compensation, was held firm throughout the planning process. Even after Brett in September publicly underlined the large profits made by *khas mahal* holders, the promise of more land to the group was kept. In the end, an unidentified number of former tenants, as well as sub-tenants from the Chowk, remained without compensation at least until 1939 when financial compensation from the government was suggested as an alternative option. The government had granted double the amount of land to those who had given up their *khas mahal* in the Chowk bazaar but Bekapur was, as Brett had anticipated at the outset, insufficient for the promise of 50 per cent extra land to the tenants. They declined the local government's offer of land in other areas and financial compensation appeared as the only way out.[211]

Temple's plan contained ideals benefitting the residents of the Chowk bazaar, but in order to fully adopt his plan of a less populated bazaar interspersed with green areas, the government would have had to settle with even fewer holdings and locate more land for relocated or displaced residents. As Gooptu points out, implementation of town planning was more pragmatic than the visions expressed at the planning stage since the government's first priority was to treat 'congested areas' to which all other goals were secondary. Another explanation provided by Gooptu, which may hold equal truth in the earthquake's aftermath: town planners and the Indian middle classes preferred fast renewal which modernised and cleaned up the towns, a process which often entailed removal of the poor.[212] The earthquake had partly facilitated steps towards transforming 'congested' areas at the centre of the bazaars, and in the planning process sub-tenants were the first to be removed from the central points to the temporary and new extended bazaar area. By September, the visionary outlook had somewhat soured, and the government claimed the envisioned town plans to be limited by financial constraints.[213] The removal of the poor appeared as the least costly alternative and partially solved the problem of overcrowding which was considered constitutive of a 'slum'. Likewise in Muzaffarpur, the same method to target the cheapest means for freeing up space was applied. Widening roads in the bazaar turned 'prohibitive in cost' and therefore the focus shifted towards 'cheaper houses' and a smaller area than in the initial plan. As a consequence, road widening was only partially implemented with space to form 'refuges' for the residents in future earthquakes.[214] In the case of Monghyr, improvements after the earthquake followed patterns of urban transformation which served to meet the interests of the propertied classes as it furthered their aspirations, not unlike the general patterns of urban planning illustrated by Gooptu.[215]

Conclusion: Redistribution and Renewal

Urban reconstruction in the aftermath was planned with sanitary conditions and trade in mind rather than earthquake safety. The many deaths due to congestion in the bazaar areas served as an argument to push for changes that resulted in 'improvements' of hygiene and trade according to the planners. This chapter has, in uncovering some of the logic that went into the planning of bazaars, highlighted how engineers and government officials conceptualised reconstruction based on established ideas of planning and the financial relations of the bazaar population.

The argument by the GSI that insufficient private assets of residents was a reason for the lack of a building code for earthquake safety served to strengthen the local government's resolve to enforce planning as a solution to earthquake safety. The government and the engineer in-charge from the outset shared the idea that insanitary conditions and congestion in the towns were of greater concern than earthquake safety. In planning the bazaars, 'improvements' of sanitary conditions—which encompassed widening roads, regulating reconstruction of houses and controlling population density—and at the same time measures for an 'improvement' of commercial interests by providing better access to the bazaars and conveniently structured spaces for trade overshadowed the concerns regarding safety and risk in future earthquakes. The government administration quickly seized the opportunity to undertake planning by either restricting or encouraging reconstruction with the help of municipal acts even before a rough sketch of what planning encompassed had been settled. The opportunity to undertake changes made the government interfere in private persons' attempts to rebuild, and by restructuring the bazaars, it disrupted or altered trade conditions.

The broader point is to note the concern of the government and the planners in adopting a pragmatic stance to accommodate improvements with financial interests. Although town planning was perceived as a project in the hands of the government, a process that provided an opportunity for reordering bazaars and facilitating communication, commercial interests of the financially strong traders and the *khas mahal* holders played a significant role in shaping the conservation of landed interests in the replanned areas. The new plan for the Chowk bazaar in Monghyr illustrated how town planning was primarily an instrument to remove a 'slum' and improve trade conditions according to the interests of the local government and its tenants. While the new bazaars were planned with lower population density, controlled constructions and widened roads that foremost sought to create hygienic living conditions and improve trade conditions, the new layout and restructuring of space also impacted tenancy relations and occupancy rights in the bazaars. Land availability and tenancy relations thereby became the major issues for the government to address as an outcome of town planning in bazaars. The arrangement of temporary housing at convenient locations and the construction of semi-permanent houses for approximately 3,000 residents in Monghyr who were displaced by town planning demanded resources and additional land. The earthquake aftermath was, given the damages to infrastructure that impeded the delivery of material, was not really an ideal opportunity to intervene by undertaking town planning. The problem of transport complicated the organisation of temporary and semi-permanent housing, and these very practical obstacles were furthered aggravated by a lack of foresight in planning and coordination, as well as an ad-hoc approach towards considering the opinion of the population, resulting in a reconstruction process slowed down and marked by disagreements. Except for those tenants who lost significant *khas mahal* holdings in the bazaar, shopkeepers appeared to have favoured town planning since it improved the standard of the area, but at the same time, they were hesitant towards the uncertainties it entailed regarding temporary displacement and relocation of shops. Even though the government to begin with protected the interests of leaseholders, its offer of leases in the newly developed bazaar areas to former sub-tenants reflected a more ambiguous position where town planning enabled redistribution. While the process of turning the disaster into an opportunity for change was early conceived and acted upon by the government, the resulting outcome with the problems encountered in implementation proved the practical solutions considerably more difficult to realise.

Notes

1. D.O. 930-J, J. E. Scott, Commissioner of Tirhut, to P. C. Tallents, Muzaffarpur, 9 February 1934, File: 'Town Planning in the Tirhut Division', BSA RE 8/1934.

2. For historical examples of reconstruction and coping with disasters in European urban history, see Ranft and Selzer, 'Städte aus Trümmern: Einleitende Überlegungen', 19–24.

3. Naomi Klein, *The Shock Doctrine: The Rise of Disaster Capitalism* (New York: Metropolitan Books, 2007). Rozario argues that disasters are part of American capitalism, see Rozario, 'What Comes Down Must Go Up: Why Disasters Have Been Good for American Capitalism', 75–77. Rozario, *The Culture of Calamity: Disaster and the Making of Modern America* (Chicago and London: University of Chicago Press, 2007). In economic theory, Joseph A. Schumpeter coined 'creative destruction' to refer to 'revolutions' in production and innovations which he argues have sustained capitalism. See ch. 7, 'The Process of Creative Destruction', in Joseph A. Schumpeter, *Capitalism, Socialism and Democracy* (London and New York: Routledge, 1994), 81–86.

4. Dyer, 'The Phoenix Effect in Post-Disaster Recovery', 279. 'Phoenix' cultures are also discussed in Rebecca Solnit, *A Paradise Built in Hell: The Extraordinary Communities That Arise in Disaster* (New York, NY: Viking, 2009); Christof Mauch, 'Phönix und Mnemosyne. Katastrophenoptimismus und Katastrophenerinnerung

in den USA: Von der Johnstown Flood bis Hurricane Katrina' (Pheonix and Mnemosyne. Disaster Optimism and Disaster Memoralization in the United States: From the Johnstown Flood to Hurricane Katrina), in *Katastrophen machen Geschichte. Umweltgeschichtliche Prozesse im Spannungsfeld von Ressourcennutzung und Extremereignis* (Disasters Make History: Environmental Historical Processes in the Context of Resource Use and Extreme Events), ed. Patrick Masius, Jana Sprenger and Eva Mackowiak, 133–51 (Göttingen: Universitätsverlag Göttingen, 2010).

5. Elizabeth McKellar, *The Birth of Modern London: the Development and Design of the City 1660–1720* (Manchester: Manchester University Press, 1999).

6. Gerrit Jasper Schenk, '"Learning from History"? Chances, Problems and Limits of Learning from Historical Natural Disasters', in *Cultures and Disasters: Understanding Cultural Framings in Disaster Risk Reduction*, ed. Fred Krüger et al., 72–87 (London and New York: Routledge, 2015).

7. Clancey, 'The Meiji Earthquake', 918–21.

8. Some of this research has previously been discussed in Eleonor Marcussen, 'Town Planning after the 1934 Bihar–Nepal Earthquake: Earthquake-Safety, Colonial Improvements and the Restructuring of Urban Space in Bihar', *Studies in Nepal History and Society* 22, no. 2 (2017): 321–54.

9. Howard Spodek, 'City Planning in India under British Colonial Rule', *Economic and Political Weekly* 48, no. 4 (2013): 53–61.

10. Nandini Gooptu, *The Politics of the Urban Poor in Early Twentieth–Century India* (Cambridge: Cambridge University Press, 2001), 78.

11. Yang, *Bazaar India*, 104–5.

12. Sinha, 'Entering the Black Hole', 325–26.

13. Veena Talwar Oldenburg, *The Making of Colonial Lucknow, 1856–77* (Princeton: Princeton University Press, 1984), 52–60.

14. Kidambi, *The Making of an Indian Metropolis*, 71.

15. Roy Chaudhury, *Monghyr*, 540.

16. Ibid., 549.

17. The reorganisation was completed by 1936–37 and an expanded scheme was completed in 1938–39 by the Public Health Engineering Department. Ibid., 333–34.

18. The total length of the *pucca* drains was 30 miles, *kuccha* drains 28 miles; *pucca* roads 47 miles, and *kuccha* roads 53 miles. Ibid., 338.

19. Ibid., 549.

20. 'Monghyr' (8 pp.), report by BCRC's Monghyr branch until end of June [July–August] 1934, BCUL PC 1028.

21. Brett, *A Report on the Bihar Earthquake*, 72.

22. Speaker K. B. Abdul Wahab Khan, from Monghyr District, 15 February 1934, *BOLCP* 30, no. 2, 158.

23. Tallents, 'No. 2628-P. R.', 17 August 1934, NAI HP 34/1/1934.

24. Speaker K. B. Abdul Wahab Khan, from Monghyr District, 15 February 1934, *BOLCP* 30, no. 2, 158.

25. Eyewitness account of the earthquake narrated by Kedarnath Goenka, '*Paramātmā kī līlā*' (The Play [or 'Way of'] of the Supreme Spirit), in Varma, *Bhūkamp pīḍitom kī karuna-kahāniyām̐*, 117–20.

26. Speech by J. D. Sifton quoted in Roy Chaudhury, *Monghyr*, 548.

27. D.O. 930-J, J. E. Scott to P. C. Tallents, Muzaffarpur, 9 February 1934, BSA RE 8/1934.

28. Yang, *Bazaar India*.

29. See 'Introduction' in Sinha, *Communication and Colonialism in Eastern India: Bihar, 1760s–1880s*.

30. About Patna's urban history and colonial governance, see Rebecca M. Brown, 'The Cemeteries and the Suburbs: Patna's Challenges to the Colonial City in South Asia', *Journal of Urban History* 29, no. 151 (2003): 151–72; Rebecca M. Brown, 'Inscribing Colonial Monumentality: A Case Study of the 1763 Patna Massacre Memorial', *The Journal of Asian Studies* 65, no. 1 (2006): 91–113; Rebecca M. Brown, 'Patnā's Golghar and the Transformations of Colonial Discourse', *Archives of Asian Art* 55 (2005): 53–63.

31. 'Monghyr Town Planning: Scheme Approved', *Behar Herald*, 12 September 1934.

32. 'Earthquake Relief: Government Communiqué', *Indian Nation*, 7 April 1934.

33. Dunn et al., 'The Bihar–Nepal Earthquake of 1934', 173.

34. Rai Bahadur Harendra Nath Banarji, Jamalpur, 14 February 1934, *BOLCP* 30, no. 1, 167. As discussed in Chapters 2 and 5 respectively, it is difficult to appreciate the actual death toll as well as the number of ruined houses in Monghyr since the sources either include different areas or provide starkly disparate figures.

35. 'Monghyr May Benefit from Earthquake Disaster: Scientific Town Planning', *The Englishman*, 26 March 1934.

36. 'Darbhanga Town Improvement; Grant of Sites; Ranchi Session of the Bihar Council Concluded', *Behar Herald*, 12 September 1934.

37. D.O. 930-J, J. E. Scott, Commissioner of Tirhut, to P. C. Tallents, Muzaffarpur, 9 February 1934, BSA RE 8/1934.

38. Tania Sengupta, 'Between the Garden and the Bazaar: The Visions, Spaces and Structures of Colonial Towns in Nineteenth-Century Provincial Bengal', *Visual Culture in Britain* 12, no. 3 (2011): 333–48.

39. Jain and Nigam, 'Historical Developments and Current Status', 2–3.

40. K. F. Nariman, 'The Great Earthquake of Japan: How It Was Fought and Won', *Hindustan Review* LVX [*sic* 60], nos. 350–52 (January, 1934): 191–94.

41. Jain and Nigam, 'Historical Developments and Current Status', 3.

42. The 1931 Mach earthquake recorded *Mw* 7.4; intensity VII on Rossi-Forel Intensity Scale of I to X, and was located about 60 kilometres from Quetta in Baluchistan. Sudhir K. Jain, 'Codes, Licensing, and Education', *Earthquake Spectra* 18, no. S1 (July, 2002): 319–39. S. L. Kumar, 'Theory of Earthquake Resisting Design with a Note on Earthquake Resisting Construction in Baluchistan', Paper No. 165, *Punjab Engineering Congress*, 1933: 154–89.

43. Jain, 'Codes, Licensing, and Education', 319.

44. Ben Wisner, 'Disaster: What United Nations and Its World Can Do' (Short Communications), *Global Environmental Change Part B: Environmental Hazards* 3, no. 3 (2001): 125–27.

45. Dunn et al., 'The Bihar–Nepal Earthquake of 1934', 174–75.

46. Although published after the Bihar earthquake, it only makes a brief note of it. A. R. Astbury, 'Earthquake-Resisting Design', Punjab P.W.D., Paper no. 84, Superintendent of Government Printing, 1934, Lahore, Punjab, 1.

47. Dunn et al., 'The Bihar–Nepal Earthquake of 1934', 166–67, 170–71, 174.

48. Dunn et al., *Preliminary Report* on the North Bihar Earthquake of the 15th January 1934*, 40.

49. The earthquake took place on 3 July 1930, not 1933 as claimed in Dunn et al., 'The Bihar–Nepal Earthquake of 1934', 168; E. R. Gee, 'Dhubri Earthquake of 3rd July 1930', *Memoirs of the Geological Survey of India* 65, Pt. 1 (pp. 1–106), 1934, 3, 8, 9, 88.

50. Dunn et al., 'The Bihar-Nepal Earthquake of 1934', 168.

51. Ibid., 252.

52. Dunn et al., *Preliminary Report* on the North Bihar Earthquake of the 15th January 1934*, 45.

53. Ibid., 40.

54. Dunn et al., 'The Bihar–Nepal Earthquake of 1934', 168.

55. Quote by 'eye-witness' in 'The Earthquake's Toll', *The Statesman*, 20 January 1934. The English Church documented in photo and text on the cover of *The Statesman*, 21 January 1934. Pusa, see Chapter 1. About the Golghar, see Brown, 'Paṭnā's Golghar and the Transformations of Colonial Discourse', 53.

56. Dunn et al., 'The Bihar–Nepal Earthquake of 1934', 171–72.

57. 'For Cheap—Earthquake Proof—Pucca Houses; Please contact Saroda Sunder Paul, Retired Superintending Engineer' (advertisement), *Behar Herald*, 7 April 1934.

58. Jain and Nigam, 'Historical Developments and Current Status', 3.

59. P. C. Roy Chaudhury, *Inside Bihar* (Calcutta; Patna; Allahabad: Bookland Private Limited, 1962), 122.

60. Brett, *A Report on the Bihar Earthquake*, 78.

61. Turnbull and Ormerod (eds.), *The Great Indian Earthquake*.

62. Advertisement for 'Earthquake Proof Buildings' by The Concrete Association of India, on the back cover of Moore (ed.), *Record of the Great Indian Earthquake*.

63. Dunn et al., 'The Bihar–Nepal Earthquake of 1934', 168.

64. See '10.1 Building Modern Cities after the Earthquake', 143–44, in Katharina Weiler, *The Neoclassical Residences of the Newars in Nepal: Transcultural Flows in the Early 20th Century Architecture of the Kathmandu Valley*, doctoral dissertation, Heidelberg University, 2009 (published 2010), available at http://archiv.ub.uni-heidelberg.de/volltextserver/10691/ (accessed 20 February 2021).

65. Ibid., 144.

66. Dunn et al., 'The Bihar–Nepal Earthquake of 1934', 166–67, 174.

67. Kidambi, *The Making of an Indian Metropolis*, 78–81.

68. Dunn et al., *Preliminary Report* on the North Bihar Earthquake of the 15th January 1934*, 48.

69. '32nd Communiqué, Patna, 5th June, 1934', R.D., Govt of B&O, NAI HP 34/1B/1934.

70. 'Extract from D.O. letter no 690 dated 1st February 1934', the Commissioner, Bhagalpur Division, to Chief Sec. to Government, B&O, BSA RE 495/1934.

71. 'Note of conversation with Dr. Dunn', James Whitty, 28 January 1934, BSA RE 495/1934.

72. The first recommendations were given in correspondence. J. A. Dunn, Assistant Superintendent, GSI, to the Chief Sec., Govt of B&O, Patna 29 January 1934, BSA RE 495/1934. (Also mentioned later in Dunn et al., 'The Bihar–Nepal Earthquake of 1934', 161) P. C. Tallents, Chief Sec., to the Director, Geological Survey of India, Calcutta, No. 104, Govt of B&O, Political Dept, Patna, 2 February 1934, BSA RE 495/1934.

73. Dunn et al., 'The Bihar–Nepal Earthquake of 1934', 5, 35.

74. The two publications are Dunn et al., *Preliminary Report* on the North Bihar Earthquake of the 15th January 1934*; Auden and Ghosh, 'Preliminary Account of the Earthquake of the 15th January, 1934, in Bihar and Nepal'.

75. Section 173, and sections 186 and 188, respectively. Notes by P. C. Tallents, Sec. to the Govt of B&O, W. G. Lacey, Sec., LSG, and Davies, Sec., Judicial Dept, Patna, 26–30 January 1934, BSA RE 45/1934.

76. Brett, *A Report on the Bihar Earthquake*, 55.

77. Notes by P. C. Tallents, Sec. to the Govt of B&O, W. G. Lacey, Sec., LSG, and Davies, Sec., Judicial Dept, Patna, 26–30 January 1934, BSA RE 45/1934.

78. Mr Gaur Shankar Prasad, 3 February 1934 to 2 March 1934; Mr Vishwanath, 7 February 1934 to 6 March 1934; Mr Shedi Narayan, 12 February 1934 to 11 March 1934; Mr M. Salimullah, 17 February 1934 to 12 March 1934. Office order by J. G. Powell, Chief Engineer, LSG, B&O, to PWD, 12 March 1934, BSA RE 76/1934.

79. Mrs P. Lacey, wife of W. G. Lacey, Secretary, LSG Department, experienced the earthquake in Patna. Her memories of the aftermath were recorded as a part of an oral history project in 1981. Interviewer: Mary Thatcher. Centre for South Asian Studies, Cambridge University, Cambridge, Oral History Archive: Interview number: 088, 'Mrs. P. Lacey (2 July, 1981)', 2 parts, http://www.s-asian.cam.ac.uk/archive/audio/collection/p-lacey/ (accessed 10 June 2011).

80. Copied Memo, signed W. G. Lacey, Sec., LSG Dept, 25 January 1934, BSA RE 45/1934.

81. 'Municipal Taxes Remission; Bihar Legislation', Behar Herald, 21 April 1934.

82. Ibid.

83. Spodek, 'City Planning in India under British Colonial Rule', 58.

84. 'B&O Council: Darbhanga Improvement Trust: Bill Referred to Select Committee', The Searchlight, 9 September 1934.

85. J. G. Powell, Chief Engineer, PWD, B&O, to the Sec., LSG, 2 February 1934, File: 'Loan of Officers for Appointment as Town Engineers', BSA RE 74/1934.

86. No. 2189E, VI A-5 of 1934, Subject: 'Loan of an Assistant Engineer in Connection with Earthquake Works', J. G. Powell, PWD, B&O, to the Sec. to the Govt of U.P., PWD (Lucknow), Patna, 14 February 1934, BSA RE 65/1934.

87. Frederick Charles Temple (1879–1957), engineer, graduated from Oxford and continued his training as assistant to Indian Military Service 1905–07, after which he joined the Public Works Dept of India, 1907–19. He was Chief Town Engineer in Jamshedpur 1919, and Administrator 1924–32. He had previously been District Engineer in Muzaffarpur District and Superintending Engineer, Public Health Dept, PWD, Bihar and Orissa. 'Builders of the New Bihar' in Moore (ed.), Record of the Great Indian Earthquake, 37. After one year as Relief Engineer and Supply Officer, he returned to London where he spent the remainder of his career in leading positions at various ministries. Antonia Brodie et al. (eds.), Directory of British Architects 1834–1914, Vol. 2: L–Z. British Architectural Library, Royal Institute of British Architects (London: Continuum, 2001): 777–78.

88. Notification, W. B. Brett to J. T. Whitty, Patna, 23 February 1934, BSA RE 19/1934.

89. J. G. Powell to Chief Secretary, 3 February 1934, BSA RE 65/1934. Harold Vinith Williams (born 9 June 1898; joined PWD 1 October 1921), D.O. 279: 'Retrenchment under the 1932 Compulsory Retirement Rules', Mr Curry, Chief Engineer, Bengal Secretariat, Irrigation Dept to J. G. Powell, PWD, B&O, Calcutta, 5 February 1934, BSA RE 74/1934. Williams served from 10 February to 10 May 1934, and Nunn from 30 January to 19 April 1934; D.O. 9554, Accountant General, B&O, to the Sec. to the Govt of B&O, PWD, Patna, 6 July 1934, BSA RE 65/1934.

90. No. 2189E, VI A-5 of 1934, Subject: 'Loan of an Assistant Engineer in Connection with Earthquake Works', J. G. Powell, PWD, Establishment Branch, B&O, to the Sec. to the Govt of U.P., PWD (Lucknow), Patna, 14 February 1934, BSA RE 65/1934. 'Statement of Expenditure on Account of Pay', Travelling Allowance and Contingencies on Account of Rai Sahib Pandit Ram Chandra (alt., Ramchandra) for the period 1 March to 1 June 1934', enclosed with 2729 R. D., W. B. Brett to Finance Dept, B&O, Patna, 26 July 1934, BSA RE 65/1934. 613 R.D''. 'Appointment of Special Engineer for Advising on Damaged Buildings', W. B. Brett to Commissioner of Tirhut, Patna, 12 March 1934, BSA RE 76/1934. Devi Dayal, senior Executive Engineer with more than 19 years of service, as Under Secretary and Assistant Chief Engineer for nearly two years. In the U.P. he had served both as district officer and in the Secretariat; also Honorary Sec. of the Assam Branch of the Red Cross Society. Notes by W. B. Brett, 7 April 1934, BSA RE 65/1934.

91. No. 613 R.D. 'Appointment of Special Engineer for Advising on Damaged Buildings', W. B. Brett to Commissioner of Tirhut, Patna, 12 March 1934, BSA RE 76/1934.

92. Letter No. F. 1338, J. E. Scott to Sec. to the Govt of B&O, PWD Dept, Patna, Muzaffarpur 21 February 1934, BSA RE 65/1934.

93. 'Detailed Programme of the Assistant Engineer', enclosed with No. F. 1338, J. E. Scott to Sec. to the Govt of B&O, PWD Dept, Patna, Muzaffarpur, 21 February 1934, BSA RE 65/1934.

94. D.O. J 2244, J. E. Scott to W. B. Brett, Muzaffarpur, 25 March 1934; D.O. J 2248, J. E. Scott to W. B. Brett, Muzaffarpur, 4 April 1934, BSA RE 65/1934.

95. Harold Easton Bruce, 'Tirhut Trivialities' (14 pp., s.d.), Mss Eur C282.

96. Notes by W. B. Brett, 8 February 1934, BSA RE 65/1934.

97. Notification, W. B. Brett to H. E. (J. T. Whitty), Patna, 23 February 1934, BSA RE 19/1934.

98. Temple received a salary of 2,150 rupees per month, and overseas pay at 13-6-8 pounds. Notification, W. B. Brett to H. E. (J. T. Whitty), Patna, 23 February

1934, BSA RE 19/1934. His office had nine staff according to 'Note' by Finance Dept S.D./25 March 1934, attached with reply by W. B. Brett to Finance Dept, 27 March 1934, BSA RE 76/1934.

99. F. C. Temple, *Report on Town Planning*. Jamshedpur Social Welfare Series (Bombay: Commercial Press, 1919).

100. Amita Sinha and Jatinder Singh, 'Jamshedpur: Planning an Ideal Steel City in India', *Journal of Planning History* 10, no. 4 (2011): 263–81, 268.

101. Volker M. Welter, *Biopolis: Patrick Geddes and the City of Life* (Cambridge, MA; London: The MIT Press, 2002), 49–50.

102. Gooptu, *The Politics of the Urban Poor*, 77–78.

103. Temple's understanding of the local context in Jamshedpur town plan is shown in his design of *adivasi* worker quarters modelled on their huts in a traditional village structure and with a well in the centre of the habitat. Sinha and Singh, 'Jamshedpur: Planning an Ideal Steel City in India', 270.

104. Temple published a number of reports and notes on drainage schemes in Patna and Muzaffarpur, 1917–20. Reports and publications in Mss Eur D926/1–3 Temple; see also reference to Temple, *Report on Town Planning*.

105. Enclosure 'Town Reconstruction Work', in 'Order no. 3162 E/VI A – 15 of 34', J. G. Powell, PWD, B&O, Patna, 30 March 1934, BSA RE 19/1934.

106. Singh, 'The Colonial State, Zamindars and the Politics of Flood Control', 248. Brett, *A Report on the Bihar Earthquake*, 34.

107. 'Waterways in North Bihar, Their Present Condition after the Earthquake and Their Possibilities for the Future', F. C. Temple to W. B. Brett, 17 July 1934; 'Sitamarhi and Darbhanga Roads Committee', Temple to Brett, Muzaffarpur, 15 January 1935, Mss Eur 926D/3.

108. The engineers' work in Motihari, Monghyr, Muzaffarpur and Darbhanga was monitored in bi-weekly reports with abstracts of figures and details of the number of applications for loans and consultations. 'Govt of B&O. Reconstruction Dept, Periodical Report from Town Engineer' (template), BSA RE 256/1934.

109. W. B. Brett to Finance Dept, 27 March 1934, BSA RE 76/1934.

110. Ibid.

111. 'Note' by Finance Dept, 30 March 1934, BSA RE 76/1934.

112. 'Organisation of the Town Engineers' (Memo, 2), W. B. Brett, 19 March 1934, BSA RE 76/1934.

113. 'Routine Notes', Temple to Brett, 2 April 1934; 'Routine Notes', Temple to Brett, Patna, 24 April 1934; 'Notes', Temple to Brett, Patna, 20 June 1934, BSA RE 76/1934.

114. Correspondence, F. C. Temple to W. B. Brett, 15 May 1934, BSA RE 76/1934.

115. Mr J. Williamson, Agent to the Bengal and North-Western Railway, in Dunn et al., 'The Bihar–Nepal Earthquake of 1934', 195.

116. Correspondence, F. C. Temple to W. B. Brett, 15 May 1934; Correspondence, W. B. Brett to H. C. Prior, Finance Secretary, 16 May 1934, and notes by H. C. Prior, 18 May 1934, BSA RE 76/1934.

117. 'Fortnightly Progress Report on District Board Bridges on Main Roads for the Fortnight Ending the 15th June, 1934', Memo. no. 488, Inspector of Local Works, Tirhut Division, Muzaffarpur, 21 June 1934, Patna, File: 'Fortnightly Progress Report of the Inspection of Local Works', BSA RE 245/1934.

118. Anon. to J. W. Houlton, Revenue Secretary B&O, 25 January 1934; D.O. 482, J. W. Houlton to J. W. Nicholson, Divisional Forest Officer, Palamau Division, Patna, 25 January 1934, BSA RE 56/1934.

119. *Shorea robusta* (Lat.), a common tree in eastern and northern India. K. Sivaramakrishnan, 'The Politics of Fire and Forest Regeneration in Colonial Bengal', *Environment and History* 2, no. 2 (1996): 145–94.

120. D.O. 1176 R.D., W. B. Brett to J. W. Nicholson, Divisional Forest Officer, Daltonganj, 20 April 1934, BSA RE 56/1934.

121. Comments on Bamboo in D.O. 775, District Officer V. K. B. Pillai to the Relief Commissioner, B&O, Patna, Chapra, 5 June 1934; D.O. 2242 R.D., W. B. Brett to the Collector of Saran, Patna, 27 June 1934; D.O. 55, Collector of Saran to Relief Commissioner, Chapra, 21 July 1934, BSA RE 56/1934.

122. D.O. 7130/12-E (23), J. W. Nicholson, Palamau Forest Division, to H. C. Prior, Finance Dept, Govt of B&O, Daltonganj, 10 March 1934; D.O. 478 VR, R.D., Relief Commissioner, Govt of B&O, to the Agent, East India Railways, Calcutta, Patna, 24 March 1934, BSA RE 56/1934.

123. Memo: 'Monghyr: Reconstruction Proposals', F. C. Temple, 14 April 1934, BSA RE 45/1934.

124. Ibid.

125. Memo: 'Monghyr Town Planning Scheme', W. B. Brett, 15 April 1934, submitted to the local government. Brett's memo was written after having consulted F. C. Temple's Memo: 'Monghyr: Reconstruction Proposals' (4 pp.), 14 April 1934, BSA RE 45/1934.

126. Brett, *A Report on the Bihar Earthquake*, 7–9, 72; 'Table II', BCRC, *Devastated Bihar*, 66.

127. Temple counted 461 plots. Memo: 'Monghyr Town Planning Scheme', W. B. Brett, 15 April 1934, BSA RE 45/1934. The reconstruction of the area was further facilitated by the land being under the control of the Deputy Collector. 'Some Political and Other Aspects of Earthquake Relief in Bihar', M. G. Hallett,

31 March 1934 (Unofficial report of a 'short visit' to Bihar of two days in Patna, two days in Monghyr and two days in Muzaffarpur, 18 unnumbered pages out of which one appear to be missing), NAI HP 34/1/1934.

128. Memo: 'Monghyr Town Planning Scheme', W. B. Brett, 15 April 1934, BSA RE 45/1934. According to Temple, 395 families would be 'allowed' to stay and 355 families had to be accommodated elsewhere. Memo: 'Monghyr: Reconstruction Proposals', F. C. Temple, 14 April 1934, BSA RE 45/1934.

129. 'Monghyr Town Planning; Government's Statement on Subject; Full Text of Mr Brett's Speech in Council', *The Searchlight*, 12 September 1934.

130. Sinha and Singh, 'Jamshedpur: Planning an Ideal Steel City', 269–70.

131. Memo: 'Monghyr: Reconstruction Proposals', F. C. Temple, 14 April 1934, BSA RE 45/1934.

132. Memo: 'Monghyr Town Planning Scheme', W. B. Brett, 15 April 1934, BSA RE 45/1934.

133. Brett, *A Report on the Bihar Earthquake*, 72.

134. For the Purabsarai road, 0.682 acres had been set aside. Memo: 'Monghyr Town Planning Scheme', W. B. Brett, 15 April 1934, BSA RE 45/1934.

135. 'Untitled note' (3), W. B. Brett, 10 June 1934, BSA RE 45/1934.

136. 'Application for Sanction (Under Section 30 of the Darbhanga Improvement Act)' (printed, 41 pp.) T. A. Freston, Chairman, 8 May 1935, 7–9. Darbhanga, MKSKF.

137. Ibid., 4–5, 10–11.

138. T. A. Freston, 'Explanatory Note. Scheme No III' [that is, to 'III: Lalbagh New Area Scheme', Darbhanga Improvement Trust] [May 1935]. Darbhanga, MKSKF.

139. '30th Communiqué, Patna, 16 May, 1934: Monghyr Town-planning Scheme', NAI HP 34/1B/1934. Brett, *A Report on the Bihar Earthquake*, 72. Memo: 'Monghyr: Reconstruction Proposals', F. C. Temple, 14 April 1934, BSA RE 45/1934.

140. A map of the new areas published by the district officer is unavailable in the archival records consulted. Memo [by Brett], 27 May 1934, BSA RE 45/1934.

141. 'Monghyr Town Planning; Government's Statement on Subject; Full Text of Mr Brett's Speech in Council', *The Searchlight*, 12 September 1934.

142. Wisner et al., *At Risk*, 254.

143. Memo: 'Monghyr: Reconstruction Proposals', F. C. Temple, 14 April 1934, BSA RE 45/1934.

144. 'Earthquake Relief: Government Communiqué', *Indian Nation*, 7 April 1934.

145. Brett, *A Report on the Bihar Earthquake*, 73.

146. Sinha, *The Bihar Earthquake and the Darbhanga Raj*, 44.

147. Published letter, J. D. Sifton, Governor of Bihar and Orissa, to Maharajadhiraja Kameshwar Singh of Darbhanga, Government House, Ranchi, 31 May 1934, in

Hetukar Jha (ed.), *Courage and Benevolence: Correspondence and Speeches of India's Prime-Estate Holder; Maharajadhiraja Kameshwar Singh of Darbhanga (1907–1962)* (Darbhanga, Bihar: Maharajadhiraja Kameshwar Singh Kalyani Foundation, 2007), 78.

148. Brett, *A Report on the Bihar Earthquake*, 14.

149. The initial budget for reconstruction of the main buildings of the Raj amounted to 665,000 rupees. 'Construction after the Earthquake 1934' ('KS Records no 50'; 4 pp.) Chief Manager to His Highness, 10 November 1934; 'RD form no 88', office note, File: Administrative Report, Confidential (printed, 8), Chief Manager R.D., 16 June 1936. Darbhanga, MKSKF.

150. P. C. Roy Chaudhury, *Darbhanga*, Bihar District Gazetteers (Bihar, Patna: Superintendent Secretariat Press, 1964), 422–23.

151. Memo: 'Monghyr Town Planning Scheme', W. B. Brett, 15 April 1934, BSA RE 45/1934. Exact numbers are difficult to ascertain, for instance, another publication claims that by June 1934 the VERF had granted 70,000 rupees for clearing the Chowk bazaar. *RPER*, 18.

152. Roy Chaudhury, *Monghyr*, 338. The amount was subdivided into 'Roads and Buildings 155,734 rupees', 'Water-supply and Sanitary Projects 56,644 rupees' and 'Other Charges 116,186'. The construction of Raja Bazaar Market [that is, Bekapur] for 116,186 rupees is listed separately, but appears to have been recorded as 'Other Charges' of Monghyr bazaar as well.

153. Land acquisition costs for the new sites, 36,510 rupees, and Purabsarai Road widening, 13,183 rupees, went under the heading of 'Land Acquisition, 50,000 rupees'. Resumption costs of 10,000 rupees for cancelling *khas mahal* leases. The following memo was submitted together with Brett's and Temple's respective memos on Monghyr's town plan, dated 14 and 15 April 1934. Memo: 'Estimate of Town Improvement Costs, Monghyr', A. Wheeler, Town Engineer, Monghyr, 13 April 1934, BSA RE 45/1934.

154. 'Supplementary Budget: Revenue; Appendix, Schedule no. 1', Supplementary Demand under the 'Land Revenue', 19 November 1936, *BLCP* 36, no. 2.

155. November 1936. Ibid.

156. Ibid.

157. Henningham, *A Great Estate and Its Landlords*, 131–34.

158. Ibid., 130–37.

159. 'Weekly Earthquake Report for the Week Ending 10 March 1934' (Muzaffarpur), D.I.G. to McDowell, Inspector General, C.I.D., BSA PS 33 III/1934.

160. 'Explanatory Note. Scheme No II' by T. A. Freston, [s.a.] in 'Darbhanga Improvement Trust.' Darbhanga, MKSKF.

161. Gooptu, *The Politics of the Urban Poor*, 83–84.

162. 'Darbhanga Improvement Bill; Citizens' Strong Opposition; Representative and Influential Manifesto', *The Searchlight*, 2 September 1934.

163. 'Extract from the proceedings of the meeting of the Darbhanga Improvement trust held on the 7th of May, 1935', 2; 'Application for Sanction (Under Section 30 of the Darbhanga Improvement Act)' (41 pp.), T. A. Freston, Chairman, 8 May 1935. Darbhanga, MKSKF, 3–4.

164. Rai Bahadur Shayamnandan Sahay, one of the richest zamindars in Bihar, see 66–67 in Arvind N. Das, 'Peasants and Peasant Organisations: the Kisan Sabha in Bihar', in *Agrarian Movement in India: Studies on 20th Century Bihar*, ed. Arvind N. Das, 40–87 (London: Frank Cass and Company Limited, 1982).

165. 'B. & O. [Bihar and Orissa Legislative] Council; Darbhanga Improvement Trust Bill Carried', *Behar Herald*, 8 September 1934.

166. In a reply to suggestions (received 25 January 1934) regarding town planning in Tirhut up for debate in the Legislative Council in Patna. D.O. 930-J, J. E. Scott to P. C. Tallents, 9 February 1934, BSA RE 8/1934.

167. 'Earthquake Relief: Government Communiqué', *Indian Nation*, 7 April 1934.

168. 'The Darbhanga Improvement Act, 1934 (Bihar and Orissa Act 4 of 1934)', Pandey, *Manual of Bihar Local Laws 1790–1985*, vol. 3 [C–E], 65.

169. 'Application for Sanction (Under Section 30 of the Darbhanga Improvement Act)' (printed, 41 pp.), T. A. Freston, Chairman, 8 May 1935, 22–25. Darbhanga, MKSKF.

170. 'Explanatory Note. Scheme No. IV [Rehousing Scheme]', T. A. Freston, May 1935, enclosed with Darbhanga Improvement Trust'. Darbhanga, MKSKF.

171. Note: 'Organisation of the Town Engineers', by W. B. Brett, Patna, 19 March 1934, BSA RE 76/1934.

172. 'Allotments from Bihar and Orissa Branch Viceroy's Earthquake Relief Fund' ('up to the end of May'), 2 pp., compiled by H. C. Prior, D.O. 1813–18 V. R. C., H. C. Prior to W. B. Brett, Ranchi, 5 June 1934, BSA RE 43/1934.

173. Memo No. 447, Ramanugrah Jha, 'Special Officer' in charge of Monghyr Municipality, to District Magistrate [Mainwaring], 3 July 1934, BSA PS 33/B/1934.

174. Communiqué, 'Temporary Housing at Monghyr', R.D., Govt of B&O, 28 March 1934, NAI HP 34/1B/1934.

175. 'Maharaja of Mayurbhanj', *ABP*, 18 March 1934.

176. Archer, 'The Bihar Earthquake', Mss Eur F236/1.

177. Ibid.

178. 'Communiqué: Progress of Temporary Housing Scheme', R.D., Govt of B&O, 28 March 1934, NAI HP 34/1B/1934.

179. W. B. Brett, 'Weekly Bulletin' (for the week ending 9 March 1934), Reconstruction Office, Patna, to M. G. Hallett, Sec. to the GOI, Home Dept, NAI 34/1B/1934.

180. Marwari Relief Society, *Report of the Behar Earthquake Relief Work*, 39.

181. The Marwari Relief Society constructed 1,500 huts as temporary quarters and erected a colony with 300 rooms, sufficient to accommodate 1,200 persons, in the Prince of Wales Garden in Muzaffarpur. Ibid., 10–12. The Servants of India Society, the Ramakrishna Mission and the Kushtia Marwari Society had built colonies in Muzaffarpur. BCRC, *Report for the Period Ending 30th June 1934*, 34.

182. See, for instance, expenditure in Monghyr of 4,267 rupees for corrugated iron sheets. Marwari Relief Society, *Report of the Behar Earthquake Relief Work*, 20.

183. 'Weekly Bulletin' (for the week ending 9 March 1934), W. B. Brett to M. G. Hallett, Sec. to the GOI, Home Dept, NAI HP 34/1B/1934.

184. 'Temporary Housing', Extract from 'Earthquake Reconstruction' report D.O. 320, 9 July 1934, enclosure to D.O. 2019, District Magistrate A. J. Mainwaring (Collector's House, Monghyr), to P. C. Tallents, Chief Sec. to Govt of B&O, Ranchi, 12 July 1934, BSA PS 33/B/1934.

185. Memo No. 447, Ramanugrah Jha, 'Special Officer' in charge of Monghyr Municipality, to District Magistrate [Mainwaring], Monghyr, 3 July 1934, BSA PS 33/B/1934.

186. Extract from 'Earthquake Reconstruction' report no. D30 320, 'Temporary Housing', 9 July 1934, to Commissioner [of Monghyr], BSA PS 33/B/1934.

187. The first telegram was sent by the postmaster to the District Magistrate, 22 June 1934, the second telegram on 23 June 1934. D.O. 2019, District Magistrate A. J. Mainwaring (Collector's House, Monghyr), to P. C. Tallents, Chief Sec. to Govt of B&O, Ranchi, 12 July 1934, BSA PS 33/B/1934.

188. Extract from 'Earthquake Reconstruction' report no. D.O. 299, 'Temporary Housing', 25 June 1934, to Commissioner [of Monghyr], BSA PS 33/B/1934.

189. Extract from the confidential diary of the Superintendent of Police, Monghyr, 2 July 1934. Forwarded as 'Memo no. 6027' to the Chief Sec., Govt of B&O, 7 July 1934. Another report claimed 'some 200 persons' attended. D.O. 304: 'Temporary Housing', Mainwaring to Commissioner of Bhagalpur, Monghyr, 2 July 1934, BSA PS 33/B/1934.

190. Among the people behind the call was the Vice-Chairman of the District Board, Sayed Rafiuddin Rizvi, and Shri Krishna Prasad, an M.L.C., as well as the two 'chief mischief makers' Sita Ram Khemka, the dispatcher of the withheld telegram, and Mansukh Ram Khemka, whom the district officer thought were behind the agitation. 'Temporary Housing', Extract from 'Earthquake Reconstruction', D.O. 299, dated 25 June 1934 to the Commissioner, BSA PS 33/B/1934.

191. Extract from the confidential diary of the Superintendent of Police, Monghyr, 2 July 1934. Forwarded as 'Memo no. 6027' to the Chief Sec., Govt of B&O, 7 July 1934, BSA PS 33/B/1934.

192. Nripado Mukherjee, president of the [Bihar] Central Relief Committee at Monghyr, accused the police and Special Officer of the Municipality of forcefully evicting residents of the Ramlila maidan. See file in previous footnote. 'Province Day by Day: Monghyr', *Indian Nation*, 7 April 1934.

193. Extract from 'Earthquake Reconstruction', D.O. 304: 'Temporary Housing', 2 July 1934, to Commissioner; Memo no. 447, Ramanugrah Jha, 'Special Officer' in charge of Monghyr Municipality, to District Magistrate [Mainwaring], 3 July 1934, BSA PS 33/B/1934.

194. D.O. 3473-C, P. C. Tallents to A. J. Mainwaring, District Magistrate, Monghyr, 9 July 1934, BSA PS 33/B/1934.

195. 'In reply to D.O. 3473-C', A. J. Mainwaring, District Magistrate, to P. C. Tallents, Monghyr, 12 July 1934, BSA PS 33/B/1934.

196. Memo No. 447, Ramanugrah Jha, 'Special Officer' in charge of Monghyr Municipality, to District Magistrate [Mainwaring], 3 July 1934, BSA PS 33/B/1934.

197. Extract from 'Earthquake Reconstruction', D.O. 304: 'Temporary Housing', District Officer Monghyr to the Commissioner [of Bhagalpur], 2 July 1934; Forwarded as 'Memo no. 6027' to the Chief Sec., Govt of B&O, 7 July 1934, BSA PS 33/B/1934.

198. Memo No. 447, Ramanugrah Jha, 'Special Officer' in charge of Monghyr Municipality, to District Magistrate [Mainwaring], 3 July 1934, BSA PS 33/B/1934.

199. Ibid.

200. Bata Shoe Co. Pvt. Ltd (founded 1894), later Bata India Ltd, was a Swiss-based Czechoslovakian shoe company with a production unit in West Bengal since 1931. Anthony Cekota. *The Stormy Years: An Extraordinary Enterprise... Bata 1932–1945* (Perth Amboy, NJ: Universum Sokol Publications, 1985), 33–34.

201. Memo No. 447, Ramanugrah Jha, 'Special Officer' in charge of Monghyr Municipality, to District Magistrate [Mainwaring], 3 July 1934, BSA PS 33/B/1934.

202. Memo: 'Monghyr Town Planning Scheme', W. B. Brett, 15 April 1934, BSA RE 45/1934.

203. 'Monghyr Town Planning; Government's Statement on Subject; Full Text of Mr. Brett's Speech in Council', *The Searchlight*, 12 September 1934.

204. Memo: 'Monghyr Town Planning Scheme', W. B. Brett, 15 April 1934, BSA RE 45/1934.

205. Ibid.

206. Memo No. 447, Ramanugrah Jha, 'Special Officer' in charge of Monghyr Municipality, to District Magistrate [Mainwaring], 3 July 1934, BSA PS 33/B/1934.

207. Memo: 'Monghyr Town Planning Scheme', W. B. Brett, 15 April 1934, BSA RE 45/1934.

208. Brett, *A Report on the Bihar Earthquake*, 73.

209. 'Monghyr Town Planning; Government's Statement on Subject; Full Text of Mr Brett's Speech in Council', *The Searchlight*, 12 September 1934.

210. One acre of the new settlement was sold to former *khas mahal* holders for 200 rupees. Memo: 'Monghyr Town Planning Scheme', W. B. Brett, 15 April 1934, BSA RE 45/1934.

211. 'Settlement of Lands with the Tenants of the Chauk [Chowk] Area, Monghyr', 34. [Question by] Rai Bahadur Deonandan Prasad Singh, reply by the Hon'ble Mr. Shri Krishna Sinha, *BLCD* 4, no. 5. Official Report. (Patna: Superintendent, Government Printing, 1939), 214–15.

212. Gooptu, *The Politics of the Urban Poor*, 83–84.

213. Governor James Sifton, 3 September 1934, *BOLCP* vol. 31, 56.

214. Brett, *A Report on the Bihar Earthquake*, 74.

215. Gooptu, *The Politics of the Urban Poor*, 84.

Conclusion

One of the larger aims of this book is to examine the earthquake as a sociopolitical process in its historical context. While doing so, I have discussed how experiences with past disasters and the contemporary sociopolitical setting affected responses in the aftermath. The very disruptive nature of an earthquake, literally throwing people off their feet, crumbling buildings and destroying lives and livelihoods, makes the event into a process of change experienced by communities and individuals on a psychological and physical level. Whether viewed as an opportunity for change or an unwanted agent of destruction, or both, the devastation wrought by the earthquake led to a set of responses that can enhance our understanding of vulnerability and resilience.

Throughout the chapters of this book, the relationships between various disaster responses, that is, the approaches of the government, civil society actors and victims are at the centre of analysis. A disaster calls into question who cares, and for whom. The diversity of needs, the invisibility and the visibility of neglected and prioritised relief receivers respectively, tell us about the unequal effect disaster have on people, not just in the long or short aftermath but also for historians relying on archival sources. Greg Clancey suggests that disaster victims 'may be the ultimate historical subalterns'.[1] In the case of the dead, the victims' voices are complicated to recover as a group, whether in a historical or contemporary disaster. Yet the dead are often instrumentalised in, for instance, disaster reconstruction where they become evidence of needful changes in construction improvements or settlement patterns. In the more recent past, the perception of the disaster body as the ultimate subaltern historical subject resonates with Henry A. Giroux's reflections on the body politics of the dead in the aftermath of the hurricane Katrina.[2] Giroux argues that the invisibility of bodies post-Katrina was the effect of a 'politics of disposability'. The bodies rendered invisible were not simply the outcome of failed governance and a natural hazard. According to Giroux, the government's disaster policy in Katrina rendered 'disposable' lives invisible by editing out bodies, death and human suffering and focusing on material destruction. His analysis places racism at the core of how citizens were negated protection, access to relief provisions, media attention and sympathy. In this way, the victims in Katrina were historically and socially produced as a vilified group of poor and therefore vulnerable people, rather than victims of a hurricane.[3] From a historian's point of view, depictions of victims or missing victim narratives in the primary sources may produce significant insights into the aftermath's politics of relief, as in the case of biopolitics after Katrina. In the reading of the archives, deeper reflection upon the representation of disaster victims, relief providers and aid may reveal the complexity of relationships that is needed to analyse the course of events in an aftermath.[4] In an attempt at such a reading of sources, the 1934 aftermath can provide an understanding of how responses to a disaster follow established patterns and yet becomes a moment for change. How disasters reveal or, as Hoffman puts it, 'unclothe' the social world, and how they give birth to transformations and adjustments[5] form the core of this book.

Patterns and Ruptures in the Politics of Relief

The book's exploration of responses in the aftermath provides an argument for seeing the earthquake as a moment of rupture in terms of political demands for change in governance. The balancing act and inter-relational character between what was in existence before the earthquake and the social processes generated in its aftermath will be discussed next. Past experiences with disasters—the development of patterns in responding to emergencies—played an important role in the aftermath. Both among civil society organisations and in the official government's approach, previous experiences with disasters partially shaped responses. The narratives of the local government's response in the earthquake's immediate aftermath and during the emergency relief phase situate the event in the context of a broader frame of governance. Through an analysis of the narratives of the aftermath in Chapter 2, I argue that the official emergency disaster response can be understood as embedded within the ideas and everyday practices of colonial governance. Communication and information played important roles in understanding the government's response as well as in its master narrative of the earthquake, as outlined in Brett's report. The breakdown in communications caused by the earthquake and a fear of losing control of government offices partially explained the government's security-oriented response. In the local colonial government's narrative of the aftermath, damages to communication infrastructure, as well as the 'natural' difficulties of navigating Bihar's landscape, explained delays and lack of information. The government's narrative of challenges and failures in responding to the earthquake followed 'the classic paradigm of British administrative writing' in disasters[6] by explaining its shortcomings as having arisen due to the lack of communication infrastructure. Instead of accepting the local government's inability to review the situation and respond accordingly, not only the earthquake's damaging effects on infrastructure but also Bihar's landscape was blamed for its administrative failure in providing emergency relief. The government's ability to overcome the hurdles in providing relief—that is, the damaged infrastructure and the volatile landscape of Bihar—was, according to its own narrative, dependent on the use of technological advancement in the form of aeroplanes and the relatively swift resurrection of an erratic telegraph connection. Even if a next-to-completely-ruined land transport system indeed affected mobility and information, the disruption of communication created a disaster narrative that justified a security-oriented response. A lack of information and communication, not instances of violence or crimes, made the local government ensure reinforcement of public institutions and mobilise the police. It was a response that reflected the government's anxieties regarding losing control of communication rather than a fear that its institutional capabilities weakened by the earthquake would be unable to maintain public order.

That the earthquake was a major jolt to the local government's administrative structure is also evident from the organisation of the Reconstruction Department and the Earthquake Branch in the weeks following the earthquake. The administrative set-up testified to the need for coordination that the initial chaos in the aftermath had only given a foretaste of. In the emergency phase of relief, previous experiences offered little opportunity for the government and civil society to have 'learnt' how to respond to specifically the large-scale, sudden and deathly destruction in urban areas, combined with the particular damages wrought on agricultural land, the waterways and communication infrastructure. A further reason to emphasise the role communication and information had in shaping the government's response and narrative of the aftermath can be gleaned from the challenging position that civil society and eyewitness reports expressed in view of government data. These so-called un-official reports on the numbers of deaths and descriptions of damages and calls for relief did not only serve to describe the government's official data as deliberate underestimates, but also fundamentally challenged the government's ability to access information about the disaster's scope. In effect, the local colonial government's faulty data and lack of knowledge in these counter-narratives illustrated the government's weak hold on the region. The publications by BCRC and those in the newspapers provided counter-narratives that undermined any belief in the government's ability to respond in a responsible manner in the extreme event of a disaster as well as its capability to gather information. In view of the role disaster narratives had in shaping responses, numbers and data from all publications should be approached carefully with their plausible methodological faults in mind.

If the local government's narrative of the aftermath justified its failure to provide relief as explainable by the disrupted communication, there were no attempts at explaining the great extent to which it relied on local and regional resources in the provision of relief material and manpower. The local government's lack of institutional coordination and infrastructure for providing emergency relief appear as part of a set strategy to rely on voluntary resources, ranging from private individuals and corporate bodies to persons connected with the government, official institutions, European enterprises and the Darbhanga Raj, civil society organisations and medical associations such as the Indian Red Cross and the Indian Medical Association. To a considerable extent, it viewed emergency and medical relief as a domain of its close cooperation partner, the Indian Red Cross. Contrary to the efficient mobilisation of police, the local government exerted less effort in providing or organising medical relief but rather viewed itself as a facilitator of provisions by the Indian Red Cross and other major established relief providers. These relief providers were, like the local government, unprepared for a disaster such as an earthquake. For instance, the local Red Cross branch used its epidemic fund for emergency relief in the aftermath and argued for the necessity to establish a permanent disaster relief fund. As such, the government's response was disjointed and depended on cooperation with local actors and their resources, many of whom were inadequately prepared to deal with the situation effectively. Notably, in the narratives of BCRC and the nationalist-friendly press, Rajendra Prasad and other civil society organs began mobilising—and importantly—coordinating with local relief providers before the local government took such an initiative.

Like humanitarian work by Indian nationalists on an international stage during the 1930s can be understood as 'political humanitarianism' in its overt articulation of political motivations,[7] earthquake relief was embedded within broader nationalist claims for sovereignty from British colonial rule. Considering civil society's central role in the provision of aid, we can also reflect on the impact that participation in disaster relief had on civil society associations. Roy suggests, compared to the nineteenth century when the market dominated relief and rebuilding, the colonial state gradually expanded response mechanisms in natural disasters in the period leading up to the 1934 Bihar earthquake and the 1935 Quetta earthquake.[8] He argues that the inclination towards a more interventionist stance coincided with the increasing involvement of civil society in relief, combined with a growing dissatisfaction with charity.[9] The BCRC represented one such mobilisation of resourceful civil society bodies that were able to exert political pressure on the government, as discussed in Chapter 3. The Congress used the committee's work in disaster relief as a site for 'parallel governance'[10] or to show 'credibility';[11] by providing relief through BCRC, INC tested and proved its ability as a political force in power. According to the colonial government, aid of all kinds could be converted into different forms of political capital: through practising parallelism in governance, pocketing the possible financial gains from disaster relief funds or by launching an oppositional political campaign of non-cooperation. The government here clearly referred to 'political capital' as moulded from financial or material resources and social power. The BCRC was an attempt at state-building by establishing parallel institutions, which sometimes filled a gap where government infrastructure was lacking, and sometimes outdid the government by providing relief provisions better in its capacity of 'knowing' the region. The attempt by Congress and Prasad to organise disaster relief for Quetta in 1935 was actively blocked by the colonial government, based on the assumption that they would earn political influence and make financial gainsout of it. The initiative to organise disaster relief in Quetta was, even though curbed by the government, an act that echoed Prasad's previous success in Bihar. The earthquakes were in these ways arenas for nationalist undertakings, a disruption that worked as a window for civil society bodies to garner political support.[12] It should, however, be noted that when it came to implementation of the envisioned tasks by its parallel institutions, the Congress was accused of a lack of accountability. Although relief served as a site for the expansion of civil society as a political force, primarily and most significantly by members of the Congress and the BCRC, government officials and the public perceived overt political agendas to be guiding the course of the relief programme.

While the aftermath saw a surge in civil society organisations partaking in the relief fund collections, foremost represented by the BCRC, Chapter 4 discussed the colonial government's attempts at reaffirming its position as the official agency for disaster relief by issuing publications and by seeking public support for the VERF. The charitable fund headed by the Viceroy had the support of the Mansion House fund in England which rested on established principles for relief of famine victims in India since the second half of the nineteenth century and was the preferred institution for the government to collect national as well as international disaster relief funds.[13] Support for the VERF was ensured by prescribing local government officers with the duty to supervise and to encourage fund collections. Monitored and put on display, this was a form of public charity controlled by the government, in terms of both collection as well as distribution of funds. It was an institutionalised form of charity, by Roy perceived as 'state-aided'.[14] The state's interventions appeared partly in reaction to the organisational abilities of a politicised civil society. Collections to the fund were reinforced with the help of financial support, information campaigns and networks by relying on the colonial government's institutions, which extended beyond disaster relief. The importance of the VERF to the government rested both with the fund's function as an auxiliary financial source and as a display of the government's authority as the principal provider of relief. The state being contested in disaster relief not only challenged its role and abilities as a relief provider, but also its authority as a political force.

Since the government's mandate to carry out relief to a certain extent depended on charitable funds from the public, the BCRC's fund collection and its coordination of voluntary associations and other fund collections challenged the government's position as the official relief provider. The 'national' support for BCRC showed that the government lacked not only credibility but also authority as a political force. In terms of governance, the government's dependency on donations for disaster aid weakened its accountability to the broader public. This was apparent as, at the same time, its ability to provide relief was a mandate granted by the public's willingness to give to its relief funds. The Congress could, with BCRC as a relief provider, display its abilities as a political force that could be counted on. In this manner, the government's reliance and utilisation of relief funds appear to have weakened its authority. The government's increasingly centralised and controlled collection of charity under the auspices of government offices can be seen as an attempt at displaying an ability to act as the provider of tangible goods and relief in times of need. At the same time as the government actively encouraged and invited civil society to contribute, its control over charitable relief from the VERF served to give it a mandate not only as the principal provider of relief, but also as a legitimate government in power.

In this context, where the display of political authority appeared in the shape of funds, the public subscribing to the VERF and the BCRC held considerable importance. The colonial government's preference for a disaster relief fund like the VERF under its control was not only a question of the political situation, but a practice well established during previous 'imperial' disasters in the British colonies. The government's level of interference in disaster relief cannot, in this case, be seen as exclusively driven by political pressure or from a loss of governance infrastructure in a certain context. Rather, the government's relatively strong presence in collecting and distributing aid depended on its ability to influence and control public charity through its administration and cooperation partners. Nowhere was the government's grasp over fund collections more evident than in the case of international aid, where its active interference and rejection of an international collection by the IRU served to maximise government-controlled funds. The government's provision of aid largely depended on its hold over public charity and organisational support provided by trusted partners with close ties to the government administration, for instance, the Indian Red Cross and its local branches. The efficient dismissal of the IRU displayed, besides the reluctance towards inter-governmental cooperation in humanitarian relief, the central role funds like the VERF held in institutionalised charity under the control of the government.

The importance of narrative in BCRC's rhetoric for collecting funds and organising disaster relief becomes most pronounced in the light of the government's and VERF's propaganda for collecting funds. As Kathleen Tierney and colleagues write on the aftermath of Hurricane Katrina: metaphors matter.[15] Media frames helped to guide and justify the actions of those assigned responsibility for the post-disaster emergency response in Katrina and in Bihar. In the historical case of Japan, too, war and conflict metaphors were deployed to describe the devastation.[16] There is, however, a fundamental difference between the examples of metaphors in the respective scenarios, that is, after the 1923 Kanto earthquake and the Hurricane Katrina in 2005. Narratives metaphorically representing the disaster-stricken city of New Orleans as a war zone, with parallels between the city and urban insurgency in Iraq, was used to legitimise the use of law enforcement and military.[17] In Japan, on the contrary, urban earthquake devastation likened to a battlefield brought in the imagery of war in order to call on the nation and the mobilisation of civil society in aid provisioning.[18] In the case of the 1934 earthquake, the BCRC's and supporting funds' use of images and narratives relied upon well-known tropes in the nationalist imaginary, namely the suffering of women and the motherland. In comparison to the VERF publications supported by the colonial government, nationalist descriptions feminising Bihar and images of victims relied upon a gendered geography. The victimised region was anthropomorphised and the target for a nationalist civil society's rescue and relief mission. Bihar was a 'sister' province 'overtaken' by disaster, and to some extent portrayed as a neighbour in need of help, according to the Mayor of Calcutta, who was divided in his support between the VERF and the BCRC. Whether portrayed as a woman, a sister, a 'dependency' of Britain or a neighbour, all fund collections stressed geographical closeness or regional bonds in creating a sense of affinity between potential givers and the earthquake victims. Contrary to the affect and physical closeness expressed in appeals organised by BCRC and by its supporters in India, appeals for contributions from England articulated remoteness to the disaster. In advertising the VERF, description of the 'Great Indian earthquake' with photographs of urban devastation generalised the local and human side of suffering into an idea of a disaster that was relatable. Geographical distance and the lack of a relationship, if ever so imagined, between the victims and the giving audience may explain why this was thought to be a more or less successful strategy to generate subscriptions to the fund. Instead, in order to create a sense of proximity and affinity to the suffering experienced, gifting was invoked with the help of familiar descriptions of war devastation. Also, European communities were singled out as affected by the earthquake, even though they comprised a small minority of the victims.

In some of these descriptions, government officials expressed the idea that colonial ties would elicit donations among the British public. At a distance, however, the geographical zone of the earthquake and its victims were both Others. The cultural construction of India as a land of 'natural' disasters, a 'tropical other' or a 'disaster zone' helped to shape an image of Bihar as the victim of a capricious nature. Helping the earthquake victims through disaster relief was depicted in publications for the VERF as a form of care that justified interventions in the form of, for instance, promoting 'better' constructions. Aid could be framed as 'palliative imperialism' in the sense that disaster relief was depicted as care to promote improvements that would save lives.[19] Simultaneously, the nationalist imagery of a feminised Bihar, a victim of nature, also served to extend relief programmes. This perceivably 'weakened' figure of Bihar represented the site of the disaster, revivable by financial aid and assistance from outside the province. A comparison might here be made with the relief process after the 1950 Assam earthquake when descriptions of the region as subjected to nature, or incapable of taking care of itself, served to re-inscribe it as a marginal space.[20] Like Assam, Bihar was an easy target to depict as disadvantaged and being in need of 'improvements', based on poverty, the lack of infrastructure and, not to forget, its troubled environment and the occurrence of floods.

Institutional capacities developed by the government and civil society during previous disasters played a key role in collecting funds. Both actors efficiently relied on established models and followed a pattern of relief that consisted of mobilisation of relief funds and civil society organisations and associations engaged in providing social services and relief to victims subject to any type of disaster. In this way, fund collection and the organisation of relief built upon previous experiences and provided a model for collecting and distributing aid. The response by both the colonial government and civil society to the exceptional event of the earthquake relied on previous disaster experiences such as 'normal' famines and floods. Nevertheless, the aftermath triggered new practices, mostly because the effects of the earthquake differed greatly from previous disasters and those experiences proved insufficient to address the specific 'needs' for relief. As soon as the emergency phase was over, relief and reconstruction schemes were conceptualised based foremost on the earthquake as an exceptional case of destruction. The destruction was turned into an opportunity for both civil society and the local colonial government to intervene by providing aid and relief funds. In this context, it is worth considering the aftermath as an opportunity for revealing or changing structures and relations that the social world consists of.

Disaster Effects: The Ambiguities of Aid

While appeals by relief funds homogenised the spectre of victims into 'sufferers', the process of allocating aid by relief organisations as well as the local government differentiated among the victims according to their social class and material losses. Losses in the present disaster and social relations transcending the disaster event were interchangeably used to argue for who the victims were and their respective needs. Rather than an event, the disaster becomes a social occasion across time and space, where its putative victims emerge as manifestation of the broader forces that shape society.[21] Similar to in famine relief, as I have argued in Chapter 5, material losses and social position played an important role in shaping categories of 'needs' and qualifying the victims for charitable relief, loans or work-based relief programmes. Significantly, this pattern of relief provisioning based on experiences with previous disaster contributed to both positive and negative consequences. The functioning and evolution of associations and institutions, both informal and formal, provided an infrastructure for relief that could relatively fast roll out relief provisions. Just like in the case of the Marwari Relief Society, the central work and engagement of many associations lay in welfare activities within a much broader spectre of relief, while sometimes also advocating more or less politicised questions. The existing infrastructure of civil society had a positive effect in the sense that earthquake relief could build upon established networks, committees and funds and were thereby able to swiftly mobilise human and material resources. Most of these pre-established institutions were largely run by community-based networks and urban middle classes. This did not necessarily lead to religious or community-based relief. Targeting their own community in relief was, in some cases, the stated purpose of the aid distributed by organisations. Historically, corruption in famine relief has been explained by the use of go-betweens, as governing elites often relied on sub-bureaucracies and local gentry to identify worthy recipients.[22] In 1934, the middle classes, as a part of urban elites and local institutions, were to a great extent involved in defining themselves as the ultimate victims of the earthquake. In line with the classificatory process in famine relief which tended to reduce a person to the status of an individual to a 'pauper' or 'destitute' and thereby shed identities of caste and occupation,[23] earthquake relief classifications revolved around the ability to labour and possession of property.

Both charitable relief funds and loan schemes by the government singled out the propertied 'middle classes' as a favoured category in the distribution of relief. The earthquake was first of all treated as a disaster for this diverse group that was clearly framed by the middle classes themselves, the authorities and civil society organisations as in 'need' of aid. Perceptions of relief categories produced intended and unintended effects. In addition, the middle classes were, when helped by relief societies, given special treatment in light of a reluctance to accept aid in public spaces. Nevertheless, the government and relief societies alike expressed difficulties in reaching out to the middle classes in the distribution of aid. Although it was argued that the middle classes reluctantly received aid, this was far from the material reality as there appeared to be no stigma attached to monetary aid or materials for the reconstruction of property. By proving to have lost what could be defined as a house, people qualified as belonging to the middle classes. The making of this relief category and its compensatory schemes intended to protect the entitlements of the propertied classes, a strategy that could be seen as strengthening this group of people's coping strategies in the aftermath.[24] At a first instance, the destruction of property motivated financial aid to this large category of relief receivers labelled as 'middle classes', yet belonging to a social class defined as unable to labour played an important role.

Apart from assistance to the middle classes, the government gave considerable practical and financial support to sugar cane planters and large landowners. Rural relief to a large extent relied upon previous practices in famine relief and the surveys of the Land and Revenue Department that formed the basis of *taccavi* and charitable relief sourced from the Provincial Famine Relief Fund and the VERF. Compared to the middle classes as a relief category, labourers and landless agricultural workers, who did not possess property according to definitions of both relief organisations and the local colonial government, remained neglected in the distribution of relief. The perception of an increased demand for workers in the undertaking of reconstruction and land rehabilitation, coupled with the idea that the 'dwellings' of labourers did not qualify as property, resulted in an official and middle-class-driven portrayal of this socio-economic class as having 'benefitted' from the earthquake. Although reports by relief societies and the colonial local government presented labourers as 'winners' and the middle classes as 'losers', members of the international organisation Service Civil International, which together with the local government and the BCRC formed the Joint Flood Committee in rural north Bihar, found labour wages to be poor and barely enough to sustain the workers. Contrary to a view articulated in the press and by relief societies of labourers profiting from the reconstruction boom while not having had anything of material value to lose in the earthquake, the SCI described their living situation as precarious and made even more vulnerable in light of floods threatening rural areas. In view of the large number of people employed on low relief wages in reclaiming land and reconstructing roads, organised by both relief societies such as the BCRC and by the local government, nothing except for arguments by the advocates of middle-class relief indicate gains made by the labourers. On the contrary, such relief schemes benefited the public since rebuilt or repaired roads and infrastructure are likely to have contributed to a speedy recovery in terms of aiding trade and reconstruction.

The local government failed in distributing grants and loans partly because of a distribution system badly attuned to its administrative capabilities, and partly since the assessment and compensation for lost property were more complicated than first anticipated. Government-subsidised loans were initially considered a viable option for relief but were gradually replaced by grants that could be expedited and required less administrative work in both a long- and short-term perspective. In the end, the provision of aid, open to change throughout the aftermath, underlined the government's approach as not just unprepared for an earthquake of this magnitude, but perhaps more so, a lack of grasp over its administrative capacities. Even if the aid and compensatory scheme was in its design adjusted to meet the needs of the middle classes, it was a failure without an administration to carry it through.

The earthquake's catastrophic impact, as it turned from a natural hazard into a 'natural' disaster, threw into sharper relief relationships between civil society and the government. Rather than breaking the structure of social relations, the aftermath showed how relief responses negotiated existing institutions and relationships. Like scholars have enquired why South Asia became more vulnerable to famine during colonial rule[25] vis-à-vis the impact the crises had on governance and society,[26] perceptions and responses to the earthquake may enhance our understanding of the socio-environmental constructions behind vulnerability in 'natural' disasters. What could have made society less acutely sensitive to earthquakes, let alone hazards or shocks in a broader sense? The focus on middle-class relief and urban 'improvements' in the reconstruction phase after the 1934 earthquake showed few traces of 'learning' from the damages or previous earthquakes in the planning process for rebuilding towns, as discussed in Chapter 6. Even if safety in future earthquakes became an argument for widening roads and controlling reconstruction and population density, engineers and administrators relied on established ideas of town planning developed during the late nineteenth century. Town planning had as its goal improvement of sanitary conditions and trade in cities across north India, and the same thinking shaped the colonial government's planning for 'improvements' of bazaars. Although earthquake-safety was used as an argument for making structural changes that entailed widening of roads, rebuilding houses with recommended 'solid' materials and housing plans with reduced population density, the planners tried, first of all, to implement 'improvements' of hygienic conditions and trade.

Therefore, town planning followed a far from comprehensive scheme or a vision of earthquake-safe constructions on a larger scale. Despite complications caused by lack of planning and taking action in the spur of the moment, the government dismissed the problems as negligible compared to the opportunity the aftermath posed for bringing about changes. These were structural changes of building designs and urban planning that in the government's vision led to improved sanitation, trade and consequently better socio-economic conditions. Sanitation and trade were the most important parts of the urban environment in need of improvements according to town planning. Reconstruction was one site where the government perceived it could influence urban life by aiding first commercial interests and improving sanitation.

Since reconstruction with better materials was contingent on private financial capabilities, the government and the GSI viewed an encompassing building code as blocked by the poor financial status of the town residents. Despite the fact that the local government, the GSI and engineers agreed on the dire need for constructions to be modified in view of public safety in future earthquakes, the local colonial government extended help to individual cases instead of attempting a building code for the region. Financial aid and engineering assistance measured out to the propertied urban classes gave the local government an opportunity to influence the reconstruction process in towns. As in the distribution of relief funds and loans, propertied classes were privileged in the planning process while poorer segments and sub-tenants were dislocated and held weaker bargaining positions in obtaining a place to trade or live. The central aim of planning was to undertake 'improvements' of bazaars as a means to remove 'slums' by decreasing population density, which would result in sub-tenants being accommodated elsewhere. Judging by the government's assistance to the propertied population and traders, its involvement in rehabilitation helped individuals and groups with social and financial influence, before taking the interests of the broader public into consideration.

It has now been more than 80 years since the 1934 Bihar–Nepal earthquake. Were Bihar to experience an earthquake like that of 1934 today, it is likely that a far larger number of people would succumb. Based on population and housing data from the 2011 census, a contemporary report issued by the Bihar State Disaster Management Authority estimates the loss of life and damages to houses in case of an earthquake of the same magnitude and scope as the 1934 earthquake. Accordingly, 222,337 deaths may occur if an earthquake takes place at night, and 72,766 if during the daytime. About 20 per cent of the houses would need reconstruction and about 45 per cent would need repairing and retrofitting.[27] There are obvious factors at work which make such estimates a baseline at best, for instance, population growth, migration, building techniques and population density. Although after the 2015 Gorkha earthquake two more recent publications provide substantially lower figures, the event of an earthquake similar to in 1934 would be devastating. One estimate states 33,000 victims in Nepal and more than 50,000 in India,[28] while another calculation appreciates about 100,000 deaths if the earthquake would occur at night in any of the densely populated regions of the Himalayas such as the Kathmandu valley.[29]

The continuing significance and relevance of this book can be appreciated from the ongoing disaster in the long aftermath of the 2015 Gorkha earthquake in Nepal where the 'natural' event triggered political decisions for the country's development agenda, its national border and the constitution. When politicians and the international funding bodies of the aid community directly or indirectly contribute to stalling rather than aiding relief and rehabilitation, answers to how vulnerability in earthquake-prone areas can be minimised appear much harder to tackle head-on than the task of engineering earthquake-safe buildings.[30] However, as discussed throughout this book, an understanding of historical disasters gives a better chance for reviewing vulnerability and building resilience and can thereby help to minimise risk during a potentially catastrophic earthquake looming large over South Asia, amongst other regions across the globe.[31]

Notes

1. Greg Clancey, 'The Changing Character of Disaster Victimhood: Evidence from Japan's "Great Earthquakes"', *Critical Asian Studies* 48, no. 3 (2016): 356–79, 357.
2. Henry A. Giroux, 'Hurricane Katrina and the Politics of Disposability: Floating Bodies and Expendable Populations', in *Schooling and the Politics of Disaster*, ed. Kenneth J. Saltman, 43–70 (New York: Routledge, 2007); Henry A. Giroux, *Stormy Weather: Katrina and the Politics of Disposability* (Boulder, C O: Paradigm Publishers, 2006).
3. Giroux, 'Hurricane Katrina and the Politics of Disposability', 43–51.
4. The body as metaphor and physical site of conflict in disaster, in Rukmini Bhaya Nair, 'Acts of Agency and Acts of God: Discourse of Disaster in a Post-colonial Society', *Economic and Political Weekly* 32, no. 11 (March 15–21, 1997): 535–42.
5. Hoffman, 'After Atlas Shrugs', 310.
6. Mukherjee, *Natural Disasters and Victorian Empire*, 43.
7. Maria Framke, 'We Must Send a Gift Worthy of India and the Congress!' War and Political Humanitarianism in Late Colonial South Asia', *Modern Asian Studies* 51, no. 6 (2017): 1969–98. Maria Framke, 'Political Humanitarianism in the 1930s: Indian Aid for Republican Spain', *European Review of History: Revue européenne d'histoire* 23, nos. 1–2 (2016): 63–81.
8. Roy, 'State, Society and Market', 289.
9. Ibid., 268, 277.
10. Kuracina, *The State and Governance in India*, 25.
11. Dang, 'The Congress and the Politics of Relief', 110.
12. Clancey, 'The Meiji Earthquake', 946.
13. Hutchinson, 'Disasters and the International Order. II', 255.
14. Term used for referring to the VERF in Roy, 'State, Society and Market', 268.

15. Kathleen Tierney, Christine Bevc and Erica Kuligowski, 'Metaphors Matter: Disaster Myths, Media Frames, and Their Consequences in Hurricane Katrina', *Annals of the American Academy of Political and Social Science* 604, no. 1 (March 2006): 57–81, 61. See also Jeffry M. Diefendorf, 'Reconstructing Devastated Cities: Europe after World War II and New Orleans after Katrina', *Journal of Urban Design* 14, no. 3 (August 2009): 377–97.

16. J. Charles Schencking, '1923 Tokyo as a Devastated War and Occupation Zone: The Catastrophe One Confronted in Post Earthquake Japan', *Japanese Studies* 29, no. 1 (2009): 111–29. For tropes and motifs, see also Gennifer Weisenfeld, *Imaging Disaster: Tokyo and the Visual Culture of Japan's Great Earthquake of 1923* (Berkeley: University of California Press, 2012).

17. Tierney, Bevc and Kuligowski, 'Metaphors Matter', 61.

18. Schencking, '1923 Tokyo as a Devastated War and Occupation Zone', 122, 126.

19. Mukherjee, *Natural Disasters and Victorian Empire*, 17–18.

20. Guyot-Réchard, 'Reordering a Border Space', 4.

21. Kathleen J. Tierney, 'From the Margins to the Mainstream? Disaster Research at the Crossroads', *Annual Review of Sociology* 33, no. 1 (2007): 503–25, 509.

22. Cormac Ó Gráda, *Famine: A Short History* (Princeton and Oxford: Princeton University Press, 2009), 206.

23. Sharma, *Famine, Philanthropy and the Colonial State*, 141.

24. Entitlements have foremost been discussed in relation to famine relief, for instance, in the 1874 Bihar famine. David Hall-Matthews, 'The Historical Roots of Famine Relief Paradigms', in *A World without Famine: New Approaches to Aid and Development*, ed. Helen O'Neill and John Toye, 107–27 (Basingstoke; London: MacMillan Press Ltd, 1998), 118.

25. Naoroji, *Poverty and Un-British Rule in India*. Arnold, *Famine: Social Crisis and Historical Change*. Sen, *Poverty and Famines*.

26. See, for instance, Ahuja, 'State Formation and "Famine Policy" in Early Colonial South India' and Benjamin Siegel, *Hungry Nation: Food, Famine, and the Making of Modern India* (Cambridge: Cambridge University Press, 2018).

27. Based on the break-up of data according to districts in Anand S. Arya, *Damage Scenario under Hypothetical Recurrence of 1934 Earthquake Intensities in Various Districts in Bihar* (Patna: Bihar State Disaster Management Authority, Government of Bihar, August 2013), 9–13.

28. Also based on the 2011 census. Sapkota, Bollinger and Perrier, 'Fatality Rates of the Mw ~8.2, 1934, Bihar–Nepal Earthquake', 7.

29. Roger Bilham, 'Himalayan Earthquakes: A Review of Historical Seismicity and Early 21st Century Slip Potential', in *Himalayan Tectonics: A Modern*

Synthesis, ed. P. J. Treloar and M. P. Searle, 423–82 (London: Geological Society, Special Publications, 483, 2019, published online 5 February 2019, https://doi.org/10.1144/SP483.16). Approximately 50 million people are at risk to large Himalayan earthquakes in the Ganges plain according to Roger Bilham, Vinod K. Gaur and Peter Molnar, 'Himalayan Seismic Hazard', *Science* 293, no. 5534 (2001): 1442–44.

30. Patrick Daly, Sabin Ninglekhu, Pia Hollenbach, Jennifer Duyne Barenstein, and Dori Nguyen, 'Situating Local Stakeholders within National Disaster Governance Structures: Rebuilding Urban Neighbourhoods Following the 2015 Nepal Earthquake', *Environment and Urbanization* 29, no. 2 (October 2017): 403–24.

31. Roger Bilham, 'Raising Kathmandu', *Nature Geoscience* 8 (August 2015): 582–84.

Glossary

acre	0.405 hectare or 4,047 square metres
anna	one-sixteenth of a rupee
bataidar	tenant-at-will paying rent in kind.
bazaar	market
bhadralok	literal meaning 'respectable people' but used as a category to imply a status group in Bengal who came from the upper castes, often economically dependent on landed rents and professional and clerical employment.
crore	10 million
ekka	a two-wheel light trap, buggy, drawn by a pony
gur	raw sugar; unrefined sugar
khas mahal	government estate
khatiyan	land register containing the full description of each holding (plots, areas, boundaries, details of ownership and tenancy, rents and dues)
khesra/khasra	official village field book containing the list of plots and showing their areas, crops and details of occupancy
kuccha	(adj.) 'raw' (anglicised from Hindi *kaccā*); with reference to buildings, it was used to refer to village houses or 'huts' made of mud and grass, or houses made of unfired brick and unslaked lime.
kuccha-pucca	used for describing a building made of kuccha and pucca materials
lakh/lac	100,000
maund	82.2 pounds or 37.3 kilograms
mohalla	locality

pie/pice/paisa/paise	1/12 of an *anna*
pucca	(adj.) 'solid' (anglicised from Hindi *pakkā*); with reference to buildings, it generally referred to constructions made of bricks or stone with mortar, or concrete as opposed to *kuccha* or *kuccha-pucca*
rabi	winter crop; crop sown after the rains and reaped in the first three or four months of the year
raiyat (*ryot*)	peasant, cultivator
thana	police station
zamindar	landholder or landlord, usually hereditary, who pays a fixed revenue to the government and collects rent from his tenants
zamindari	(adj.) land-revenue system under zamindars; (noun) the land covered by a zamindar
zarpeshgidar	holder of a *zarpeshgi* lease, that is, holder of a mortgage with possession
zirat	private land of a zamindar

Bibliography

Primary Sources

Unpublished Government Records

Bihar State Archives, Patna

Political Department – Special Branch/Section, 1934–1937
Revenue Department – Lands Branch, 1934–1936
Revenue Department – Lands and Revenue Branch, 1934–1936
General/Reconstruction Department – Reconstruction/Earthquake Branch, 1934–1936
Local Self Government – Local Self Government and Sanitation Branch, 1934–1936

National Archives of India, New Delhi

Home Department – Political Branch, 1934–1937
Home Department – Public Branch, 1934–1937
Foreign Department – Political Branch, 1934–1937

Asia and Africa Collections, India Office Records (IOR), British Library, London
Bihar and Orissa Gazette, IOR/V/11/1153
Bihar and Orissa Local Government's Reports
Confidential fortnightly reports, IOR L/P.J/12/59 or IOR/L/P.J/12/743
Indian [sic] and Earthquake, IOR/20/A/3658
Earthquake Relief, IOR/R/20/A/3607.
Preliminary Report* on the North Bihar Earthquake of the 15th January, IOR/V/27/410/25
Nepal, Earthquake IOR/L/PS/12/3036
Darbhanga Improvement Act 1934, IOR/L/PJ/7/719
Newspaper Cuttings (1934–1936) IOR/20.165 L/I/2/57

Archival Manuscripts and Private Papers

Maharajadhiraj Kameshwar Singh Kalyani Foundation, Darbhanga
Correspondence, 1934–1935
Darbhanga Improvement Trust, 1934–1935
Photo albums, 1934–1936

European Manuscripts (Mss Eur), British Library, London
Harold Easton Bruce, Mss Eur C282
Vincent Ellis Davies papers, Mss Eur D833/22
Samuel Solomon, Mss Eur D883
F. C. Temple, relief engineer and supply officer, Mss Eur D926/1–3
C. F. Andrews, Mss Eur D1113/5-6-9-10
Samuel Hoare, Mss Eur E240
Cornelia Sorabji, Mss Eur F165/96–97, 170
Papers of W. G. Archer and Mildred Archer, Mss Eur F236
James David Sifton (1878–1952), Mss Eur F266/5
AICC and relief work, Mss Eur F341/167
Satow Collection, Mss Eur F290, 1082/6

Library of the Gandhi Seva Sangh, Sevagram, Maharashtra
Village Industries: Entry 4, Nr. 17: Bihar Central Relief Committee

School of Oriental and African Studies (SOAS), Archive Section, London
Banks Photography Collection, Ms 380389 (1934–1937)

Library and Museum of the Order of St John (St John Ambulance Service), London
Bihar and Quetta Earthquakes

Bibliothèque Cantonale et Universitaire BCU Lausanne (Lausanne Cantonal and University Library)
Private Papers of Pierre Ceresole

Bibliothèque de la Ville, La Chaux-de-Fonds (BVCF, The City Library) Switzerland
International Archives of Service Civil International

Centre for South Asian Studies, Cambridge University, Cambridge
Mrs P. Lacey, Oral History Archive

BFI National Archive, The British Film Institute (BFI), London
British Movietone News No. 243a 'Earthquake in India Spreads Desolation' (BFI ID: 380164): http://www.colonialfilm.org.uk/node/1437
Quetta Earthquake, May 31st 1935 (BFI ID: 9607): http://www.colonialfilm.org.uk/node/4587

Ramakrishna Mission, Belur Math
Papers pertaining to the 1934 Bihar–Nepal Earthquake:
Ramakrishna Mission. *The Eight General Report of the Ramakrishna Mission (1934–35)*. Kolkata: Ramakrishna Mission, Belur Math, Reprint (s.d.; photocopied March 2010).

Newspapers and Periodicals

Monthly and Weekly Publications (1934–37)
The Friend (London)
Hindustan Review (Allahabad)
Illustrated Weekly of India (Bombay)
Mithila Mihir (Darbhanga)
Modern Review (Calcutta)
Nature (London)
Prabuddha Bharata (Chennai)
Royal Society of Arts, Journal (London)
Vishāl Bhārat (Calcutta)

Newspapers (1934–37)
Amrita Bazar Patrika (Calcutta)
Behar Herald (Patna)
The Englishman (Calcutta)
Forward (Calcutta)
Gorkhapatra (Kathmandu)
Harijan (Madras)
The Leader (Allahabad)
The Indian Nation (Patna)

The Nation (Kolkata)
The Searchlight (Patna)
Servant of India (Poona)
The Statesman (Calcutta)
Yugantara (Lahore)

Published Works and Reports

Andrews, Charles Freer. *The Indian Earthquake*. London: George Allen and Unwin Ltd, 1935.

Astbury, A. R. *Earthquake-Resisting Design*. Punjab P. W. D., Paper No. 84. Lahore, Punjab: Superintendent of Government Printing, 1934.

Auden, J. B. and A. M. N. Ghosh, 'Preliminary Account of the Earthquake of the 15th January, 1934, in Bihar and Nepal', 177–239. In *Records of the Geological Survey of India* 68, pt. 2, 1934.

Bhaduri, Satinath. *Dhoday Charitmanas*. Original in Bengali, part 1, 1949; part 2, 1951; Hindi translation by Madhukar Gangadhar, 2nd ed. Allahabad: Lokbharati Prakashan, 1981.

Bihar Central Relief Committee. *Devastated Bihar: An Account of Havoc Caused by the Earthquake of 15th January, 1934 and Relief Operation Conducted by the Committee*. Patna: Bihar Central Relief Committee, 1934, 67 pp. + map.

Brett, William Bailie. 'Report on the Progress of Earthquake Reconstruction in Bihar'. 1934, 18 pp.

———. *A Report on the Bihar Earthquake and on the Measures Taken in Consequence thereof up to the 31st December 1934*. Patna: Superintendent, Government Printing, 1935.

Bureau of Public Information, GoI, *India in 1933–34*. New Delhi: Manager of Publications, 1935.

Caldwell, K. S. 'Note on Sand Deposit', dated 17 March 1934, printed by the R.D. at the B&O Govt Press, 28 March 1934.

Cliff, A. M. P. *Bālū kaise haṭegī? Bhūkamp ke kāraṇ khetoṃ meṃ jo bālū jamā ho gayā hai uske miṭne ke kucch upāy* (How to Remove the Sand? Some Remedies for Removing the Sand in the Fields Caused by the Earthquake). Calcutta: Published on behalf of Muzaffarpur District Board. Published and Printed by R. P. Roy Sharma, 70 Dharmatala Street [Calcutta]: Rashtrabandhu Press [1934], 8 pp.

Dunn, J. A., J. B. Auden and A. M. N. Ghosh. *Preliminary Report* on the North Bihar Earthquake of the 15th January 1934* [*Certain Portions of the Report Have Been Omitted]. Patna: Superintendent, Government Printing, 1934.

Dunn, J. A., J. B. Auden, A. M. N. Ghosh and D. N. Wadia (Officers of the Geological Survey of India). 'The Bihar–Nepal Earthquake of 1934'. In *Memoirs of the Geological Survey of India*, vol. 73. Calcutta: Geological Survey of India, 1939.

Earthquake Number: Which Hand Is Yours. Edited by Syed Abdullah Brelvi and B. G. Horniman. Special Issue by Chronicle-Sentinel, Bombay (March 1934).

'Earthquake (Relief Measures)'. In House of Commons Debates, 19 February 1934, vol. 286 cc3–4. http://hansard.millbanksystems.com/commons/1934/feb/19/earthquake-relief-measures#S5CV0286P0_19340219_HOC_17 (accessed 11 February 2021).

East Indian Railway. *Report on the Earthquake on 15th January 1934*. Calcutta, 1934, 36 pp.

Fermor, L. L. 'General Report of the Geological Survey of India for the Year 1934'. In *Records of the Geological Survey of India*, vol. 69, 1–108. Calcutta, Geological Survey of India, 1936.

Flight. 'Bengal Flying Club'. No. 1309 (25 January 1934): 78.

———. 'Capt. C.D. Barnard for India'. No. 1298 (9 November 1933): 1130–31.

———. 'The Barnard Tour' (Correspondence). No. 1323 (3 May 1934): 448.

———. 'The Bengal Flying Club'. No. 1318 (29 March 1934): 302.

———. 'The "Jupiter" in India'. No. 1334 (19 July 1934): 754.

———. 'The Indian Earthquake: An Aerial View—Taken by the Air Survey Co., Ltd.—of the City of Muzaffarpur, Bihar State, Showing Many of the Buildings in Ruins'. No. 1311 (8 February 1934): 119.

Gee, E. R. 'Dhubri Earthquake of 3rd July, 1930'. *Memoirs of the Geological Survey of India*, vol. 65, Pt 1, 1–106. Calcutta: Office of the Geological Survey, 1934.

Gorgé, Camille. *The International Relief Union: Its Origin, Aims, Means and Future*. Geneva: International Relief Union, 1938.

Government of Bengal. *Annual Report on Indian Papers Printed or Published in the Bengal Presidency for the Year 1934*. Alipore, Bengal: Superintendent, Government printing, Bengal Government Press, 1935.

———. *Report on Newspapers and Periodicals in Bengal 1934*. Alipore, Bengal: Superintendent, Government printing, Bengal Government Press, 1935.

Government of Bihar. *Bihar Legislative Council Debates*. Vol. 3. Official Report. Patna: Superintendent, Government Printing, 1939.

———. *Bihar Legislative Council Debates*. Vol. 4. Official Report. Fourth Session, 23rd January to 18th March 1939. Patna: Superintendent, Government Printing, 1940.

———. *Bihar Legislative Council Proceedings*. Vol. 36. Official Report. Fourth Council, Fourteenth Session, 18th to 21st November, 1936. Patna: Superintendent, Government Printing, 1937.

Government of Bihar and Orissa. *Bihar and Orissa Legislative Council Proceedings.* Vol. 30. Official Report, Fourth Council-Eighth Session, 14th February to 23rd March, 1934. Patna: Superintendent, Government Printing, 1934.

———. *Bihar and Orissa Legislative Council Proceedings.* Vol. 31. Official Report. Fourth Council-Ninth Session, 3rd to 18th September 1934. Patna: Superintendent, Government Printing, 1934.

———. *Bihar and Orissa Legislative Council Proceedings.* Vol. 32. Official Report. Fourth Council-Tenth Session, 15th January to 27th March 1935. Patna: Superintendent, Government Printing, 1935.

———. *Bihar and Orissa Legislative Council Proceedings.* Vol. 34. Fourth Council-Twelfth Session, 9th January to 28th March, 1936. Patna: Superintendent, Government Printing, 1936.

———. *Final Report on the Survey of Lands Damaged by Earthquake in North Bihar in 1934.* Department of Land Records and Surveys. Superintendent, Government Printing, Bihar and Orissa, Patna, 1934.

———. *History of Services of Gazetted and Other Officers Serving under the Government of Bihar and Orissa.* (Corrected until 1 July 1930) Part I. Patna: Superintendent, Government Printing, 1930.

———. *Bihar and Orissa Natural Calamities Loans Act, 1934. Bihar and Orissa Act I of 1934.* Patna: Superintendent, Government Printing, Bihar and Orissa, 1934. 7 p; 25 cm.

Government of India. *Legislative Assembly Debates* (Official report), vol. I, 1934. 24 January–16 February 1934, Seventh Session of the Fourth Legislative Assembly.

———. *Quetta Earthquake, 1935.* Published by authority of the Government of India. Simla: Government of India Press, 1935, 26 pp.

———. *Quetta Earthquake. Collection of Information Made Available to the Press in the Form of Communiqués, Statements and Reports Regarding the Situation and of the Measures Taken in Connection with Relief, Supplies, Evacuation and Salvage.* Simla: Bureau of Public Information, Government of India Press, 1935.

———. *The Council of State Debates.* Vol. 1, 1934 (8 February to 27 April, 1934). Seventh Session of the Third Council of State, 1934. Published by Manager of Publications, Delhi. Printed by the Manager, Government of India Press, New Delhi, 1934.

Hammond, C. B. 'The Song of the Seismologist: Manchester Meeting, 1911'. *Bulletin of the Seismological Society of America* 2, no. 4 (December 1912): 224–25.

Hart, Bernard. *Psychopathology: Its Development and Its Place in Medicine.* Cambridge: At the University Press, 1927.

Hoyland, John S. *Digging for a New England: The Co-operative Farm for Unemployed Men*. London: Alden Press, 1936.

Imperial Gazetteer of India, The. The Indian Empire, vol. 1, Descriptive. Oxford: Clarendon Press, 1909.

———. The Indian Empire, vol. III, Economic. (New Edition) Published under the Authority of His Majesty's Secretary of State for India in Council. Oxford: Clarendon Press, 1908.

Indian Red Cross Society. *Proceedings of the Annual General Meeting. Held in the Council Chamber, Viceregal Lodge, Simla, on the 24th June, 1931, at 4 p.m.* Delhi: Thakur Das and Sons, Government Printing at the Delhi Printing Works.

———. *Annual Report 1934. Headquarters Simla (summer); New Delhi (Winter)*. Delhi: Thakur Das and Sons, Government Printing at the Delhi Printing Works.

———. *Proceedings of the Annual General Meeting. Held on the 25th March, 1936, at The Viceroy's House, New Delhi*. Delhi: Thakur Das and Sons, Government Printing at the Delhi Printing Works.

———. *Proceedings of the Annual General Meeting. Held on the 20th March, 1935, at The Commander-in-Chief's House, New Delhi*. Delhi: Thakur Das and Sons, Government Printing at the Delhi Printing Works.

———. *Proceedings of the Annual General Meeting. Held at 'The Viceroy's House', New Delhi, on the 22 March, 1934, at 4:45 p.m.* Delhi: Thakur Das and Sons, Government Printing at the Delhi Printing Works.

Indian Franchise Committee. *Volume I: Report of the Indian Franchise Committee*. Calcutta: GOI Central Publication Branch, 1932 (2nd edition).

Jha, Hetukar (ed.). *Courage and Benevolence: Correspondence and Speeches of India's Prime-Estate Holder; Maharajadhiraja Kameshwar Singh of Darbhanga (1907–1962)*. Darbhanga (Bihar): Maharajadhiraja Kameshwar Singh Kalyani Foundation, Darbhanga, 2007.

Kumar, S. L. 'Theory of Earthquake Resisting Design with a Note on Earthquake Resisting Construction in Baluchistan,' Paper No. 165. *Punjab Engineering Congress*, 1933: 154–89.

Lacey, W. G. *Census of India, 1931. Vol. VII, Bihar and Orissa Part II – Tables*. Patna: Superintendent, Government Printing, 1932.

Loveday, A. *The History and Economics of Indian Famines*. London: G. Bell and Sons Ltd., 1914.

Marwari Relief Society, Calcutta, The. *Report of the Behar Earthquake Relief Work*. Published by Jwalaprasad Kanoria, General Secretary. Calcutta: March 1935.

Mitra, Nripendra Nath (ed.). *The Indian Annual Register: An Annual Digest of Public Affairs of India*. Volume II (July–December). Calcutta: The Annual Register Office, 1934.

Moore, William Arthur (ed.). *Record of the Great Indian Earthquake: To Help the Earthquake Relief Work*. Special Issue of *The Statesman*, Calcutta: Printed and Published for *The Statesman*, 1934.

Nariman, K. F. 'The Great Earthquake of Japan: How It Was Fought and Won'. *Hindustan Review* LVX [*sic* 60], nos. 350–52 (January, 1934): 191–94.

Nasu, Nobuji. 'No. 30, The Great Indian Earthquake of January 15, 1934'. *Department Bulletin Paper* 13, 2, Earthquake Research Institute, Tokyo Imperial University, 30 June 1935: 417–32, pl. XVII–XXIII. Tokyo University, http://repository.dl.itc.u-tokyo.ac.jp/dspace (accessed 12 January 2010).

———. [alt. Nasu, Shinji]. 'Seismic Damages Caused by the Great Indian Earthquake of Jan. 15, 1934'. *Journal of Architecture and Building Science* 48, no. 591 (11 May 1934): 1182–1293.

Nehru, Jawaharlal. 'The Humiliation of India'. *The Nation* 138, no. 358 (April 1934): 410–11.

———. *An Autobiography: With Musings on Recent Events in India*. London: The Bodley Head, 1949 [1936].

Nixon, C. R. C. 'The Indian Earthquake'. *Journal of the Royal Society of Arts* 82, no. 4142 (9 March 1934): 486.

Pinhey, Louis Alexander Gordon. *Report on the Quetta Earthquake on the 31st of May 1935*. Delhi: Manager of Publications, 1938.

Prasad, Jamuna. 'The Psychology of Rumour: A Study Relating to the Great Indian Earthquake of 1934'. *British Journal of Psychology* 26, no. 1 (1935): 1–15.

———. 'A Comparative Study of Rumours and Reports in Earthquakes'. *British Journal of Psychology* 41, no. 3/4 (1950): 129–44.

Prasad, Rajendra. *Autobiography*. New Delhi: Penguin Books India, 2010 [1946].

———. *Devastated Behar: The Problem of Reconstruction*. Patna: Published by Publicity Officer, Bihar Central Relief Committee and Printed by Murli Manohar Pd. at the Searchlight Press, s.d. [end February to 10 March 1934], 23 pp.

Ravenhill, D. W. and G. Wilson. 'The Reconstruction of the Inchcape Bridge, Bengal and North Western Railway'. *Journal of the ICE* 7, no. 1 (1 November 1937): 49–56.

Report of the Central Executive Committee, Indian Famine Charitable Relief Fund, 1900: With Complete Accounts and Proceedings, Including the Reports of the Provincial Committees. Calcutta: Office of the Superintendent of Government Printing, 1901.

Roy Chaudhury, P. C. *Muzaffarpur*. Bihar District Gazetteers. Bihar, Patna: Superintendent Secretariat Press, 1958.

———. *Monghyr*. Bihar District Gazetteers. Bihar, Patna: Superintendent Secretariat Press, 1960.

———. *Inside Bihar*. Calcutta; Patna; Allahabad: Bookland Private Limited, 1962.

———. *Darbhanga*. Bihar District Gazetteers. Bihar, Patna: Superintendent Secretariat Press, 1964.

Saksena, Mohanlal. *Devastated Bihar through Jawaharlal's Lenses/Bihār-bhūkamp Javāhar Lāl ke Citrom̐ Dvārā*. (Written in English and Hindi) Lucknow: Mohanlal Saksena; Allahabad: Mahendra Nath Pandey, Allahabad Law Journal Press, 1934, 74.

Saraswati, Swami Shahajanand, *Mera Jivan Sangharsh* (Hindi, Autobiography). Patna: Sitaram Ashram, Bihta, 1985 [1950].

———. 'Terrible Plight of the Kisans [peasants], Relentless Machine of Landlordism, Remission of Rent the Only Remedy'. *The Searchlight*, 18 March 1934. Sempill, Lord. 'Private Flying: Developments in India'. *Flight*, no. 1360 (17 January 1935): 75.

'Servindia ['Servants of India'] Earthquake Relief'. *Servants of India* 27, no. 9, edited by P. Kodanda Rao, Poona. (1 March 1934), 97.

Shumsher Jung Bahadur Rana, Major General Brahma, *Nepālko Mahābhūkamp (1990 Bikram Samvat (BS) [1934])* (in Nepali). Kathmandu: Babaramahal, 1936 [1935], 249 pp. [Ratnakar Press, Calcutta, also printed a 2nd ed. in 1936; 3rd ed., Sahayogi Press, 2041 BS (1984)].

———. *The Great Earthquake in Nepal (1934 A. D.)*. Translated from Nepali by Kesar Lall. Kathmandu: Ratna Pustak Bandar, 2013, 136 pp.

Sinha, Kumar Ganganand. *The Bihar Earthquake and the Darbhanga Raj*, 2nd ed. Calcutta: Thacker's Press & Directories, Ltd. and published by the Darbhanga Raj, 1936 [first published in April 1936 by the Darbhanga Raj].

Solomon, Samuel. *Bihar and Orissa in 1934–35*. Patna: Superintendent, Government Printing, 1937.

Sorabji, Cornelia. 'Earthquake in Bihar'. *The Nineteenth Century and After* 115, no. 687 (May 1934): 535–47.

Sharma, Sriram. 'Bhūkamp-Pīḍit Bihār' (Hindi, 'Earthquake-Suffering Bihar'). *Vishāl Bhārat, bhāg* 13, *ank* 2 (February 1934): 129–40.

Temple, F. C. *Report on Town Planning*. Jamshedpur Social Welfare Series, Bombay: Commercial Press, 1919.

'Trial and Imprisonment of Pandit Jawaharlal Nehru'. *Modern Review (A Monthly Review and Miscellany)*, 55, no. 3, Calcutta, edited by Ramananda Chatterjee (March 1934): 351–53.

Turnbull, W. J. and H. E. Ormerod (eds.). *The Great Indian Earthquake*. Special Issue of *The Indian Concrete Journal* 8, no. 10 (15 October 1934).

Vangmaya, Rahul. *Jīvan Yātrā*. Part I, 4 volumes. New Delhi: Radhakrishna Prakashan Private limited, 1994.

Varma, Ramchandra (ed.). *Bhūkamp pīḍitoṃ kī karuna-kahāniyāṃ: Bihār ke bhūkamp-pīḍitoṃ kī param āścarya-janak aur karuṇāpūrṇ saccī ātma-kathāeṃ* (Hindi; Stories of the Victims of the Earthquake: Bihar's Earthquake Victims' Most Astonishing and Pitiful True Narrations). Compiler Radhanath Mishra. Kashi (Varanasi), Rajmandir: Chunnilal Malviya, (May) 1934.

Wasi, S. M. *Bihar and Orissa in 1936–37*. Patna: Superintendent, Government Printing, Bihar, 1938.

Wilcock, J. S. *Bihar and Orissa in 1933–34*. Patna: Superintendent, Government Printing, Bihar, 1935.

Secondary Sources

Published Books and Articles

Abe, Kitao. 'Levels of Trust and Reactions to Various Sources of Information in Catastrophic Situations'. In *Disasters: Theory and Research*, edited by E. L. Quarantelli, 159–72. Beverly Hills, California: Sage Publications, 1978.

Abramovitz, Janet. 'Unnatural Disasters'. In *Worldwatch Paper 158*, edited by Linda Starke. Washington, DC: Worldwatch Institute, October 2001.

Ahuja, Ravi. 'State Formation and "Famine" Policy in Early Colonial South India'. *Indian Economic and Social History Review* 39, no. 4 (2002): 351–80.

Alexander, David. 'The Study of Natural Disasters, 1977–1997: Some Reflections on a Changing Field of Knowledge'. *Disasters* 21, no. 4 (1997): 284–304.

Ali, Daud. 'Recognizing Europe in India: Colonial Master Narratives and the Writing of Indian History'. In *Contesting the Master Narrative: Essays in Social History*, edited by Jeffrey Cox and Shelton Stromquist, 95–130. Iowa City: University of Iowa Press, 1998.

Allison, M. A. 'Historical Changes in the Ganges-Brahmaputra Delta Front'. *Journal of Coastal Research* 14, no. 4 (1998): 1269–75.

Ambraseys, Nicholas. 'Three Little Known Early Earthquakes in India' (Commentary), *Current Science* 86, no. 4 (2004): 506–08.

Ambraseys, Nicholas and D. Jackson. 'A Note on Early Earthquakes in Northern India and Southern Tibet' (Research Communications). *Current Science* 84, no. 4 (2003): 570–82.

Ambraseys, Nicholas and Roger Bilham. 'A Note on the Kangra Ms = 7.8 Earthquake of 4 April 1905' (General Articles). *Current Science* 79, no. 1 (2000): 45–50.

Anderson, Mark D. *Disaster Writing: The Cultural Politics of Catastrophe in Latin America*. ProQuest Ebook Central; University of Virginia Press, 2011.

Archer, William G. and Mildred Archer. *India Served and Observed*. London: BACSA, 1994.

Arnold, David. *Famine: Social Crisis and Historical Change*. Oxford: Basil Blackwell, 1988.

———. *The Problem of Nature: Environment, Culture and European Expansion*. New Perspectives on the Past. Oxford: Blackwell publishers, 1996.

———. *Science Technology and Medicine in Colonial India*. The New Cambridge History of India, vol. 3, pt. 5. Cambridge: Cambridge University Press, 2004 [2000].

———. *The Tropics and the Traveling Gaze: India, Landscape, and Science, 1800–1856*. Nature, Culture, Conservation Series. Delhi: Permanent Black, 2005.

Arya, Anand S. *Damage Scenario under Hypothetical Recurrence of 1934 Earthquake Intensities in Various Districts in Bihar*. Patna: Bihar State Disaster Management Authority (Disaster management Authority), Government of Bihar, August 2013.

Bankoff, Greg. 'Dangers to Going It Alone: Social Capital in the Origins of Community Resilience in the Philippines'. *Continuity and Change* 22, no. 2 (2007): 327–35.

———. 'Rendering the World Unsafe: "Vulnerability" as a Western Discourse'. *Disasters* 25, no. 1 (2001): 19–35.

———. *Cultures of Disaster: Society and Natural Hazard in the Philippines*. London: Routledge Curzon, 2003.

Bapat, Arun, R. C. Kulkarni and S. K. Guha. *Catalogue of Earthquakes in India and Neighbourhood from Historical Period up to 1979*. Roorkee: Indian Society of Earthquake Technology, 1983.

Batabyal, Rakesh. *Communalism in Bengal: From Famine to Noakhali, 1943–47*. New Delhi; Thousand Oaks, CA: Sage Publications, 2005.

Bayly, Christopher A. *Origins of Nationality in South Asia: Patriotism and Ethical Government in the Making of Modern India*. Delhi: Oxford University Press, 1998.

———. *Empire and Information: Intelligence Gathering and Social Communication in India, 1780–1870*. Cambridge Studies in Indian History and Society. Cambridge: Cambridge University Press, 1996.

Beck, Ulrich. *Risk Society: Towards a New Modernity*. London: Sage Publications, 1992 [*Risikogesellschaft. Auf dem Weg in eine andere Moderne*. Frankfurt am Maine: Suhrkamp, 1986].

———. 'Living in the World Risk Society'. *Economy and Society* 35, no. 3 (2006): 329–45.

Beckerlegge, Gwilym. *The Ramakrishna Mission: The Making of a Modern Hindu Movement*. New Delhi: Oxford University Press, 2000.

———. *Swami Vivekananda's Legacy of Service: A Study of the Ramakrishna Math and Mission*. New Delhi: Oxford University Press, 2006.

Benson, John. 'Colliery Disaster Funds, 1860–1897'. *International Review of Social History* 19, no. 1 (1974): 73–85.

Benthall, Jonathan. *Disasters, Relief and the Media*. Wantage, UK: Sean Kingston Publishing, 2010 [1993].

Bergman, Jonathan. 'Disaster: A Useful Category of Historical Analysis'. *History Compass* 6, no. 3 (2008): 934–46.

Bhabha, Homi K. *The Location of Culture*. London and New York: Routledge, 1994.

Bhargava, Meena. 'Changing River Courses in North India: Calamities, Bounties, Strategies—Sixteenth to Early Nineteenth Centuries'. *The Medieval History Journal* 10, nos. 1 and 2 (2007): 183–208.

Bhatia, Bal Mokand. *Famines in India: A Study in Some Aspects of the Economic History of India with Special Reference to Food Problem, 1860–1990*. 3rd rev. ed. Delhi: Konark Publishers, 1991 [1967].

Bhatnagar, Ramratan. *The Rise and Growth of Hindi Journalism (1826–1945)*. Edited by Dhirendranath Singh. Varanasi: Vishwavidyalaya Prakashan, 2003 [1947].

Bhatta, Braja Bandhu. *The Natural Calamities in Orissa in the 19th Century*. New Delhi: Commonwealth Publishers, 1997.

Bhattacharyya, Debjani. *Empire and Ecology in the Bengal Delta: The Making of Calcutta*. Cambridge: Cambridge University Press, 2018.

Bhattacharya, Sabyasachi (ed.). *The Mahatma and the Poet: Letters and Debates Between Gandhi and Tagore 1915–1941*. New Delhi: National Book Trust, 1997.

'The Bihar and Orissa Natural Calamities Loans Rules, 1934'. In *Manual of Bihar Local Laws: 1790–1991* [Civil, Criminal, Revenue, Labour & Taxation Laws], edited by S. K. Pandey, 91–108, vol. 12. Allahabad: S. B. Malik for National Law Agency, 1991.

'The Bihar Famine Relief Fund Act, 1936 (Bihar Act V of 1936). In *Manual of Bihar Local Laws: 1790–1991* [Civil, Criminal, Revenue, Labour & Taxation Laws], edited by S. K. Pandey, vol. 3 [C-E]. Containing: Bihar Acts, Rules, Orders & Notifications issued by State Government with Up-to-date Amendments with Latest Case-laws. Allahabad: National Law Agency, 1985.

Bilham, Roger. 'Location and Magnitude of the 1833 Nepal Earthquake and Its Relation to the Rupture Zones of Contiguous Great Himalayan Earthquakes'. *Current Science* 69, no. 2 (1995): 101–28.

———. 'Slip Parameters for the Rann of Kachchh, India, 16 June 1819, Earthquake, Quantified from Contemporary Accounts'. In *Coastal Tectonics*, edited by I. S. Stewart and C. Vita-Finzi, 295–318. London: Geological Society, 1999.

———. 'Slow Tilt Reversal of the Lesser Himalaya between 1862 and 1992 at 78°E, and Bounds to the Southeast Rupture of the 1905 Kangra Earthquake'. *Geopysical Journal International* 144, no. 3 (2001): 713–28. https://doi-org.proxy.lnu.se/10.1046/j.1365-246x.2001.01365.x.

———. 'Earthquakes in India and the Himalaya: Tectonics, Geodesy and History'. *Annals of Geophysics* 47, nos. 2/3 (April/June, 2004): 839–58.

———. 'Raising Kathmandu', *Nature Geoscience* 8, no. 8 (August 2015): 582–84.

Bilham, Roger and Susan E. Hough. 'Site Response of the Ganges Basin Inferred from Re-Evaluated Macroseismic Observations from the 1897 Shillong, 1905 Kangra, and 1934 Nepal Earthquakes'. *Journal of Earth System Science* 117, no. S2 (November, 2008): 773–82.

Bilham, Roger, Vinod K. Gaur, and Peter Molnar. 'Himalayan Seismic Hazard'. *Science* 293, no. 5534 (2001): 1442–44.

Birkland, Thomas. 'Natural Disasters as Focusing Events: Policy Communities and Political Response'. *International Journal of Mass Emergencies and Disasters* 14, no. 2 (1996): 221–43.

———. *Lessons of Disaster: Policy Change after Catastrophic Events*. Georgetown University Press, 2006.

Birla, Ritu. *Stages of Capital: Law, Culture, and Market Governance in Late Colonial India*. Durham: Duke University Press, 2009.

Blaut, James Morris. *Eight Eurocentric Historians*. New York and London: The Guilford Press, 2000.

Boltanski, Luc. *Distant Suffering: Morality, Media and Politics*. Translated by Graham Burchell. Cambridge: Cambridge University Press, 2004 [French edition 1993].

Bondi, Liz and Joyce Davidson, 'Troubling the Place of Gender'. In *Handbook of Cultural Geography*, edited by Kay Anderson, Mona Domosh, Steve Pile and Nigel Thrift, 325–44. London: Sage Publications, 2003.

Bordia, Prashant and Nicholas DiFonzo, 'When Social Psychology Became Less Social: Prasad and the History of Rumour Research'. *Asian Journal of Social Psychology* 5, no. 1 (2002): 49–61.

Borland, Janet. 'Capitalising on Catastrophe: Reinvigorating the Japanese State with Moral Values through Education Following the 1923 Great Kanto Earthquake'. *Modern Asian Studies* 40, no. 4 (2006): 875–907.

Borst, Arno. 'Das Erdbeben von 1348. Ein historischer Beitrag zur Katastrophenforschung' (The Earthquake of 1348: A Historical Contribution to Disaster Research). *Historische Zeitschrift* 233, no. 1 (1981): 529–70.

Bose, Sugata. *His Majesty's Opponent: Subhas Chandra Bose and India's Struggle Against Empire*. New Delhi: Penguin Books, 2011.

Brancati, Dawn. 'Political Aftershocks: The Impact of Earthquakes on Intrastate Conflict'. *Journal of Conflict Resolution* 51, no. 15 (2007): 715–43.

Brennan, Lance. 'The Development of the Indian Famine Codes: Personalities, Politics, and Policies'. In *Famine as a Geographical Phenomenon*, edited by Bruce Currey and Graeme Hugo, 91–111. Dordrecht: D. Reidel, 1984.

———. 'Government Famine Relief in Bengal, 1943'. *Journal of Asian Studies* 47, no. 3 (1988): 542–67.

Brewis, Georgina. '"Fill Full the Mouth of Famine": Voluntary Action in Famine Relief in India 1896–1901'. *Modern Asian Studies* 44, no. 4 (2010): 887–918.

Brodie, Antonia, Alison Felstead, Jonathan Franklin, Leslie Pinfield and Jane Oldfield (eds.). *Directory of British Architects 1834–1914*, vol. 2: L–Z. British Architectural Library, Royal Institute of British Architects. London: Continuum, 2001.

Brown, Judith M. *Gandhi's Rise to Power: Indian Politics 1915–1922*. New York: Cambridge University Press, 1972.

———. *Gandhi: Prisoner of Hope*. New Haven: Yale University Press, 1989.

Brown, Rebecca M. 'The Cemeteries and the Suburbs: Patna's Challenges to the Colonial City in South Asia'. *Journal of Urban History* 29, no. 151 (2003): 151–72.

———. 'Patnā's Golghar and the Transformations of Colonial Discourse'. *Archives of Asian Art* 55 (2005): 53–63.

———. 'Inscribing Colonial Monumentality: A Case Study of the 1763 Patna Massacre Memorial'. *Journal of Asian Studies* 65, no. 1 (2006): 91–113.

Brunsma, David and J. Steven Picou. 'Disasters in the Twenty-First Century: Modern Destruction and Future Instruction'. *Social Forces* 87, no. 2 (2008): 983–91.

Butler, David. 'Focusing Events in the Early Twentieth Century: A Hurricane, Two Earthquakes, and a Pandemic'. In *Emergency Management: The American Experience, 1900–2005*, edited by Claire B. Ruben, 11–48. Fairfax, VA: Public Entity Risk Institute, 2007.

Cekota, Anthony. *The Stormy Years: An Extraordinary Enterprise…: Bata 1932–1945*. Perth Amboy, NJ: Universum Sokol Publications, 1985.

Chakrabarti, Shirshendu, 'The Matrix of History: A Study of Satinath Bhaduri's *Dhorai Charit Manas* (1949–51)'. *Journal of Arts and Ideas*, no. 9 (October–December, 1984): 49–56.

Chakrabarti, Bidyut. *Subhas Chandra Bose and Middle Class Radicalism: A Study in Indian Nationalism, 1928–1940*. London: London School of Economics & Political Science, 1990.

Chakrabarty, Dipesh. *Rethinking Working-Class History: Bengal 1890–1940*. Princeton: Princeton University Press, 1989.

———. 'The Climate of History: Four Theses'. *Critical Inquiry* 35, no. 2 (Winter 2009): 197–222.

Chandra, Bipan, Mridula Mukherjee, Aditya Mukherjee, Şucheta Mahajan and K. N. Panikkar. *India's Struggle for Independence 1857–1947*. New Delhi: Penguin Books, 1988.

Chandra Ray, Prafulla. *Life and Experiences of a Bengali Chemist*. Calcutta: Chuckeryvertty, Chatterjee & Co., Ltd; London: Kegan Paul, Trench, Trubner & Co., Ltd., 1932.

Chatterjee, Kumkum. *Merchants, Politics, and Society in Early Modern India: Bihar, 1733–1820*. Leiden: E. J. Brill, 1996.

Chatterjee, Partha. 'The Nation in Heterogeneous Time'. *Indian Economic and Social History Review* 38, no. 4 (December 2001): 406–40.

———. 'The Subalternity of a Nationalist Elite'. In *The Middle Class in Colonial India*, edited by Sanjay Joshi, 94–117. New Delhi: Oxford University Press, 2010.

Chowdhury-Zilly, Aditee Nag. *The Vagrant Peasant: Agrarian Distress and Desertion in Bengal; 1770–1830*. Beiträge zur Südasienforschung, Band 71. Wiesbaden, Franz Steiner Verlag, 1982.

Clancey, Greg. *Earthquake Nation: The Cultural Politics of Japanese Seismicity, 1868–1930*. Berkeley: University of California Press, 2006.

———. 'The Changing Character of Disaster Victimhood: Evidence from Japan's "Great Earthquakes"'. *Critical Asian Studies* 48, no. 3 (2016): 356–79.

Clark, Nigel. 'Geo-Politics and the Disaster of the Anthropocene'. In *Disasters and Politics: Materials, Experiments, Preparedness*, edited by Manuel Torini, Israel Rodriguez-Giralt and Michael Guggenheim, 19–37. Oxford; West Sussex: Wiley Blackwell/Originally published in *The Sociological Review* 62: S1 (2014): 19–37.

Clarke, Lee. 'Possibilistic Thinking: A New Conceptual Tool for Thinking about Extreme Events'. *Social Research* 75, no. 3 (Fall, 2008): 669–90.

Cohen, Charles and Eric D. Werker. 'The Political Economy of "Natural" Disasters'. *Journal of Conflict Resolution* 52, no. 6 (2008): 795–819.

Courtney, Chris. *The Nature of Disaster in China: The 1931 Yanqzi River Flood.* Cambridge, UK: Cambridge University Press, 2018.

Crosbie, Barry. 'Ireland, Colonial Science, and the Geographical Construction of British Rule in India, c. 1820–1870'. *The Historical Journal* 52, 4 (2009): 963–87.

———. *Irish Imperial Networks: Migration, Social Communication and Exchange in Nineteenth-Century India.* Cambridge: Cambridge University Press, 2012.

D'Souza, Rohan. *Drowned and Dammed: Colonial Capitalism and Flood Control in Eastern India.* New Delhi: Oxford University Press, 2006.

Daly, Patrick, Sabin Ninglekhu, Pia Hollenbach, Jennifer Duyne Barenstein, and Dori Nguyen. 'Situating Local Stakeholders within National Disaster Governance Structures: Rebuilding Urban Neighbourhoods Following the 2015 Nepal Earthquake'. *Environment and Urbanization* 29, no. 2 (October 2017): 403–24.

'The Darbhanga Improvement Act, 1934 (Bihar and Orissa Act 4 of 1934)'. In *Manual of Bihar Local Laws 1790–1985*, edited by S. K. Pandey, 62–64 [Civil, Criminal, Revenue, Labour and Taxation Laws]. Containing: Bihar Acts, Rules, Orders & Notifications issued by State Government with up-to-date Amendments with latest Case-laws, vol. 3 [C-E]. Allahabad: National Law Agency, 1985.

Das, Arvind N. 'Peasants and Peasant Organisations: The Kisan Sabha in Bihar'. In *Agrarian Movement in India: Studies on 20th Century Bihar*, edited by Arvind N. Das, 40–87. London: Frank Cass and Company Limited, 1982.

Das, Debojyoti. '"Majuli in Peril": Challenging the Received Wisdom on Flood Control in the Brahmaputra River Basin, Assam (1940–2000)'. *Water History Journal* 6, no. 2 (2014): 167–85.

Davis, Mike. *Ecology of Fear: Los Angeles and the Imagination of Disaster.* New York, NY: Vintage Books, 1999.

Deb Roy, Rohan. 'Quinine, Mosquitoes and Empire: Reassembling Malaria in British India 1890–1910'. *South Asian History and Culture* 4, no. 1 (2013): 65–86.

Dey, Sarmistha. *Marginal Europeans in Colonial India: 1860–1920.* Kolkata: Thema, 2008.

Diamond, Jared M. *Collapse. How Societies Chose to Fail or Succeed.* New York: Viking, 2005.

Diefendorf, Jeffry M. 'Reconstructing Devastated Cities: Europe after World War II and New Orleans after Katrina'. *Journal of Urban Design* 14, no. 3 (August 2009): 377–97.

Dixit, Amod M., L. R. Dwelley-Samat, M. Nakarmi, S. B. Pradhanang and B. Tucker. 'The Kathmandu Valley Earthquake Risk Management Project: An Evaluation'. 12WCEE: 12th World Conference on Earthquake Engineering, Auckland, New Zealand. 30 January–4 February 2000. Upper Hutt, New Zealand: New Zealand Society for Earthquake Engineering, 2000, 8. http://www.iitk.ac.in/nicee/wcee/article/0788.pdf (accessed 1 May 2015).

Dutta, Krishna and Andrew Robinson (eds.). *Selected Letters of Rabindranath Tagore*, vol. 53. University of Cambridge Oriental Publications. Cambridge: Cambridge University Press, 1997.

Dyer, Christopher L. 'The Phoenix Effect in Post-Disaster Recovery: An Analysis of the Economic Development Administration's Culture of Response after Hurricane Andrew'. In *The Angry Earth: Disaster in Anthropological Perspective*, edited by Anthony Oliver-Smith and Susannna M. Hoffman, 278–300. New York: Routledge, 1999.

Dynes, Russell R. 'Interorganizational Relations in Communities under Stress'. In *Disasters: Theory and Research*, edited by E. L. Quarantelli, 49–64. London: Sage Publications, 1978.

Edgerton-Tarpley, Kathryn Jean. 'From "Nourish the People" to "Sacrifice for the Nation": Changing Responses to Disaster in Late Imperial and Modern China'. *The Journal of Asian Studies* 73, no. 2 (May 2014): 447–69.

Enarson, Elaine, Alice Fothergill and Lori Peek. 'Gender and Disaster: Foundations and Directions'. In *Handbook of Disaster Research*, edited by H. Rodriguez, E. L. Quarantelli and R. R. Dynes, 130–46. Handbooks of Sociology and Social Research. New York: Springer, 2006.

Felgentreff, Carsten and Wolf R. Dombrowsky. 'Hazards-, Risiko- und Katastrophenforschung'. In *Naturrisiken und Sozialkatastrophen*, edited by C. Felgentreff and Thomas Glade, 13–29. Berlin; Heidelberg: Spektrum Akademischer Verlag, 2008.

Felgentreff, C. and Thomas Glade. 'Naturrisiken—Sozialkatastrophen: zum Geleit'. In *Naturrisiken und Sozialkatastrophen*, edited by C. Felgentreff and T. Glade, 1–10. Berlin; Heidelberg: Spektrum Akademischer Verlag, 2008.

Festinger, Leon. *A Theory of Cognitive Dissonance*. Stanford, CA: Stanford University Press, 1962 [1957].

Fischer, Henry W. III. *Response to Disaster: Fact versus Fiction and Its Perpetuation: The Sociology of Disaster*. Lanham, Maryland: University Press of America, 1988.

Framke, Maria. '"We must Send a Gift Worthy of India and the Congress!" War and Political Humanitarianism in Late Colonial South Asia'. *Modern Asian Studies* 51, no. 6 (2017): 1969–98.

———. 'Political Humanitarianism in the 1930s: Indian Aid for Republican Spain'. *European Review of History: Revue européenne d'histoire*, 23, nos. 1–2 (2016): 63–81.

Frömming, Urte Undine. *Naturkatastrophen. Kulturelle Deutung und Verarbeitung.* Frankfurt and New York: Campus Verlag, 2006.

Gadgil, Madhav and Ramachandra Guha. *This Fissured Land: An Ecological History of India.* New Delhi: Oxford University Press, 1992.

Galloway, J. H. 'Sugar'. In *The Cambridge World History of Food*, vol. 1, edited by Kenneth F. Kiple and Kriemhild Coneé Ornelas, 437–49. Cambridge: Cambridge University Press, 2000.

Ghosh, Papiya. *The Civil Disobedience Movement in Bihar, 1930–1934*. New Delhi: Manak Publications, 2008.

Giroux, Henry A. 'Hurricane Katrina and the Politics of Disposability: Floating Bodies and Expendable Populations'. In *Schooling and the Politics of Disaster*, edited by Kenneth J. Saltman, 43–70. New York: Routledge, 2007.

———. *Stormy Weather: Katrina and the Politics of Disposability*. Boulder, CO: Paradigm Publishers, 2006.

Gooptu, Nandini. *The Politics of the Urban Poor in Early Twentieth-Century India*. Cambridge: Cambridge University Press, 2001.

Goswami, Manu. *Producing India: From Colonial Economy to National Space.* Chicago and London: The University of Chicago Press, 2004.

Goswami, Omkar. 'Collaboration and Conflict: European and Indian Capitalists and the Jute Economy of Bengal, 1919–39'. *The Indian Economic and Social History Review* 19, no. 2, 1982: 141–79.

Gould, William. 'Hallett, Sir Maurice Garnier (1883–1969)'. In *Oxford Dictionary of National Biography*. Oxford: Oxford University Press, 2004; online edition, May 2007 (doi: 10.1093/ref:odnb/67176, http://www.oxforddnb.com/view/article/67176 [accessed 16 June 2011]).

Greenough, Paul Robert. *Prosperity and Misery in Modern Bengal: The Famine of 1943–1944*. New York: Oxford University Press, 1982.

Gregson, Sarah. '"Women and Children First?" The Administration of Titanic Relief in Southampton, 1912–59'. *English Historical Review* 127, no. 524 (February 2012): 83–109.

Groh, Dieter, Michael Kempe and Franz Mauelshagen. 'Einleitung. Naturkatastrophen—wahrgenommen, gedeutet, dargestellt', 11–33. In *Naturkatastrophen: Beiträge zu ihrer Deutung, Wahrnehmung und Darstellung in Text und Bild von der Antike bis ins 20. Jahrhundert*, edited by D. Groh, M. Kempe, F. Mauelshagen.Tübingen: Gunter Narr Verlag, 2003.

Grove, Richard H. *Green Imperialism: Colonial Expansion, Tropical Island Edens and the Origins of Environmentalism, 1600–1860*. Cambridge: Cambridge University Press, 1995.

Guggenheim, Michael. 'Introduction: Disasters and Politics—Politics as Disasters'. In *Disasters and Politics*, edited by Torini, Rodriguez-Giralt and Guggenheim, 1–16. Originally published in *The Sociological Review* 62: S1 (2014): 1–16.

Guha, Ramachandra. *The Unquiet Woods: Ecological Change and Peasant Resistance in the Himalaya*. Berkeley: University of California Press, 2000 [1989].

Guha, Ranajit. *Elementary Aspects of Peasant Insurgency in Colonial India*, 2nd ed. London, Durham: Duke University Press, 1999 [1983].

Guidoboni, Emanuela and John E. Ebel. *Earthquakes and Tsunamis in the Past: A Guide to Techniques in Historical Seismology*. Cambridge: Cambridge University Press, 2009.

Guyot-Réchard, Bérénice. 'Reordering a Border Space: Relief, Rehabilitation, and Nation-Building in Northeastern India after the 1950 Assam Earthquake'. *Modern Asian Studies* 49, no. 4 (July 2015): 931–62.

Hall-Matthews, David. *Peasants, Famine and the State in Colonial Western India*. New York: Palgrave and Macmillan, 2005.

———. 'The Historical Roots of Famine Relief Paradigms'. In *A World without Famine: New Approaches to Aid and Development*, edited by Helen O'Neill and John Toye, 107–27. Basingstoke; London: MacMillan Press Ltd, 1998.

Hannigan, John. *Disasters without Borders: The International Politics of Natural Disasters*. Cambridge, UK: Polity, 2012.

Hardgrove, Anne. *Community and Public Culture: The Marwaris in Calcutta*. New Delhi; New York: Oxford University Press, 2004. E-book, http://www.gutenberg-e.org/haa01/main.html (accessed 12 October 2011).

Hastrup, Frida. *Weathering the World: Recovering in the Wake of the Tsunami in a Tamil Fishing Village*. Oxford and New York: Berghan Books, 2011.

Hauser, Walter. 'The Indian National Congress and Land Policy in the Twentieth Century'. *Indian Economic and Social History Review* 1, no. 1 (1964): 57–65.

———. *The Provincial Kisan Sabha 1929–1942: A Study of an Indian Peasant Movement*. PhD dissertation, University of Chicago, 1960; New York: Routledge, 2019.

——— (ed.). *Sahajanand on Agricultural Labour and the Rural Poor*. New Delhi: Manohar Publishers and Distributors, 2005 [1994].

Haynes, Douglas E. 'From Tribute to Philanthropy: The Politics of Gift Giving in a Western Indian City'. *Journal of Asian Studies* 46, no. 2 (May, 1987): 339–60.

———. *Rhetoric and Ritual in Colonial India: The Shaping of Public Culture in Surat City, 1852–1928*. Berkeley and Los Angeles: University of California Press, 1991.

Henningham, Stephen. *Peasant Movements in Colonial India: North Bihar, 1917–1942*. Canberra: Australian National University, 1982.

———. 'Bureaucracy and Control in India's Great Landed Estates: The Raj Darbhanga of Bihar, 1879 to 1950'. *Modern Asian Studies* 17, no. 1 (1983): 35–57.

———. *A Great Estate and Its Landlords in Colonial India: Darbhanga 1860–1942*. Delhi: Oxford University Press, 1990.

Hill, Christopher V. *River of Sorrow: Environment and Social Control in Riparian North India, 1770–1994*, Monograph and Occasional Paper Series, no. 5. Ann Arbor, Michigan: Association for Asian Studies, 1997.

Hoffman, Susanna M. 'After Atlas Shrugs: Cultural Change and Persistence after a Disaster'. In *The Angry Earth: Disaster in Anthropological Perspective*, edited by Anthony Oliver-Smith and Susanna M. Hoffman, 302–25. London: Routledge, 1999.

Hoffman, Susanna M. and Anthony Oliver-Smith (eds.). *Catastrophe and Culture: The Anthropology of Disaster*. Santa Fe, NM: School of American Research Press, 2002.

Holenstein, Andre. 'Introduction: Empowering Interactions: Looking at Statebuilding from Below'. In *Empowering Interactions: Political Cultures and the Emergence of the State in Europe 1300–1900*, edited by Wim Blockmans, André Holenstein and Jon Mathieu, 1–31. Farnham, UK: Ashgate, 2009.

Hough, Susan Elizabeth. *Earthshaking Science: What We Know (and Don't Know) about Earthquakes*. Princeton and Oxford: Princeton University Press, 2002.

Hutchinson, John F. 'Disasters and the International Order: Earthquakes, Humanitarians, and the Ciraolo Project'. *International History Review* 22, no. 1 (2000): 1–36.

———. 'Disasters and the International Order. II: the International Relief Union'. *International History Review* 23, no. 2 (2001): 253–98.

Iqbal, Iftekhar. *The Bengal Delta: Ecology, State and Social Change, 1840–1943*. London: Palgrave Macmillan, 2010.

Jain, Sudhir K. 'Indian Earthquakes: An Overview'. *Indian Concrete Journal* 72, no. 11 (November 1998): 555–61.

———. 'Codes, Licensing, and Education'. *Earthquake Spectra* 18, no. S1 (July 2002): 319–39.

Jain, Sudhir K. and N. C. Nigam. 'Historical Developments and Current Status of Earthquake Engineering in India', *Proceedings of the Twelfth World Conference on Earthquake Engineering*, Auckland, New Zealand, 30 January–4 February 2000, Paper no. 1792.

Jamasji-Hirjikaka, Daleara and Yasmin Qureshi. *The Merchant-Knight, Adamjee Haji Dawood*. Karachi: Adamjee Foundation, 2008 [2004].

Janku, Andrea, Gerrit J. Schenk and Franz Mauelshagen. 'Introduction'. In *Historical Disasters in Context: Science, Religion, and Politics* edited by Gerrit J. Schenk and Franz Mauelshagen, 1–14. New York; London: Routledge, Taylor and Francis Group, 2012.

Janku, Andrea. 'From Natural to National Disaster: The Chinese Famine of 1928–1930'. In *Historical Disasters in Context: Science, Religion, and Politics*, edited by Andrea Janku, Gerrit J. Schenk and Franz Mauelshagen, 227–60. New York: Routledge, 2012.

Jatana, B. L. 'Fail-safe Large Dams in Earthquake Prone Himalayan Region'. *ISET Journal of Earthquake Technology* 36, no. 1 (1999): 1–13.

Jayal, Niraja Gopal. *Citizenship and Its Discontents: An Indian History*. Cambridge, MA: Harvard University Press, 2013.

Jhala, Jayasinhji. 'In Time of Fear and Terror: Seeing, Assessing, Assisting—Understanding and Living the Reality and Consequence of Disaster'. *Visual Anthropology Review* 20, no. 1 (2004): 59–69.

Jigyasu, Rohit. 'From 'Natural' to 'Cultural' Disaster: Consequences of Post-Earthquake Rehabilitation Process on Cultural Heritage in Marathwada Region, India'. UNESCO-ICOMOS Conference. Earthquake-safe: Lessons to be Learned from Traditional Construction. Istanbul, 2001.

Jones, Eric L. *The European Miracle: Environments, Economies, and Geopolitics in the History of Europe and Asia*, 3rd ed. New York: Cambridge University Press, 2003 [1981].

Jones, Samantha, Katie J. Oven and Ben Wisner. 'A Comparison of the Governance Landscape of Earthquake Risk Reduction in Nepal and the Indian State of Bihar'. *International Journal of Disaster Risk Reduction* 15 (2016): 29–42.

Johns, Alessa (ed.). *Dreadful Visitations: Confronting Natural Catastrophe in the Age of Enlightenment*. New York and London: Routledge, 1999.

Joshi, Sanjay. 'Introduction.' In *The Middle Class in Colonial India*, xv–lvi, edited by Sanjay Joshi. New Delhi: Oxford University Press, 2010.

———. 'The Spectre of Comparisons: Studying the Middle Class of Colonial India'. In *Elite and Everyman: The Cultural Politics of the Indian Middle Classes*, by Amita Baviskar and Raka Ray, 83–107. New Delhi: Routledge, 2011.

Juneja, Monica and Franz Mauelshagen. 'Disasters and Pre-Industrial Societies: Historiographic Trends and Comparative Perspectives'. *The Medieval History Journal* 10, nos. 1–2 (2007): 1–31.

Kapur, Anu. *On Disasters in India*. New Delhi: Foundation Books, Cambridge University Press India Pvt. Ltd., 2009.

———. *Vulnerable India: A Geographical Study of Disasters*. Shimla: Indian Institute of Advanced Study, Sage Publications, 2010.

Khilnani, Sunil. 'The Development of Civil Society'. In *Civil Society: History and Possibilities*, edited by Sudipta Kaviraj and Sunil Khilnani, 11–32. New Delhi: Cambridge University Press, 2001.

———. 'Nehru's Faith'. *Economic and Political Weekly* 37, no. 48 (2002): 4739–99.

Kidambi, Prashant. *The Making of an Indian Metropolis: Colonial Governance and Public Culture in Bombay, 1890–1920*. Historical Urban Studies. Aldershot, U.K.: Ashgate Publishing, 2007.

Kingsbury, Benjamin. *An Imperial Disaster: The Bengal Cyclone of 1876*. New Delhi: Oxford University Press, 2018.

Klein, Ira. 'When the Rains Failed. Famine, Relief, and Mortality in British India'. *The Indian Economic and Social History Review* 21, no. 2 (1984): 185–214.

Klein, Naomi. *The Shock Doctrine: The Rise of Disaster Capitalism*. New York: Metropolitan Books, 2007.

Kreps, Gary A. 'Disaster: Systemic Event and Social Catalyst'. In *What Is a Disaster? Perspectives on the Question* edited by E. L. Quarantelli, 25–50. London, New York: Routledge, 1998.

Kumar, Arun. *Rewriting the Language of Politics: Kisans in Colonial Bihar*. Delhi: Manohar Publishers, 2001.

Kumar, Deepak. 'Economic Compulsions and the Geological Survey of India'. *Indian Journal of History of Science* 17, no. 2 (1982): 289–300.

Kumar, Manasi. 'A Journey into the Bleeding City: Following the Footprints of the Rubble of Riot and Violence of Earthquake in Gujarat, India'. *Psychology & Developing Societies* 19, no. 1 (2007): 1–36.

Kumar, N. *Journalism in Bihar*. Bihar District Gazetteers. Patna: Government of Bihar, Gazetteers Branch, Revenue Department: Secretariat Press, 1971.

Kuracina, William F. *The State and Governance in India: The Congress Ideal*. Routledge Studies in South Asian History. New York: Routledge, 2010.

Lal, Vinay. 'The Gandhi Everyone Loves to Hate'. *Economic and Political Weekly* 43, no. 40 (2008): 55–64.

Lee, William H. K., Paul Jennings, Carl Kisslinger, Hiroo Kanamori. *International Handbook of Earthquake and Engineering Seismology*, Part B. Amsterdam: Academic Press, 2002.

Lefebvre, Georges. *The Great Fear of 1789: Rural Panic in Revolutionary France*. New York: Vintage Books, 1973 [Translated by Joan White; publication 1932].

Low, D. A. 'Thomas, Freeman Freeman, First Marquess of Willingdon (1866–1941)'. In *Oxford Dictionary of National Biography*. Oxford University Press, 2004; online edition, January 2008, http://www.oxforddnb.com.ubproxy.ub.uni-heidelberg.de/view/article/33266 (accessed 13 May 2015).

Lu, Yi and Jiuping Xu. 'The Progress of Emergency Response and Rescue in China: A Comparative Analysis of Wenchuan and Lushan Earthquakes'. *Natural Hazards* 74, no. 2 (2014): 421–44.

Ludden, David. *An Agrarian History of South Asia*. Cambridge: Cambridge University Press, 1999.

Macalister-Smith, Peter. 'The International Relief Union of 1932'. *Disasters* 5, no. 2 (1981): 147–54.

Manyena, Siambabala Bernard, Geoff O'Brien, Phil O'Keefe and Joanne Rose. 'Disaster Resilience: A Bounce Back or Bounce Forward Ability?' (Editorial). *Local Environment* 16, no. 5 (May 2011): 417–24.

Marcussen, Eleonor. 'Explaining the 1934 Bihar–Nepal Earthquake: The Role of Science, Astrology, and "Rumours"'. In *Historical Disaster Experiences: Towards a Comparative and Transcultural History of Disasters across Asia and Europe*, edited by Gerrit Jasper Schenk, 241–66. Transcultural Research–Heidelberg Studies on Asia and Europe in a Global Context. Heidelberg: Springer, 2017.

———. 'Town Planning after the 1934 Bihar–Nepal Earthquake: Earthquake-Safety, Colonial Improvements and the Restructuring of Urban Space in Bihar'. *Studies in Nepal History and Society* 22, no. 2, Kathmandu: Mandala Book point (2017): 321–54.

———. 'Cooperation and Pacifism in a Colonial Context: Service Civil International and Work Camps in Bihar, 1934–1937'. In *Her Story. Historical Scholarship between South Asia and Europe: Festschrift in Honour of Gita Dharampal-Frick*, edited by R. Klöber and M. Ludwig, 83–101. Heidelberg: CrossAsia-eBooks, 2018.

Markovits, Claude. *Indian Business and Nationalist Politics 1931–1939: The Indigenous Capitalist Class and the Rise of the Congress Party*. London: Cambridge University Press, 1985.

———. *Merchants, Traders, Entrepreneurs: Indian Business in the Colonial Era*. Ranikhet: Permanent Black, 2008.

———. 'What about the Merchants? A Mercantile Perspective on the Middle Class of Colonial India'. In *The Middle Class in Colonial India*, edited by Sanjay Joshi, 118–31. New Delhi: Oxford University Press, 2010.

Massard-Guilbaud, Geneviève. 'Introduction: the Urban Catastrophe—Challenge to the Social, Economic, and Cultural Order of the City'. In *Cities and Catastrophes: Coping with Emergency in European History*, edited by G. Massard-Guilbaud, Harold L. Platt and Dieter Schott, 9–42. Frankfurt am Main: Lang, 2002.

Mauch, Christof. 'Phönix und Mnemosyne. Katastrophenoptimismus und Katastrophenerinnerung in den USA: Von der Johnstown Flood bis Hurricane Katrina'. In *Katastrophen machen Geschichte. Umweltgeschichtliche Prozesse im Spannungsfeld von Ressourcennutzung und Extremereignis*, edited by Patrick Masius, Jana Sprenger and Eva Mackowiak, 133–51. Göttingen: Universitätsverlag Göttingen, 2010.

McDonald, G. 'Unity on Trial: Congress in Bihar, 1929–39'. In *Congress and the Raj: Facets of the Indian Struggle 1917–47*, edited by Donald A. Low, 289–314. 2nd ed. New Delhi: Oxford University Press, 2004 [1977].

McGregor, R. S. (ed.). *The Oxford Hindi–English Dictionary*. New Delhi: Oxford University Press, 1993.

McKellar, Elizabeth. *The Birth of Modern London: The Development and Design of the City 1660–1720*. Manchester: Manchester University Press, 1999.

McNeill, John R., José Augusto Pádua and Mahesh Rangarajan. *Environmental History: As If Nature Existed*. New Delhi: Oxford University Press, 2010.

Mehta, Lyla. 'Reflections on the Kutch Earthquake'. *Economic and Political Weekly* 36, no. 31 (August 2001): 2931–36.

Mishra, Dinesh Kumar. 'Bihar Floods: The Inevitable Has Happened'. *Economic and Political Weekly* 43, no. 26 (September 2008): 8–12.

Misra, Girishwar. 'Obituary: Professor Durgananda Sinha (1922–1998)'. *Cross-Cultural Psychology Bulletin* 32, no. 3 (1998): 6–10.

Mitchell, James K. 'Including the Capacity for Coping with Surprises in Post-Disaster Recovery Policies. Reflections on the Experience of Tangshan, China'. *Behemoth: A Journal on Civilization* 1, no. 3 (2008): 21–38.

Mitra, S., Himangshu Paul, Ajay Kumar, Shashwat K. Singh, Siddharth Dey and Debacharan Powali. 'The 25 April 2015 Nepal Earthquake and its Aftershocks' (Research Communications). *Current Science* 108, no. 10 (May 2015): 1938–43.

Monastier, Hélène. *Pierre Ceresole: Ein Kämpfer für den Frieden*. Vienna: Sensen-Verlag, 1950 [Translated from French first ed., 1947].

Mosse, David. *The Rule of Water: Statecraft, Ecology, and Collective Action in South Asia*. Delhi: Oxford University Press, 2003.

Mukherjee, S. N. Afterword to *Disasters: Image and Context*, edited by Peter Hinton, 187–96. Sydney: Sydney Studies, 1992.

Mukherjee, Upamanyu Pablo. *Natural Disasters and Victorian Empire: Famines, Fevers and the Literary Cultures of South Asia*. Basingstoke, UK: Palgrave Macmillan, 2013.

Mundargi, Tirumal. 'Congress and Zamindars: Collaboration and Consultation in Bihar, 1915–36'. *Economic and Political Weekly* 25, no. 22 (June 2, 1990): 1217–22.

Muralidharan, Sukumar. 'Religion, Nationalism and the State: Gandhi and India's Engagement with Political Modernity'. *Social Scientist* 34, nos. 3/4 (March–April 2006): 3–36.

Nair, Rukmini Bhaya. 'Acts of Agency and Acts of God: Discourse of Disaster in a Post-colonial Society'. *Economic and Political Weekly* 32, no. 11 (15–21 March 1997): 535–42.

Nandy, D. R., A. K. Choudhury, C. Chakraborty and P. L. Narula. 'Geological Survey of India, Bihar–Nepal Earthquake, August 20, 1988'. *Special Publication, Geological Survey of India* 31, 1993.

Naoroji, Dadabhai. *Poverty and Un-British Rule in India*. London: Swan Sonnenschein & Co., 1901.

Nixon, Rob. *Slow Violence and the Environmentalism of the Poor*. Cambridge, MA; London: Harvard University Press, 2011.

Oezerdem, Alpaslan and Tim Jacoby. *Disaster Management and Civil Society: Earthquake Relief in Japan, Turkey and India*. New York: I. B. Tauris & Co. Ltd, 2006.

Ó Gráda, Cormac. *Famine: A Short History*. Princeton and Oxford: Princeton University Press, 2009.

O'Keefe, Phil, Ken Westgate and Ben Wisner. 'Taking the Naturalness out of Natural Disasters'. *Nature* 260, no. 5552 (1976): 566–67.

Oliver-Smith, Anthony and Susanna M. Hoffman (eds.). *The Angry Earth: Disaster in an Anthropological Perspective*. London: Routledge, 1999.

Olson, Richard Stuart. 'Towards a Politics of Disaster: Losses, Values, Agendas, and Blame'. *International Journal of Mass Emergencies and Disasters* 18, no. 2 (August 2000): 265–87.

Page, Scott E. 'Are We Collapsing? A Review of Diamond's *Collapse: How Societies Chose to Fail or Succeed*'. *Journal of Economic Literature* 43, no. 4 (December 2005): 1049–62.

Pandey, Gyanendra. *The Ascendency of Congress in Uttar Pradesh: Class Community and Nation in Northern India, 1920–1940*. Anthem South Asian Studies. London: Anthem Press, 2002.

Pandey, M. R. and Peter Molnar. 'The Distribution of Intensity of the Bihar–Nepal Earthquake of 15 January 1934 and Bounds on the Extent of the Rupture Zone'. *Journal of Nepal Geological Society* 5, no. 1 (1988): 22–44.

Paranjape, Makarand R. '"Natural Supernaturalism?" The Tagore–Gandhi Debate on the Bihar Earthquake'. *Journal of Hindu Studies* 4, no. 2 (2011): 176–204.

Parthasarathy, Rangaswamy. *Journalism in India*, 4th ed., rev. and enlarged. New Delhi: Sterling Publishers, 1997 [1989].

Pfister, Christian. 'Die "Katastrophenlücke" des 20. Jahrhunderts und der Verlust traditionalen Risikobewusstseins' ('The "Disaster Gap" of the 20th Century and the Loss of Traditional Disaster Memory'). *GAIA* 18, no. 3 (2009): 239–46.

———. 'Learning from Nature-Induced Disasters: Theoretical Considerations and Case Studies from Western Europe'. In *Natural Disasters, Cultural Responses: Case Studies toward a Global Environmental History*, edited by Christof Mauch and Christian Pfister, 17–40. Lanham, MD: Lexington Books, 2009.

Pickren, Wade E. and Alexandra Rutherford. *A History of Modern Psychology in Context*. Hoboken, New Jersey: Wiley & Sons, 2010.

Pouchepadass, Jacques. *Champaran and Gandhi: Planters, Peasants and Gandhian Politics*. French Studies in South Asian Culture and Society. New Delhi: Oxford University Press, 1999.

———. *Land, Power and Market: A Bihar District under Colonial Rule, 1860–1947*. New Delhi: Sage, 2000.

Prasad, Shambhu. 'Towards an Understanding of Gandhi's Views on Science'. *Economic and Political Weekly* 36, no. 39 (2001): 3721–32.

Quarantelli, E. L. 'Emergent Behaviors and Groups in the Crisis Time Period of Disasters'. Preliminary Paper No. 206. Disaster Research Centre, University of Delaware, Newark, DE, 1994.

Quittmeyer, R. C. and K. H. Jacob. 'Historical and Modern Seismicity of Pakistan, Afghanistan, Northwestern India, and South-Eastern Iran'. *Bulletin of the Seismological Society of America* 69, no. 3 (1979): 773–823.

Raj, Yogesh. 'Management of the Relief and Reconstruction after the Great Earthquake of 1934' (Notes from the Archive). *Studies in Nepali History and Society* 20, no. 2 (December 2015): 375–422.

Ramaswamy, Sumathi. 'The Goddess and the Nation: Subterfuges of Antiquity, the Cunning of Modernity'. In *The Blackwell Companion to Hinduism*, edited by Gavin Flood, 551–68. Oxford: Blackwell Publishing, 2003.

———. *The Lost Land of Lemuria: Fabulous Geographies, Catastrophic Histories*. Berkeley: University of California Press, 2004.

Ranft, Andreas and Stephan Selzer. 'Städte aus Trümmern: Einleitende Überlegungen'. In *Städte aus Trümmern: Katastrophenbewältigung zwischen Antike und Moderne*, edited by Andreas Ranft and Stephan Selzer, 9–25. Göttingen: Vandenhoeck & Ruprecht, 2004.

Rangarajan, Mahesh and K. Sivaramakrishnan. Introduction to *Shifting Ground: People, Animals, and Mobility in India's Environmental History*, edited by M. Rangarajan and K. Sivaramakrishnan, 1–29. Oxford University Press, 2014. DOI:10.1093/acprof:oso/9780198098959.001.0001 (accessed 5 July 2015).

Ray, Rajat Kanta. *Urban Roots of Indian Nationalism: Pressure Groups and Conflict of Interests in Calcutta City Politics, 1875–1939*. New Delhi: Vikas, 1979.

Reynolds, Reginald. *The White Sahibs in India*. London: M. Secker and Warburg, 1937.

Rothermund, Dietmar. *India in the Great Depression: 1929–1939*. Perspectives in History. New Delhi: Manohar, 1992.

———. *An Economic History of India: From Pre-Colonial Times to 1991*. New York, London: Routledge 1993 [1988].

Roy, Tirthankar. *Rethinking Economic Change in India: Labour and Livelihood*. London; New York: Routledge, 2005.

———. 'State, Society and Market in the Aftermath of Natural Disasters in Colonial India: A Preliminary Exploration'. *Indian Economic Social History Review* 45, no. 2 (2008): 261–94.

———. '"The Law of Storms": European and Indigenous Responses to Natural Disasters in Colonial India, c. 1800–1850'. *Australian Economic History Review* 50, no. 1 (2010): 6–22.

———. *Natural Disasters and Indian History*. Oxford India Short Introductions. New Delhi: Oxford University Press, 2012.

Rozario, Kevin. 'What Comes Down Must Go Up: Why Disasters Have Been Good for American Capitalism'. In *American Disasters*, edited by Steven Biel, 72–102. New York: New York University Press, 2001.

———. *The Culture of Calamity: Disaster and the Making of Modern America*. Chicago and London: University of Chicago Press, 2007.

Said, Edward W. *Orientalism*. Repr. with a new afterword, 1978. London: Penguin Books, 2003.

Saikia, Arupjyoti. 'Jute in the Brahmaputra Valley: The Making of Flood Control in the Twentieth-Century Assam'. *Modern Asian Studies* 49, no. 5 (2015): 1405–41.

Sanderson, David and Anshu Sharma. 'Winners and Losers from the 2001 Gujarat Earthquake'. *Environment and Urbanization* 20, no. 1 (2008): 177–86.

Sapkota, Soma Nath, Laurent Bollinger and Frédéric Perrier. 'Fatality Rates of the Mw ~8.2, 1934, Bihar–Nepal Earthquake and Comparison with the April 2015 Gorkha Earthquake'. *Earth, Planets and Space* 68, no. 40 (2016): 1–9.

Sarkar, Sumit. *Modern India, 1885–1947.* Cambridge Commonwealth Series. Basingstoke: Macmillan, 1989 [1983].

Schenk, Gerrit Jasper. 'Historical Disaster Research: State of Research, Concepts, Methods and Case Studies'. *Historical Social Research* 32, no. 3 (2007): 9–31.

———. '"Learning from History"? Chances, Problems and Limits of Learning from Historical Natural Disasters'. In *Cultures and Disasters. Understanding Cultural Framings in Disaster Risk Reduction,* edited by Fred Krüger, Greg Bankoff, Terry Cannon, E. Lisa and F. Schipper, 72–87. Routledge Studies in Hazards, Disaster Risk Reduction and Climate Adaptation. London and New York: Routledge, 2015.

Schenk, Gerrit Jasper and Jens-Ivo Engels (eds.). 'Historische Katastrophenforschung: Begriffe, Konzepte und Fallbeispiele' (Historical Disaster Research. Concepts, Methods and Case Studies), Theme Issue, *Historische Sozialforschung (Historical Social Research)* 32, no. 3 (2007): 1–236.

Schencking, J. Charles. '1923 Tokyo as a Devastated War and Occupation Zone: The Catastrophe One Confronted in Post-Earthquake Japan'. *Japanese Studies* 29, no. 1 (May 2009): 111–29.

Schumpeter, Joseph A. *Capitalism, Socialism and Democracy.* London and New York: Routledge, 1994.

Sen, Amartya Kumar. *Poverty and Famines: An Essay on Entitlement and Deprivation.* Oxford: Clarendon Press, 1981.

Sen, Anindya. *Ramakrishna Mission and Community Service in Eastern India, 1922–1962: A Qualitative and Quantitative Analysis,* reworked Jadavpur University dissertation, 1996. Kolkata: Readers Service, 2005.

Sengupta, Tania. 'Between the Garden and the Bazaar: The Visions, Spaces and Structures of Colonial Towns in Nineteenth-Century Provincial Bengal'. *Visual Culture in Britain* 12, no. 3 (2011): 333–48.

Sharma, Sanjay. *Famine, Philanthropy and the Colonial State: North India in the Early Nineteenth Century.* New Delhi: Oxford University Press, 2001.

Shaw, Rajib and Katsuihciro Goda. 'From Disaster to Sustainable Civil Society: The Kobe Experience'. *Disasters* 28, no. 1 (2004): 16–40.

Simpson, Edward. 'The "Gujarat" Earthquake and the Political Economy of Nostalgia'. *Contributions to Indian Sociology* 39, no. 2 (2005): 219–49.

———. *The Political Biography of an Earthquake: Aftermath and Amnesia in Gujarat, India.* New Delhi: Oxford University Press, 2014.

Simpson, Edward and Malathi de Alwis. 'Remembering Natural Disaster: Politics and Culture of Memorials in Gujarat and Sri Lanka'. *Anthropology Today* 24, no. 4 (2008): 6–12.

Simpson, Edward and Stuart Corbridge. 'The Geography of Things That May Become Memories: The 2001 Earthquake in Kachchh-Gujarat and the Politics of Rehabilitation in the Prememorial Era'. *Annals of the Association of American Geographers* 96, no. 3 (2006): 566–85.

Singer, Wendy. *Creating Histories: Oral Narratives and the Politics of History-Making*. Delhi: Oxford University Press, 1997.

Singh, Praveen. 'The Colonial State, Zamindars and the Politics of Flood Control in North Bihar (1850–1945)'. *Indian Economic Social History Review* 45, no. 2 (2008): 239–59.

Sinha, Amita and Jatinder Singh. 'Jamshedpur: Planning an Ideal Steel City in India'. *Journal of Planning History* 10, no. 4 (2011): 263–81.

Sinha, Durgananda. 'Behaviour in a Catastrophic Situation: A Psychological Study of Reports and Rumours'. *British Journal of Psychology* (General Section) 43, no. 3 (1952): 200–09.

Sinha, Nitin. *Communication and Colonialism in Eastern India: Bihar, 1760s–1880s*. Anthem Modern South Asian History. London: Anthem Press, 2012.

———. 'Entering the *Black Hole*: Between 'Mini-England' and 'Smell-Like Rotten Potato', the Railway Workshop Town of Jamalpur, 1860s–1940s'. *South Asian History and Culture* 3, no. 3 (2012): 317–47.

———. 'Fluvial Landscapes and the State: Property and the Gangetic Diaras in Colonial India, 1790s–1890s'. *Environment and History* 2, no. 20 (May 2014): 209–37.

Sinha, Sachchidananda. 'The Devastation of Behar and the Problem of Reconstruction'. *Hindustan Review* LVX [*sic* 60], nos. 350–52 (January 1934): 151–57.

Sivaramakrishnan, K. *Modern Forests: Statemaking and Environmental Change in Colonial Eastern India*. Stanford: Stanford University Press, 1999.

Sivaramakrishnan, K. and Gunnel Cederlöf. 'Introduction. Ecological Nationalisms: Claiming Nature for Making History'. In *Ecological Nationalisms: Nature, Livelihoods, and Identities in South Asia*, edited by G. Cederlöf and K. Sivaramakrishnan, paperback ed., 1–40. Seattle and London: University of Washington Press, 2014 [2006].

Slettebak, Rune T. 'Don't Blame the Weather: Climate-related Natural Disasters and Civil Conflict'. *Journal of Peace Research* 49, no. 1 (2012): 163–76.

Solnit, Rebecca. *A Paradise Built in Hell: The Extraordinary Communities that Arise in Disaster*. New York, NY: Viking, 2009.

Spodek, Howard. 'City Planning in India under British Colonial Rule'. *Economic and Political Weekly* 48, no. 4 (2013): 53–61.

Srivatsan, R. 'Concept of 'Seva' and 'Sevak' in the Freedom Movement'. *Economic and Political Weekly* 41, no. 5 (February 4–10, 2006): 427–38.

Stafford, Robert. 'Geological Surveys, Mineral Discoveries and British Expansion, 1835–1871'. *Journal of Imperial and Commonwealth History* 12, no. 3 (1984): 5–32.

Stallings, Robert A. 'Disasters and the Theory of Social Order'. In *What Is a Disaster? Perspectives on the Question*, edited by E. L. Quarantelli, 127–46. London and New York: Routledge, 1998.

———. 'Methodological Issues'. In *Handbook of Disaster Research*, edited by H. Rodriguez, E. L. Quarantelli and R. R. Dynes, 55–82. Handbooks of Sociology and Social Research. New York: Springer, 2006.

Steinberg, Ted. *Acts of God: The Unnatural History of Natural Disaster in America*. New York, NY: Oxford University Press, 2000.

Stern, Gary. *Can God Intervene? How Religion Explains Natural Disasters*. West Port, CT, and London: Praeger, 2007.

Talwar Oldenburg, Veena. *The Making of Colonial Lucknow, 1856–77*. Princeton: Princeton University Press, 1984.

Tierney, Kathleen J. 'From Margins to the Mainstream? Disaster Research at the Crossroads'. *Annual Review of Sociology* 33, no. 1 (2007): 503–25.

Tierney, Kathleen, Christine Bevc and Erica Kuligowski. 'Metaphors Matter: Media Frames, and Their Consequences in Hurricane Katrina'. *Annals of the American Academy of Political and Social Science* 604 (2006): 57–81.

Timberg, Thomas A. *Marwaris: From Traders to Industrialists*. New Delhi: Vikas Publishing House Pvt Ltd, 1978.

'Tributes to Earthquake Victims: Residents Pay Homage to More than 1000 People Who Lost Lives in 1934'. *The Telegraph* (online edition). http://www.telegraphindia.com/1150116/jsp/bihar/story_8626.jsp#.VmVQOnYrLIU (accessed 12 February 2015).

Twomey, Christina and Andrew J. May. 'Australian Responses to the Indian Famine, 1876–78: Sympathy, Photography and the British Empire'. *Australian Historical Studies* 43, no. 2 (2012): 233–52.

United Nations. *2009 UNISDR Terminology on Disaster Risk Reduction*. Geneva: United Nations International Strategy for Disaster Risk Reduction (UNISDR), 2009.

van Bavel, Bas, Daniel R. Curtis, Jessica Dijkman, Matthew Hannaford, Maïka de Keyzer, Eline van Onacker and Tim Soens. *Disasters and History: The Vulnerability and Resilience of Past Societies*. Cambridge: Cambridge University Press, 2020.

Voss, Martin and Klaus Wagner. 'Learning from (Small) Disasters'. *Natural Hazards* 55, no. 3 (2010): 657–69.

Wagner, Kim A. *The Great Fear of 1857: Rumours, Conspiracies and the Making of the Indian Uprising.* Oxford: Peter Lang, 2010.

Watt, Carey Anthony. *Serving the Nation: Cultures of Service, Association, and Citizenship.* Partly Cambridge University dissertation. New Delhi: Oxford University Press, 2005.

———. '"No Showy Muscles": The Boy Scouts and the Global Dimensions of Physical Culture and Bodily Health in Britain and Colonial India'. In *Scouting Frontiers: Youth and the Scout Movement's First Century*, edited by Nelson R. Block and Tammy M. Proctor, 121–42. Newcastle: Cambridge Scholars Publishing, 2009.

Weiler, Katharina Maria Lucia. *The Neoclassical Residences of the Newars in Nepal: Transcultural Flows in the Early 20th Century Architecture of the Kathmandu Valley.* Vol. I: *Text*; Vol. 2: *Figures.* Doctoral dissertation, Heidelberg University, 2009 (published 2010). Online resource http://archiv.ub.uni-heidelberg.de/volltextserver/10691/ (accessed 10 August 2011).

Weise, Kai. Summary and Commentary to *Revisiting Kathmandu: Safeguarding Living Urban Heritage*, edited by K. Weise, 1–47. International Symposium Kathmandu Valley, 25–29 November 2013. Paris, UNSECO, 2015.

Weisenfeld, Gennifer. *Imaging Disaster: Tokyo and the Visual Culture of Japan's Great Earthquake of 1923.* Berkeley: University of California Press, 2012.

Welch, Stuart Cary and Diane M. Nelson. 'William G. Archer (1907–1979)'. *Archives of Asian Art* 33 (1980): 109–11.

Welter, Volker M. *Biopolis: Patrick Geddes and the City of Life.* Cambridge, MA, and London: The MIT Press, 2002.

Williams, Stewart. 'Rethinking the Nature of Disaster: From Failed Instruments of Learning to a Post-Social Understanding'. *Social Forces* 87, no. 2 (2008): 1115–38.

Wisner, Ben. 'Disaster: What United Nations and Its World Can Do' (Short Communications). *Environmental Hazards* 3, no. 3 (2001): 125–27.

Wisner, Ben and Henry R. Luce. 'Disaster Vulnerability: Scale, Power and Daily Life'. *GeoJournal* 30, no. 2 (1993): 127–40.

Wisner, Ben, Piers Blaikie, Terry Cannon and Ian Davis. *At Risk: Natural Hazards, People's Vulnerability, and Disasters*, 2nd ed. London: Routledge, 2004 [1994].

The World Bank, and United Nations. *Natural Hazards, Unnatural Disasters: The Economics of Effective Prevention.* Washington, DC: The International Bank for Reconstruction and Development/The World Bank, 2010.

Yang, Anand A. *The Limited Raj: Agrarian Relations in Colonial India, Saran District, 1793–1920.* Berkeley, CA: University of California Press, 1989.

———. *Bazaar India: Markets, Society, and the Colonial State in Gangetic Bihar.* Berkeley: University of California Press, 1998.

Unpublished Dissertations

Dang, Kokila. 'The Congress and the Politics of Relief: 1920–1940'. Unpublished MPhil thesis, Jawaharlal Nehru University, 1992.

———. 'Colonial Ideology, Nationalist Politics and the Social Organization of Relief in the Late Nineteenth and Twentieth Centuries'. Unpublished PhD dissertation, Jawaharlal Nehru University, 1998. Open access: http://hdl. handle.net/10603/17082 (accessed 30 January 2015).

Jha, Murari Kumar. 'The Political Economy of the Ganga River: Highway of State Formation in Mughal India, c.1600–1800'. Doctoral thesis, Leiden University, Institute for History, 2013. Available online: http://hdl.handle.net/1887/20931 (accessed 3 February 2015).

Kirpes, Martha Patricia. 'Bringing Environmental Justice to Natural Hazards: An Earthquake Vulnerability and Reconstruction Case Comparison from India'. Doctoral dissertation, University of Michigan. UMI number 9825270, 1998.

Mulvany, Aaron Patrick. 'Flood of Memories: Narratives of Flood and Loss in Tamil South India'. PhD dissertation, University of Pennsylvania. Philadelphia. UMI number: 348516, 2011.

Raju, Emmanuel. 'Exploring Disaster Recovery Coordination: Stakeholder Interfaces, Goals and Interdependencies'. Doctoral dissertation, Faculty of Engineering, Lund University, 2013.

Sabhlok, Anu. 'Sewa in Relief: Gendered Geographies of Disaster in Relief in Gujarat, India'. A Thesis in Geography and Women's Studies, Doctor of Philosophy, Pennsylvania State University, Philadelphia. UMI number: 3266196, 2007.

Singh, Praveen. '"Colonising the Rivers": Colonial Technology, Irrigation and Flood Control in North Bihar, 1850–1950'. Unpublished PhD thesis. Centre for Historical Studies, School of Social Sciences, Jawaharlal Nehru University, New Delhi, India, 2003. Open access: http://hdl.handle.net/10603/29310 (accessed 30 January 2015).

Index